THE SCENTS OF EDEN

ALSO BY CHARLES CORN

Distant Islands: Travels Across Indonesia

DISCARD

THE
SCENTS
OF
EDEN

❧❧❧

A Narrative of the Spice Trade

CHARLES CORN

PUBLIC LIBRARY
EAST ORANGE, NEW JERSEY

KODANSHA INTERNATIONAL
NEW YORK · TOKYO · LONDON

959.8
C812
cop.1
DISCARD

Portions of this book appeared in slightly different form in *The Sophisticated Traveler,* *The New York Times,* and *San Francisco Focus.*

Cover illustration credit: *Amsterdams Historisch Museum*

Kodansha America, Inc.
114 Fifth Avenue, New York, New York 10011, U.S.A.

Kodansha International Ltd.
17-14 Otowa 1-chome, Bunkyo-ku, Tokyo 112, Japan

Published in 1998 by Kodansha America, Inc.

Copyright © 1998 by Charles Corn
All rights reserved.

Library of Congress Cataloging-in-Publication Data
Corn, Charles.
The scents of Eden : a narrative of the spice trade /
Charles Corn.
p.   cm.
Includes bibliographical references and index.
1. Maluku (Indonesia)—History.   2. Spice trade—Indonesia—History.   I. Title.
DS646.67.C67   1997
959.8'5—dc21   97-36839

ISBN 1-56836-202-1

Book design by Debbie Glasserman

Map on pp. xxvi–xxvii drawn by Heather Saunders

Manufactured in the United States of America on acid-free paper

98 99 00   10 9 8 7 6 5 4 3 2 1

To Ann, Lovick, and Susan,
and to Tom, all with love;
and to Rosalie, fidus Achates fide et amore

There was all the East before me, and all life, and
the thought that I had been tried in that ship and
had come out pretty well. And I thought of men
of old who, centuries ago, went that road in ships
that sailed no better to the land of palms, and
spices, and yellow sands, and of brown nations
ruled by kings more cruel than Nero the Roman,
and more splendid than Solomon.

—Joseph Conrad, *Youth: A Narrative*

This was of course a luxury trade—but have not luxuries
always been what instinctively "seems the most
necessary to man"?

—Fernand Braudel

Contents

PART I: IBERIAN DREAMS

PART II: NORTHERN DESIRE

PART III: NEW ENGLAND PASSION

Time Line

1920 B.C. The Bible tells of Joseph with his coat of many colors being sold to a spice caravan by his brothers.

1700 B.C. A recent archaeological dig in Mesopotamia (today Syria) unearthed cloves from an ordinary household kitchen dating from this period.

992 B.C. The Queen of Sheba visits King Solomon with "camels that bear spices" as her main gift.

400 B.C. Hippocrates, the "Father of Medicine," assembles a lengthy list of remedial uses for spices and herbs.

A.D. 17 Hippalus, a Greek sea captain, discovers a method of employing monsoon winds in sailing, a finding that opens direct sea trade between the Eastern Mediterranean and India.

65 The funeral rites in Rome for Nero's wife, Poppaea, require a year's supply of cinnamon.

410 Alaric the Visigoth demands three thousand pounds of pepper as ransom from Rome. Two years later he begins to extract three hundred pounds of pepper as an annual tribute.

595 Mohammed, founder of Islam, marries a spice-rich widow; his followers combine missionary zeal with spice trading in the East, thereby building the first spice monopoly while spreading Islam.

900 Venice has risen as a commercial power, principally in spices, as she begins to lead Europe out of the Dark Ages.

1095 The Crusades begin, thus alerting opportunists to the possibilities of Eastern trade as well as the need to free the Holy Land from the Muslims.

1165 A famous forged letter supposedly written by Prester John is circulated widely in Europe, tantalizing readers with the possibility of a Christian kingdom in the East.

1298 Marco Polo returns to Venice from his long Asian trip with tales of where spices were to be found. Thus Europe is awakened to the possibilities of direct Eastern trade.

1400 *The Travels of Sir John Mandeville* is published by an English knight describing real and fantastic experiences in the East. The invention of the printing press at midcentury allows this narrative a wide readership.

1402 The port of Malacca is founded on the Malay Peninsula by Prince Paramesvara, a refugee from Sumatra. Work on the cathedral in Seville is begun.

1418 Portugal's Prince Henry the Navigator founds his navigation academy to spur the Eastern spice quest.

1477 Chaucer's *Canterbury Tales* are printed. Botticelli paints his *Primavera*.

1492 Leonardo da Vinci draws a flying machine. Lorenzo de Medici, "The Magnificent," dies. Moorish Granada falls to Christian Spain. The Inquisition gives Jews three months to accept Christianity or leave Spain. Ferdinand and Isabella finance Columbus's voyage to the New World.

1493 With the stroke of a pen the Borgia Pope Alexander VI divides the unexplored world between Spain and Portugal by the Treaty of Tordesillas.

1498 Michelangelo completes his *Pietà* at St. Peter's in Rome. Vasco da Gama rounds the Cape of Despair (later the Cape of Good Hope) to open a sea route to India.

1504–1506 Venice sends ambassadors to the sultan of Turkey proposing construction of a canal across the Isthmus of Suez. Portuguese found spice factories on India's east coast. Francis Xavier, "the Apostle of the Indies," is born. Columbus dies.

1507 Luther is ordained. America is named after Amerigo Vespucci, and the New World is finally described as distinct from Asia.

1509 Eighteen-year-old Henry VIII ascends to the throne of England and marries his brother's widow, Catherine of Aragon. Magellan and Serrão, on a reconnoitering mission to Malacca, barely escape to India with their lives. Michelangelo is suspended beneath the ceiling of the Sistine Chapel painting his frescoes.

1510–1512 The painter Botticelli dies. The American east coast is discovered up to Charleston. Leonardo da Vinci designs the horizontal water wheel (principle of the water turbine). The Portuguese under Albuquerque conquer Malacca, and three ships set sail for the Spice Islands. Serrão begins his new life on Ternate.

1519 Financed by Charles V, the eighteen-year-old Holy Roman Emperor, Magellan sets sail westward from Spain in search of the Spice Islands. Cortés brings Arabian horses from Spain to North America. Leonardo da Vinci dies.

1521 Magellan is killed in the Philippines, while Serrão is poisoned by island intriguers. Cortés assumes control of Mexico. Luther is cross-examined before the Diet of Worms.

1522–1524 The single surviving ship of Magellan's expedition returns to Spain with sufficient spices to pay for the entire expedition. Vasco da Gama dies. Giovanni da Verrazano discovers New York Bay and the Hudson River.

1531 Henry VIII is recognized as supreme head of the Church of England. The "Great Comet" (later Halley's Comet) arouses superstition in Europe.

1546 Francis Xavier sails from Malacca for the Spice Islands. Martin Luther dies.

1552 Xavier dies off the coast of China. Titian paints his *Self-Portrait.*

1556 Charles V abdicates, assigning Spain to his son Philip II. Ignatius Loyola dies.

1564 Shakespeare is born. John Calvin and Michelangelo die. Spaniards occupy the Philippines and begin to build Manila.

1575–1580 The Portuguese surrender their colony on Ternate. England's Sir Martin Frobisher discovers Labrador in the course of seeking a northwest passage to the Spice Islands. Francis Drake returns to England as a hero after circumnavigating the globe.

1584 Sir Walter Raleigh discovers and claims Virginia.

1591–1592 James Lancaster sets sail from Plymouth on the first English voyage to the East Indies and sails around the Malay Peninsula.

1595 The Dutch begin their efforts at colonizing the East Indies. Shakespeare writes *A Midsummer Night's Dream.*

1597 Willem Barentsz, Dutch navigator, dies on his return from Nova Zembla, having attempted to find a northeast passage to the Spice Islands.

1600 Shakespeare writes *Hamlet.* The English East India Company is founded.

1602 The Dutch East India Company is established, having evolved from an earlier company.

1603 Upon the death of Queen Elizabeth, James of Scotland ascends to the English throne. Raleigh is arrested and imprisoned in the Tower of London. England's first colony is founded on the tiny island of Run in the Banda Islands.

1609 Hugo Grotius writes *Mare Librum,* advocating freedom of the seas. Rubens paints his self-portrait with his wife. The Bank of Amsterdam is founded. Tea from China is shipped to Europe for the first time by the Dutch East India Company. The Banda islanders ambush the Dutch in a "vile treachery."

1611–1612 The King James Bible is published. Henry Hudson, who had discovered Hudson Bay the year before, dies. John Donne composes his elegy "An Anatomy of the World." Tobacco is planted in Virginia. The Dutch use Manhattan as a fur-trading center. El Greco paints *Baptism of Christ.*

1614 Raleigh writes *The History of the World* while imprisoned. Pocahontas, an Indian princess, marries the Englishman John Rolfe.

1616 Shakespeare and Miguel de Cervantes die. Raleigh is freed from the Tower of London to lead his expedition to Guiana in search of El Dorado. Galileo is prohibited from further scientific work by the Catholic Church. The Banda islands of Run and Ai take England as an overlord, thus provoking the wrath of the Dutch.

1618 Raleigh returns to England after a disastrous expedition and is beheaded. Francis Bacon is made lord chancellor. The hard-liner Jan Pieterszoon Coen is promoted to governor-general of the Dutch East Indies and institutes a reign of terror in the islands.

1623–1626 The Ambon Massacre occurs. James I of England dies and is succeeded by his son Charles I. The Dutch colony of New Amsterdam is founded on the Hudson River.

1649–1651 Charles I goes to the block, and England is declared a commonwealth. Cromwell invades Ireland. Tea is first drunk in England. The first English Navigation Act is directed against the Dutch. The Dutch settle the Cape of Good Hope.

1658 The Dutch oust the Portuguese from Ceylon, thus seizing control of the cinnamon trade. John Dryden eulogizes Cromwell in "Heroic Stanzas."

1661–1664 The coronation of Charles II marks the beginning of the Restoration. Daniel Defoe is born.

1666 The Great Fire of London rages and is recorded by the diarist Samuel Pepys, following the Great Plague of the previous year, chronicled later by Defoe.

1667 The treaty known as the Peace of Breda is signed, giving Manhattan to the English and the island of Run to the Dutch. Milton's "Paradise Lost" is published. The Cathedral in Mexico City, a hundred years in the building, is completed.

1697 Peter the Great, posing as Peter Mikhailov and determined to Europeanize Russia, begins an eighteen-month journey through Prussia, Holland, England, and Vienna to study European ways of life. The last remains of the Mayan civilization are destroyed by the Spanish in Yucatán.

1701–1706 Yale Collegiate School is founded at Saybrook and Yale College is established in New Haven, Connecticut, on Elihu Yale's proceeds from the spice trade. Captain Kidd is hanged for piracy. Benjamin Franklin is born.

1721 A great plague from the East sweeps through southern France.

1732 George Washington is born. Franklin's *Poor Richard's Almanack* is issued by the twenty-six-year-old author.

1755–1760 A major Lisbon earthquake kills thirty thousand people and destroys the original letters exchanged between Magellan and Serrão as well as other important correspondence. Clive leaves India a hero. Marie Antoinette is born. George III ascends to the English throne.

1769–1770 Captain James Cook sails for Tahiti and discovers Australia.

1770 Pierre Poivre's associate, Provost, manages to smuggle clove and nutmeg seedlings out of the Spice Islands to Mauritius, thus ending the Dutch monopoly of the spice trade. The Boston Massacre erupts, a brawl between civilians and British troops. Beethoven is born.

1775–1783 The American Revolution is under way the year Jane Austen is born. James Watt perfects the steam engine. By the Treaty of Paris, Great Britain finally recognizes the independence of the United States. Mozart composes his Mass in C minor.

1789 The Paris mob storms the Bastille, beginning the bloody period of the French Revolution. Fletcher Christian and the other mutineers of the HMS *Bounty* settle on

Pitcairn Island in the East Pacific, while Captain William Bligh and his eighteen loyalists sail 3,600 miles from Tonga to Timor in the Dutch East Indies.

1793 The Reign of Terror begins, and France's king and queen are carted to the guillotine. The Louvre becomes a national art gallery, and the building of the Capitol in Washington, D.C., begins. Eli Whitney invents the cotton gin.

1796 The Napoleonic Wars are gearing up in Europe. The Spice Islands briefly revert to England. Captain Jonathan Carnes of Salem, Massachusetts, secretly sails his schooner *Rajah* to Sumatra to acquire bulk pepper. John Adams defeats Thomas Jefferson in the U.S. presidential election.

1803 President Thomas Jefferson consummates the Louisiana Purchase with a financially strapped Napoleon, prompting the Lewis and Clark expedition through the Pacific Northwest. Emerson and Berlioz are born. Robert Fulton propels a boat by steam power.

1807 Thomas Jefferson signs the Tyrannical Embargo Act (aimed against Britain and France), crippling American sea trade. Explorer Alexander von Humboldt publishes the first of thirty volumes on Spanish America.

1812–1819 After mounting tensions, the United States declares war on Britain. Lord Byron writes "Childe Harold's Pilgrimage," which makes him quite literally famous overnight. Beethoven composes his Seventh and Eighth Symphonies. The British found Singapore.

1831 As Boston continues its rise, ultimately to overtake Salem as New England's most important port, Nat Turner leads a Virginia slave revolt. Charles Darwin begins his voyage as a naturalist on the HMS *Beagle* to the South Pacific. Bellini composes his operas *La Sonnambula* and *Norma,* and Chopin arrives in Paris. The American frigate *Potomac* sails to Sumatra's coast to avenge an attack on Salem's merchant ship *Friendship*.

1838 Queen Victoria is crowned. Chopin's liaison with George Sand begins. Navy statistics reveal that Great Britain has ninety active ships, Russia fifty, France forty-nine, and America fifteen.

1839 The First Opium War between Britain and China breaks out. Poe writes "The Fall of the House of Usher." Army officer Abner Doubleday designs the first baseball field and oversees the first baseball game ever played, in Cooperstown, New York.

1842 The Opium Wars between Britain and China are ended by the Treaty of Nanking, and Hong Kong is ceded to Great Britain. Charles Dickens publishes *American Notes.* Wagner composes his early opera *Rienzi*.

1850–1855 Donald McKay's clipper *Flying Cloud* sets a record. A year after Hawthorne's *The Scarlet Letter,* Melville's *Moby Dick* is published, followed three years later by Thoreau's *Walden* in 1854. Walt Whitman's *Leaves of Grass* creates a sensation. Livingston discovers Victoria Falls of the Zambezi River. The first iron Cunard steamer crosses the Atlantic in nine and a half days.

1861 The American Civil War breaks out. T. S. Mort of Sydney, Australia, builds the first machine-chilled cold-storage unit, thus relegating spices to the role of flavoring agents rather than that of preservatives. Louis Pasteur puts forth his germ theory of fermentation.

1871–1873 The Dutch declare war on the Acehnese. Piracy and native attacks finally halt America's direct pepper trade with Sumatra, marking the last of 967 pepper voyages.

1877 Queen Victoria is proclaimed empress of India. Thomas Edison invents the phonograph, a year after Alexander Graham Bell invented the telephone. Henry James writes *The American.*

1880 Joel Chandler Harris writes *Uncle Remus.* Thomas Edison invents the lightbulb. Canned fruits and meats first appear in stores.

1900 The Boxer Rebellion erupts in China, pitting Chinese against American marines. Picasso paints *Le Moulin de la Galette.* The zeppelin has its first trial flight. Joseph Conrad publishes his novel *Lord Jim.*

1907 The American Spice Trade Association is formed.

1937 Albert Szent-Györgyi is awarded the Nobel Prize for discovering vitamin C in his research with paprika.

1939–1945 World War II sharply curtails the world's spice supply.

1955 Hurricane Janet destroys 75 percent of Grenada's nutmeg trees. At the time, this loss represents 40 percent of the world's supply.

1959 An American survey reveals that spices in whatever form have become the fastest-selling grocery items.

Note: While many of the entries in the preceding chronology are original, many others have been adapted from the American Spice Trade Association's 1966 pamphlet *A History of Spices* and Dr. Bernard Grun's *The Timetables of History,* revised edition (Simon and Schuster, 1991).

PROLOGUE

LATE IN THE spring of 1994, I returned to the cluster of tiny volcanic and coral islands—some no larger than atolls—that float in the Banda Sea at the eastern end of the Indonesian archipelago. The Banda Islands are mere dots on a map of any size. You reach them by small aircraft out of Amboina, the capital of the Moluccas, a hundred miles to the north, or by the occasional native freighter, as I did when I first fetched up there during the monsoon of 1988. This forested, spice-scented mini-archipelago, dominated by a lofty volcano and surrounded by gin-clear waters caressing brilliant coral gardens, is as stunningly beautiful as any island group in the world.

Scattered in the strange seas between Celebes (today Sulawesi) and New Guinea, the Bandas (also referred to collectively as Banda) are the southernmost of a larger group, the Moluccas. The Moluccas are the Spice Islands of history and legend that fired the imagination of the Roman scholar Pliny and beckoned Sinbad the Sailor. The Bandas themselves were a particular prize because of a lofty, fruit-bearing tree with dark green foliage that thrived nowhere else in the world—*Myristica fragrans,* the nutmeg.

The walnut-size nutmeg has proliferated for millennia in idyllic circumstances that long predate man's comparatively recent arrival here, and the fruit's abundance speaks to a unique natural alchemy that teases the mind and excites the imagination. Situated between Southeast Asia and Australia, the Banda Islands share some of the characteristics of each continent, while belonging to neither by virtue of their remoteness and the earth's geological upheavals. This is a point that was noted in 1869 by the Victorian naturalist Alfred Russel Wallace in his masterwork *The Malay Archipelago.* While monkeys and snakes are unknown here, boar and pigeons abound. It is the latter, birds with soft cries habitually flying the short distances between islands to deposit what they have ingested whole, that have allowed the nutmeg to flourish in Banda, and only in Banda, over countless thousands of years.

Likewise, the clove tree—*Eugenia aromatica*—is native only to the five small Moluccan islands of Ternate, Tidore, Moti, Makian, and Bacan, located some four hundred miles north of Banda on the other side of the equator. The two most prominent of these clove-producing islands, Ternate and Tidore, are active volcanoes that rise a mile into the sky. As in Banda, the periodic eruptions within this ring of fire enrich the adjacent spice gardens with nutrient-laden dust.

Everywhere and nowhere, the location and even the existence of the Spice Islands were far from a geographical certainty as the Age of Discovery opened. Clothed in mystery and lost in equatorial seas, they teased the European imagination to the point of obsession. Compounding their remote, elemental setting was the fact that it was not known until the mid-eighteenth century that trees and plants could be grown in places other than where they were native. This botanical ignorance prompted European sailors to sail boldly, embracing whatever hardships hostile oceans could inflict, to reach a remote corner of the earth in search of spices, for the only place the nutmeg tree then grew was half a world away on a sprinkling of islands with a total area of forty square miles. The clove groves to the north were as uniquely sized, situated, and pedigreed. It may seem to us today incomprehensible that such a horticultural circumstance could occasion the rise and fall of empires whose seats of power stood on the other side of the world, but so it was.

From the late fifteenth century, as European powers sought to colonize Asia, overriding Chinese and Arab traders in the process, the Portuguese, Dutch, English, and to a lesser degree the French were magnetized by and waged wars over these islands in successive waves as each nation sought to establish a trade monopoly over their produce. The quarry was spices: delicious flower buds, sweet-smelling dried pieces of bark, small aromatic seeds—prized for their aphrodisiacal, medicinal, and preservative qualities as well as their scent and taste. The Spice Islands themselves became a theater, peopled with representatives of Eastern cartels and Western nations, with each season bringing a new rage while successors with new leases of affection waited in the wings. It was a stage, at once romantic and inglorious, that had no precedent in history.

Why were spices, which drove the world's economy four hundred years ago much as oil does today, so universally and highly prized? Their uses were many and diverse, especially the clove, known for hundreds of years as the "black rose" among the caravansaries dotting the limitless Asian steppes. For the locals who harvested them, cloves functioned as a remedy as well as a delicacy. When picked green and sugared, the fruit could be transformed into conserves. Salted and pickled, it became a flavoring for vinegar. In whole or powdered form, the clove functioned as a medicine. The Chinese were keen on the clove for flavor in cooking and prized it as an analgesic. They also used it in religious ceremonies, and courtiers and courtesans of the Han dynasty in the third century B.C. sweetened their breaths with cloves whenever they addressed their emperor. Europeans believed that the essence of clove when applied to the eye strengthened the vision. When rubbed on the forehead, it was thought to relieve head colds. Added to food or drink, the clove supposedly stimulated the appetite and cleared the bladder and intestines. Taken with milk, the fruit was thought to enhance the pleasures of sexual intercourse. The Dutch held that the uses of the clove were "too many to recount."

Nutmeg functioned as both an aphrodisiac and a hallucinogen as well as a condiment, while ginger, cinnamon, and pepper were especially prized as preservatives. Tacitus informs us that after murdering his wife, Poppaea, in A.D. 65, Nero used a year's supply of Rome's cinnamon to bury her. In the Middle Ages a pound of ginger was worth a sheep, while a similar weight of mace could buy three sheep or half a cow. Pepper, counted out berry by berry, was nearly priceless. It could pay taxes and rents, dowries and tributes. Nor did these uses and values lessen in time before the invention of artificial refrigeration in the mid-nineteenth century. Eighteen centuries after Nero, the body of a Salem, Massachusetts, sailor was embalmed in a coffin of pepper in Sumatra and after months at sea was returned to New England, where he was pronounced as looking "very natural."

For Europeans intent on reaching their source, spices had an association at once worldly and otherworldly. To be sure, spices conjured up a legendary, if not mystical, continuum, a story deeply rooted in antiquity. For thousands of years these curls of bark, small seeds, and dried buds flowed like a great fragrant river along the well-rutted trade routes, while, with a seeming life of their own, they invaded man's history and infused his legends. Perfuming the bath, lending aromatic grace to the hearth, and enrichening tributes to the gods, spices had worked their magic since biblical times.

Nineteen hundred years before Christ, Joseph was sold by his brothers to "a company of Ishmaelites come from Gilead, with their camels bearing spicery and balm and myrrh, going to carry it down to Egypt." This "company" was the Arabs, over three thousand years ago already monopolists of the spice trade, acquiring their precious stores from Indian as well as Chinese and Javanese traders who visited ports of the Indian subcontinent. For centuries Arabs had kept secret the source of their supply, telling only of dark and menacing distant lands, while their caravans, numbering sometimes as many as four thousand camels laden with silks and gold as well as spices, crossed vast Asian wastes along several routes that have been known collectively as the Silk Road. These priceless commodities of long-distance trade were in demand from China all the way to Europe via the markets of Nineveh and Babylon, and later Carthage, Alexandria, and Rome.

Other biblical references document the use of spices. The book of Exodus tells that when the children of Israel fled Egypt, they took with them "principal spices," and that at the rich port of Tyre, trade was conducted "of all spices, and with all precious stones and gold." It is believed that King Solomon, around 1000 B.C., had amassed some of his great wealth from spices through a trade agreement with the Phoenician king Hiram. When the Queen of Sheba calls on Solomon, she is escorted by "camels that bear spices," an extravagant gift. One measure of their widespread use in antiquity is a recent archaeological dig at the Mesopotamian site of Terqua (today Syria), dating from 1700 B.C., which unearthed cloves in the kitchen of an ordinary household.

In ancient times the produce was carried from the islands by local people in shallow-drafted, native boats, known as prahus, to the Chinese traders aboard their junks in the larger ports of the archipelago, who would then disseminate them throughout Asia's waterways. By the fourteenth century northeastern Javanese ports, with their ruling Arab, Chinese, and Javanese elite, provided a means to link the Spice Islands' trade network with the rest of the world. Eventually, Muslim traders entered the picture by exploiting the sea route from the prosperous Malay entrepôt of Malacca to Bassorah, on the Persian Gulf, where spices were transported overland to Damascus or Aleppo on the Mediterranean. In turn, the spices were delivered by Muslim merchants to such ports as Constantinople, Genoa, and Venice, markets for an expectant Europe. The produce arrived, however, at exorbitant prices; a conservative estimate is that they rose in value one hundred percent each time they changed hands, and this route required that they change hands hundreds of times.

The Arabs' monopoly, always strong, had strengthened during Europe's Dark Ages. After the fall of Rome left much of western Europe to languish in darkness, a young camel driver named Mohammed, from Mecca on the eastern shore of the Red Sea, was fortunate enough to make an auspicious marriage to the widow of a wealthy Arabian spice merchant. A religious visionary of a new faith known as Islam (literally, "submission"), Mohammed cunningly saw that faith and trade were anything but mutually exclusive. While Europe stagnated until the tenth century, when Venice rose under new winds of trade, Mohammed's followers—missionaries and traders—spread Islam to the East, reaching the Malay Archipelago in the thirteenth century. Though Venetian galleys were laden with spice sacks, Europe still remained ignorant of the sources of this great wealth, while Muslims knew them only too well.

It was only a question of time before secular and ecclesiastical authorities in a Christianized Europe would seek to throw off an economic yoke imposed by its Islamic enemies and attempt to gain control of their own spice trade. Portugal's Prince Henry the Navigator was the first to sponsor an agenda of discovery in the early fifteenth century, emphasizing the search for a sea route to Asia. Bartholomeu Dias rounded Africa's southern cape in 1488, and he was followed a decade later by Vasco da Gama's successful expedition to India's west coast. The ultimate goal of the Portuguese, as with the nations that followed them, was to reach the source of the fabled holy trinity of spices—cloves, nutmeg, and mace—while seizing the vital centers of international trade routes, thus destroying the long-standing Muslim control of the spice trade. European colonization of Asia was ancillary to this purpose, and it would prove to be as undesirable for all concerned as it was inevitable.

There were also subtler factors at work on the European imagination and its notions of time and progress that would contrast starkly with Eastern ideas of the cyclical and episodic when the two worlds finally collided. Since the time of Homer, tales of fabulous lands with their fantastic peoples and monsters lying far beyond the perimeters of the Greek world provided a framework for the West's appreciation of the unknown. (It was a Greek sea captain, Hippalus, who in the year A.D. 17 discovered a method of using the force of monsoon winds in sailing, thereby allowing direct sea trade between Egypt and India.) Herodotus wrote of monsters in India, and such notions persisted during Roman times with Pliny's *Historia Naturalis*. During the Middle Ages views of the wondrous East were held with the authority of the Bible in mind, and St. Augustine posited that monstrosities were not against God and nature but real phenomena.

A best-seller of medieval times perpetuating this traditional view was *The Travels of Sir John Mandeville,* by an English knight who claimed to have served the sultan of Egypt and the Great Khan of Cathay during his decades of travel between 1322 and 1356. The book, a compendium of the real and chimerical about the East, had by the year 1400 been translated not only into Latin but into every other European language, reaching an unprecedented audience with the invention of the printing press in the mid-fifteenth century. The narrative, a mingling of prosaic renderings of daily life and lurid, grotesque accounts of monster races, was as vigorously influential among mapmakers of the age as it was widely read. Atlases relying upon the information brought back by Marco Polo and Odoric de Pordenone continued to incorporate the mythical with real peoples and geography.

There was another important obsession nurturing the European sensibility, and it was deeply rooted in the Christian tradition. On the eve of the age of discovery there was an abiding belief in Europe that the Garden of Eden was a real place, and that it lay in Asia. This potent image, handed down from the Middle Ages, impelled Columbus, believing he had reached Asia, to write the Spanish monarchy after his third voyage to the New World: "There are great indications of this being the terrestrial paradise, for its site coincides with the opinion of the holy and wise theologians . . . all of whom agree that the earthly paradise is in the East." The image, similar in effect to the Holy Grail, was to become a driving force.

The association of Eden and the East was sufficiently strong to be embraced not only by the Church as an ecclesiastical certainty but as well by the common consciousness as the Prester John legend, long a part of the European oral tradition. A bishop in 1144 claimed to have met a man known as Prester John, the Christian king of an astonishingly wealthy land in Asia, and this claim was substantiated around 1165 in the form of a letter (later discovered to have been forged) from this alleged ruler that was circulated widely in Europe. Addressed to Immanuel I, emperor of Byzantium, it read in part: "I Prester John, who reign supreme, surpass in virtue, riches, and power all creatures under heaven. Seventy kings are our tributaries. . . . For gold, silver, precious stones, animals of every kind, and the number of our people, we believe there is not our equal under heaven. . . . Every month we are served in rotation by seven kings, sixty-two dukes, and 265 counts and marquises. . . . And if we have chosen to be called by a lower name and inferior rank, it springs from humility. If indeed you can number the stars of heaven and sands of the sea, then you may calculate the extent of our dominion and power."

So inspired, a number of travelers, Marco Polo and Odoric of Pordenone among them, searched for this ruler and claimed to have found him among Christian Turkish tribes in Central Asia. By the fourteenth century, Prester John's kingdom was believed to be in Ethiopia, and an emissary was dispatched by the Portuguese court only to discover that the discovered ruler, although Christian, was not the almighty ruler self-described in the famous letter. The legend, however, had seized the European fancy, and no effort was spared to seek out this wealthy bastion of Christendom in a land of Muslims. Among the pictorial details in a chart of the Indian Ocean by Diogo Homem dating from 1558 is a drawing of Prester John enthroned.

Thus Europe's compulsion to reach the source of spices for the procurement of earthly riches was tempered as well by faith, an equally strong compulsion, as merchants and politicians, geographers and seafarers pushed back the limits of the unknown world to reach the Spice Islands.

Today these islands lie largely forgotten and are visited only by the adventurous traveler with time on his hands. But not so in their heyday, and with good reason. In 1603, when the first English colony anywhere was founded on the Bandanese island of Run, ten pounds of nutmeg could be bought from its natives for a halfpenny a pound and resold in Europe for a profit, at least by one estimate, of a staggering 32,000 percent.

Similarly, Ternate and Tidore and three smaller islands adjacent to the sprawling island of Halmahera in the Northern Moluccas, the exclusive home of the clove tree, were equally prized destinations. Although the California-size island of Sumatra was a major source of pepper (as was India's Malabar Coast), it was not the home of the holy trinity of spices, and the Moluccas were. Hence the first European gaze to the Far East settled on the fabled Spice Islands of the Moluccas.

Four centuries ago the most dangerous and competitive game in the world, the spice trade, was joined on these remote "spiceries." The theater on which this centuries-old drama was played out, determining the fortunes of nations, soon became the world itself, prompting unprecedented explorations and discoveries, adventures and misadventures, which form the narrative of this book.

By the end of the fifteenth century, the development of oceangoing vessels and improved navigational aids enabled Europe to open trade routes to Asia, for the West's appetite for spices by this time was nearly insatiable. It should come as no surprise, then, that the European voyages were enormously profitable.

Vasco da Gama returned to Lisbon in 1499 with a cargo that paid for his expedition's cost sixty times over. Francis Drake's world voyage, 1577–80, during which he called at the Spice Islands, gained its investors a return of 4,700 percent. During the two hundred years of its existence, the Dutch East India Company paid an average annual dividend of eighteen percent, and the profits of the English East India Company during the same period were much higher, with the wealth generated by this trade a great stimulus to commerce in general.

Put in more grandiose terms, the spice trade was the lifeblood of civilization and brought with it a tide of wealth sweeping through a still largely barbaric Europe. Literally worth their weight in gold, the cloves, nutmeg, mace, cinnamon, ginger, and pepper spawned a new age of revolutionary economics based on credit, the rise of a rudimentary banking system, and ultimately free enterprise.

• • •

I WAS STRUCK on my first trip to the Moluccas by the astonishing historical mystery of these tiny islands and how they held an expectant world hostage for hundreds of years. This book finds its origins in a trivial incident that invoked that very question. One afternoon, as I was exploring one of Banda's scented nutmeg forests, I paused to pick up a nutmeg that had just fallen from a nearby tree. I split the nut, once more valuable than gold, with my knife, and inhaled the aroma. For an instant, I imagined I held in my fingers a passkey to history.

This is the story of the spice trade from the Age of Discovery onward, told through select individuals who embodied different periods in this trade—among them Ferdinand Magellan and his friend and probable cousin Francisco Serrão in the early sixteenth century; Francis Xavier, cofounder of the Jesuits and "the Apostle of the East" a half century later; the infamous Jan Pieterszoon Coen, governor-general of the Dutch East India Company, in the next century; Pierre Poivre, the enterprising Frenchman who broke the Dutch monopoly in the late eighteenth century; and the Salem, Massachusetts, sea captain Jonathan Carnes, who made a fortune in the pepper trade with Sumatra in the years following the American Revolution, anticipating America's first millionaires in the finest neoclassical city of the American enlightenment.

Each is a participant within a larger story, a stage arrayed with famous and obscure, noble and venal players alike, but always a compelling cast of characters whose circumstances and actions set others in motion, creating a rippling effect leading to often extraordinary associations. It is, then, first and foremost a story about people associated with exploration and colonization in Asia, the connections they made, and the crucial impact they had on the individuals and events of their day.

The participants not only gathered unto themselves the dream of several ages, but also lived and struggled in their own time for the material fortune to be gained from the spice trade. To be sure, there were enormous discrepancies between their visions of glory and what they actually discovered. Whatever were the cravings of such exceedingly diverse men, they mirror also the aspirations of their age.

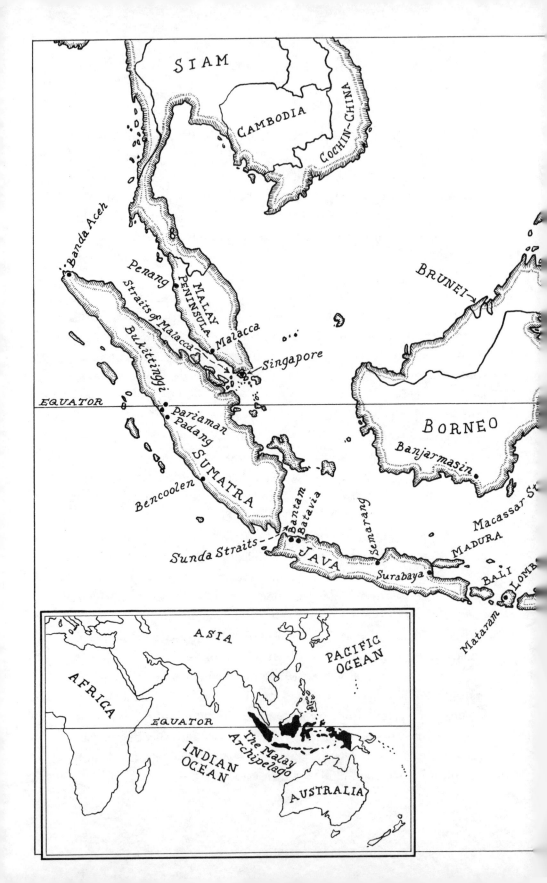

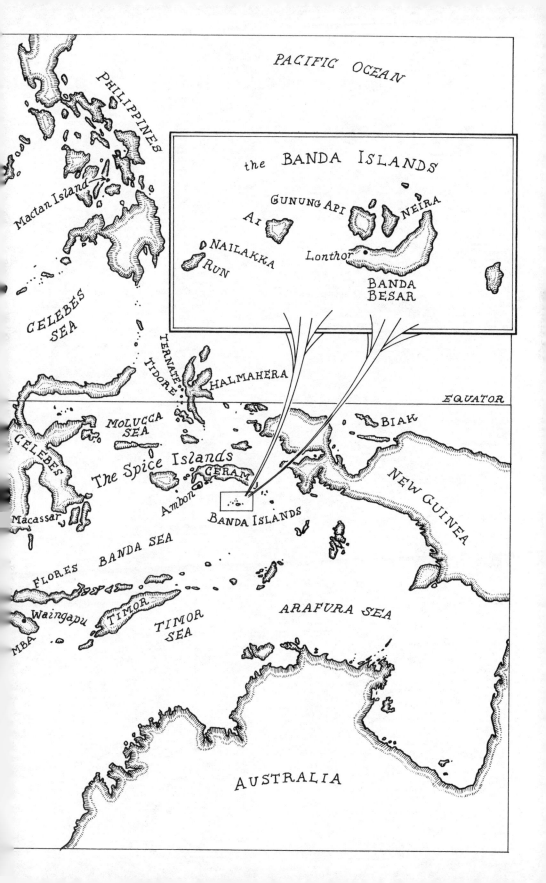

Part V

IBERIAN
DREAMS

Over the Eastern Oceans cast your eyes
To see where islands numberless are spread:
Tidore, Ternate view, mountains whence arise
Flames undulating round the burning head:
Trees of hot clove thou shall behold, likewise,
With blood of Portugal e'en purchased;
Here are the golden birds, who ne'er descend
On earth, while living, but when life doth end.

—LUIS DE CAMÕES, *Os Lusiadas* (1572)

Chapter 1

"WHOEVER IS
LORD OF MALACCA . . ."

EUROPEAN COLONIZATION OF the Far East began in July of 1511 when a Portuguese fleet, commanded by Afonso de Albuquerque and including a young captain named Fernão de Magalhães, rode at anchor just off the strategic port of Malacca's deepwater channel, within sight of the river bisecting the city and the sultan's palace on the fortified port's highest hill.

Malacca is tucked away on the southwestern coast of the Malay Peninsula in the narrowest part of the straits separating the mainland from the island of Sumatra. Today this ancient port city, lying midway between the Malaysian capital, Kuala Lumpur, and Singapore, is a neglected terminus —a seaside pastel of narrow streets and old ruins whitened by the sun, a detour for the curious traveler. But at the beginning of the sixteenth century, Malacca was fabled and golden: one of the most important destinations on earth. Malacca was the most prized port along the legendary spice route that stretched from the Moluccas, or Spice Islands, in the East across Asia to the West. As the major entrepôt trading center in Asia, the riches of the Orient—especially spices—passed through the city on their way to an expectant Europe, a trade for centuries controlled by Arab and Chinese merchants.

That summer day the ships rode in place under a monsoon their sailors knew well, for it had raged at the flotilla as it sailed east from India. At northern Sumatra the Europeans had managed not only to secure provisions, but also to commandeer a few junks. Now the winds funneled up the straits, boiling the seas under the strained anchor ropes and tearing at the furled sails—dull gray for the European ships and bright red, green, and yellow for the junks.

The Portuguese were intent on seizing control of the spice trade, but to do so required the siege and capture of Malacca, for the fortress-port guarded the bottleneck between the Indian Ocean, the Java Sea, and the South China Sea, and hence monopolized mercantile activities in this part of the world. The deepwater channel separating the mainland from Sumatra passed close to the city, and merchant dhows riding the seasonal monsoons from Arabia and India called here, as did junks from China. Likewise, *lanchara,* the small single-sailed, square-rigged vessels from the islands to the east of Java, were familiar sights in the harbor.

An early-sixteenth-century visitor put a fine point on the city's importance. "No trading port as large as Malacca is known, nor anywhere else do they deal in such fine and highly priced merchandise. Goods from all over the world are sold here. It is at the end of monsoons when you find what you want, and sometimes more than what you are looking for."

Urged on by the dictum "Whoever is lord of Malacca has his hand on the throat of Venice," the Portuguese, with no fond memories of the Moors' three-hundred-year occupation of Iberia, were primed for invasion in July 1511.

Since the year 1000 the Venetian fleet had controlled the Asiatic scene, dominating the route to the Holy Land and the Far East, and by the 1400s Venetian ships were returning from the East loaded with its most precious cargo, spices. Venice in its prime was extravagantly rich, much as Amsterdam would become in the seventeenth century. Its spirit of taste and adventure may be perceived in a single individual of the thirteenth century, Marco Polo (1254–1324).

The pen of this Venetian merchant yielded one of the world's most important and timely books, *The Adventures of Marco Polo,* while Polo suffered captivity as a Genoese prisoner of war. With the enforced leisure to chronicle his travels, which began in 1271, Polo in his narrative awakened Europe's interest in the Far East. Though many of his contemporaries—unwilling to believe that Asia was in many ways ahead of the West in matters economic, cultural, and technical—branded Polo as a boaster and liar, his narrative had a profound influence in exciting the European imagination and giving shape to the way the Western mind began to perceive Asia.

Alexandre Dumas later wrote of Venice in *Grand Dictionnaire de Cuisine:* "The intellectual faculties seem to have soared in an enduring exaltation under the influence of spices. Is it to spices that we owe Titian's masterpieces? I am tempted to believe it." Therefore, it did not augur well for Venice when Portuguese mariners in the wake of Vasco da Gama waded ashore in India with the cry "For Christ and spices!" In the city of St. Mark, Girolamo Priuli noted in his journal in July 1501 that the loss of the spice trade "would be like the loss of milk to a newborn babe."

Fernão de Magalhães (who would later take the *nom de guerre* Fernando de Magallanes, which in turn would become anglicized to Ferdinand Magellan) and his friend Francisco Serrão were both in their early thirties, Magellan older by two years. Though neither was famous, their lives were to become curiously intertwined and lead a decade later to Magellan's leadership of the first expedition to circumnavigate the globe in his search for the Spice Islands. But there was little in the summer of 1511 to suggest that such a feat was even a remote possibility.

Born in northwestern Portugal of provincial nobility, the young men served in 1495 as court pages in Lisbon. It was the eve of Vasco da Gama's expedition around southern Africa's Cape of Good Hope to reach India, and the palace talked of little else than overseas conquests. Caught up in the brash times, the two had embarked by 1505 on a campaign several years long in the Indian Ocean, when the Portuguese sought military and, more important, mercantile supremacy over the hated Venetians. Venice, with the combined forces of Egypt and India, had secured a monopoly on Europe's trade, and Portugal was keen to see it ended. It signaled a bloody period.

Magellan, not a tall man, had the stocky build of a wrestler and carried a large, square head with a high, strong nose, his prominent features framed by a black beard giving off an air of unrelenting intensity. No less determined was the younger Serrão, who cut a more poetic figure in his suit of armor than his friend's prosaic one. Magellan had saved Serrão's life more than once, as Serrão had Magellan's, each earning scars in battle.

In the midsummer of 1511, as the Portuguese awaited the signal for the offensive, the two men—now bachelor officers in their prime—were hardened, cocksure veterans of the wars.

The soldiers and sailors of the expedition were dirty and stank from weeks of crowded living aboard the sixty-ton caravels, which forced on the men a diet of bitter wine, hard bread, and salt meat: staples of the adventurer's life. Rations, however, were not always so mean. Though the scarcity of fruit and vegetables on long voyages inevitably raised the specter of scurvy, the Portuguese did discover a plentiful source of protein in the meat of green sea turtles. These docile creatures were especially vulnerable on tropical moonlit beaches when they emerged from the surf to lay their eggs, only to be seized by human predators. Flung on their backs in the watery holds of caravels to flail helplessly in the swill for days and weeks, they were slaughtered one by one to feed hungry seamen. But turtles were not always to be found, and a steady diet of barely edible victuals had been forced on these men in a confined space not much larger than a modern school bus.

By contrast, some of the Chinese vessels that called at Malacca were floating cities, with room for as many as four hundred men, women, and children, as well as onboard fruit and vegetable gardens. There were even larger Malay ships called *jongs,* twice the height of Portuguese ships; these rode low in the water and sailed slowly and awkwardly when carrying a full cargo of a thousand tons and a thousand men.

Since its founding, Malacca had been impregnable to siege, and many believed it to be unassailable. There were four gates in the surrounding city wall, each with a watch and drum tower. Inside the walls was a second, smaller enclosure of palisades where individual godowns on the river housed wares for trade. Malacca's defenses were not readily seen from the sea, for good reason. The fortress-port was a warren of confused levels and narrow streets that descended to the protected harbor at the mouth of the river. A crucial tactical consideration was the river itself, for it divided the city, which clung to the estuary like seaweed to rock.

Serrão and Magellan were no strangers to Malacca. Two years before, they had tasted the city's wealth in an expedition that ended in disaster, nearly costing them their lives. In September of 1509 Diogo Lopes de Sequeira carried orders from Portugal's King Manuel to reconnoiter the fabled port and establish a base there from which to reach the Spice Islands. Magellan and Serrão, eager for adventure and riches, signed onto the voyage in Cochin, on the subcontinent. The small group got under way, a force of seventy men driven by high-handedness and greed and possessed of a near-total ignorance of the world they were about to confront.

When the Portuguese anchored off the fortified city and came ashore in longboats, they were greeted by vast, enthusiastic crowds of Malays. "These are white Bengalis," the natives said to each other in wonder as they surrounded the visitors, some pulling their beards and patting their heads while others seized the hats or clasped the hands of the newcomers. At first Malacca's sultan, Mahmud Shah, received the strange, ragtag visitors courteously, and after signing a peace treaty on the third day, Sequeira immediately traded for spices to fill his ships. It was the commander's intention to ride the seasonal winds back to India before they shifted.

Despite warnings by Chinese merchants and a Persian woman who had taken one of the "white Bengalis" as a lover, the Portuguese were seemingly oblivious to a treacherous plot that was being urged on the royal house by rival Arab traders. This was a desperate card played by the Muslim merchants, who resented the interlopers as Christians, but more so as their competitors in trade. In this regard, the Ming merchants, Chinese, were neutral, unless they had intermarried with the Malays, in which case they were forced to convert to Islam, thereby siding with the Arabs.

To the Malaccans, business as usual generally precluded bald betrayal of a potential trading partner. But there were unique forces at work in this encounter between two such vastly disparate peoples. Among them was the issue of two antagonistic faiths confronting each other. The newly arrived, infidel Portuguese were of a culture that had waged war against Islam for the duration of the Crusades. Then there was the question of protocol. Especially galling to Malacca's court was Portuguese ignorance of palace etiquette, for the visitors had no sense of the homage due a head of state and his prime minister.

During an audience with the sultan, one of the outlanders, Jeronimo Texeira, addressed the ruler in a loud, rude voice and in a tone familiar and demanding. It was a devastating breach of courtesy, and it became clear to the Malaccans that such boorishness should reap no reward. Then Sequeira himself attempted with his left hand—the one Muslims used for cleansing oneself, thus rendering the member unclean—to hang a gold chain around the neck of the prime minister, whose name was Tun Mutahir. Though the court was visibly angry, the sultan calmed his attendants, saying, "Leave the men alone; they know no better." But the affronts festered in the royal house, which waited for a propitious moment to strike. It came the following day.

The sultan sent a messenger to inform Sequeira that large quantities of pepper and other goods had been collected for his fleet and that he had only to send his boats and men ashore to load them. When the unsuspecting Portuguese commander split his forces between the four ships and the shore where his men were collecting spices in bulk from a warehouse on the river, the Malays attacked the shore party, cutting the men off from the longboats at the beach. Simultaneously, the Malay prahus approached the anchored caravels as if to trade, virtually surrounding the ships. With a hundred men ashore, the caravels were now lightly defended, and the remaining crew members were oblivious to what was occurring onshore as the Malays scampered aboard.

In the commander's cabin high over the square stern, Magellan discovered a half-naked Sequeira entertaining a Malaccan trader over a chessboard, surrounded by a roomful of armed Malays, and he warned Sequeira of what might be happening. Historians have roundly criticized Sequeira's credulity. Damião de Góis writes that the commander behaved "as if he were in the port of Lisbon." A lookout spotted smoke ashore and then watched in horror as a mob intercepted the Portuguese as they made their way to the beach and their longboats.

Serrão, commanding one of the loading parties, was among them, and with his men tried to slash his way through the frenzied Malays swarming the beach. The captain's pointed, high-combed helmet and metal breastplate were a prize for his attackers, and the hapless Serrão would have been killed had Magellan and two companions on shipboard not seized a skiff and paddled furiously to the beach to counterattack, allowing Serrão's group to reach a longboat, which they retook with their swords. The outnumbered Portuguese fought their way through the surf, greeted by arrows and shrieks from enemy prahus, as they rowed back to the ships, leaving behind sixty men dead or captured.

Sequeira waited a day before weighing anchor, hoping to ransom his men held by the Malays, but it was a vain hope. Determined, however, not to allow the sultan's treachery to go unpunished, he executed two captives he held aboard by having a crossbowman put an arrow through their brains, after which he deposited the bodies ashore with a message pinned to their bodies: "Thus the king of Portugal avenged the treason of his enemies."

Portugal's first dream of establishing a post at Malacca in 1509 ended in defeat and humiliation, and the expedition began the slow voyage back to India seething with the instincts of pirates. Life to these Portuguese was fierce, savage, and uncertain; it was the vast gamble that had brought them here. As consolation for the Malaccan failure, they attacked a merchant transport in the Andaman Sea, but even their attempts at piracy backfired. The crew of the junk put up a good fight, beating off the Portuguese, and then in retaliation swarmed aboard Serrão's caravel and pinned him against the mast. Again, Magellan's sword saved his friend from certain death as he and his men repelled the counterattackers. The Europeans sailed onward and as a balm to their woes took another, less resistant junk.

AS CITIES GO, Malacca was not an ancient place. Barely more than a century old, this maritime kingdom was established in 1402 by Prince Paramesvara, a fugitive driven out of southern Sumatra's Sriwijaya kingdom (today Palembang) by the powerful Majapahit rulers of East Java. Its founding is shrouded in Malay legend. The prince had been hunting in an area just out of sight of the Sumatran coast on a site known as Water Island. He was resting under a tree when one of his hounds was kicked by a white mouse-deer, sending the dog into the river.

"This is a good place," said Paramesvara, according to Malay annals. "Even its mouse-deer are full of fight! We shall do well to make a city here."

The prince ordered that a city be made, asking as he rose from his place of rest, "What is the name of this tree under which I am standing?"

"It is called *malaka,* Your Highness," his courtiers answered.

"Then Malaka shall be the name of this city," he is said to have declared, and his followers set to work laying out a settlement of wide streets lined with raised houses of split coconut palms and thatched roofs beside the river. The images of a malacca tree and a startled deer soon adorned the new settlement's coat of arms.

As the new city-state grew, it prospered. Settlers came from Java, Sumatra, Siam. Soon Malacca gained control over the straits, making Paramesvara heir to the maritime influence and power earlier enjoyed by the Sumatran kingdoms. In due time the visitation of ships from China and India were enhancing its reputation as an important trading port. And with such features as the commanding hill where the sultan's palace stood (it would become the site of St. Paul's Church in Christian times) and the sinuous river surrounded by jungle, the city was easy to defend.

Superstition as well as fortification protected Malacca. Estuarine crocodiles, believed to be dragons by Chinese traders, lurked in the coastal waters, as did tigers in the forested hills behind the port, both predators believed by Malacca's citizens to be capable of assuming human form and entering the city.

As early as 1403 the Chinese emperor sent the eunuch admiral Yin Ch'ing as envoy to this new country with presents of silks woven with golden flowers. Yin Ch'ing spoke to Paramesvara of the power and rank of China. Siam, which had claimed dominion over the peninsula, was a constant threat to overrun Paramesvara's kingdom, so the prince quickly sought protection from the imperial envoy. Other visits followed. Then the Ming court received Paramesvara in 1411, when the upstart mercantilist arrived with an entourage of 540 persons. The prince himself was received by the emperor, then lodged in the building of the Board of Rites, where he received lavish gifts and daily provisions of bullocks, goats, and wine from the imperial buttery.

When the visitors were prepared to leave, more gifts marked their departure. The emperor personally passed to Paramesvara a girdle with precious stones, horses with saddles, a hundred ounces of gold, five hundred ounces of silver, 400,000 koan in paper money, 2,600 strings of copper cash, three hundred pieces of silk gauze, a thousand pieces of plain silk, and two pieces of silk with golden flowers. Paramesvara returned home freed of the Siamese yoke, and Malacca grew overnight into the most important port in the East.

A generation later, following his conversion to Islam and his marriage to a north Sumatran princess, the second king of Malacca took the name

Iskander Shah, and the port became a center for the diffusion of Islam throughout Southeast Asia and the Malay Archipelago.

By 1477, just seventy-five years after Paramesvara established his kingdom, Malacca (contrary to the legend, the name is actually derived from the Arabic word *malakat,* meaning "market") had become the talk of Europe, while its court intrigues—marriages, divorces, murders—rivaled any in Renaissance Italy. Hindu Indian merchants arrived and settled, bringing with them theology and scholarship to adorn lustful lives at an ambitious court obsessed with war and women. A favorite tale at the court was the saga of Alexander the Great, which had arrived with Islam. Soon the Javanese quarter brought such Hindu artistry as the shadow play. Chinese traders imported Buddhism, Taoism, and Confucianism. Islam introduced a new rhythm to court life, while a succession of Malacca's sultans willingly sat at the feet of India's missionaries and absorbed the mystical doctrines of the subcontinent.

From the city's bazaars ships carried off rich cargoes of sandalwood seed, pearls, porcelain, white silk, gold, tin, and the sought-after bird of paradise feathers that found their way to Malacca from the remote islands near New Guinea. But the most coveted treasures that passed through this great emporium were spices—cloves, mace, nutmeg—from the islands known as the Moluccas. With trade came growth, and Malacca's faith became the mosque wedded to the marketplace.

As befits a storied kingdom, Malacca's past evolved into a mingling of fact and myth. One fable told of a foreign sultan's miraculous courtship of Malacca's fairy princess, whose haunted domain was the nearby mountain known as Gunung Ledang. The princess demanded a dowry of seven trays of mosquitoes' hearts, seven trays of mites' hearts, a vat of juice from sapless young areca palms, and a cup of the sultan's blood and another of his son's.

At the time of the impending Portuguese invasion in July 1511, Malacca was still ruled by the autocratic Mahmud Shah, who had absolute power over life and death within his empire, a role now deeply rooted in a century's tradition. The sultan imposed on his domain an astonishing tapestry of ritual, orchestrated down to the smallest detail. In his excursions within the city, he dressed in ceremonial costume, a black velvet suit with gold and silver braiding and buttons with a red sash. Carrying the royal white umbrella, he was "borne about on high," on the back of an ele-

phant or the shoulders of a slave or in a litter. Heading the procession was
a band: drums, fifes, gongs, and a silver trumpet mimicking a dragon's call.

There were secret, forbidden quarters of the magnificently gabled
palace where brides of many races lived for the royal pleasure. Malay
records provide vivid accounts of the sultan's harem. "He took all the
beautiful daughters of the Parsee merchants and Klings who pleased him
to be his concubines, made them turn Moors when he had to give them
in marriage and he married them to mandarins' sons and gave them
dowries, and this custom of marrying people of different sects caused no
surprise in Malacca." So well supplied was this private collection of fetching young women that it became a constant scene of scandal.

When the sultan held court in the audience hall, he sat at the head of a
long raised dais surrounded by heralds and warriors, awarded proximity to
the royal presence by virtue of noble birth or individual prowess and deed.
Here the officers of the state, dressed in long silken sarongs and shawls decorated by pins and other ornaments, sat in order of precedence. Behind
them stood young nobles, selected as personal servants. A visitor fortunate
enough to win an audience—a Ming or Indian trader, or Majapahit envoy—
approached with many signs of deference before prostrating himself before
the royal presence. Likewise, a convict seeking pardon was unceremoniously
flung by guards before his despot to receive judgment: a reprieve carefully
measured or dispatch to the headsman after unspeakable torture.

It was Sultan Mahmud Shah, son of Sang Purba, who descended from
Mount Si-Guntang to become ruler of Malacca, who gave the remarkable
Maritime Laws of Malacca, the codification of a century's customs and
legal practices:

> The captain is a king on board his ship, and a ship rigged and ready to sail
> is like a king about to leave his palace.
>
> The changing of the watch should be witnessed by the midshipmen and
> announced by one beat on the drum. The man on watch is issued opium to
> keep him awake.
>
> The navigator should not fail to pray to Allah and his Prophet, for he is
> an imam on board a ship.
>
> Whoever uses a mirror facing toward the bow commits a serious offense,
> for the captain's wife or concubine might be on board. The punishment is
> seven lashes and a fine of 1¼ tael of gold.

Surrounded by sandy, saline soil, Malacca had no agriculture or industry to speak of, so its economy was a narrow one based on foreign commerce. Rigid customs duties, port taxes, fixed weights and measures, and coinage of tin, gold, and silver propelled daily trade, and one visitor in 1508 counted five hundred money changers on one street alone in the city. An aristocracy of wealth through trade quickly evolved.

The monsoons and trade winds permitted traders from East and West to convene in Malacca. Ships from India usually sailed in March on the northeast monsoon and returned by late summer, before the subcontinent was sealed off by the southwest winds. Likewise, the Chinese descended with the northeast trade winds early in the year, returning on the southeast monsoon in early summer. Ships from Java also made use of the southeast winds, arriving in summer and departing later in the year with the fall northwesterlies.

Extravagant and mysterious, Malacca by the beginning of the sixteenth century had drawn the world into its orbit. To the European imagination, Malacca was as bright and vivid as a bird of paradise's plumage. It was all the more exotic because, beyond its strategic location as the richest of trade emporia, little was known about it, least of all its past, a history some later said was worthy of noblest theater or grandest opera, ripe for a Shakespeare or Verdi.

IT WAS A cosmopolitan city where the East and West met half a world away from Europe, this emporium awaiting the Portuguese fleet. Now the swollen sails of caravels and junks had wound down the straits to lay to off Malacca in July 1511. The Portuguese were determined to take control of the spice trade to ensure regular shipment of the condiments and preservatives back to Lisbon, but first they had a score to settle. Magellan and Serrão had bitter memories of the Portuguese humiliation of two years before. So first they must take Malacca, then it would be a question of finding the mysterious source of spices. A window of distance was about to be shattered, never to be pieced back together. Though few realized it, an expanding world was to be set in violent motion.

Chapter 2

THE SIEGE

THE INVADING CARRIERS, an odd armada of fifteen Lisbon-made, round-tucked and square-stern carracks and caravels as well as the captured junks, a total of fifteen ships, carried an assault force of fifteen hundred men, including eight hundred Portuguese soldiers and six hundred Malabar Indian archers pressed into service on the subcontinent.

The intoxicated Portuguese, including Serrão and Magellan, were returning to Malacca from India with a score to settle. The fleet of 1511, having embarked from Goa on India's southwest coast, was now under the command of Governor and Admiral Afonso de Albuquerque, whose aim was to reach the sources of Europe's trade with the Far East.

It would seem an uneven match, for the Portuguese were outnumbered at least twenty to one. The attackers waited and feared, for within those walls lay as fine a prize as existed this side of paradise—or even on the far side, some said. So extravagant was this treasure that the invaders would gladly have sailed into the teeth of any storm or endured whatever hardship any of the seven seas had to inflict to reach it. Where the Malacca River met the sea was the treasure of all estuaries.

The Portuguese were obsessed by Malacca, and their obsession had to do with more than a wounded pride that sought revenge for the earlier debacle. Back in India, the odd pieces of information supplied by such men as Serrão and Magellan, who had returned as if from a forbidden city, confirmed the choice strategic location of Malacca as the gateway to the Moluccas and nutmeg, mace, and cloves. But Albuquerque needed more intelligence before he would press the invasion, and it would reach him, quite unsolicited, in a strange fashion.

Malacca's court had suffered an intrigue after the Portuguese failure in 1509 that played into the hands of the invaders. Prime Minister Tun Mutahir took in marriage the beautiful Tun Fatimah, much to the sultan's annoyance, for the despot wanted the young woman for himself.

An intriguer concocted a tale purporting the prime minister's plans to overthrow the sultan, who responded by sending Tun Mutahir and his family to the executioner, while sparing Tun Fatimah and her brother. Tun Mutahir died bravely. Later, when Mahmud Shah learned that he had been duped, he ordered the plotter's death, but the damage was irreparable. The sultan now ruled a Malaccan court and people bitterly divided over the fate of Tun Mutahir, an extraordinarily instrumental and popular figure.

Meanwhile, the handful of Portuguese captured in the 1509 skirmish had not fared poorly, due to the intercession of an influential Indian trader named Nina Chatu, who had prospered in Malacca and was crucial in later dealings with the Portuguese. As a realistic businessman, he believed it prudent to curry favor with the Europeans determined to displace Malacca's sultanate. Secretly, he lobbied for a measure of freedom for the prisoners so that they could engage in trade and maintain themselves. Some even took Malay wives, and others wrote letters to Afonso de Albuquerque on India's Malabar Coast that were smuggled out of the port by Muslim traders in Nina Chatu's confidence.

One such letter with the date February 6, 1510, written by the leader of the prisoners, Rui de Araujo, and signed by his eighteen companions, gave a detailed account of Malacca and its trade. The letter's author also informed Albuquerque that the sultan feared reprisals by the Portuguese, and this explained why the captives had not been mistreated, beyond an enforced conversion to Islam. He stated further that Malacca could never have fallen while the scrupulous and capable Tun Mutahir was alive. But now the prime minister had been murdered, creating an unsettling vacuum in both court and kingdom. Here was the opening the Portuguese had been waiting for.

As for Magellan and Serrão, shared combat had fostered a rare brand of friendship in the two men, forging the strongest of bonds. But there was more between Serrão and Magellan than soldierly fidelity and familial loyalty. Kinsmen with a common background, together they embodied the restless spirit of a daring age, which would lead to greater, and quite different, exploits for each. But for now they thought of little else but the conquest of Malacca.

Vivid contemporary accounts of this great battle survive, though the specific roles Magellan and Serrão played in the siege are unknown, other than that they "gave good account" of themselves. One can only imagine these salty comrades in arms caught up in the frenzy of what became one of the decisive invasions in history, an incursion that was to determine much of the fortune and fate of the world over the next two centuries.

Albuquerque, as the drawing by his secretary Gaspar Correa reveals, was small in stature but possessed an admonishing demeanor, with prominent eyes and a strong nose above a long beard. At fifty-six he was ambitious to consolidate Portuguese control over the spice trade, but at the same time he knew his force to be outnumbered. Bravado crossed with caution, he decided, was key. On the first evening after his fleet cast anchor off Malacca, he ordered a sounding of trumpets and a volley of cannon fire to announce his arrival.

By chance, the arrival of Albuquerque and his armada coincided with the wedding of Sultan Mahmud's daughter to a Pahang prince. Though the fleet's artillery was aimed seaward, the reports of the heavy guns reverberated through Malacca's walls, disrupting the royal nuptials and causing panic.

The next day Albuquerque received an emissary from Sultan Mahmud, who wished to know whether the Portuguese had come in the name of peace or war. Albuquerque responded with an ultimatum that the Portuguese prisoners taken in the ill-fated expedition of two years before were to be delivered and compensation paid for their internment.

The sultan then made a show of his riverboats, while his armed Malays watched from stockade walls. Stalling for time, Mahmud insisted that terms of peace had to be negotiated before he released any prisoners, while declaring that he was having clothes made for them in the event of their safe return to Albuquerque's ships. Privately, the sultan confided to his advisers that he hoped to string out negotiations until the monsoon winds were unfavorable to the invaders, thus putting the Portuguese at his mercy. Several days passed while Albuquerque pondered with his captains his next move. Through friendly Hindu merchants, he was already in communication with the chief of the captured Portuguese, Rui de Araujo, who advised Albuquerque to do what he thought best without regard for their own fate.

In the meantime, a handful of Chinese traders was given safe passage to board the flagship to provide intelligence reports on the sultan's armament: artillery, poisoned darts and arrows, concealed entrenchments, and a herd of elephants trained for battle, as well as a healthy stock of food supplies from Java. Citing the sultan's cruel and capricious rule, as evidenced by his summary execution of the popular prime minister, they allied themselves with the Portuguese, at once urging an attack on a fortified city whose forces greatly outnumbered the Europeans. One estimate of the sultan's strength was put at twenty thousand men. Another estimated thirty thousand, and the sultan was believed to have three thousand cannon. However, in a siege, the Chinese merchants reasoned, the Portuguese would gain an unexpected ally: Foreign merchants, with everything to lose if the city was sacked, would implore that the sultan sue for peace. Mahmud would have no choice, for foreign trade was Malacca's lifeblood.

Albuquerque grew bolder and more confident of success as the days passed. He weighed the odds. The Portuguese had faced war elephants in India and were not as intimidated as the sultan might have hoped. Though his force was inferior in numbers, it had superior weapons and more sophisticated tactics, and was a battle-hardened army from campaigns on the subcontinent. Moreover, the design of the protective armor and pointed helmets worn by Portuguese soldiers had allowed them a surprising mobility in previous battles against armies clad similar to the Malays, in turbans and pantaloons. Albuquerque decided to act.

On the evening of July 25 he dispatched clandestine parties to the beach to bombard the city, while armed bands set fire to waterfront houses. Merchant ships anchored in the harbor—except for Chinese junks and Indian dhows and feluccas—were torched. The sultan's response was immediate, declaring that the Portuguese should lay off while he decided terms of a peace.

Albuquerque's bombardment continued, less to inflict damage on the city than to ascertain how the enemy would rally at the alarm and what measures they would take to defend their port. Through his intelligence sources Albuquerque now knew that many of Malacca's inhabitants were sympathetic to the Portuguese. So rather than destroy the enemy, which was likely to include entire Malay families, he wanted to take the city with as little damage to its trading capacity as possible.

But it was mainly a waiting game that Albuquerque played, though he continued shelling the city over the next several days. Without warning, the group of Portuguese captives, inexplicably freed by the sultan, approached a landing party crying for peace, and a signal was given to lift the bombardment. Once aboard the flagship, the former prisoners told of tortures inflicted by Muslims upon Christians, and Albuquerque swore by his beard that he would take vengeance on the Malays. Rui de Araujo's advice was to invade, then negotiate. The Malays, the captain of the prisoners told the commander, "thought more of a subtle treason than of all the chivalry in the world."

Albuquerque then sent two forces to the beach in a split attack, but the assault was beaten back with many men severely wounded. Some of Albuquerque's advisors lost heart and recommended returning to Goa, but the commander was adamant. A lull followed as Albuquerque continued his wait while the ranks of Chinese merchants supporting the European cause swelled. With renegade junks at his disposal, Albuquerque's fleet was now much larger than when he announced his arrival.

A devotee of the Apostle James, Albuquerque waited until the evening of that saint's day to resume the attack. By now, on the advice of Rui de Araujo, a strategy had been decided. To capture the city and its compounds filled with what they dreamed to be the riches of the East, Araujo insisted that it was crucial for the Portuguese to take the bridge over the river. This tactic would best be achieved by dividing the attack: Albuquerque would strike at both the north and south sides of the city, at the mosque and the bridge, thus confusing the enemy as to the assault's main objective and splitting its defenses.

At midnight Albuquerque ordered his fleet to bombard the city, and the shelling by bronze single-shot cannon lasted the entire night. "It was a frightening thing," recorded Albuquerque's secretary, Gaspar Correa, "to hear in the darkness the whole city thrown into uproar, the cries and shouts, people fleeing with their children and household goods on their shoulders without knowing which way to go."

Two hours before dawn a trumpet summoned the invading officers to the flagship's deck for confession and absolution. When first light spilled into the city, the attackers began swarming to the beach in the teeth of the first volley of the Malay artillery, explosions from bronze "esmerils, falconets, and sakers," the contribution of Italian gunsmiths introduced ten years before by Arab dealers in weaponry. When that fury was spent, the Portuguese shrieked the war cry "Santiago!" and under the interdicting fire of superior cannon that outranged less potent Malay guns, they fell upon the stockades of the bridge, defended by shielded Malays who fought back with a hail of arrows, poisoned darts, and lances.

The two-pronged assault wreaked confusion and havoc. The mosque, the spiritual home of the sultanate and the seat of its morale, was weakly defended and easily taken. The battle now blazed to a white heat at the bridge, where landing parties fought hand to hand against Malay defendants, most of whom were cut down on the spot, while others jumped into the water only to be slaughtered by Portuguese in boats.

Realizing that a number of his men were wounded and dying from the poisoned arrows and darts, Albuquerque, on counsel from Rui de Araujo, ordered sails spread at a vertical angle on spars anchored in barrels of earth to ward off the deadly missiles while his forces held the bridgehead. The protection worked, for the thick canvases shielded the Portuguese from the aim of Malay marksmen. Then he dispatched a tall junk filled with reinforcements to the bridge, but the awkwardly built ship struck a sandbar, where it remained a sitting target for nine days while the battle raged. Malays sent barges of firewood, pitch, and oil on the falling tide to set it afire, while the Portuguese protected the junk with bowsprits and harpoons hung with iron chains. Finally on August 10 the junk, a tall tower of death with its loopholed bulwarks and artillery and stores of weaponry, was freed by a surge of high tide, and it churned through the estuarine surf to the bridge while bombardment of the city continued, with the sultan's palace and the mosque now reduced to rubble.

While the men were grappling the junk to the bridge under heavy fire, its captain, Antonio d'Abreu, took a bullet in the jaw from a matchlock, costing him several teeth and a piece of tongue. He was relieved "more by force than by his own wish," according to a witness, but not before he had cleared the bridge of the enemy, who fled to fortifications between it and the destroyed mosque only to find themselves cut off by the other attacking party. Meanwhile, two boats with heavy cannon took up positions on both sides of the harbor to protect the flanks of the invaders, while the bridge was fortified with barricades mounted with guns and sheltered against the brutal sun with thatches of palm.

With the bridge secured, the Portuguese advanced on the city with canvas shields and slaves carrying planks for crossing the pitfalls and mines of gunpowder that the Malays had planted in the streets. Late in the day the invaders positioned their large cannon with a straight field of fire down the broad, grassy, palm-shaded avenues, thus preventing the digging of new trenches.

The defenders were soon joined by the sultan himself and his son astride war elephants, with others being readied for a counterattack. But before the beasts could be mobilized into a fighting force, they were soon routed by lance thrusts to eye, ear, and belly, and they trampled their keepers and many other Malays as they fled.

The sultan and his son, whose name was Ahmad, took to the jungle with their parties and found refuge a day's journey away at the village of Bertam Ulu, though they were to be hunted and pursued by the invaders to preclude any restoration of the sultanate. The prime minister, Tun Mat, who had succeeded the ill-fated Tun Mutahir, was already an old man with paralysis in the legs, and he refused to leave the palace. Though preferring to meet a warrior's end, he was unwillingly borne away by his subordinates and left to die alone.

By morning Malacca's streets were cleared of the remaining defenders, the invaders giving no quarter to man, woman, or child who fled, while sparing those who surrendered for slave labor. Now the city was ripe to be sacked, and it quickly yielded the richest plunder of any of the Eastern campaigns of the Portuguese before or since. They seized warehouses of golden chairs, intricately fashioned jewelry, gold nuggets, precious stones, silks, two thousand bronze cannon, brocaded howdahs, and gold-plated palanquins, and in the spice godowns they inhaled the heavenly scents of Eden: cinnamon, nutmeg, and clove. A collection of bronze-skinned, beautiful young women skilled in embroidery and dancing, as well as those of noble birth, were also taken. They too were the spoils of victory, and Albuquerque intended personally to see them back to Portugal as a royal gift for King Manuel.

Albuquerque's consolidation of his victory after the six-week siege was swift. Though the city was sacked, his men were instructed not to touch the house or possessions of Nina Chatu, the Hindu merchant who had befriended Rui de Araujo and was now advising Albuquerque on Malacca's need for a new currency. Appreciating the necessity of a system of administration, Albuquerque retained the sultanate system, but named one Rui de Brito governor and Nina Chatu prime minister. The commander allowed the several foreign settlements in the city—Javanese, Hindu, Chinese, Japanese—to manage their own affairs. Parties were sent into the jungle to round up frightened Malays who had fled the carnage.

Having been slaves under Sultan Mahmud's reign, these Malays were now servants of King Manuel and were immediately put to use in building a fortress against counterattack. Rui de Araujo drew the assignment of overseeing its construction southeast of the river, which he managed by salvaging stone and masonry from the destroyed palace, mosque, and adjacent royal tombs: enough material, in his words, that "two fortresses might well have been constructed." After the fortress—prominently marked by a five-story-high tower between the hill, estuary, and river—was finished by the labor of fifteen hundred slaves, "and stood complete," noted an observer, "with its artillery and garrison of soldiers, it created among the Malays a feeling of intense dread and astonishment which lasted permanently to the great credit and honor of the Crown of Portugal."

Albuquerque by now was anything but complacent. He remained on his guard and eager to respond in kind to the sort of treachery that he believed to be endemic in the port's politics from the beginning. Having learned through Hindu traders of a plot hatched by the elderly and venerable Javanese leader Utimata Raja (who had earlier pleaded allegiance to the Portuguese) to overthrow the Portuguese and restore the sultan to his throne, the commander arranged a meeting with the old chief and his entourage at the fortress. The unsuspecting Utimata Raja, now well into his eighties, was seized, along with his son, son-in-law, and grandson, and sentenced to die. Despite attempted bribes by the headman's wife, the conspirators were beheaded on a lofty scaffold in the middle of the square, where the bodies were displayed from morning until evening. Other suspected followers were put to the sword in the streets.

Keen to reestablish Malacca's trading activities, Albuquerque dispatched an ambassador aboard a junk to the king of Siam. He knew that news of the Portuguese victory had spread quickly throughout the nations and archipelagos of Asia, and he needed to ally himself with this powerful monarch. The emissary offered trade and the friendship of the Portuguese king to the Siamese throne and was in turn greeted with royal honors. So in Albuquerque's view it would seem that little had altered Malacca beyond a new stewardship to oversee a proven commercial enterprise.

In fact, Portuguese Malacca became much more vulnerable than the port had been during the reign of the sultans, for it was now surrounded by enemies. The deposed sultan's authority still extended to neighboring lands as well as across to the Sumatran shore. With the straits unsafe, the Portuguese fleet was needed to protect the city. Further, Utimata Raja's Javanese rebellion, quickly crushed by Albuquerque, anticipated other unrest, as Asian Muslims bitterly resented the Christian Europeans in Southeast Asia.

This resentment festered and found expression in more armed conflicts, first with Malaccan Javanese; then with the Gujarati, the Muslim traders of Malacca who had hated their Portuguese rivals from the beginning; and with the Acehnese, a fiercely independent Muslim tribe of northern Sumatra, who waged bloody wars in efforts to dominate this main artery of trade. Likewise, the kingdom of Johore at the southern tip of the Malay Peninsula, founded by the remnants of Malacca's deposed royal house, vied with Portugal for control of the straits.

Because of these threats, Malacca's reputation as the main entrepôt of Southeast Asia became tarnished, and the port suffered a gradual economic decline over time. It remained for Albuquerque to harvest whatever golden eggs he could from the nest of the slain goose, so he directed his gaze eastward to the Spice Islands.

Malacca's streets were scarcely cleared of the rubble of the battle when Albuquerque dispatched three ships under the leadership of Antonio d'Abreu to journey to the Moluccas, with Francisco Serrão captaining the second of the ships and Simão Afonso Bisagudo commanding the third.

With the fall of Malacca having major repercussions throughout Asia,

the reverberations in the Moluccas themselves might have been catastrophic had Albuquerque not planned the expedition carefully before it
got under way. The governor first gave d'Abreu most explicit orders that
contradicted earlier Portuguese strategy in the Indian Ocean campaigns.
Neither prizes nor ships were to be pursued and taken, and at every landfall the explorers would honor local customs and laws. Albuquerque even
sent a junk captained by a Malaccan trader named Nakoda Ismail to pre-
cede the expedition, hoping to ensure a favorable reception for it. Ismail
knew the seas and commerce of the islands, and his mission was to spread
word that the Portuguese were coming.

Anticipating a brisk trade resuming at a Malacca under Portuguese
rule, Albuquerque made plans to return to his governorship in Goa,
anticipating a later hero's welcome in Lisbon. Preparations for his leave-
taking aboard the flagship *Flora de la Mar* were elaborate, and Albuquerque made sure the treasures taken in the siege were loaded, as were
the scores of Malay ladies, embroiderers, and dancers. Accompanied by
two other ships, his flagship set sail from Malacca in mid-January 1512,
five months after the port had fallen.

The *Flora de la Mar* was a big, broad-beamed, three-masted galleon
with a fore and aft castle capable of transporting six hundred people and
five hundred tons. On the face of it, this was a ship fit for a governor. The
overloaded ship leaked, however, and six days later she foundered in a
storm off Sumatra, carrying with her to the bottom of the Indian Ocean
the greatest wealth ever lost in a single shipwreck, as well as the ladies who
had been handpicked by the governor himself to adorn King Manuel's
court in Lisbon. Albuquerque and several of his officers survived by fash-
ioning a raft from split ship's masts, then fending off with lances other
would-be survivors who might have swamped their craft, thus drowning
them all.

Chapter 3

LORD JIM

THE EXPEDITION Albuquerque had ordered to reconnoiter the Spice Islands left a month before the governor's own ill-fated voyage for India. In December 1511 the tiny armada led by d'Abreu, who had still not recovered from his ugly bullet wound in the face, lifted anchor. The ships —two fifty-ton caravels and a small Indian vessel seized at Goa, together carrying a force of a hundred men—dropped into the deepwater channel of the Straits of Malacca, sailed southeast past the Johore River and the confusion of islands at the peninsula's tip, and, crossing the equator, entered the Java Sea with the southern tip of Sumatra still visible to starboard. Avoiding the shallows, they plowed through deep blue, whitecapped water, steering clear of the crocodile-infested cloudy green palmettoes that reached seaward. Sumatra was soon lost to sight as they made southeast for Java.

It was a bold voyage. The Portuguese were seeing new expanses of azure water with schools of flying fish skipping across the surface and billows of cumulus clouds gathered on the horizon. But the three craft were guided by experienced Malay pilots recruited in Malacca, whose forefathers had sailed these waters for centuries. The ships kept within sight of each other as they rode the monsoon, following the ancient route of Chinese traders.

The knowledge that they were not the first Europeans to venture into this part of the world steeled the confidence of d'Abreu and his men. Ludovico de Varthema, an Italian from Rome, had departed Europe in 1502 to wander for many years in the Far East, and a record of his travels was published in 1510. It is from Varthema that we have the first description of Borneo—which lay some two hundred miles to the northeast of d'Abreu's expedition at this point—and, more important, the flotilla's destination, the Spice Islands.

Varthema had entered into the service of the Portuguese in India, distinguished himself in battle, and was knighted before returning to Lisbon and then to Rome in 1508. Albuquerque's decision to dispatch d'Abreu's convoy immediately after taking Malacca was undoubtedly based on the information Varthema had provided the Portuguese five years earlier. The Italian explorer's accounts of "Maluch" and its cloves, and of Banda (the *"isola molto brutta & trista"*) and its nutmegs, were more tantalizing to the Portuguese imagination than America's rumored El Dorado, with its lakes of silver and gold. For d'Abreu's seamen, now within striking distance of the mysterious and unknown Moluccas, a destination that had been seen by no other white man but Varthema, that perfumed vision became a movable feast.

Within days they sighted the changing patterns of Java's great green and purple folds. From the decks the mariners marveled at the terraced rice fields flashing in the sun against a nexus of austere, moss-colored mountains, and gazed at the island's succession of smoking peaks that pushed up through the rising foliage like moonscapes. The sailors passed Christmas half a world away from Christendom under a slice of Islamic moon gesticulating over the deep black ribbon of sea.

Time was measured in half-hour intervals with the Venetian sand clock. Success and safety were so counted in these forty-eight daily increments, with eight glasses to the watch and by the grace of God. On the aft deck the crew gathered in the evenings for prayers, concluding with an ancient Benedictine chant, "Salve Regina," the hymn most favored by sailors. This praise to the Queen of Heaven provided a measure of comfort to men sailing uncharted seas under the strange, new stars of the Southern Hemisphere, where they were dreaming of further conquests in a world they did not yet know. Dawn was the favorite hour for sailors who stood the night watch, when the unseen dangers of the dark were past, and water and sky mingled at an indistinct horizon before the breaking of day and the promise of God's benediction on their voyage.

As it was the rainy season for this part of the Malay Archipelago, the sailors rode out the squalls lathering over the decks, scattering the hencoops. Their first taste of Java, when the storms were spent, were the sparkling beaches at Gresik, where they lay to for provisions; then they coasted for other settlements along Java's north coast. The Portuguese made such landfalls in calms. They would anchor their ships in indigo water, then guide their longboats through the emerald green shallows of the reefs to the lush, palm-fringed shore, where they could fill their casks with water and stretch their cramped limbs in welcome interludes of tropical sun. Threading the narrow strait separating East Java from the small island of Madura, the sailors discovered the teeming port of Surabaya, founded two centuries before, where lateen-rigged junks and feluccas colored the harbor.

Java was scarcely in their wake when the purple rise of Bali's volcano Gunung Batur, crowned in supernal haze, loomed out of the sea. Then followed one after the other the southeastern islands that lay south of Celebes: Lombok, Sumbaya, and Flores. In the early new year, the expedition was soon positioned north of Sumba and Timor, and, having sailed nearly three thousand miles east of Malacca, the Malay pilots set a northeast course through the Banda Sea before a following wind.

By commanding the second of d'Abreu's ships encroaching on the Spice Islands, Francisco Serrão was drawing nearer to an experience that would not only change radically his own life but have a profound effect on Magellan's as well. As was so often the case, the weather played a prominent role when the three ships were separated for several days by a storm. Serrão's Indian vessel, already in poor condition, was nearly lost as long swells ground under the keel and pounded the hull, flinging up mast-high veils of water. But the fleet managed to reunite in a calm just as the men sighted Ceram, the largest island of the Moluccas and the hub of a wheel of islands and centrifugal seas that created its own climate.

The sailors made landfall at a harbor known as Guli-Guli, at the eastern tip. Ceram was a wild, forested island, inhabited by a near-naked race of warrior cannibals who feasted on the hearts of their enemies. Warned by the Malay pilots that these natives resented strangers, the Portuguese were watchful. The voyage had been mercifully spared of the kinds of catastrophe that often, almost routinely, overtook such missions. Despite the poor condition of Serrão's ship, which had plagued him nearly from the outset, each day had glowed with promise.

But now, damaged and leaking badly, his vessel was unseaworthy for a return to Malacca. When the pilots advised him that he could buy a replacement junk in Banda, he ordered the ship to be burnt. Transferring himself and his crew to the two remaining caravels of d'Abreu's fleet, he left the smoking wreck in the small harbor and set sail from Ceram for Banda, a two-day push before a north wind.

By the second evening they were in the harbor of Neira, the small, idyllic island guarded by the volcano Gunung Api, and were surprised to find the natives not as Varthema had described them, "rascally and beastly," but handsome, friendly, and eager to trade. News traveled quickly in this part of the world, and a rumor that they were coming in search of Banda's golden fruit, the nutmeg, which grew here and nowhere else in the world, had preceded their arrival. The first order of business for Serrão was to procure his means of returning to Malacca, so he bought a junk from a Chinese trader.

D'Abreu's party remained a month, buying and loading nutmeg as well as clove, which had come from the islands several hundred miles to the north. Expected to outbid regional merchants with their own trade goods, the Portuguese did so, but still at prices so cheap that they could expect a profit of at least 1,000 percent in Lisbon.

Now having taken on three shiploads of spices, d'Abreu intended to ride the shifting monsoon back to Malacca. He ordered the flotilla to prepare to sail, assigning Serrão nine Portuguese sailors to expand his crew of a dozen Malays. What followed is one of history's odd stories, a seeming fictional blend of hearsay, myth, prophecy, and romantic fancy that might have sprung from a novelist's imagination were it not true. Again, weather was key on another fateful occasion.

The two caravels departed Banda with Serrão dropping in their wake. Suddenly a furious storm struck, separating the three ships. The baffling winds and treacherous currents hurled Serrão's junk upon a reef off an uninhabited isle called Lusi Para about 150 miles west of Ambon. While several of his men were lost, Serrão and a few survivors managed to make their way ashore.

Reminded by his native sailors that the waters were infested with pirates, Serrão conceived a plan. He ordered half his handful of men, armed, to hide in the underbrush, while posing the rest of his party as castaways, helpless now with useless wealth. In time, a scavenging prahu approached the wrecked junk, still upright but pounded by breakers on the reef. Then, seeing a frantic signal from shore, its crew, sensing easier plunder, put in to the beach. When their boat grated on the sand, the Portuguese ambushed them, seizing both craft and crew. The ruse, with no loss of life, saved the Portuguese. It was later reported that "if they met not their death from thirst and hunger, they might expect it from these corsairs."

Now, with their craft in hand and his muskets aimed, Serrão threatened to maroon the scavengers, which would have meant their death from starvation, not to mention dehydration. He could see that the island lay uninhabited for good reason. With no springs, there was only rainwater to drink and virtually nothing to eat beyond what fish could be caught. In the Malay Archipelago the pirates knew that if abandoned, they would die with no hope of rescue. On bended knee they pleaded for their lives.

Serrão, whose men were already loading whatever spices they could salvage from the foundering junk into the beached prahu, relented, striking a bargain. He would not maroon them, he proposed, if these Malays agreed to sail the Portuguese to the nearest habitable island. Having no choice, the pirates readily agreed. The two parties quickly muscled the prahu back through the surf, trimmed sails, and put to open sea for Ambon, which lay just south of the larger island of Ceram, where Serrão had torched his crippled ship a few weeks earlier.

A two-day sail brought them to Hitu, the island's northern peninsula. Having suffered enough Malay deviousness in his service, Serrão refused to be intimidated on this new island. Upon beaching, he ordered his men to brandish their weapons before the curious onlookers, though he need not have bothered: Stories of the fall of Malacca had already carried across the seas to the Spice Islands, and the Hitu chiefs had been summoned to welcome the strangers.

And welcome them they did, with feasts and comely young women. Toasting the Portuguese with cups of arak, they explained that the Hitu people were at war with villagers on Ceram, a people more backward than the Hitu. Sensing an opportunity, Serrão had his men display their armor, muskets, and marksmanship. The chiefs, astonished and riveted by this martial display, implored the captain to lead an army against their rivals.

Serrão, recalling the savages who might have attacked them at Guli-Guli, considered the proposal. He had faced native weaponry before in the siege of Malacca, and the Ceramese were far more primitive fighters. He welcomed the test. If he was successful, as he knew he would be with firearms against the islanders' bows and arrows and spears and blowguns, stories of his routing the enemy would be on the lips of every Malay trader whose prahu plied Moluccan waters. Fortune favored the bold. Serrão gathered his handful of Portuguese in their armor. Backed by his new allies, he led his small army in a surprise raid, slaughtering whatever Ceramese were foolish enough to stand up to the Europeans.

Serrão was shrewd on the heels of this victory, doing nothing to dissuade the natives from believing that the Portuguese were masters not only of military science and tactics, but of magic and astrology as well. His hosts were willing believers, and word carried as if by the wind to other islands. Reports of the victory soon reached the two rival clove-producing island kingdoms to the north, Ternate and Tidore, each seeking to extend its empire. Their sultans both rushed emissaries to Hitu with invitations of a state visit, but Ternate's ruler, in an incredible show of force, sent his own brother Prince Jubila in the flagship of a fleet of nine *kora-kora,* ten-ton outrigger war canoes, each manned by a hundred warriors.

Ternate won the day, and Serrão and his men set out northward with the prince's festive flotilla, the beating of drums and ringing of gongs sounding the rhythm for the paddlers while colorful banners carried on the breeze. Once under way, the newcomers clanked themselves into reclining postures on cushioned, shady decks and were plied with food and drink by their royal hosts.

After the three-hundred-mile journey of six days, they crossed the equator and shortly sighted the twin islands of Ternate and Tidore separated by a mile-wide channel, each a rugged, towering volcanic cone forested with clove trees and encircled by treacherous coral reefs, and lying just three or four miles off the larger island of Halmahera.

Serrão was entranced with the lavish flora and fauna distributed about the most beautiful landscape he had ever seen. Streams cascaded down the volcanic slopes. The air sang with the cries of sulfur-crested white cockatoos and brightly plumaged parrots, as well as the mournful cries of plump green pigeons, a local delicacy. Sago palms provided materials for shelter, food, arak, and other daily necessities, while a profusion of sea life swam within and without the reefs.

As the nutmeg tree was native only to Banda, the supreme gift of nature to these two islands—as well as the neighboring vassal islands of Moti, Makian, and Bacan—was the clove tree, which carpeted the lower slopes of the volcanoes. Serrão could scarcely believe the good fortune that had befallen him. Sheer chance had fetched him up in the richest garden the world had ever known.

As he pondered his marvelous predicament, two merging realizations struck Serrão simultaneously as a single epiphany: The birthplace of cloves was still unknown to the European world; and, excepting Varthema, Serrão himself was the first white man to see the minuscule islands where God had given the clove tree to the world. Dazzled, he took stock of himself and his own life's possibilities. Had he met his destiny?

Gradually a picture of a bold, potentially glorious experiment settled in his mind's eye. The people of Ternate, both high and low, had received him as if he were royalty or a sort of god. His fellow officers back in Malacca probably thought him killed in a shipwreck, which he very nearly had been. He had soldiered valiantly for his king and bore the scars to prove it. The obvious course was to return to Malacca. But what if he remained in the islands to serve the interests of the Crown? His presence would ensure that cloves would be channeled into the holds of Portuguese ships, and at the right price, too. It made perfect sense to establish himself as the Portuguese king's representative on Ternate. How could he possibly fail? He would write to Magellan, sharing his good fortune; Magellan would somehow join him. Then there was the question of Serrão's own private interests. The island women were very fetching indeed. If he were to take a wife, then he would belong on Ternate; his position would be consolidated, and he could make his own personal fortune in the clove trade. That was expected of a seasoned campaigner; it was the way things were done. What if he stayed here?

He had already learned that Ternate was a smoothly cut gem among some rough ones. While savages inhabited the neighboring island of Halmahera, Ternate's sultanate had evolved over the years into a worldly seat of power and learning. Ternate's chiefs, called *kaicil,* held sway over their regional counterparts, whom they regarded as vassals. The *kaicil* had mastered the craft of piracy, sought politically advantageous marriages, waged war, and conducted diplomacy. With this mix they exercised authority over their subservient neighbors, seeking an alliance one moment, answering with animosity the next. Arab, Chinese, and Javanese merchants had been lured here to share their skills of weaving and boat and house building. Manners were refined and rituals sharpened for court and home life. With Islam had come scholarship. Ternate's influence was carried over the waters throughout the Moluccas and even far beyond the islands. Serrão suspected that he could be very useful among such people.

Ludovico de Varthema had preceded Serrão by only a few years. But the Italian, now in Portuguese employ, had not appreciated Ternate's pretenses at culture. "The inhabitants," he had written, "are much worse than those of Banda; for, were it not for man's shape, they should in manner differ nothing from beasts." Serrão in 1512, however, was mesmerized by the islands and the islanders. Now, inhaling the scented sea air just seven years after Varthema's visit, he believed himself to have discovered paradise on earth. As far as Serrão was concerned, the Portuguese search for their Holy Grail had ended; the "Carreira da India" had not found it, but he himself had.

Sultan Bolief (variously known as Boleyse, Abu Lais, and Abdul Hassan), who now occupied the throne, ordered feasts for his European guests. Renowned among his people as a prophet, the sultan let it be known that his dreams had told him of the coming arrival of a force of men dressed in iron who would serve his realm and "extend the dominion and glory of Molucca." Simply put, the fair-skinned Portuguese, especially Serrão, were the embodiment of a royal vision that just happened to confirm a recent turn of events.

The sultan pledged to deliver cloves to the Portuguese on the condition that when Serrão returned to Portugal, he would persuade King Manuel to build a fortress on Ternate "and in no other place," meaning, of course, Tidore, which was ruled by his bitter enemy Sultan Almanzor. Spelling out conditions in a letter to the Portuguese king, Bolief entrusted the monarch with "his land and all in it" and requested arms so that the Ternateans could defend themselves, especially against the rival Tidoreans.

Serrão, anxious to prove that his diplomatic skills matched his soldierly prowess, had by now made his decision to remain.

Still caught up in the fervor of his own prophecy, the sultan sent two of Serrão's crew members back to Malacca to request "more Portuguese men, arms, and a factory for the clove trade." The factory, while of Portuguese origin in Asia, descended from the medieval *fondachi,* the residential quarters of Genoese and Venetian merchants in the Muslim seaports scattered throughout North African and Ottoman harbors. Eventually they appeared in Asian trading ports from the Persian Gulf to the South China Sea, where foreign traders resided in special districts, as had the Tamil, Gujarati, and Javanese traders of Malacca. They were nonetheless under the mercy of the local ruler, who could claim a merchant's daughter for his harem or sell the trader's estate on his death.

So the Portuguese set a precedent that the Dutch and English would follow. To ensure security in Asian trading centers, they were convinced of the need for sanctuaries where persons and goods could not be arbitrarily seized and ships could be safely provisioned and repaired. Thus factories and fortifications to protect them evolved into today's foreign naval base. To the administration in Malacca the sultan wrote, "I have heard that the king of Portugal helps all those kings who are one with him, thus enhancing their kingdoms. . . . I want to say to you that in this land of Molucca there is trade in cloves, nutmeg, and mace, and this kingdom is yours to command. Sir, I have heard of the king of Cochin who received the mercies shown him by the king of Portugal."

The sultan's reference was to Cochin's ruler on India's west coast, whose pepper trade with the Portuguese had ensured him wealth and power. Word of this success had reached Bolief. Envisioning a similar arrangement thus fulfilling his prophecy, Bolief asked of the Malacca authorities a dachin stamped by the seal of the Portuguese king. The dachin was an ancient measure of currency brought by the Chinese and had been widely used in the archipelago until the fall of Malacca. Since traders, who were keenly aware of the vast shift in power after the Portuguese invasion, were reluctant to use the Ternate sultan's currency, he hoped an official Portuguese dachin would be reassuring to merchants.

Because news of Malacca's conquest by the Europeans had already reached the "spiceries" through other traders before Serrão's arrival, there had been a sense of expectation in the islands. Trade, however, by definition was a reciprocal enterprise. Malacca had been not only the major center for the collection and redistribution of cloves, nutmeg, and mace supplied by Ternate's sultanate, but also the Spice Islands' main source of both common and luxury goods, from clothing and kitchen utensils to gold and silks.

The island sultans, while dismayed that such a lucrative market had been disrupted, were keen to reestablish trade in Malacca with the port's new rulers. Survival depended upon business as usual. If the Portuguese were equally intent on pursuing this shared goal, what did it matter that the strangers were a new race shaped by an alien god and a vastly different way of perceiving the world?

The commerce resumed, at first with junks and other Asian craft. Then, as Serrão surely anticipated as a result of Sultan Bolief's letter, the first of what was to become an annual Portuguese trading fleet called at Ternate in early 1513. It was commanded by Captain Antonio de Miranda de Azevedo, who quickly established a factory and stationed merchants on the island to ensure business on a continuing basis.

There was, however, other business on Azevedo's mind: namely, the Serrão situation. Azevedo was amazed and dumbfounded by his fellow officer's lofty, influential status on the island. Prior to Azevedo's leaving Malacca, stories had circulated in the port telling of a European who by happenstance had arrived on Ternate, seeking ordination as a white god among island savages. Now Azevedo discovered that the interloper was not only a Portuguese, but a comrade in arms, a captain who had sailed with d'Abreu's expedition the year before, but never returned.

Questions needed to be asked, and the commands in Malacca and Goa wanted the answers. Serrão was an officer in the Portuguese army. Granted, his ship had been lost and the rest of d'Abreu's force had given him and his crew up for dead. But here was Serrão, thriving. Other, more enterprising members from his party had managed to return to Malacca. Why, then, had he not made his way back to the Malay port on one merchant junk or another that plied the route? For a Portuguese soldier, disobeying orders, and particularly desertion, meant a death sentence.

There was something else. Serrão, though a good soldier, had a reputation as a troublemaker. Three years before, in 1510, he had incurred Albu-

querque's fury after the siege of Goa. That April, Albuquerque had ordered
Serrão south to Cochin for supplies. Plagued again with an inferior ship,
Serrão, without so much as a by-your-leave, decided to have it repaired
before sailing back up the Malabar Coast. The delay enraged the governor,
and he accused his captain of dereliction of duty, then had him arrested
and jailed. Now, Azevedo was thinking, here was the same Serrão, even
more culpable, affecting royal airs among a band of brown heathens.

But if the Portuguese command considered reprimanding Serrão, or
worse, it thought better of confronting one of their own who in local affairs
had the status of a prime minister. Not only was he influential, he was indispensable. Because he had lost his ship in a storm and survived through sheer
pluck and luck, Serrão now managed the choicest piece of real estate in the
world. For the moment, it was decided that Serrão, having quickly developed a sense of the strange political imbroglio in which he found himself on
Ternate, was a man of such importance that it was best to leave him alone.
It was a reluctant decision but the only possible one. Portuguese Malacca
seethed with resentment and envy over this upstart who would be king.

Meanwhile, if Serrão on Ternate had any anxious moments about
charges of desertion by his superiors in Malacca, they were displaced by
what he perceived as his new subsidy, waiting to be exploited as commercial plunder by Portugal. Elegant and European, the tall, fair (to his island
hosts) knight was an exotic, offering Ternatean aristocrat and commoner
alike their escape and their curse.

So it happened that Ternate rather than Banda became the first
Portuguese—and first European—colony for trade in the Spice Islands.
Before Serrão's arrival, this scattering of specks over the seas between
Celebes and New Guinea had been largely a state of mind for those who
lived west of the Bay of Bengal. Now the Moluccas were becoming a more
precise geographical location, resulting in the publication of new maps of
arcane places for an enthralled Europe. One immediate result of this gradually developing picture was that contemporary Portuguese accounts
began to draw a careful distinction between the two island destinations
on each side of the equator, confused by names that conjured up either
cloves or nutmeg. The irony, however, is that Serrão became the orches-
trator of that trade with his own country that now regarded him as a renegade: a prophet without honor and turncoat who went native.

The Europeans saw themselves as culturally and morally superior to a people who were less than civilized, while island natives distrusted strangers as a people excluded by island myth and legend. Though Serrão had seized upon a native prophecy to his own great advantage, as well as Portugal's, the meeting of these two cultures in the sixteenth century inevitably led to rancor and confrontation.

In the meantime, and with no reason to disabuse his hosts, Captain Francisco Serrão soon became the sultan's personal counselor, taking his place among the trusted advisors of the island kingdom. In a gesture designed to give greater credence to the sultan's reputation as a seer, Serrão took to dressing for state occasions in his shining armor, striking an anomalous pose among the silk-robed, turbaned figures of the royal court. To this day, Portuguese helmets are worn by Moluccans in elaborate ceremonies rooted in ancient tradition. Thus was Ternate's rival kingdom of Tidore eclipsed, at least for the time being.

The anachronism aside, a twentieth-century reader familiar with the work of Joseph Conrad might find something decidedly Conradian about Serrão and his circumstances. If Serrão was a master by virtue of the muted colonialism he represented, likewise he was a slave—imprisoned, caught up in a play of opposites he did not fully understand or reconcile, a plight assuming many forms. The condition would prove to be his undoing. In the meantime, he thrived in his paradisaical surroundings, which he enjoyed through no fault of his own beyond his decision to remain in the Spice Islands. Like Captain Lingard winding up his secret river from the sea to the island's heartland as a great white father of commerce, Serrão anointed himself as the indispensable arbiter of trade between two vastly disparate cultures, blissfully unaware of the darker implications of his role. Delighted with his lotus-eater's station after years of soldiering, he began to amass wealth through his conciliatory position.

Spurning his own culture and holdings in Portugal, Serrão made another decision that would ensure a lifelong fate as a willing expatriate in the Spice Islands: He took a wife. Accounts vary as to who she was. While some identify her as Javanese, more credible evidence has her as a daughter of Almanzor, the sultan of neighboring and rival Tidore, a mile to the southeast by small sailboat or canoe.

According to contemporary accounts, Almanzor had a harem of two hundred women, with an equal number of servants for them. He had four wives, as permitted by Islamic law, who had provided the sultan with eight sons and eighteen daughters. Sensing a diplomatic opening, Serrão worked at resolving the differences between the two royal houses. Believing he had succeeded and with a signed treaty between the two sultans to show for it, he claimed one of Almanzor's beautiful princesses in marriage, who bore him a son and daughter.

The specter of obscurity never haunted Francisco Serrão. On the contrary, having made his separate peace while others dreamed of El Dorado, he embraced his "new world." Full of curiosity and lacking all bias toward native customs, he made himself belong, seeing himself as a harbinger of a new and better world in a marriage of East and West. Most important, because of him there was a roaring trade with Portugal in spices. It was perhaps with an exalted notion of his own infallibility that he took quill in hand to write a series of extraordinary letters to his friend Magellan.

Chapter 4

"I HAVE FOUND
A NEW WORLD . . ."

BUT SERRÃO, in rhapsodizing to his friend about the idyllic life in the Spice Islands, was hardly aware that Magellan had abandoned himself to more desperate courses shortly after his return to Portugal. It was a strange, unnerving time for Magellan, and the period before he actually found himself once again in his homeland is shrouded in mystery.

While Serrão sailed with d'Abreu to the Spice Islands in late 1511, Magellan left few clues as to his activities. Though he had spent seven years of service in India and Southeast Asia, this period is a blank page in Magellan's life story and a riddle that has provoked spirited debate among historians and biographers.

A view held by some, including the late Samuel Eliot Morison, has it that the third ship of d'Abreu's expedition to the Spice Islands was commanded not by Simão Afonso Bisagudo, but by Ferdinand Magellan. On the face of it, this position is logical. If Magellan and Serrão had been comrades in arms throughout the Indian Ocean campaigns and had saved each other's life repeatedly in battle, including the first incident at Malacca, what sensible order would have separated them now?

The argument gains strength when one considers that the Moluccas were the choicest prize in the entire world, to the point that to reach them from the west soon became Magellan and Serrão's obsession. Given the inseparability of the two men, would Magellan not have first journeyed to these fabled isles with Serrão? The demands of psychology aside, still-stronger evidence exists in a letter written in September 1519 to Charles V (Carlos V), in which Magellan speaks with authority of the islands' geographical position.

Each of these points, however, is open to rebuttal. Though Magellan may have acquired some knowledge of the Spice Islands from merchants in Malacca, it was Serrão's letters that enticed him. Interestingly, the Portuguese historians João de Barros, Fernão Lopes de Castanheda, Gaspar Corrêa, Damião de Góis, and Antonio Galvão do not mention his presence on d'Abreu's expedition, while the early-seventeenth-century Spanish historian Leonardo de Argensola tells us plainly that Magellan captained the third ship. But in 1519, when he began his circumnavigation, Magellan sailed for the Spanish crown, not the Portuguese, and one must take into account each historian's nationalistic bias.

Argensola's position has been popularly accepted because he was the Spanish authority for Magellan's expedition. The implication of this view is that Magellan was the first to circumnavigate the globe by virtue of his having sailed eastward from Malacca with Serrão to the Spice Islands, then having voyaged west from Spain a decade later to a similar longitude in the Philippines before he met his death. Considered in cold light, however, Argensola's assertion is not supported by Portuguese ship rosters or other records.

Another story that gained and lost currency had Magellan on an unofficial, secret mission that in 1512 took him to the Philippines. A Florentine merchant named Giovanni da Empoli, according to the account, had come to the East to oversee his spice firm's trading business and commissioned Magellan to reconnoiter the islands beyond the South China Sea. It was an illicit undertaking that supposedly angered the government in Goa and led to Magellan's recall.

The truth may never be known. What is known, however, is that Magellan had returned to Lisbon by June 12, 1512, because his signature and the date is affixed to a document that survives in the Lisbon archives, a receipt for his monthly salary paid by the court. If d'Abreu's expedition to the Spice Islands left Malacca in December 1511, or even as early as November that year, it would have been nearly impossible for

Magellan to have returned to Portugal by the following June, especially in view of the west monsoon, against which any ship of the day would have struggled. The east monsoon, which habitually powered fleets back to Europe from Malacca, was not well established until July. The same considerations would weigh heavily against the alleged voyage to the Philippines in early 1512.

A reasonable assumption drawn from records is that Magellan remained in Malacca before returning to Lisbon, gathering his own intelligence about the Spice Islands from various sea captains, pilots, masters of godowns, and traders. It is known that he acquired a Malay slave, whom he named Enrique de Malacca; he returned with Magellan to Portugal and later claimed to be the first person to circumnavigate the globe.

Of paramount importance in firing Magellan's drive to set out again for the Spice Islands were the letters from his friend. Serrão wrote to Magellan, and in his letters he lyricized about the captivating beauty and fertility of the Spice Islands. These communications, lost in the earthquake of 1755 that reduced Lisbon to ruins, were perused by early Portuguese chroniclers. "I have found a New World," Serrão wrote on one occasion, "richer, greater, and more beautiful than that of Vasco da Gama. . . . I beg you to join me here, that you may sample for yourself the delights which surround me." It was a correspondence that played no small part in convincing Magellan to undertake his search for the Spice Islands by following Columbus's original design: sailing west.

Before that expedition lifted anchor in 1519, however, Magellan spent a miserable seven years, an unhappy time that began to unfold on his return to Lisbon. The Crown owed him money for his services but refused to pay him. Then in August 1513 his sovereign, Dom Manuel, dispatched him from Portugal on a punitive expeditionary force to Morocco's Atlantic coast to quell a colonial rebellion, where Magellan on one occasion lost a horse under him and on another took a lance in the knee, a wound that gave him a permanent limp. Never one to mince words, he had a talent for making enemies easily, and in Morocco trumped-up charges of corruption were leveled against him. An investigation later revealed that the charges were groundless, a development that made him even more a subject of contempt by his superiors.

Sailing back to Lisbon, he sought and was given an audience with the king. Petitioning the Crown for an increase in his *moradia,* an advance in prestige as well as money, he was refused. Although regarded as a fair "Frank," as were all Europeans in Malacca, in Lisbon he was perceived at court as short, swarthy, and rough, cutting a tactless, outlandish figure among Manuel's bedizened, sycophantic courtiers. Nuance eluded him. When he reminded his sovereign of his noble origins, the court ridiculed such a pretension on the part of a peasant aristocrat. Attempting to win over Manuel with his integrity, he catalogued the wounds he had suffered in battle, most recently in Morocco, in a long career of faithful service. There was a vicious rumor abroad in the royal house, however, that his limp was an affectation. The king had no use for him.

Though Lisbon suffered a devastating earthquake in the mid-eighteenth century, in Magellan's day it rivaled Venice as Europe's greatest city. Moorish in origin and situated on the Bay of the Tagus, it was a pastel metropolis of steep streets and terraces overlooking the wide expanse of the bay, where ships from all over the known world rode at anchor. The English novelist Henry Fielding's sketch in the eighteenth century may apply to the sixteenth: From the sea the city appeared as "one vast high hill and rock, with buildings rising above one another, and that in so steep and almost perpendicular a manner that they all seem to have but one foundation."

In 1515 the city was infused with the restless and inquisitive spirit of an earlier royal figure, Prince Henry the Navigator. Though Henry had died in 1460, the year Vasco da Gama was born, it was Henry, a king's fourth son who never ruled, to whose energy, intelligence, and foresight must be traced all the fortune and fame that Portugal achieved on the seas in the fifteenth and sixteenth centuries. Explorers sent out at his instigation discovered the Azores and unknown regions on the African coast. They sought gold beyond the Sahara and the lost Christian kingdom of Prester John. Vasco da Gama had rounded the Cape of Good Hope in 1497 to open up commerce with the East by colonizing India's Malabar Coast. Though he sailed under the reign of Manuel, Vasco's voyage was Henry the Navigator's legacy, as was Albuquerque's expedition from India to sack Malacca a little more than a decade later.

Magellan, it would seem, might have embodied the spirit of that city and age. In a sense he did, but he was also strangely at odds with it. At cross-purposes with the same court that had lionized Gama, Magellan must have stood perplexed before the still-unfinished Convento dos Jeronymos de Belém. Its church was where Gama had spent the night of July 8, 1497, before he embarked on his voyage of discovery, and where the king received him on his return. The king had vowed to erect here a convent to the Virgin if the enterprise was successful, and he laid the foundation stone of the building within a few weeks of the explorer's homecoming. The blunt-spoken Magellan, by contrast, would be treated as a pariah by the same monarch.

The church and cloisters were an exuberantly rich development of Gothic architecture, the details of which had been largely borrowed from the decorative forms of the early Renaissance, from the sumptuous buildings of India, and from the Moors. It was a blended style that was often fantastic, with a decided tendency to overelaboration and extravagance. That style, the personal taste of Dom Manuel, was mirrored in the manners of his court, where Magellan's boorishness would have no place.

Months passed, and Magellan sought other ways to press for service and recognition. Aware that the Spanish had designs on the coveted Moluccas, he implored his king to send him with men and supplies to join his friend Serrão, thereby consolidating Portugal's early advantage in the spice trade. Again, he was refused. The Crown knew about Serrão, who by 1515 was permanently branded a renegade for his refusal to return to Malacca from Ternate, where by now he was legendary as a white man who prospered in splendid, royal isolation as advisor to the native rajah.

The correspondence passed to and from the other side of the world by way of Malacca, with Serrão's letters tantalizing Magellan to the point of anguish. In one communication, Serrão greatly overestimated the distance of the Spice Islands from Malacca, a mistake that had two fateful repercussions for Magellan. The first was a practical one: the possibility that the Moluccas were so far west that they might lie in the Spanish domain as defined by the Treaty of Tordesillas. The second was an outgrowth of the first, but it was anything but practical. A seed was planted in Magellan's imagination that the Spice Islands were so far east that they might lie no great distance from Spanish and Portuguese America.

The Treaty of Tordesillas, one of the most curious and unlikely in history, addresses a problem brought on by the Age of Discovery, when it began to dawn on the emerging European nations, especially after Columbus's coming upon America, that vast colonizing possibilities were open to them. The chief contenders, of course, were Spain and Portugal, and theirs was an uneasy alliance when it came to territorial matters. Pope Alexander VI, the father of Cesare and Lucrezia Borgia as well as a native of Valencia, was naturally sympathetic to Spain, though Portugal had evolved into the Roman Catholic world's greatest sea power. Both nations looked to the Holy See to adjudicate their contentions.

As if the earth were an apple to be split with a knife, this Borgia pope, in a bull issued on May 4, 1493, simply divided the world into two halves, giving Portugal the Eastern Hemisphere and Spain the Western, with the line of demarcation drawn from pole to pole.

The inexactness of longitudinal measurement induced each nation to claim that with the line extended over the poles, thus bisecting the other side of the world, the Moluccas lay within its boundary. The Portuguese claimed the islands by right of discovery and Francisco Serrão's exploitative residence there, while the Spaniards felt no less justified in claiming that the islands belonged to them. Despite posturing to the contrary in each royal house, both sides were intractable, and the matter would not be settled until the middle of the sixteenth century.

To Magellan, meanwhile, it was a challenge to forestall any Spanish claims, while Dom Manuel fretted that Portugal's new colony in the Moluccas might be illegitimate. Magellan's surmise that the Spice Islands lay in such close proximity to America goaded him further, and this insistence before Manuel's court ensured his alienation from his sovereign.

The sixteenth-century Portuguese historian João de Barros put it well and succinctly: "The demon that always in secret drives men to do ill made Magellan quarrel with the King." Magellan received a final audience. Being told that the Crown no longer valued his services and that he could take them anywhere he pleased dropped like a curtain of final humiliation. Magellan knelt to kiss the hand of his king, but the latter withdrew it. Stunned and angry, Magellan in his imagined cell saw a window, and through it blue sky. He limped from the court, but he strode toward Spain.

• • •

MAGELLAN CAME TO Seville in October 1517, nearly two years after his disgrace at Dom Manuel's court in Lisbon, a driven man known to be "very knowledgeable in matters concerning navigation." This reputation was an extraordinary one for a mere soldier, whose only naval command had been of an oared barge in East Africa. But he spent days at India House in Lisbon examining manuscripts and charts, and he stayed with relatives in Oporto, where he was constantly seen in the company of pilots; this, together with his own knowledge gained from service in Malacca, meant that he had amassed as much practical information as he could in his day. With his study of a map of the Java and Banda Seas gained from d'Abreu's expedition, and, of course, Serrão's letters, he was now a man obsessed with reaching the Spice Islands.

Thus it became the dubious question of finding sponsors in a land that was an enemy to his own, which had cast him out. So it was that Magellan worked both sides of this argument. Having been rebuffed by the court at Lisbon for urging the bolstering of Serrão's possibly illegitimate Portuguese colony, he now sought Spanish support to exploit what many believed to be really Spain's.

Before departing Portugal he had shrewdly sat at the feet of a fellow Portuguese equally disgruntled with Dom Manuel, a man who in his day also happened to be the finest mathematician, astronomer, and scholar of the nautical sciences: the famously eccentric Rodriguo Faleira. It was said that on the island of Madeira, Faleira had advised Columbus that a New World existed to the west.

Faleira and Magellan pored over maps, the finest and most accurate of their day—but by no means accurate at all—drawn by Pedro and Jorge Reinel, who were the most notable cartographers of that time. These mapmakers were Portuguese, and the maps they produced prior to 1519, the year Magellan departed Seville on his voyage, plainly showed the Moluccas to be in Spain's sphere. With this knowledge, Magellan arrived in Seville seeking an audience with a young and eager Charles I of Spain, who would later become known as Charles V of the Holy Roman Empire.

In Seville Magellan discovered an ancient port dating from Roman times, a labyrinth of narrow streets inherited from the Moors and as gay and bright a city as he had ever seen. Almost every open space was planted with trees, and the houses were nearly all whitewashed with balconies and patios paved with marble, enclosed by arcades and adorned with fountains, flowers, and foliage plants. La Tierra de María Santisima, as Seville's citizens proudly called the surrounding countryside, produced olives, wine, oranges, cork, and grain, combining the peculiarities of a harbor town with the exuberant fertility of a southern landscape. Here roses blossomed throughout the winter, while hyacinths and crocuses appeared as early as January.

The discovery of America had advanced Seville to an undreamed-of importance. On Palm Sunday 1493, Columbus was formally received here on his return from his first voyage. The city, invested with the monopoly of the transatlantic trade, was chosen as the seat of the Tribunal de las Indias, and soon became the chief port of Spain.

Seville's position on the tawny Rio Guadalquivir was unique. The great river described a curve around the west side of the city, parting it from the district of Triana. The fall of the Guadalquivir was so slight that the flood tide was perceptible more than sixty miles from its mouth. The highest tide rose nearly six feet above the mean level, while the ebb sank fully three feet below it. Since ancient times, deep-drafted seagoing vessels could ascend with the flood to the quays of Seville, which enjoyed the advantages of a seaport, though more than fifty miles from the sea.

Residing in Seville came to bring about a quiet change in Magellan's personal life. Marriage would seem an ancillary feat at this obsessive point in his life, and so it was. Without fanfare and before the end of 1517, he took as a wife Beatriz Barbosa, the daughter of his host in Seville, Diego Barbosa. She bore him a son and had conceived a second child before his departure two years later. Magellan had another marriage of sorts with Faleira, and when they signed a final contract allocating the profits from their forthcoming joint venture, Magellan for the first time signed his name not in the customary Portuguese form Fernão de Magalhães, but in the Spanish fashion, Fernando de Magallanes.

Invited for a royal audience in Valladolid, the two men traveled in February 1518 north from Andalusia to this favorite residence of the sovereigns of Castile, situated among grain fields in a fertile plain on the left bank of the Rio Pisuerga. Ferdinand and Isabella had been married here in 1469. It was at Valladolid that Columbus, broken in health and vainly hoping for the fulfillment of royal promises, spent the last two years of his life before he died in 1506. Now overflowing with King Charles's Flemish and German entourage, the old capital was a lively place, with inns and taverns filled to capacity and a dark underworld of prostitutes, spies, and criminals preying on the unwary.

Magellan met first with Charles's ministers and then the king himself. Charles, the grandson of Columbus's sponsors Ferdinand and Isabella, had just turned eighteen, and wore an air of enthusiastic but thoughtful caution. Advised by his native Flemish counselors, he listened to Magellan's arguments that the Spice Islands lay within Spain's domain as decreed by the pope himself, while hearing contrary asides from his ministers that the islands belonged to Portugal.

The very first evidence Magellan produced was Serrão's letters, emphasizing his friend's claim that if he wanted to get rich, he should come to the Moluccas. "I have found a New World," he read aloud, "richer, greater, and more beautiful than that of Vasco da Gama. . . ." Then he proceeded to describe with remarkable authority the geographical configuration of the Spice Islands, with most of his knowledge having been gained from Serrão. He presented his slave, the multitongued Enrique, as well as a slave girl from Sumatra, "who understood the tongues of many islands." He argued that South America turned westward as the Cape of Good Hope turned toward the east, and that it was a question of sailing the coast of the continent until he discovered that corresponding cape which he would navigate to reach the Spice Islands.

Then Magellan produced the Reinels' globe, which he had brought with him from Portugal, showing the continent and his intended route. The globe suggested that Japan was no great distance from the west coast of America. All these things gave weight to a case that could never have been made had the reality been known: that Ptolemy had greatly underestimated the earth's circumference; that Serrão had cavalierly overestimated the distance of the Spice Islands from Malacca; and that Magellan had not the faintest idea of the vast width of the Pacific Ocean, as he pleaded his case for an expedition to find a strait leading to what was then known as the Great South Sea. Faleira completed the argument, emphasizing that the prized islands lay within the line of demarcation.

Charles was stirred, and, seeing him stirred, Christopher de Haro of the Haros of Antwerp, the Rothschilds of the age, volunteered to outfit the expedition, a major measure of enthusiasm beyond the court. But Charles declined his offer. If it was to be the Crown's gain, it would be the Crown's risk. Magellan's expedition would be financed by the royal treasury.

Contracts were drawn up, detailing such matters as payments, profits, the size of the armada that would be assembled without delay (five ships provisioned for two years, manned by 234 officers and crewmen), and the stipulation that the exploration not violate the territories of Charles's "dear and well-beloved uncle and brother the King of Portugal." On March 22, 1518, after less than a month of negotiations, the commission was awarded.

Faleira's unstable temperament eventually resulted in his removal as cocommander. Magellan alone received the royal standard in a solemn ceremony at the church of Santa Maria de la Victoria de Triana. On August 10, 1519 the fleet, composed of the *San Antonio, Trinidad, Concepción, Victoria,* and *Santiago,* ranging in tonnage from 75 to 120, departed Seville to cannon salutes. The ships were carried on the ebb downstream on the Guadalquivir, thus beginning the fateful expedition that shrank the globe, dispelling a profound, enduring ignorance of it.

TWO YEARS AND three months later, the two remaining ships of Magellan's armada, the *Trinidad* and *Victoria,* having sailed southeast from the Philippines through the Celebes Sea, entered Moluccan waters, and on November 6, 1521, their crews sighted the towering peak of Ternate's volcano. The *Santiago* had been wrecked in Patagonia; the *Concepción,* in abominable condition after the Pacific crossing, scuttled; and the *San Antonio* seized by mutineers and sailed back to Spain from Patagonia. Now, more than halfway around the world from Seville, a native pilot informed the Spaniards that they were gazing upon the Maluco of history and fable, where the clove tree thrived.

In their wake were a series of desultory horrors and tests that only the cruelest of gods could have inflicted: mutiny in Brazil, with the ringleaders left decapitated and quartered; a brutal Patagonian winter; and

the endless frustrations in the search for the elusive strait at South America's tip. Scurvy and starvation during the Pacific crossing had reduced
those who had survived to eating rats and leather and drinking water
befouled by the rodents' urine and droppings. The expedition had lost
three ships and at least 153 men and suffered mortal attacks by unfriendly
natives. But the supreme disaster, as we shall see, was the needless death
eight months before of Magellan at the hands of a native prince on Mactan Island to the north, who had resented his intrusiveness within his
domain.

That Magellan had earned the title by which history would know
him—the Great Navigator—points to the expedition's successes, but at a
great price, including his own life. Magellan had discovered and traversed
the hostile strait that today bears his name, and he had led his ships across
a vast, pathless ocean colossally indifferent to the plight of men, a body of
water three times the width of the Atlantic.

It would seem that a leader who had taken his charges on a series of
adventures through hell in his search for his friend Serrão and the Spice
Islands would have seen that the prize for which he had sailed was within
his grasp. But it was not to be. Why Magellan did not seek a calmer
course than the one he chose when he reached the archipelago we know
today as the Philippines can only be conjectured. What followed, the
events leading to Magellan's death, provide an acute account, as sharp as
any ever recorded, of a maniacally misplaced focus, fueled by a crazed
hubris.

Ironically, Magellan was *not* a wild, flamboyant, arrogant, and reckless
flouter of convention. On the contrary—his strengths lay in his ferocious
devotion to a cause and his uncanny ability to discern the difference
between dream and achievement. The vision of the Spice Islands and
their potential for Europe had been not his but Serrão's. Magellan was
a doer, drivingly so, seeking the goal at hand: to find the Spice Islands,
and with them, Francisco Serrão. In the meantime there were other, more
immediate tasks, such as feeding his men, whose ranks were thinning
daily from scurvy. He had himself managed to ingest enough vitamin C
by eating preserved quince served in the officers' mess to survive the savage crossing of the Pacific.

That achievement past, he found himself in a world of islands seen by no other Europeans before the arrival of his expedition. Now he saw an opportunity for a demonstration of Spanish might to win over the locals, at little or no cost. He was also determined to spread the Roman Catholic faith among the fiercely independent islanders, who clung to animist or Islamic faiths, and often both. Though with knees hardly scarred from prayer, Magellan was in his fashion a devout believer in the Holy Trinity. It was in the interest of Spain to see Christianity take root half a world away in a land Magellan was bent on exploiting.

Magellan's eagerness to realize these achievements was crossed with a misguided conviction of his own invincibility. Combined with the profound determination with which he went about executing his goals, these proved his own undoing.

After landfall and provisioning in Guam, the flotilla found itself in March 1521 off the island called Limasawa, a name with a lilting cadence familiar to Magellan's Malaccan slave Enrique. When a canoe of natives approached the ships, Enrique engaged them in their own dialect. Magellan was then struck with twin realizations. He had fulfilled Columbus's dream of discovering the easternmost part of the world as it was known, and he was in waters specified by treaty for Portuguese, not Spanish, exploration. He seemingly paid this transgression no mind, however, but announced to the natives that the expedition had come in peace.

On Good Friday, entertained lavishly by a local chieftain named Colambu, who ruled over the islands of Limasawa and Suluan as well as a portion of the larger island of Mindanao, Magellan quickly sought to consolidate his triumph. Gifts and blood were exchanged in a fraternal ritual known as *casi-casi*. On Easter Sunday, March 31, Magellan conducted services on the beach, startling onlookers by having his cannon fire six rounds as a sign of peace.

The men feasted on meat, fish, fresh fruit, and an abundance of palm wine, but encountered only ginger as a spice. Determined to press on, Magellan needed staples for his ships. Cebu was the trading center of the region, and Colambu offered to guide them there in exchange for help with the rice harvest. Eager for these immediate stores, Magellan agreed, and on April 7 they anchored in the channel off the port of Cebu, a humming settlement with houses on stilts reaching out into the water, not far from the island called Mactan.

A cannon salvo frightened the population, panicking them to flee to the jungle and hills. The local leader, Sultan Humabon, a short, portly man covered with tribal tattoos, was impressed but guarded. Hearing that the strangers had come in peace, he wanted to know why they had come at all. A Muslim trader suspected aloud that these were the same Franks who had sacked Malacca, but Enrique played this card to Magellan's advantage. They were Spanish, he emphasized, not Portuguese, and they served the emperor of all Christians. Humabon quickly suggested a trade agreement, and another blood oath was exchanged.

Thanking God in heaven, Magellan began to press for the locals' conversion as the latter looked curiously and intently on the Christian funeral services that were being conducted for two men recently dead of scurvy. Touched and bewildered, Humabon converted, as did many of his people, while Magellan busied himself founding a trade base in Cebu. Pagan idols were destroyed, while his men reveled, ravishing the island women and angering the men. Announcing that successful trade would require that he return to Spain for reinforcements, Magellan then went too far. Stating that he would need a reliable ally, a Christian one, he ordered that the cluster of islands of which Cebu was the nucleus, and all its diverse peoples, must be ruled by a single king, Humabon. On the day of the ruler's baptism Magellan sent word abroad that local chiefs refusing to pay tribute and submit to Humabon's rule would do so on pain of death and destruction or confiscation of property.

Lapulapu, a chief on the island of Mactan, flatly refused, daring the Spaniards to attack. Magellan was happy to oblige him. What native force could stand up to Spanish arms protected by the Holy Virgin? Wiser heads tried to dissuade Magellan, but in vain. Moved by the spirit of Serrão's success on Ternate, which Magellan sensed could not be far distant, he named himself leader of the attacking force and boasted that he could take Mactan with sixty men.

Early on April 27, 1521, three boats mounted with swivel guns and with a full armed fighting force converged on the mangrove-fringed village beside a bay on Mactan's northeast end. Immediately there was trouble. The force was attacking in the predawn hours and in a low tide, which Magellan, normally thorough, had not considered. A reef prevented his boats from beaching, and his swivel guns were unable to provide covering fire at a distance of a thousand yards. He ordered his men out of the boats and then led them toward the beach, a distance, according to a survivor, of "two crossbow flights."

They landed without incident and made for the town. Finding it evacuated, they began setting fire to the thatched huts. Within minutes the force was enveloped on two sides by armies of natives. Hours passed as the flight of crossbow bolts and arrows greeted the dawn, and the reports of musket fire seemed to shatter it. The Spaniards' supply of powder was soon depleted and their crossbow bolts spent.

Magellan ordered a withdrawal to the beach, but seeing the invaders on the run only increased the determined rage of Lapulapu's pursuit as his men sent poisoned arrows and lances at the backs of the fleeing Spaniards. Magellan and a group of eight tried to cover the retreat, but they were easily outnumbered. Magellan took an arrow in the leg, only a graze, but then he was surrounded and pelted with rocks, knocking his helmet off. A *bolo* cut his leg, and he fell. Then the mob set upon him. Bamboo lances pierced his body in countless places, and one found his throat.

When the remnants of the attacking party returned to Cebu, Humabon wept upon learning of Magellan's death, but several days later he turned upon the Spaniards, ambushing a shore group and cutting their throats. Among the victims was João Serrão, Francisco's brother, who had been one of two men elected to succeed Magellan in a dual command. Enrique somehow escaped, and the ships managed to leave Cebu.

Endless days and weeks became months of wandering among the countless islands scattered across the China Sea. Sailing between the Philippines and Borneo produced a succession of misadventures, as the Spaniards sought clues to the exact location of the Spice Islands. They strayed as far afield as Brunei, in the northern part of Borneo, where the sultan feted the Europeans with sumptuous banquets and local transport on silken howdahs mounted on the backs of elephants. After three weeks of provisioning, the crew fought off an attack on their ships, then repaired north to a safe harbor to shore up the vessels.

Piracy, blackmail, betrayal, and hostage taking, the Spaniards had learned, were a way of life in these waters. But as local merchants and pilots were furtive and misleading as to where the Spice Islands precisely were, the Iberians took to looting junks as they crisscrossed these strange seas, taking silks, silver, spices, and whatever other lucrative plunder they came upon, while piecing together any isolated shreds of evidence about the Moluccas they could find. Then an unlikely coincidence off Sakul Island near the Philippine Zamboanga Peninsula proved singularly crucial.

Closing on a native vessel, whose crew put up a gallant fight with scimitars and shields, the Spaniards killed seven men but managed to take several survivors prisoner. One was a brother of a rajah from Mindanao, and the news he gave overjoyed his captors. He claimed to have been a guest in the house of Francisco Serrão on Ternate.

The *Trinidad* and *Victoria,* now with shanghaied local guides, altered their course. They pushed south, then southeast, eventually guided by the spine of mountains on Celebes, then followed the lush coastline of Moro and Batching on the island of Halmahera before sighting Ternate rising from the sea. Soon the gentle, smoky rise of that island's twin, the volcanic cone of Tidore, was sketched against the sky. Two afternoons after sighting it, a Friday, the two ships hove to close to Tidore's shore in the lee off the southern tip of the island, firing a cannon barrage as the anchors plunged through the twenty-fathom depths to the bottom.

"The pilot who had remained with us," writes Antonio Pigafetta, an Italian who would gain fame in Europe for publishing his account of the circumnavigation, "told us that they were the Moluccas, for which we thanked God, and to comfort us we discharged all our artillery. Nor ought it to cause astonishment that we were so rejoiced, since we had passed twenty-seven months, less two days, always in search of these Moluccas, wandering hither and thither for that purpose among innumerable islands."

The principal European pilot of the expedition was a Greek mariner named Francisco Albo, an independent-minded man aloof from politics, who determined through a previous astronomical fix that they were uncomfortably west of the line of demarcation, hence in Portuguese territory. Pigafetta most likely later altered the record of their position to please the Spanish court, for in his account he placed the longitude of the Moluccas east of the line.

As a practical matter, the command thought it prudent to ingratiate itself with Tidore's sultan, the sultan of Ternate's old enemy, thereby gaining an ally in a probable territorial dispute with the Portuguese. At the same time, haunted by the spirit of Magellan, the sailors were desperate to

meet the man they had endured such acute hardships to see: Francisco
Serrão.

As the Spaniards plotted their next move, Tidore's sultan surprised
them with an initiative of his own. On November 9, the very day after
their arrival, a curious scene unfolded for the mariners on the decks of the
Trinidad and *Victoria* as a prahu bedecked with a silk awning was rowed
through the water toward the ships. After so many disasters in the islands
to the north, the Spaniards immediately were on their guard, suspecting
trickery, until it became apparent that the approaching vessel was no
ordinary one. Under the silks reclined Tidore's sultan, Almanzor, and
his courtiers. A ship's boat was dispatched to escort the royal party to the
flagship.

When the party reached the sultan's *kora-kora,* the men discovered a
well-built man of royal presence in his mid-forties dressed in a delicate
white shirt with gold-embroidered sleeves and a long sarong reaching
from his waist to his bare feet. His head was wrapped in a silk turban
crowned with a garland of flowers, though the even features of his face
were strangely at odds with the garish red smears—betel nut stains—
across his mouth. Before him sat a son with the royal scepter, and the
royal couple was preceded by two attendants bearing gold jars with water
for the sultan's washing, while two others held gilded baskets filled with
betel.

Once aboard the Spanish vessel, the sultan was escorted to the stern
cabin, which he refused to stoop to enter. Instead, he was invited to
descend from above and sit in a red velvet chair and then was clothed in
a yellow velvet Turkish robe. The mariners, anxious to please, showered
him with gifts: delicate linens and damasks, scarlet cloths, brocaded silks,
beads, knives, mirrors, scissors, combs, gilded drinking cups. They gave
similar gifts to his son and each of the nine other members of his
entourage, who were all chiefs.

After the gifts were dispensed, the sultan held court. He welcomed the
strangers, explaining that his own powers as a visionary and astrologer
had been at work. Not so long before he had dreamed of the arrival in his
kingdom of strange ships from distant lands, and now the prophecy had
been fulfilled. "After such long tossing upon the seas, and so many dangers," he stated, "come and enjoy the pleasures of the land, and refresh

your bodies, and do not think but that you have arrived at the kingdom of your own sovereign." He went on to say that his island kingdom was to be no longer called Tidore, but Castile, because of his great love for Spain's king.

Having been made welcome, the officers and crew, filthy and half starved, now expected the man whom they had traveled so far to see to greet them. It was an anticipation that transcended considerations of country or creed. Though most of the surviving mariners were Castilian, Portugal was well represented, and there were sailors from Aragon, the Azores, Brazil, England, Flanders, France, Genoa, Germany, Greece, India, Ireland, Lombardy, Malacca, Naples, Navarre, Norway, the Philippines, Rhodes, and Sicily as well. They had survived a mutiny and other threatened insurrections, the death of a leader, and everything a hostile nature dealt to them. Whatever their differences, their hardships duly shared had forged a fraternity, and Francisco Serrão was its absent member-in-waiting. Where was he? they asked discreetly, sensing immediately a shift in mood.

Almanzor now wore another face, one of the mendacity and wiliness the Spanish had grown accustomed to seeing in the islands to the north. The Ternateans were no longer friendly to Europeans, he began, drawing a marked contrast between the manner of the Spaniards' reception here and what they might have expected on Ternate. For their part, the Spaniards may have been taken aback by this revelation. Had Francisco Serrão not mediated between the two sultanates? Almanzor's next words, however, were grave indeed

Francisco Serrão was dead, he stated impassively. But how? the men asked. The mariners were told only that Serrão had died under mysterious circumstances, for much of his stay on Ternate was shrouded in enigma. They learned further that he had died only recently, after eight years of service as grand vizier to the sultan of Ternate. One rumor had it that he was poisoned by his erstwhile friend and protector on Ternate, Sultan Bolief. Others claimed that he was victim of a court intrigue fueled by Portuguese villainy, for Sultan Bolief met his end a few days later, both deaths lingering and attributed to poison. The sultan's death may have been at the hands of his own daughter, who bitterly resented her father's quarrel with her husband, the sultan of the vassal island of Bacan, and Bolief's refusal to condone their marriage.

Whether or not his fellow countrymen had a hand in Serrão's murder may never be known, but there was ample motive in these violent, ambitious times, when a man's career could rise or fall on a superior's whim. Early on, Serrão had been given free rein by his king, but later when he was ordered to return to Malacca, he refused and instead requested reinforcements and materials with which to build a fort, adding that he was serving Portuguese interests in Ternate far more effectively than he could anywhere else. But Serrão, though he was unaware of it, was maligned in reports by envious colleagues forwarded to Albuquerque back in Cochin and then on to the royal court in Lisbon. Such reprimands predisposed the Crown against Serrão and, by extension, Magellan's enterprise.

Certain accounts of Serrão's fate, perhaps the closest to the truth, attribute his death to the royal figure now aboard the *Trinidad,* the sultan of Tidore, who two days later, when the loading of cloves began and the Spaniards still suspected a trap, swore on the Qu'ran his allegiance to Spain. Almanzor had allegedly killed Serrão during a state visit, when Serrão had made the narrow crossing to buy spices. Sultan Almanzor, still seething over the Portuguese captain's high-handed efforts at peace by forcing him to give a daughter in marriage not only to Serrão but to his archenemy Sultan Bolief of Ternate, invited him to a royal dinner and then poisoned him. But the Spaniards knew none of these things.

As the *Trinidad* and *Victoria* were being provisioned and loaded with spices for the long voyage home, a *kora-kora* bearing a Ternatean prince, the widow of Serrão (who may have been Almanzor's daughter), her two children, and a company of courtiers and musicians approached the ships. Not wishing to offend Almanzor, the Spaniards did not invite the royal party immediately to board, but offered gifts instead. The slight did not pass unnoticed, and haughtily the prince ordered his rowers to push off. A dialogue of sorts, however, had been established. Seizing an opportunity, some of the expedition crew members decided to venture over to the other island to call on Serrão's widow.

Examining Serrão's personal effects, they discovered a letter from Magellan and read what he had written: "God willing, I will soon be seeing you, whether by way of Portugal or Castile, for that is the way my affairs have been leaning: you must wait for me there, because we already know that it will be some time before we can expect things to get better for us."

But the two men never met again, and now both were dead, dying within seven weeks and a mere thousand miles of each other half a world away from Europe.

Only the *Victoria* completed the circumnavigation, returning to Spain with twenty-one survivors and a cargo of spices—mostly cloves—worth ten thousand times what it had cost on the other side of the world. On September 6, 1522, the *nau* lay to off the mouth of the Guadalquivir after a voyage of three years less fourteen days.

Chapter 5

BLACK DOG

THE REMAINING SHIP of Magellan's expedition, the *Trinidad,* met with disaster. As she needed months of refitting to be seaworthy, her command hatched a bold plan to ride the west monsoon to Spanish America in April, while the *Victoria,* with nothing to gain by the delay, would meet the already prevailing east monsoon for her return to Spain. After taking on cargo of cloves and nutmeg and leaving a small contingent of Spaniards on Tidore at Sultan Almanzor's urging, a provocative reminder to the Portuguese on Ternate that Spain now laid claim to the Spice Islands, the *Victoria* sailed from Tidore after an emotional leave-taking just before Christmas Day 1521.

In early April 1522, after more than three months of careening and repairs with the help of Almanzor's workers, the *Trinidad* pushed northeast through the Philippines with the vain hope of riding westerlies eastward across the Pacific. Instead, the caravel reached a midocean latitude only to be beaten back by strong headwinds in a totally unexpected weather system. A five-day raging storm sheared the mainmast and damaged the forecastle and poop; stores, save for rice, were depleted; and the men, accustomed to equatorial warmth and ill-prepared for the cold winds tearing at them, succumbed to disease.

The ship's command decided to return to Tidore. After six weeks most of the scurvy-ridden crew had died, and the *Trinidad* was more a ghost ship than a vessel of the living. When she limped southward for an anchorage dangerously close to the enemy stronghold on Ternate, the Portuguese, now a fleet of seven ships and three hundred men determined to oust the Spaniards, made their move, taking possession of the ship under a repellent, deadly stench hovering over her decks where her men lay helplessly ill. The ship's records and cargo were confiscated and her remaining crew members were imprisoned, to be forced into the hard labor of building a fort on Ternate. Only four of the *Trinidad*'s crew saw Spain again, and a Portuguese trader who had cast his lot with the Spaniards was declared a traitor and publicly beheaded.

Soon after, the *Trinidad*'s anchor rope was severed in a storm and the ship was swept aground. Broken by the gales and waves, she was dismembered by the Portuguese, who managed to salvage her cannon and timbers. These would be useful at a new fort they were building to consolidate their holdings. It was completed on February 15, 1523, and named after St. John the Baptist.

The Portuguese had not needed a fortress on the island when Francisco Serrão was alive and mediating on Ternate as a self-styled white rajah. But now with the death of Serrão, the skeletal Spanish force on Tidore, and the Ternateans' own proclivity for intrigue and mischief, that omission was corrected, with its strong-arm implications not lost on the island hosts. The fortress encompassed a large space surrounded by six-foot walls with a two-level tower rising to thirty feet. Alarmed at such a fortification, the islanders sought reassurances from the Portuguese, who simply turned to their advantage Sultan Bolief's earlier prophecy of an arriving savior force of white, ironclad men. The fort, they insisted, would ensure that the sultan of Ternate "become the greatest lord of all the isles, have many islands and lands under his dominion, and be the greatest servant of His Highness."

The fortification, however, stood between white-skinned and brown as a revelation to each group of its utter unlikeness to the other. It soon became a practical as well as symbolic underlining of the vast differences between the islanders and the Portuguese. An unnatural blight on a pristine, tropical landscape, the Fort of São João Bautista enclosed an Iberian world far from home in which the Europeans managed their own imported customs, food, and dress, insofar as they could, untainted by those they perceived to be the uncivilized savages who lived beyond its walls. The disposition and temperament of the officers and men were a far cry from those of Francisco Serrão, whose fancy had been captured by the same paradisaical alienage that these current visitors barely tolerated.

The contemporary Portuguese historian João de Barros understood his countrymen's attitude toward the islands and their people, putting it in a passage that might have been written by anyone in the succession of haughty Portuguese commanders: "The land of these islands is ill-favored and ungracious to look at. The sun is always very near. The air is loaded with vapors. The coast is unwholesome.

"The people," Barros continues, "are of a tawny complexion, have lank hair, are robust in person, strong-limbed and addicted to war. In everything but war they are slothful; and if there be any industry among them in agriculture or trade, it is confined to the women. They are agile on land and still more so on water; for in swimming they are fish, and in fighting, birds. Altogether they are a lascivious people, false and ungrateful, but expert in learning anything. Although poor in wealth, such is their pride and presumption that they will abate nothing from necessity; nor will they submit, except to the sword that cuts them, and through to blood of their bodies. Finally, these islands, according to the account given by our people, are a warren of every evil, and contain nothing good but their clove tree."

A pattern was quickly established of one Portuguese captain being recalled only to be replaced by another capable of equally arbitrary and cruel behavior, and it became a leitmotif of Portugal's colonial rule in the Moluccas. In its overriding, often violent strategy to control the spice trade, brutal confrontation was key, as an antagonistic European culture pitted itself against another society it deemed primitive, each with little appreciation of the other.

Attending and exacerbating this conflict was the clash of two fundamentally different religions. The Portuguese Christian's hatred of the Muslim long predated the siege of Malacca. Central to this prejudice was the centuries-old Islamic occupation of the Iberian Peninsula, followed by the long succession of bloody wars against the Moors in North Africa, not to mention the Crusades, which left more than a residue of bitterness on both sides. Conversely, it was writ large in the Muslim mind and heart that the invading Franks were spiritually bereft infidels, a resentment of which the Portuguese were well aware.

Despite the Portuguese muscle and contempt, relations might have proceeded smoothly, even without the intercession of Serrão, had the Europeans not begun meddling in island affairs. Moreover, the Portuguese were seemingly oblivious to the fact that such intrusiveness had cost Serrão his life. But there was maladroitness all around, and nowhere is the viper's nest of island politics and the contentions of all parties better illustrated than in the strange case of the poisoned Sultan Bolief's brother, Prince Darwis. This sinister figure, who in another incarnation might have intrigued at a Borgia court, managed affairs on behalf of the late sultan's successor, Bolief's seven-year-old son. While Islamic law forbade a brother's ascendancy to the sultan's chair, it did not preclude his acquiring the lion's share of power behind a throne that would have been his for the taking in the days before Islam came to these shores.

Complicating the entanglement was the queen mother and Sultan Bolief's widow, the beautiful and willful Niay Tsjili, who, as the daughter of Sultan Almanzor of Tidore, was another figure ambitious for power. Darwis, realizing that she was disadvantaged because of Islam's prohibition against a woman inheriting the throne, made a series of Machiavellian moves to strengthen his own position. In the first he convinced the Portuguese command to invade Tidore, taking six hundred heads in the process and effectively neutralizing its sultan, who was later poisoned by the Portuguese command's physician. Darwis's next move was to order the young prince and his brother seized and placed in Portuguese custody, explaining to an outraged queen mother that it was for their own protection, for Ternate and Tidore were at war. As one Portuguese commander was recalled to Goa to be replaced by another, Darwis continued his machinations, urging the islanders of both Ternate and Tidore to put aside their differences and galvanize themselves as a single force against the Portuguese, while himself currying favor with the Europeans as he continued plotting against them by inciting a siege of their castle.

In the meantime, more Spanish ships were appearing on the scene, bolstering the Spanish claim for the Spice Islands and clearly alarming the Portuguese authorities in Goa. This led to another change of commanders on Ternate, and then another, with the revolving commands provoking internecine quarreling among the officers and in one case drawn swords, the clashing of steels, and a near mutiny. The Northern Moluccas, with the Spanish threat and the devious doings of Darwis, were, as the Portuguese perceived them, a powder keg with a burning fuse.

The Portuguese, however, were slow to see that the Spanish threat was an impotent one, best illustrated by the fate of Magellan's flagship. Out of a fleet of twenty ships and fifteen hundred men sailing west from Acapulco to lay legitimate claim to the Spice Islands, the only ship to survive the disastrous crossing was the same *Victoria* that three years earlier had struggled back to Spain with the survivors of Magellan's expedition.

The reconditioned flagship found herself again in Moluccan waters in early 1527. Worm-eaten below the waterline, her bottom covered in barnacles and her rigging in tatters, she was in a decrepit state when she appeared off Tidore as a challenge to Portuguese caravels. The Portuguese fired on her, and it was no match. The Portuguese sailors watched the *Victoria* sink out of sight, while some of her crew of 117 men swam to shore at Tidore.

Ironically, though neither side could know it, the tensions between the two Iberian nations in the Moluccas contrasted sharply with developments back home. King Charles and King John were exchanging conciliatory signals. The papal treaty of 1529 redrew not only north-south lines of demarcation, but east-west ones as well. If Mindanao, the large southern island of the Philippines, was ceded to Spain, Spanish claims southward to Molucca would be difficult to justify.

Another domestic development came into play. Charles, now nearing thirty, was on the threshold of marriage to John's sister and was in desperate need of money. In exchange for 350,000 cruzados, cash in hand, he renounced all claims to the still imprecisely defined Moluccas. His Spaniards on the other side of the world, however, were in no haste to comply, and final resolution was slow to crystallize.

Meanwhile on Ternate, the latest in the line of Portuguese commanders had to deal with the two rival contenders for the power behind the throne on Ternate, who for the time being were working in concert: Prince Darwis and Queen Niay Tsjili. Their common cause became the release of the two young princes who had been held hostage in the Portuguese fortress for nearly seven years, ironically at Darwis's instigation, since they were seized as currency against Ternatean treachery. Both Darwis and the queen mother wanted both princes, now ages thirteen and twelve, freed and the older youth placed on the long-vacant throne, but for vastly different reasons.

Darwis had intentions of eventually disposing of the two princes and seizing the throne for himself. The queen mother was equally ambitious, wishing to isolate her sons from both Darwis and the Portuguese command, and then establishing herself as ruler in the capacity of regent. For its part, the Portuguese command was intent on keeping the royal sons in custody for the same reason they had been taken in the first place. As long as the boys were in Portuguese hands, there was little fear of an outright native rebellion. Moreover, such tender, impressionable minds could be tutored in Catholicism as well as the civilized culture and languages of the West. Thus, once on the throne, the young king would be as malleable as clay by Portuguese hands in the prosecution of Portugal's interests: control of the spice trade.

But a sudden upheaval shattered these plans. The older boy destined to be king was poisoned. By whose hand? The distraught queen mother turned on Darwis, who in turn accused the Portuguese, who, having no reason to see the young king dead, suspected a Spanish-Tidorean conspiracy hatched by Darwis.

Darwis by now had made an infamous name for himself, even in distant Goa. His days were numbered, and the beginnings of his undoing sprang from an incident that is the stuff of black comedy. A pig belonging to a Chinese merchant escaped from its pen to root about in the town. Abhorring swine as unclean, the Muslim villagers killed it. The Chinese complained to the command, who saw the incident as an opportunity to display Portuguese justice. Seeking to place specific blame, the resident captain accused an important elder of ordering the animal's death. This elder was the uncle of Ternate's late king and of Darwis himself, a factor that made the accusation all the more humiliating to the islanders.

The Portuguese command had the old man arrested and would have had him executed, were it not for appeals for clemency from Darwis. Nonetheless, as the freed prisoner was leaving the fort, a sergeant under the captain's orders smeared the elder's face and mouth with pig fat, a supremely mortifying insult to a Muslim. The old man found refuge on outlying islands, where he sought vengeance against the Portuguese, preaching the necessity of a jihad to destroy the infidels. His sermons resulted in a siege, and the Portuguese found themselves isolated in their fortress and unable to resupply themselves.

Weeks passed, and the condition of the blockaded Portuguese grew more desperate by the hour. Short on stores and reinforcements due to the tardiness of a supply ship from Malacca, the captain organized a foraging party and ordered his men to venture outside the fortress and take what they could from the nearby islands. A war party of local inhabitants ambushed the group, killing several Portuguese soldiers. Learning of the incident, the enraged captain demanded from Darwis custody of the chief who was responsible for the ambush and two elders. Darwis, assuming this *sangaji,* or chief, and his advisors would only be held several days as a reprimand, obeyed. In so doing, he let his customary guard down. But the Portuguese had other plans, threatening the trio with dreadful punishment unless their villagers delivered food and provisions to the beleaguered fort. The chief angrily defied the European authorities.

On order, guards drew their swords and cut off the hands of the captives. Then they tied the arms of the maimed *sangaji* behind his back and set two fierce mastiffs upon him, much to the amusement of the Portuguese. Unable to defend himself, the chief's legs carried him to the sea, his bound twin stumps trailing blood across the sand, while the pair of pursuing dogs tore at his flesh. The three figures flailed about in the surf, where in a supreme effort the chief seized each of the dogs with his teeth, drowning them in turn and then himself.

There remained for the command to deal finally with Darwis, who was secretly organizing a joint rebellion by Ternateans and Tidoreans alike against the Portuguese. Word of this treason reached headquarters. When paid a visit by an imprudent and incautious Darwis, the Portuguese commander had him seized and placed on the rack to extract a catalogue of confessions. On a bright Sunday morning in early 1530, Darwis's head was stricken from his body, which in turn was quartered and so exhibited on the fortress ramparts.

The queen mother required less drastic measures. The command simply kept her at bay by holding her surviving son hostage. When this latest commander was recalled to Goa and an eventual hero's return to Portugal, the queen mother's lamentations were long and agonizingly heartfelt. "This," Niay Tsjili anguished to a new captain, another in a long line of capricious and cruel commanders, "is our reward for allowing the Portuguese in our land."

THE SPANIARDS, meanwhile, had made sporadic but ineffectual excursions into the Moluccas to reclaim what they believed to be theirs. But it was not to be. Despite eager acceptance by both sultanates to reestablish their vassal status with Spain, the Spanish forces were too weak and piecemeal to mount an effective Moluccan campaign. Finally, the Spaniards were forced to leave the Moluccas, exposing Tidore and its ally islands to greater danger than before. Subsequent Spanish expeditions to the islands in 1528 and again in 1543 raised false hopes that Tidore might be sufficiently strengthened to counter Portuguese Ternate, but these ventures failed. The islands to the north, however, were uncontested, and by 1565 a Spanish colony was established in the Philippines.

Free of the Spanish threat, the Portuguese had only to exercise control over the Moluccans, for at last they had the Spice Islands to themselves. As for the Spaniards, they did not submit happily to banishment from Eden. Magellan's incomplete achievement, inspired by his friend's epistolary supplications to join him in paradise, had not won for them the Spice Islands after all. Before a fair monsoon the Spanish withdrew in their ships with a deep, abiding sadness, a sickness similar to but different from the "melancholy of the East" that would plague homesick Dutch sailors in these same waters a century later, driving many to madness and suicide.

The malaise of the Spaniard lingered in his blood and ruled his temperament. Though homegrown on the lofty plains of Castile and the vast, desolate wastes of Andalusia, it was eminently transportable by carrack and galleon to the ends of the earth, perhaps at the very gates of the terrestrial paradise. Now this "black dog" of despair was crossed with tropical heat, resentment, and fury. Among European nations only the wretched Portuguese possessed the Spice Islands . . . at least for the time being.

Chapter 6

"THE TOUGHEST CLAY HE EVER MOLDED . . ."

IN JUNE 1540 a thirty-three-year-old priest traveling alone on horseback arrived in Lisbon after an arduous journey from Rome. Known to all Europe as the "Gateway to the Orient," Lisbon by this day had displaced Venice as the continent's greatest port by gaining the monopoly in the spice trade. The appearance of the new stranger—he was tall, strikingly handsome, extroverted, and athletic—suggested nobility. The solitary figure was in fact a dispossessed aristocrat from the windswept Basque country of Navarre in Northern Spain.

Now in Lisbon the priest, whose name was Francis Xavier, noticed immediately the myriad races wandering its hilly, cobbled streets: Indian rajas, African slaves, Singhalese princes, even Malays. The exotic was quick to catch his alert eye, for Xavier was about to embark on a lifetime of journeys that would eventually take him thirty-eight thousand miles in his ministry—all the way to the Spice Islands at the eastern edge of the known world.

The summer passed quickly. In September the bull promulgating the Society of Jesus was signed. It was an ecstatic day for Xavier, one of spiritual communion with his mentor Ignatius Loyola and his other absent brothers, whose society bore the aristocratic stamp of its Spanish fathers. The Church had become weakened from within, even as the spirit of

Martin Luther swept across a Europe seized by the fervor of ecclesiastical reform. Xavier and Loyola, however, had refused to join the ranks of a weakened hierarchy or embrace the forces of the Reformation. As Loyola and his swelling ranks of followers saw it, the Church, with corruption at every level, was in dire need of a new heroism. With a mind to chivalric tradition, Loyola forged a secret oath, a courtly rite binding the men to a new brotherhood in service of the King of Heaven. So it was that he called his unofficial new order the Society of Jesus. "From now on in this life, I think we shall meet only by letter," Xavier wrote to Loyola, not without regret.

These were exciting times for the Church. With the spice trade now controlled essentially by Portugal, exploration of the East by that Christian country was a certainty. Likewise, hand in glove, the spread of the faith of Rome to a darkened side of the world was an auspicious inevitability, and Francis Xavier embodied this new energy. The Prester John legend still carried forth the notion promoted by early Christian writers that earthly paradise—Eden—was somewhere in the East, and the story gained widespread credence and popularity thanks to the invention of the printing press and the refinements of woodcut and engraving techniques.

The potency of the image of Eden in the East was already an ancient one by Xavier's day. Since the end of the eighth century with the Beatus map (after the Spanish priest Beatus), the European mind perceived Eden as a geographical reality to be sought and found. The Beatus map reveals a flat earth with Jerusalem in its center and the terrestrial paradise in the East. The top of the map is marked with Adam, Eve, and the serpent, and the four westward-flowing rivers of paradise. Below the Twelve Apostles are depicted. Such images were integral to the maps of the Middle Ages. The power of these renderings by mapmakers descended to Columbus, who stated in a letter to Ferdinand and Isabella his belief in the eastern paradise, and the same images tantalized the explorers who followed him.

The Church seized on this belief as a spiritual challenge, and the ensuing excitement was infectious, especially as news reached Europe of the discovery of America and a sea route to Asia. New lands meant new people to convert. That these fallen creatures were "primitives" only increased the Church's determination to convert them. As new worlds and peoples were discovered, a latent yearning for the poverty and simplicity of the early church likewise grew. Do we not wish to return, ecclesiastical authorities asked rhetorically, to the innocence of man before the fall of Adam and the expulsion from the Garden of Eden? The "primitives" of the New World and Asia raised that expectation. Moreover, the Church could regain much of its equilibrium lost to the forces of the Reformation by converting such freshly discovered souls. The Counter-Reformation had revitalized the Church, and Francis Xavier was soon to become its most adventurous and vigorous exponent. Magnetized by a vision of earthly paradise somewhere in the land of spices, he determined that it would be his life's mission to minister to the fallen creatures of the East.

His first audience with King John lasted an hour. The sovereign wanted Xavier to serve in his own kingdom of Portugal, but Xavier was resolute: Loyola had assigned him the whole of Asia. John reluctantly agreed. In the wake of the Crown's navigators, especially Albuquerque's signal conquests of Goa in India and the spice emporium of Malacca on the Malay Peninsula, followed by the attainment of the fabled Spice Islands themselves by d'Abreu's expedition and Serrão's checkered exile on Ternate, the king had effectively abandoned Africa for the Far East. Xavier immediately set about putting himself in touch with anyone who had returned from Asia.

MISSIONARY WORK was a strange turn for a man who had chosen the Church as his career not because of humble aspirations or mystical idealism. Humility, in fact, often eluded this Basque priest, who claimed on his mother's side descent from the kings of Aragon. Xavier was clear-eyed, ambitious, and convinced that a life of practical servitude would be its own reward. If service to Rome would lead to personal advancement as well as the search for the Holy Grail, so much the better.

When he had come to Paris's Latin Quarter fifteen years before for study, Xavier had little sense that he would never see his family again. Nor was he aware of an impending association that would irrevocably alter not only his life, ultimately sending him to Asia, but the direction of the Roman Catholic Church as well. Paris in the first quarter of the sixteenth century was second only to Rome as the bastion of spiritual authority. Hundreds of sails plied the Seine in the shadow of the great cathedral

Notre Dame. A city of faith, it was also a great urban city of new cross-currents of ideas and artistic expression seeking to free themselves from the medieval tradition. French was rapidly evolving into the language we know today. The Paris of 1525 was an impassioned, maddened city, feverishly desirous of a new set of intellectual clothes under the watchful gaze of the greatest mind of the day, Desiderius Erasmus.

In time Xavier fell under the spell of an older student, a fellow Spaniard and former soldier turned mystic, Ignatius Loyola, who was nearly forty. Neither man knew what a fateful meeting it was. Xavier and other students were oddly drawn to this grave older man with a strange self-possession, though in a period lasting five years, Xavier and Loyola were constantly at odds, even as they grew closer. "I once heard it said by our great shaper of souls," Juan Polanco, Loyola's secretary, later wrote, "that the toughest clay he ever molded was, at the start, the young Francis Xavier, whom God has used, nevertheless, more than any other subject of our time."

In this spirit they conceived of themselves in chivalrous terms, as knights, which some of them had actually been. Nurturing this ideal, the men came to draw honest parallels between themselves and the heroes of the Arthurian legend. Most likely they read and discussed *Perceval, or the Story of the Grail,* by Chrétien de Troyes, which in 1182 was the first such treatment of what was regarded as the glorious, most central quest in European literature.

Xavier, who had been a champion high-jumper at the university, took to rigorous fasting and mortification, and Loyola chastened him for going too far. The body, bearing for a time a human soul, he counseled, must not be misused unreasonably. For his part, Xavier was not so much embracing asceticism as punishing his body to test his will.

Loyola dreamed of nothing less than establishing his order as the Praetorian of the Church, after the manner of Caesar Augustus's Roman imperial guard as an army to combat idolatry and heresy. He envisioned a Church born anew to reclaim the power it had known in the thirteenth century, when the Franciscan and Dominican orders—preachers, missionaries, and mystics—were born. The order Loyola conceived, however, was designed to serve the Church at a time when the institution was shaken by agitation from within and buffeted by winds of change from without.

It was during a journey to Rome in March 1537 that the course of

Xavier's life's ministry began to declare itself for him. With his fellow Jesuits he set out first on foot. Day after day found them trudging in the rain, surviving on whatever they could forage. The group managed to ford the overflowing Po, in water up to the neck. As the pilgrims were unable to pay its captain a fare, a coastal ship put them off at Ancona on the Adriatic, where one member pawned his breviary while the others begged in the streets for food. Crossing the Apennines and then the Sabine Mountains, the men at last reached Rome, exhausted and filthy, where they won a papal audience and Paul III's benediction and authorization to become priests. The experience, however, had marked Xavier, and he began to imagine his life and work as a journey.

After service in Bologna, Xavier returned to Rome feverish with the malaria that would plague him until his death. Here he remained for two years, hearing confessions at the church of St. Louis and walking Rome's ocher streets in the shadow of the rising basilica of Saint Peter's, which had not yet borne the stamp of Michelangelo. He did not shy away from the wretched parts of the city, where the strays were at least aware that God had taken on human flesh as a carpenter's son. But something else gnawed at him.

In his quest for spices, Vasco da Gama's rounding of the Cape of Good Hope in 1497 had opened this world not only to trade but to Truth. Was it not the moment to strike a decisive blow to the infidel by ransoming India and the Far East from tainted spiritual influence? What of the millions of lost souls in the world that lay beyond the seas, those under the vast Arab dominions who had embraced the false god of Islam, thus remaining severed from Christianity's historic heroism and doomed to outer darkness? If the Portuguese had wrested the spice trade from the Arabs in those distant lands, then why shouldn't a people enslaved by a false doctrine be likewise freed? This rhetorical question became for Xavier his ultimate concern. It was Portugal's supremacy on the seas and in the spice trade that allowed it to flourish.

Meanwhile, Loyola lobbied furiously for papal recognition of his order, while remaining fully aware that he had enemies in the Vatican who were consumed with resentment and envy. "Many," he wrote, "thought that we would be burned or sent off to the galleys." When it became clear that the Holy See would confirm Loyola's order, the game became political on a larger scale. Rumors of a radically new step the Church was about to take visited the far corners of Europe, prompting every royal house to lay claim to this new breed of thoroughbred priest. Ignatius, shrewdly, ignored all except King John III of Portugal, a devout Catholic and ruler of the one European nation that, by gaining the spice trade monopoly, had made a military conquest of the fallen East. There remained the task of bringing Asia to its knees spiritually. Thus it was that Xavier found himself in Lisbon awaiting passage to the world of India and beyond it to the Spice Islands.

After innumerable preparations and false starts, Xavier sailed from Lisbon for India on April 17, 1541, aboard the carrack *Santiago*. His possessions were three woolen robes, a breviary, a catechism, and an anthology of quotations from St. Gregory, St. Jerome, and other ecclesiastical writers. Offered a valet by the king's representative at the expense of the Crown, he demurred, not wanting such an encumbrance.

"You must at least take an ordinary servant to attend to your wants on the voyage," said the noble, "for it would diminish your credit and authority with the other passengers, were they to see you washing your clothes at the side of the ship, and preparing your meals, just like themselves."

Xavier answered with some heat, stunning the king's man into silence by his reply: "Señor Conde, it is credit and authority acquired by the means you suggest which have reduced the Church of God and her prelates to their present plight. The right way to acquire them is by washing one's own clout and boiling one's own pot, without being beholden to anybody, while at the same time busying oneself in the service of souls."

The Jesuit sailed with a human cargo of soldiers, black slaves, and criminals sentenced to a life of penal servitude in Ormuz, with the latter lashed to the rigging. The voyage was typical of its day, marked by raging storms, violent spasms of seasickness in the Jesuit, and forty-two deaths, until the carrack reached the coast of Guinea on the great bend of the west coast of Africa two months later. After a prolonged calm, winds filled the *Santiago*'s sails again, and the ship began its long navigation of the Cape, sailing from one ocean into another, then pushing north for Mozambique, where Xavier remained for six months, waiting for the shifting monsoon and another ship, the *Coulam,* to take him to India.

The *Coulam,* commanded by Afonso de Sousa and unescorted, lifted anchor from Mozambique before the southwest monsoon set in, but Sousa had his reasons for forcing the voyage and its risks. As the newly appointed governor of Goa, Sousa had suspicions about the man he was to relieve, Estevam da Gama, and hoped to catch him in a financial indiscretion, thus gaining favor for himself with King John. Closer to the truth, he hoped to garner his predecessor's secret funds, thereby assuring his own fortune. As a precaution, he arrested in Mozambique Estevam's brother Alvaro, the third son of the great Vasco, and placed him in the *Coulam*'s hold, chained to a cannon for the entire voyage.

This circumstance faced the Jesuit with a dilemma: if he visited Alvaro as a priestly duty, how would it sit with Sousa, who had developed an extraordinary fondness for Xavier? Sousa was the governor-appointee of India, and his friendship and support would be essential to Xavier's implantation of the Society of Jesus on the subcontinent. Hence, Xavier regarded Alvaro as a matter of state and thought it best not to show an imprudent charity, lest he risk losing the governor's protection of the Jesuit order.

Xavier's aloofness, however, aroused Alvaro's suspicions of complicity with Sousa, and the crouching prisoner in chains vowed to get even for the slight. His vindictiveness would come to haunt Xavier ten years later and even contribute to the priest's premature death.

WHEN XAVIER DEPARTED Lisbon, a lifetime of travels had scarcely begun. True rest for the Jesuit was to be found in motion, a restlessness embodying the chivalric code of Loyola's new order. Life for such a man was a journey, the crucial attribute distinguishing mankind from the rest of the natural world and a perpetual, perilous, but joyous torment leading his race to God. He had discovered this truth on his first journey to Rome.

Xavier, when he sailed to India, was a priest but no saint. Canonization would come later, seventy years after his death. He was, however, a man of his age: a cracked mirror reflecting the beliefs and prejudices in the day of the auto-da-fé. As a student in Paris, he had witnessed the grim spectacle of the stake on the Place de Grève. Fearful of a divided Christianity, he had dutifully served the Inquisition and walked with condemned heretics to be burned, remaining with them until the end.

These were merciless doings. *Truth,* not truth, was at issue in the flames, and total submission to it was required. To be a non-Christian for lack of teaching was one thing, but to resist instruction in God's gift of sacrifice was twisted and criminal. Christ Himself had preached sternly about the folly of casting pearls before swine. There was no hope for such souls, in this world or the next. For Xavier and his fellow Jesuits, such condemnations were not an issue. The obstinate were put to the torch.

With his high, broad forehead and quick, penetrating black eyes, Xavier cut a commanding figure in his white robes descending the gang-plank at Goa on May 6, 1542, after thirteen months at sea. Though he seldom exercised his power, as Pope Paul III's apostolic nuncio he had complete authority over India's clergy.

Goa repelled Xavier. He saw it as an indolent city where greed and sensual pleasures were rampant. There were numerous markets, including one for slaves, where girls from all parts of India were sold. In the pago-das smelling of incense the gods had eyes of precious stones, and the temple maidens wore bejeweled rings on their hands and feet.

His antidote to the spells of depression that visited him more and more frequently was flight and work. He journeyed to Cape Comorin to minister to the pearl fishers and remained for two years among the Tamil-speaking Paravas, converting some twenty thousand natives to Christianity. In northern India he walked by day through a wretched desert and mountain country, seeking solace through prayer by night in a hostile land inhabited by cobras, jackals, and tigers. Despite attacks of malaria, within a month he had baptized ten thousand additional men, women, and children in this land at the foot of the Himalayas.

Back in Cochin, a traveler had pictured the port of Malacca in Southeast Asia for him, then supplied enthusiastic descriptions of the sprinkling of perfumed islands known as the Moluccas that lay to the east. A marvelous country of azure seas and spice-fragrant, forested volcanoes that glowed in Xavier's imagination, it awaited conversion. He made his decision to leave India for Malacca, and from that port on the Malay Peninsula he could take ship for the Spice Islands.

Having sowed the seeds of Christianity on the subcontinent, he advised his brethren in Goa and the fathers in Rome to send others to the remote corners of India to finish what he had begun. He wrote Loyola, telling of his plans, adding a hint of his loneliness: "During the four years of my absence from Portugal, there has been but one letter from you."

Xavier spent Holy Week of 1545 at São Thome in a tiny house with a garden overlooking the sea. The vista reached eastward across the Indian Ocean toward the Malay Peninsula and the mysterious islands beyond Java that held Europe enthralled. Here he meditated and prayed through many a night at the tomb of the almost forgotten St. Thomas, his predecessor of many centuries before, who, according to Marco Polo, had been venerated by Christians and Saracens alike.

On one such evening, he wrestled with the devil. Fate had woven for the Jesuit a skein of mingled pride and humility, with the latter clearly subservient to the former. Who was he, Xavier, to take it upon himself to convert the great unwashed of Asia? Was it an assignment from God or the fruit of his own superiority? Where was humility before so divine a task? The struggle lasted the entire night. When the bells summoned him to matins, the evil one who had stood between Francis Xavier and the Apostle of the East lay defeated. Xavier and the Apostle became the same man, and his calling crystallized as a divine revelation. The East beckoned as never before.

In September, Xavier sailed from Madras for Malacca, the seat of the Portuguese empire in the Far East and the most important spice emporium in the world. The month-long voyage carried the small vessel southeast through the Sombreiro Channel of the Nicobar Islands into the Straits of Malacca, separating the Malay Peninsula from the large island of Sumatra. Now that he was recovered in health, the stormy voyage tested Xavier's strength as well as that of the crew, a fearful lot clinging to rail and rigging. "Our ship raced before a violent wind and constantly scraped the bottom of the sea," wrote Xavier. "If we had struck a rock, the ship would have splintered; with one single shoal we would have gone aground. Many were the tears on board. . . . Without the shadow of a doubt, all creation obeys its creator."

Malacca, the seething, sweltering port barely a degree above the equator near the tip of the Malay Peninsula, awaited Xavier, for his fame as a priest had preceded him. But here his career took a fateful turn. Perhaps unbeknownst to him, Xavier had crossed a threshold to enter a part of the world where the supernatural was not regarded with suspicion but was accepted as a matter of course. It was in Malacca and the Spice Islands to the east where Xavier's own extraordinary powers began to declare themselves. Even his disembarkation was auspicious.

When the small, unescorted merchantman entered the harbor, Xavier looked with satisfaction upon St. Paul's Church atop the hill, presiding as if ordained by heaven over the confusion of mosques and shops in the lower city. The estuary had begun to silt in from the deposits of the Malacca River that snaked through the city, and as the vessel crept cautiously to the quay huge crowds flocked to waterside to greet the holy father.

All eyes were upon a man whose reputation as a living saint, however deserved, had been carried to the fortress-port as if by the wind. Stepping ashore, Xavier greeted a small Portuguese boy, who recorded the encounter. "The father beckoned to us boys, greeted each one of us by our own name, and asked us how our fathers and mothers were. He had never seen us before and there were quite a few of us, and certainly no one had told him our names. So how could he have known them, except, as I and many others believed, miraculously?"

In the nearly thirty-five years of Portuguese occupation, this most important spice entrepôt had seen better days. Its sultan, defeated at the hands of Albuquerque's forces in 1511, had sought refuge in Johore, adjacent to the later settlement of Singapore, and his successors had harassed and besieged the Portuguese as well as they could. More significantly, the sultans had strong, fierce allies in Aceh's forces at the northwestern tip of Sumatra. As a result, the Portuguese were threatened from all sides. The Acehnese, people of a strongly Islamic sultanate, would never become reconciled to Christian domination in the Straits of Malacca, and Xavier came to regard them as the forces of darkness, convinced "that God, the all-faithful, abided not with infidels and took no pleasure in their prayers."

In the meantime, however, this holy city of commerce presented its own challenges to Xavier, who had been advised of its iniquities by Padre Valignano, Malacca's only priest, who castigated the port for "abominations, lewdness, impurities, and evil." This father had laid the blame of Malacca's sinking into licentiousness in large part on the beauty, charm, and availability of Malayan women. There had been many mixed marriages as well as illicit unions, and the Eurasian population resulting from these unions were among Xavier's first challenges here, while he reminded himself that his real work lay in the distant, mysterious eastern archipelago known as the Spice Islands.

For the time being, the whole of Malacca was the Jesuit's parish, and he ministered to it at every stratum of society. Charm crossed with a measure of worldly wisdom infused his forceful personality as he worked at winning the hearts of its sinners. The lofty priest became a prominent sight as he walked Malacca's streets at will, engaging potential parishioners as he found them. He once approached a group of soldiers who were gambling at the waterfront as clove and nutmeg were being unloaded from ships that had returned that very day from Ternate and Banda. As the men were reticent to continue in his presence, he invited them to resume and amused himself by watching. "You are soldiers," he told them, "so there is no reason why you should live like monks. To be merry without offending God is better any day than grumbling and quarreling."

In the same spirit Xavier habitually invited himself to dinner with the port's spice merchants, and his natural gregariousness made him a popular guest. On each occasion he invariably played the same card. At the evening's end, he asked his host to summon the cook, whom he greeted very solicitously, praising her meal. "You are destined for sainthood," he told her on leaving. Thus did Malay concubines and slaves come to appreciate this new embodiment of a strange spiritual force, who walked through every part of Malacca, announcing his approach by ringing a bell.

Xavier often set himself about to arrange marriages among the military officers and merchants who kept concubines. Typically, he said that the girl of the house was beautiful and deserved a good husband. The man, embarrassed, confessed that he loved her very much, whereupon Xavier responded, "Why, then, not marry her, honestly and holily, instead of living in sin with her and damning both her and yourself?" The result would be a wedding ceremony.

With others he employed an opposite tactic. He once asked a spice merchant, for example, why he made himself a laughingstock in the city by living sinfully with a native woman of ill repute, when he could do so much better for himself. "If you like," he said, "I can find you a wife beautiful and good enough to be the consort of a king." He was as good as his promise, and a marriage ensued. If confronting a man with a harem of six, Xavier stuck with his subject until he had persuaded him to dispense with his concubines one by one, before marrying him to the last.

The pure Malay and Javanese subjects of Malacca, however, proved to be harder cases, eschewing Christianity for the more familiar Islam. The Jesuit came to regard this race of magicians and spiritists with despair. Charmed by them, he could not convert them so readily, and though their children were always ready to march through the streets singing with him, Xavier began directing his energies elsewhere, away from these handsome, winning people with their demons.

His gaze was east to the Spice Islands, scattered over the sea "as birds after a storm." He wrote to his brethren in Goa of his plans to leave Malacca: "I am now preparing to go to Amboina. . . . When I reach my destination I shall write to you again telling you, out of my experience at Cape Comorin and Goa, as also, please God, in Amboina and the Moluccas, how I think He can best be served and our holy faith advanced in these parts."

Chapter 7

THE CRAB AND
THE CRUCIFIX

THOUGH IT WAS only a fresco of the imagination springing from his work among a strangely mutant people, Xavier at last mentioned the name that conjured up the aromas of Eden: the same Spice Islands that had lured Columbus, Vasco da Gama, and Magellan over uncharted seas. Aware that Francisco Serrão had preceded him more than three decades before, Xavier was keen to minister to these magical islands where "there are already many Christians and bright prospects of making more." Christianity had established itself against Islam in the Moluccas, and the Jesuit was bent on expanding and consolidating this spiritual beachhead in an exiled world. It was a self-assignment that set his blood afire.

He sailed on New Year's Day, 1546, commencing a six-week voyage of nearly three thousand miles. Threading these seas, wrote the Victorian naturalist Alfred Russel Wallace, was regarded by Malays as "a rather wild and romantic expedition . . . the unachieved ambition of their lives." Curiously, Xavier had little to say of this journey over the strangest, most beautiful, and most perilous waters in the world.

Xavier most likely shipped aboard a Portuguese merchant ship or an oversized Malay prahu, junk-shaped with a thick bamboo mainyard supporting a large oblong sail. The vessel followed the route taken by d'Abreu's expedition so many years before—through the South China, Java, Flores, and Banda seas—that had brought Francisco Serrão to the Spice Islands with the belief that he had discovered paradise on earth.

One searches Xavier's writings in vain for his take on Java's wild beauty, the miraculous dawns at sea, and the tinted skies of early evening, and can only conjecture that he was obsessed with the terrible plight of his fellow men—primitive people of India and of the Indies, who in worshiping false gods had severed themselves from the True One—to the exclusion of all else.

Xavier arrived in Ambon (Amboina) on February 14, 1546, though he would have to wait until the monsoon shifted in May before dispatching a letter to Europe. He wrote from Ambon to his brother priests in Goa: "Immediately on arrival here I visited the villages and baptized a large number of children who had not received the Sacrament. One hundred and thirty leagues from Amboina there is another country called the Coast of Moro where, I am told, there are many totally uninstructed Christians. I am going there as soon as I can. I give you this account so that you may see how sorely you are needed in these parts."

Xavier also wrote of another destination to his brethren in Europe as well as the King of Portugal: Morotai, the deadly island north of Halma-hera, which Xavier refers to as Omoro, "a most dangerous place because the natives are full of treachery and put various poisons in the food and drink which they offer strangers. . . . I have made up my mind to go there myself to help them in their spiritual needs and to baptize their children. I feel it incumbent upon me to sacrifice my temporal life for the sake of the spiritual life of my neighbor, and so, putting all my trust in God our Lord, I have offered myself to danger and death in whatever shape it may come, longing as I do to be conformed in my small and feeble way to that saying of our Redeemer."

Xavier's few friends in Ambon vainly attempted to dissuade him from undertaking such a dangerous journey to sinister Morotai, where the use of poisons was rampant and ritual head-hunting was practiced. But Xavier was adamant, reminding his advisors that once in a Venetian hos-pital he had ingested the pus from a patient's hideous open sore to com-bat his own fastidious nature, thus subduing his revulsion through force of will.

Even so, the Jesuit was brutally, frankly uncompromising in his appraisal of the islanders. "The people are a very barbarous lot and full of treachery, brownish yellow in complexion rather than black, and extremely disagreeable. There are islands whose folk eat the bodies of enemies killed in their tribal wars. When one of them dies from sickness his hands and heels are eaten, and considered a great delicacy."

Xavier continues by describing how aged parents are served up as dishes on the pagan feast days. He notes the inaccessibility of the islands, covered with dense mountainous rain forests, racked continually with earthquakes as well as the more harmful seaquake, and whose mountains cast forth fire and vomited huge masses of rock, described by the Jesuit as if it were a vision of hell itself. "Within a month, I hope to go to an island where such things happen, as the people want to be Christian."

Meanwhile, he ministered to the islands near Ambon before traveling to the dangerous north islands of poisoners and head-hunting cannibals, among them Ceram, the closest island, hovering over Ambon like a giant parasol. It was on the easternmost point of this largest island of the Moluccas where Francisco Serrão had burned his unseaworthy Indian vessel, crippled and incapable of returning to Malacca in early 1512, thus beginning his unexpected, protracted stay in the Spice Islands. Now Xavier saw the accessible island just across the channel from Ambon as fair game, and he made periodic excursions there, admitting by letter with a tincture of irony that after baptizing thirty thousand souls, his arm had grown paralyzed from pouring the baptismal waters.

Regardless of whatever faith—Hindu, Islam, Christian—had been imported to the Malay Archipelago, it remained a veneer, superimposed upon ancient animist cultures that differed from island to island. Superstition was rife. The belief that an extraordinary individual possessed unusual and potent spiritual powers was widespread in Xavier's monsoon Asia, especially in the Spice Islands. Belief in miracles, however, was not exclusively the province of natives. Europeans as well regarded Asia as a part of the world where the "marvelous" occurred, and any nexus of "marvels" ran parallel to their belief that the terrestrial paradise lay somewhere in the East.

As for the Moluccan natives themselves, they relied heavily on the oral tradition of aphorisms or poetic tales to explain the inexplicable and foretell the future. An individual's powers as a prophet and a miracle worker clearly asserted themselves to be recognized. Though Xavier had performed near-superhuman feats in India by virtue of his energy and determination, it was in the Spice Islands that European and Moluccan alike would come to regard Xavier as especially spiritually gifted.

During a routine crossing to Ceram, clearly within sight of Ambon, the most famous documented miracle attributed to the Jesuit occurred. Headwinds gathered, and the prahu transporting Francis Xavier and his small party began to be tossed in the waves like a coconut, a fearful development. Seeking to calm the waters through divine power, Xavier took from his neck a crucifix no longer than a finger and eased it into the sea by its cord. Suddenly it slipped from his hand and disappeared. Despondent over the loss, he grieved openly.

The next day on Ceram, he happened to be walking on the beach with a Portuguese named Fausto Rodriguez when the two men saw a crab emerge from the sea with the crucifix held upright in its pincers.

The messenger scuttled to a position before Xavier, who had fallen to his knees to receive the crucifix, whereupon the crab retreated to the surf. According to Francisco de Sousa in his *Conquest of the East:* "[Xavier] kissed his recovered treasure a thousand times and pressed it to his heart. He remained on his knees in prayer for half an hour, as did his companion also, both giving God their profoundest thanks for so illustrious a miracle. That, and nothing more, is known of the sworn testimony taken from Fausto Rodriguez."*

After three months on Ambon with excursions to Ceram, Francis had been nearly devoured by insects in his crusade to consolidate Christianity's hold in this part of the Spice Islands. He made arrangements to journey north to Ternate with two purposes in mind. He would first convert Sultan Hairun, who sought to strengthen both Ternatean and Portuguese autonomy in the Northern Moluccas. Then he would proceed to Christianize the even more dangerous pagan island of Morotai.

In mid-June the small party set out by *kora-kora* on a voyage similar to Francisco Serrão's so many years before, but without the royal trappings—

---

* Rodriguez, the only authority for this event—whether invention, miracle, or neither—bore witness under solemn oath as to its veracity, and an authenticated copy of his deposition survives in Rome today. Later Jesuit scholars have insisted, with varying degrees of certainty, that the story is borrowed from Japanese or Indian mythology.

silks, awnings, and cushions—extended to the original "white Bengalis." Xavier's expedition consisted of two boats manned by a muscular crew who paddled to the beat of wooden drums meant to keep demons of the deep sea at bay. One day in early July, the Jesuit stepped ashore on Ternate, the "perfumed gem of the seas," and marveled at the forest-carpeted volcano island with the scent of cloves wafting in the air. Simultaneously, he saw concealed in the island's loveliness something Francisco Serrão had not seen, and Xavier described it with a poet's dark insight: "an impassable region of mangroves, an aqueous wood holding only shadows, where grisly stems projected from the sledge like the elbows and knees of the drowned."

By this time in his ministry, Xavier, known as a miracle worker, was a nearly irresistible force. Tall and majestic in his robes, he walked Ternate's main settlement trailed by a group of children singing in Malay the catechism he had translated with great difficulty in Malacca. He noted, "Thanks be to God it has become the custom in Ternate for the boys in the street and the girls and women in the houses, day and night, for the toilers in the plantations and the fishermen at sea to sing, instead of vain songs, holy chants . . . in a language understood by all, whether recent converts to the faith or people still pagans."

Hairun and Xavier immediately took to each other, and the sultan quickly condoned Francis's efforts to make converts within his court. One of his half sisters, known as Doña Catarina, became a Christian and married a Portuguese merchant, while another became the bride of the Christian sultan of Bacan, an extraordinary conversion and one motivated, as skeptical Jesuits later supposed, by Portuguese protection against rival sultanates rather than the promise of life in the hereafter.

Despite Xavier's efforts, however, Hairun himself remained unconverted, a point wryly noted by the Jesuit. "If he fails to become a Christian it is not because of any devotion to Mohammed, but because he is in thrall to carnal sins. The only thing Moorish about him is that he was circumcised as a child, and then as a man took unto himself a hundred principal wives and many other less important ones."

It was at this time that Xavier's gifts as a clairvoyant became evident, bewildering the Church no less than his Portuguese and native hearers. In a sermon preached one Sunday, Francis paused in midspeech to tell his startled listeners, "Let us offer an Our Father for the soul of João Galvano who has been drowned." In three days the wreckage of Galvano's *kora-kora* was washed up on Ternate's outlying coral reef. In a later mass at the offertory, Xavier turned to the congregation, saying, "João Araujo has died this moment in Amboina. I offered mass for him yesterday and this mass is for the repose of his soul. I beg you to commend him to God in your prayers." This death also proved to be true.

Voyaging again by *kora-kora* with the volcanic mountains of Halmahera to the east, he reached the northern end of this large island without incident, then made the twenty-five-mile crossing to the island of Morotai to labor among the wild people. Of his prolonged stay in these northern islands, Xavier tells us little, beyond his visiting the Christian settlements and baptizing numerous babies. "They were a great comfort to me and I to them," he wrote, while in a letter to Rome he harbored no illusions about the islands and their natives:

> They are dangerous places by reason of continual strife between the barbarous tribes. . . . It is their habit to poison anybody toward whom they feel ill-disposed, and in this way they kill large numbers. It is a very craggy part of the world, with mountains everywhere which make journeying a real misery. . . . There is a heathen tribe called the *Tabaru* in these parts which makes a pastime of murder. I am told that when they can find nobody else to kill, they slaughter their own sons or wives. They have also slaughtered many Christians. . . .
>
> One of these islands is in an almost constant state of tremor caused by a mountain which continually ejects fire and ashes. Often, rocks as big as the biggest trees are hurled out of the flaming mountain. . . . They asked me what this awful mountain was, and I told them it was a hell to which went all those given to the adoration of idols.

Xavier clearly had made his presence felt among the people of Ternate. "When the time came to leave Maluco," he recounted in a softer tone, "I embarked about midnight so as to avoid the weeping and mourning of my devoted friends, men and women. But it was no good, and I did not escape the tears, for my friends found me out and I could not hide from them. The night and the parting from these my spiritual sons and daughters helped me to feel my unworthiness, and the thought came to me that perhaps my absence might contribute to the salvation of their souls."

After a two-month sail aboard a merchant ship from Ambon, Xavier found himself back in Malacca, welcomed by three priests who, following his example, were to spend in essence the rest of their lives in the islands of Moro, meeting martyrs' deaths. One of them, Juan Beira, passed nearly a decade in the deadly islands. During one period of Muslim persecution, this Spanish priest was nine months on the run, hiding out in the wilds of Halmahera while subsisting on roots and grasses and comforting whatever Christians he could find who had not been slaughtered. On two occasions he was betrayed and sold into slavery. Tortured for his faith, he was an object to be broken. His captors forced him to watch while they snatched newly baptized babies and dashed their heads against rocks.

Each time, Beira managed to escape slavery, continuing his life as a fugitive while ministering to his scattered flock. Visiting Morotai and the nearby smaller island of Rau in a seagoing canoe, he was wrecked countless times, once surviving by clinging to a plank for two days and nights before he was washed up on a desolate, rocky beach in the territory of the wicked Tabaru tribe. Here he lost his breviary and what few grains of rice he had, and he lived on meals of seaweed.

Gradually he began to take leave of his senses, but Beira's derangement, according to his fellow priests, seemed to give him a greater purity. On his return to India, they saw him as a living martyr. His mind cleared on occasion, and he was able to say mass, making the sign of the cross with a mutilated hand. Death came to him in a lucid moment, and he died believing himself to be the worst of sinners.

Though Xavier wrote little of his own experiences in these forbidden islands, he undoubtedly underwent at times equally horrific inflictions. With Beira in mind, he wrote in a letter: "I know not whether anywhere else in the whole world men zealous for the glory of God and the salvation of souls have as much toil and hardship to face and perils of death to brave as in the Isles of Moro. I beg you to intercede with God for the ones who have gone thither and for those who are later to go."

The Jesuit discovered upon his return to Malacca an unsettled city, disease-ridden and more fearful than before of invasion. The port had declined remarkably, and a Dutch visitor put a fine point on one aspect of its moribund state: "It is a very unwholesome countrie . . . , and commonly there is not one that cometh thither and stayeth any time, but is sure to be sicke, so that it costeth him either hide or hair before he departeth from thence. And if any escapeth with life it is holden for a wonder, wherby the countrie is much shunned, notwithstanding covetousness and desire of gaine."

The Portuguese in Malacca, however, had more to fear than malaria and other equatorial diseases. Control of Malacca meant control of the spice trade, and a new Muslim confederation was determined to wrest back both. The forces of the deposed sultanate southward in Johore had united with the powers of Bintang and the militant Muslims of northwestern Sumatra's Aceh. Together they resolved to destroy the fortress built by Albuquerque and slaughter Malacca's Christian inhabitants.

One August night of 1547 shortly after Xavier's return, the Acehnese in a fleet of fustas, speedy shallow-drafted vessels with lateen sails, crept into Malacca's harbor to raid merchant ships riding at anchor.

Taking a group of seven Malay spice traders by surprise, they cut off their noses, ears, and feet, and sent the fortress commandant a challenge written in the blood of the victims. In the darkness the cannon of the fortress roared with little effect, and the pirates withdrew, confidently biding their time while a terror-stricken Malacca waited for the Acehnese's next move. In the meantime, the combined forces of Johore and Bintang had sailed into the estuary of the nearby Muar River to threaten Malacca by land.

As Xavier regarded the Muslim Acehnese as forces of darkness that were devil-sent, the incident inflamed him with angry purpose, provoking the emergence of another side of his personality: that of the crusading warrior-priest. With a shrewd tactician's sense, the Jesuit quickly convinced the military authorities to equip a fleet and send it in pursuit of the Acehnese. He reasoned that it would surprise the enemy at sea, while Malacca could hold its own against the other forces who were waiting, thus waging a war of nerves. Only by thus dividing and weakening the enemy would the Portuguese prevail, counseled Xavier.

A fleet of ten ships went in search of the elusive Acehnese, who concealed their smaller vessels in the crocodile-ridden rivers and bays of Sumatra's vast mangrove coast. It was a cat-and-mouse game that continued for three weeks, and even then no word reached Malacca, while the fleets of Bintang and Johore continued to wait in the nearby river. Their sultans had sent spies into Malacca to spread rumors of disaster befalling the Portuguese fleet; and because it was a fate that seemed all too probable, it was believed. The commandant, Simão de Mello, sent patrols of ballams, small craft driven by paddles, up the coast to reconnoiter, but they returned without news. A mood of gloom, if not outright terror, descended upon vulnerable Malacca.

Weeks passed, December approached, and still there was no word from the fleet, manned by Portuguese who had taken Malay wives, sired children, and were keen to seize the offensive to protect their homes in Malacca and maintain a safe harbor for the spice ships. Xavier encouraged and consoled the Malaccans, urging them not to mourn but to put trust and confidence in God, who would, with Malacca's fleet, be victorious over the enemy. His advice went largely unheeded as Malay Christians sought out the comfort of sorcerers and diviners, whose incantations spelled doom. They claimed there was no word from the pursuing force for good reason: It had perished at the hands of the Acehnese.

On Sunday, December 4, a crowd gathered in the spacious church of Our Lady of the Assumption to hear Xavier preach. After finishing his sermon, he was suddenly struck as though by a vision. After a profound silence, he spoke: "There are women and others here who practice divining and consult fortune-tellers, only to hear from them that our fleet has been destroyed and that their husbands are dead. Rather ought they to lift up their hearts to God in thankfulness . . . for *I* tell you that today, this very day, our fleet has won a great victory and scattered the enemy."

That same evening, the Jesuit preached to a group of native women at the church of Our Lady of the Mount and, advancing his theme, told his thrilled congregation the precise day on which they might expect news of the victory and their husbands' safe return. By chance, one of the first victors to return was one Afonso Fernandez, who was eagerly surrounded with questioners. On what day and hour had the victory been won? He told them, and it was exactly as Xavier had said. It had taken forty days because the Portuguese were forced to explore many of Sumatra's river estuaries before cornering the enemy about sixty miles north of Kedah on the Malay Peninsula.*

---

* Xavier quickly became known as the "Creator of the Fleet," and of all the incidents in his life suggesting his powers as a visionary, none is better attested to than this precise announcement of the Portuguese victory over the Acehnese. There are at least fifty references to it in official investigations cited in *Monumenta Xaveriana*, vol. 2, and most of the witnesses cited were present at the famous sermon on December 4 to hear Xavier's words with their own ears.

A letter from Europe with the news that an old friend and cofounder of the Jesuit order had died was a blow to Xavier, giving him a vivid sense of his own mortality while prompting him to reconsider the priorities in his work. Japan, a civilized, wealthy, and mysterious land, began to loom large on his horizon. From all reports, it was soil as fertile for spiritual conversion as the Spice Islands had been barren, and Xavier resolved to expand his ministry there. His experiences in the Spice Islands, especially Morotai, while the most intense of his life, had left him disillusioned over their suitability as an anchor for the Church in Asia.

He advised Loyola by letter that he was leaving for Japan. "I could write you indefinitely of the inner consolations which come to me as I look ahead to this voyage so filled with the deadly perils of storms, winds, shoals, and pirates," he wrote. Then he added a poignant note: "I so keenly hope, dear Father, that for one year you will ask some member of the Society, each month, to offer a Mass for me." On June 24 he boarded a junk for the long journey.

THE JESUIT'S MINISTRY in Japan, a success despite unanticipated factions and hardships, lasted for more than two years, after which he returned to Malacca. Upon his return he discovered in the harbor a forest of burned masts and the occasional capsized boat, telling of the latest failed attempt by Johore's sultanate to reclaim the port. Here Xavier received a letter from Ignatius Loyola apprising him of his appointment as provincial of the Society of Jesus for the Indies "and countries beyond." The Indies included all countries east of Africa, and "beyond" was clearly a reference to Japan and China.

Loyola had wanted his "exile" to return to Europe. There was a new pope, and Loyola felt it essential to provide an oral account of the Society's progress in the Indies. Xavier, however, having spent eleven years in Asia, was obsessed with completing his exploratory mission. The East was in his blood, and China beckoned.

Loyola was vexed by this decision but honored it, leaving Xavier's fate in his own hands. Though neither knew Xavier had only a few months to live, the Jesuit's letters reveal a man who sensed that his odyssey was drawing to a close and that he would never see Europe again. He did, however, make a brief return to India. When his ship departed Goa for Malacca, a voice cried out to the ship just lifting anchor: "When shall we meet Your Reverence again?" Xavier, seized by a premonition, called back from the deck, "In the valley of Josaphat."

Compounding this presentiment was Xavier's discovery on reaching Malacca in May that the atmosphere in the port city had changed. Pedro da Gama, who had financed his Japanese expedition, had been supplanted as grand captain of the port of Malacca by his embittered brother, Alvaro, another of the great navigator's sons, but a black sheep who was nursing an old grudge. More than a decade before, Alvaro had been Afonso de Sousa's prisoner in the hold of the same *Coulam* that had transported Xavier from Mozambique to Goa, when the priest had paid him no mind.

Now with vicious disregard for papal authority, or any authority save his own, Alvaro refused entry to Xavier's ship, the *Santa Cruz,* only to later impound its rudder and tiller. Then, enraged and envious that so important and lucrative a post should have gone to a mere trader, he confiscated the ambassadorship to China of Xavier's companion Diego Pereira, which had been conferred by the viceroy in India. This was a crucial diplomatic blow to the Jesuit's mission. Afterward, Alvaro did Xavier another great wrong. Alvaro had his agents seek out Malacca's underworld of criminals and assassins, inciting them to turn against Xavier as an object of abuse and scorn. Rocks and curses were hurled at him by thugs in the streets.

Xavier responded quickly. To an intermediary, Father Perez, he delivered this message: "Tell the Captain that I beg him by the Passion and death of our Lord Jesus Christ not to incur so grave an excommunication, entailing, let him have no doubt, the terrible chastisement of God." Though Alvaro also had left himself open not only to ecclesiastical censure but also to charges of high treason for his disobedience to king and viceroy, he remained adamant. India and Portugal, after all, were distant lands, all but forgotten in Malacca, where he held power and exercised it with ruthless determination.

"After the documents and letters had been read to him," reported Father Perez, "[Alvaro] jumped up from his chair and burst into a flood of imprecations such as my pen dare not write. Then he spat upon the ground and, stamping his foot, said, 'That's what I think of the viceroy and his instructions.'" As for the priest, he might go to China or to the devil for all he cared, but Pereira, he swore, would not accompany him as ambassador to the court of Peking.

The feelings against Xavier fanned by Alvaro had become so violent that the Jesuit seldom went to the streets for fear of being set upon by hired thugs. Resigned that Pereira would not accompany him, Xavier wrote to his merchant friend, "I have done with Dom Alvaro. . . . It grieves me to think of the heavy punishment which awaits him from God." Though some accounts hold that Xavier said mass daily for Alvaro, it seems unlikely that the Jesuit would have so spiritually attended the excommunicated captain who had effectively doomed his mission to China.

While he may have prayed for Alvaro's soul, such charity, according to Malay annals, hardly attended the scene of Xavier's final departure from Malacca aboard the spice ship. As Alvaro had sole command of the harbor and roadstead with its shipping, including the *Santa Cruz,* which he inexplicably released from quarantine, he forbade any assistance to the priest in reaching his ship riding at anchor. It was low tide, and Xavier was forced to wade through the debris and muck, then swim to an exposed coral head awash in the tide, where a ship's boat would meet him. Emerging from the water disheveled, soaked, and muddy, the angry Jesuit turned and, shaking his fist, rained curses on Dom Alvaro. Then, as the ship's boat eased to the rock, he set about cleaning himself as best he could.

By the end of September, the *Santa Cruz* dropped anchor in the Bay of Canton off a sinister island covered with brambles called Sancian. With no possessions and no official pretext to enter China, Xavier attempted to negotiate passage to the mainland with smugglers, the island's only inhabitants. But the contrabandists, fearing death if caught by Chinese authorities, were reluctant to make a nocturnal crossing. Pondering more drastic methods, Xavier was warned against contracting with a fishing boat's crew, who would have no compunction about departing in the evening with the Jesuit, only to rob him and throw him overboard.

In a letter to Goa, he wrote: "I arrived in this harbor of Sancian which is 30 leagues away from the town of Canton. Each day I am hoping to go. Arrangements have already been made with someone to take me there, for 200 cruzados . . . all in Christ."

On November 21, Xavier was offering a requiem mass on the island for a smuggler when he was shaken with a violent fever. He was rowed to the *Santa Cruz*, where he retired to his bunk, but the spice vessel was tossed about by heavy seas throughout the night, and by dawn he could no longer see. He asked to be taken ashore again, carrying under his arm a change of clothes and a fistful of almonds he was unable to swallow.

A Portuguese merchant bled him in his hut, and Francis murmured his thanks. One of his servants was attentive, while another remained callous and disrespectful. Xavier was alert enough to dismiss him. It was his last fully conscious move. Delirium soon followed, and the Jesuit murmured prayers, his lips moving in a hodgepodge of Latin, French, bits of Tamil and Japanese, Malay, and finally the Basque of his childhood.

On December 1, he regained some sense and resumed prayers, continuing the barely audible chant as he lapsed in and out of consciousness, repeating, "Jesus, Son of David, have mercy on me," and "O Virgin Mother of God, remember me!" At dawn two days later, his good servant Antonio saw that he was near death and placed a lighted candle in his hand, but by then, Francis was gone. He was forty-six.

Antonio dressed the body in silk, and after the viewing and veneration by ship's officers, he placed it in a lime-filled wooden casket, which he buried facing the sea. In the spring, when the *Santa Cruz* prepared to depart for Malacca, Antonio begged that his master be exhumed and returned. Amazingly, the body had not decomposed.

Throngs greeted the ship in Malacca's harbor on March 22. The body was carried with great solemnity past a drunken Alvaro da Gama, gambling with a group of sailors. Alvaro, who would die of leprosy, turned his back on the procession. Atop St. Paul's Hill, Xavier was buried shrouded only in his vestments in an ocher grave hewn from the rock within the church—a temporary resting place that may be seen today within the ruins of the roofless church. On August 15, 1553, Diego Pereira, the merchant who had been denied the ambassadorship to China, unearthed Francis's body by lantern light and bore it to his house as though it were a living person.

On December 11, the Jesuit was transported in a silken casket to Goa, where in a basilica the incorrupt body of the patron saint of India and all the East has since resided to be revered by all faiths. Francis Xavier was beatified in 1619 and canonized in 1622 in the company of St. Ignatius Loyola.

• • •

THE SPICE TRADE had become a spring tide of wealth flooding a largely barbaric Europe, already in a state of radical flux. The continent welcomed this sweeping commerce, unprecedented in human history, and with it a lifeblood of new ideas, eroding the old feudal order and authority of Charles V's Holy Roman Empire and its Church. There were new initiatives and doubts, directions and perplexities. A world was dying, while a new one struggled to be born.

On August 18, 1521, Martin Luther was summoned before the Diet of Worms to retract his writings. It was here that he uttered the fateful words in a firm, clear voice: "Unless I am convinced by the testimony of scripture or by an evident reason—for I confide neither in the pope nor in council alone, since it is certain that they have often erred and contradicted themselves—I am held fast by the Scriptures adduced by me, and my conscience is taken captive by God's Word, and I neither can nor will revoke anything, seeing that it is not safe or right to act against conscience. God help me. Amen."

Afterward, several of the stunned onlookers screamed, "Put him to the flames," and Luther responded with a defiant German salute, a raised fist.

Great events have small, often fortuitous, beginnings. Eight years later in a humble university lodging in Paris's Latin Quarter, a handful of exceedingly diverse students were by chance cast together. Sensing the disorder of the age, they began to found a new religious order, a gestation that eventually gave birth to the Counter-Reformation.

From the beginning Francis Xavier was seized by the impatient spirit of his changing age. As with Magellan and Serrão, his rendezvous with fate occurred in the Far East, realized in a quest that was dissimilar but parallel to theirs. It was the religious beliefs of the age, which Xavier embodied, that impelled him to embark on his spiritual journey to Asia and the Spice Islands.

A popular and potent belief of Xavier's day was the placement of the Garden of Eden, a spicy paradise yet undiscovered by Christians, as a real place in this part of the world. Interestingly, it is this legend, which evolved from medieval times, that accounts for the use of incense in the modern mass. A second belief, entwined with the first, held that Christian sects from the early Church had reached the East, established spiritual strongholds there, and were awaiting discovery. Such was Prester John's kingdom. Another belief, accounting for Xavier's determination to visit China, posited that St. Thomas, as well as other early Christians known as "Adorers of the Cross," had ventured into China to make converts. These beliefs, documented by numerous Church studies and inquiries, were shared by Xavier. It was a spice merchant returning from China whom he chanced upon in the Moluccas, however, who told him such sects actually existed. Xavier's fervor fed on itself, multiplying.

A man of his time, Xavier on his journey into the unknown carried these stories with him as essential spiritual baggage, unseen talismans, as he bore a real crucifix and breviary. Earthly hope drove the explorers to seek the source of spices, while Xavier, ever mindful that his ultimate quest was redemption of himself and his fellow man, correspondingly sought out the Spice Islands, the Moluccas with their paradisaical aromas, which he called "islands of divine hope."

Chapter 8

THE END

OF THE PORTUGUESE

CENTURY

FRANCIS XAVIER'S thirty-eight-thousand-mile ministry, for its day a near-miraculous feat in itself, is all the more exceptional in light of the skepticism of journeys held by the very Church he served. This prejudice was institutionalized by the saying *"Qui multum peregrinatur, raro sanctificatur,"* or "He who travels much is seldom canonized." The Holy See of the Renaissance and Counter-Reformation, while beatifying the singular Xavier and endorsing religious pilgrimages, essentially regarded the life of the wanderer as highly suspect.

The road not taken was infinitely preferable to the one that was, for it was held that the latter path invariably led the heedless to stumble before the gates of hell. If travel, then, was essentially a profane, not sacred, business, it reached its apotheosis in Xavier's curious contemporary and acquaintance Fernão Mendes Pinto.

Between 1537 and 1558 this intriguing Portuguese voyaged to many different parts of Asia, including Sumatra, Java, and the Spice Islands, and by his own account of his adventures, published posthumously in 1614 as *The Travels of Mendes Pinto,* was captured thirteen times, sold into slavery sixteen times, and shipwrecked five times. A case can be made that Mendes Pinto's work was the most important literary achievement of the Portuguese Renaissance. The cunning tale was certainly the most widely read, and in it the underside of Portugal's Asian colonialism as a direct result of the spice trade is depicted in sharp relief.

Immediately another contrasting work of the period comes to mind. Luis de Camões's complex extended poem *Os Lusiadas* (1572) tells of the Portuguese incursion into the Far East in Homeric style and Virgilian character. The work sings in ringing nationalistic terms of the epic of commerce realized by the Carreira da India, the Iberians' exploitation of the route to the Far East around the Cape of Good Hope. It celebrates an unprecedented maritime success—Portugal's gaining the spice trade monopoly—that resulted in the disruption of former trade routes and the displacement of Venice as a world power.

Mendes Pinto, however, had other, less festive things on his agenda. On the face of it, his *Travels* is an imaginative and rousing adventure tale of the exotic, spicy East, a grand prose epic combining fact and fancy in the picaresque tradition. "Fortune saw fit to carry me off to the Indies, where, instead of my lot improving as I had hoped, the hardship and hazards only increased with the passing years. . . . I was perfectly willing to accept, for better or worse, whatever fate had in store for me." But on another, more biting level, Mendes Pinto reorganizes and reemphasizes historical facts as he sees fit and, through the point of view of a guileless narrator, unfolds a wicked satire of Portugal's expanding religious and political institutions. As this was an age of the strictest censorship by church and state, his was no ordinary achievement.

Obscured by the persona and the purposeful inaccuracy of his tale, Mendes Pinto's actual biography is sketchy. Born of an impoverished family distantly related to the affluent Mendes family of Lisbon and Antwerp (merchants who earlier in the century had been deeded the spice trade monopoly by the Crown), the author as a young man was apprenticed into the house of a Lisbon noblewoman. After more than a year and in his own words, "something happened that placed me in such great jeopardy that I was forced to leave the house at a moment's notice and flee for my life. And I kept on running, so crazed with fear that I didn't know where I was going, for I thought I saw death staring me in the eyes, keeping pace with me every step of the way."

Thus began for Mendes Pinto a life on the run, taking the wanderer over a period of twenty-one years to India, Malacca, and the seas of

Southeast Asia, China, and Japan, where he was employed variously as an ambassador, doctor, merchant, missionary (he befriended Francis Xavier and loaned the Jesuit money to found his mission in Japan), pirate, slave, and soldier.

His success as a merchant enabled him finally to return to Portugal, where he married, reared a family, and composed his *Travels*. "I find that there is not as much reason to complain about my past misfortune as there is reason to give thanks to the Lord for my present blessings, for he saw fit to preserve my life, so that I could write this awkward, unpolished tale." He received shortly before his death in 1583 a stipend from the Crown in recognition of service to God and king.

However, it is not the historical author but the narrator of *Travels* that is of interest here. Adopting the artless persona of the picaro-naïf in the tradition of *Don Quixote* and *The Life of Lazarillo de Tormes*, Mendes Pinto, the guileless "poor me," embarks with his readers on an unblinking exotic voyage of derring-do, often tempered by the fantastic, through the Portuguese imperial and ecclesiastical scourging of Asia.

At one point he overhears a Tartar king who comments, "The fact that these people [Portuguese] journey so far from home to conquer territory indicates clearly that there must be very little justice and a great deal of greed among them," whereupon an old man observes: "It would certainly seem so, for when men, by dint of industry and ingenuity, fly over all the waters in order to acquire possessions that God did not give them, it means either that there is such great poverty among them that it makes them completely forget their homeland, or that the vanity and blindness engendered in them by their greed are so great as to cause them to deny God and their fathers."

The Church's evangelical zeal in prosecuting its Asian interests parallel to the Crown's is likewise unspared by the author's satiric bent. A Patani king remarks: "Wouldn't it be better for these people, as long as they are exposing themselves to such great hardship, to go to China to get rich rather than to foreign kingdoms to preach nonsense?"

Nor are Asians themselves untainted in the author's dark tale of human cunning and frailty. Mendes Pinto's Far East is marked by violence, hypocrisy, and greed, as his black human comedy of the absurd is peopled by natives as well as Europeans. Each in this weighty catalogue of encounters is measured with a quick, seemingly careless but artful take. Behind the laconic telling lurks a clear-eyed moral vision that, because of the posed disinterest of the former, seems if anything amoral.

Representative is the following incident relating the actions of a Malay tyrant. "At the time we arrived in Kedah, the king was in the midst of conducting elaborate funeral services for his father, whom he had stabbed to death in order to marry his mother, who was pregnant with his child." We are then told that to stamp out public indignation over such a crime, the king proclaimed that any gossiper of the affair would be brutally put to death, as were seventeen partygoers whose tongues were loosened by drink: "He had them all executed by an extraordinarily cruel method . . . which consists of sawing a live man to death, starting with the feet, then the hands, the neck, and the chest, all the way down the back to the bottom of the spine, which is the way I saw them afterwards."

Summoned before the king, the narrator expects to be similarly dispatched and begs for his life, but the ruler benignly explains the murder of his father. "'I found out that he was planning to kill me, all because of a plot hatched against me by some evil men who told him that I had made my mother pregnant—something I never even dreamed of doing. But since my father believed this baseless accusation and had already decided to kill me, I had no choice but to kill him first. God only knows how I hated to do it, because I had always been a good son to him. And since I did not want to see my mother remain poor and defenseless—which is the fate of many widows—I married her; and as a result I had to refuse many other good offers of marriage I had been considering to . . . sisters and daughters of kings who would have brought me fabulous dowries.'"

Scenes of horrible religious frenzy—reminiscent of the phantasmagoria attending the Hindu cult festival of Jagganath—are vividly drawn in *Travels*. They may or may not be dreadful parodies of Christian sacraments, but they are nonetheless memorable as the maverick narrator renders them:

> Then there were others, extremely ugly and frightful looking, called *nuca-ramoes,* who went about dressed in tiger skins, holding copper pots under their arms filled with a certain concoction of putrid urine mixed with human feces that was so noxious and so evil smelling that no one could bear to be within a whiff of it. They would go among the people begging for alms, saying as they did so, "Quick, give me some alms or I will eat the

devil's food and spray you with it so that you will be as accursed as the devil himself!" At which everybody hastened to give them alms, for if they delayed but a moment in granting his wish, he would put the pot to his mouth, take a long draft of that malodorous concoction and spray it over those he wanted to harm. In the meantime, all the others who had seen them get sprayed would consider them accursed and mistreat them so badly that the poor wretches did not know what to do, for if anyone failed to dishonor them, he would in turn be considered just as unworthy of the respect of his fellow men as they were. Thus, everybody would beat them and push them about and point to each one as having been excommunicated for causing that saintly man to eat the devil's filth, thereby becoming eternally foul in the eyes of God, so that he could neither go to paradise nor be seen by the eyes of men.

Thus, there are amongst these people, who otherwise are not lacking in good judgment and wit, many other kinds of blind spots and brutish customs that are so far beyond all reason and human understanding, that they serve as a great motive for us to offer thanks continually for the infinite mercy and goodness He has shown us, by giving us the light of true faith wherewith to save our souls.

The narrator's voice of passivity has the last say, as the book ends on a bleating, fatalistic note: "Therefore, I give many thanks to the King of Heaven, who has seen fit in this manner to carry out his divine will on me, and I am not complaining about the kings of the earth, since I did not deserve any better, for having sinned so deeply."

THE GRIM SPECTACLES described in such riveting detail by the author of *Travels* are rooted in real earth, standing as indices of a cruel age in which neither East nor West monopolized brutality. But it was not long after Mendes Pinto's Asian odyssey and Francis Xavier's ministry in the Spice Islands that the Portuguese century in the Moluccas began to wane, signaling the coming of an ignoble end for these Europeans.

Ternate had enjoyed a period of peace with Tidore mainly due to the efforts of Governor Galvão, whose leadership dates from 1536. Galvão found a Ternate in shambles and ruin, as anarchy had traditionally followed a change of rulers, whether native or Portuguese. On adjacent Tidore as many as twenty thousand men advised by a handful of Spaniards were poised to attack Ternate. With a small striking force, Galvão led a nighttime raid and put the Tidoreans to flight, thus inducing Tidore's sultan to sue for peace. The upshot was that Galvão for the time being ended the bickering between the Moluccan sultans and introduced an enlightened administration, while sponsoring both the spread of Catholicism and exploration, with the two often converging. This exceptional Portuguese ruler, a bright interlude in the sordid line of villainous predecessors and successors, immediately seized this opportunity to ensure a lasting peace by arranging a marriage between the two rival sultanates. But at this moment of great public acclaim, Galvão's downfall was to come as a result of his rigorous attempt to enforce the spice monopoly in the face of widespread promiscuous dealings in cloves on the part of natives and Portuguese alike. Eventually, he alienated Sultan Hairun, who had befriended Francis Xavier, and with small support from his own subordinates, Galvão was eventually recalled, replaced by a succession of tyrants.

Two actors played prominent roles in the final act of the Portuguese-Ternatean drama: the fortress's commander, Captain Mesquita, and Sultan Baab (Babullah), son of Hairun. It was the collision of these two that resulted in the expulsion of the Portuguese. As in the Prince Darwis episode years earlier, the fiery actions of each antagonist sprang from two vastly differing views of the world and their place in it. Once again, unrelenting fury in confrontation was central to the outcome.

Sultan Baab boasted that he ruled over seventy-two islands stretching from Celebes to New Guinea. Summoning warriors from as close as Ternate's ancient rival Tidore and as far away as Macassar on the southwestern peninsula of Celebes (quickly emerging as a rival in its own right), Sultan Baab put the Portuguese fortress to a siege that lasted five years. Entrapped within a strangely European world of dress and custom, the defenders were reduced to surviving on sago, sweetened by the meat of whatever rat, cat, or fruit bat strayed their way.

The siege was Sultan Baab's personal vendetta against the fortress's Captain Mesquita, who had honed a keen hatred for the followers of the Prophet Mohammed after his service in the Persian Gulf. Following a public ceremony of goodwill, Mesquita had lured Baab's father, Sultan Hairun, Ternate's ruler, into the fortification and managed to separate him from his retinue. Mesquita's soldiers quickly turned on the royal visitor. After stabbing him to death, they displayed his head on a pike and his quarters on the castle ramparts as exhibits of Portuguese power.

When word reached Goa of this wanton murder, the command was irate over such a colossal blunder. It ordered Mesquita relieved and returned in chains to Goa, while the grieving, enraged Ternateans placed the castle under protracted attack.

Moral considerations aside, Mesquita's deceitful murder of Hairun was a lethal setback for the Portuguese and their efforts to consolidate their colonial holdings. Not only did it encourage Baab, Hairun's eldest son, to rally support for a burning popular cause, but it enabled him to consolidate his empire and eventually be acclaimed as Molucca's greatest ruler for ousting the Portuguese. An overtaxed Goa did send reinforcements, but they were so meager that little could be done to counter the siege.

In negotiations, Baab agreed to lift the siege on the condition that Mesquita be handed over for punishment. If this was done, Baab assured Mesquita's replacement, he would also renew the oath of loyalty to Portugal, and resume trade in cloves, much in the spirit of cooperation that had existed between his revered grandfather Sultan Bolief and Francisco Serrão, whose name still brought murmurs of approval from the islanders. When the captain replied that Mesquita had already been spirited off the island, Baab's efforts to bring him to native justice became relentless, and the issue festered.

In a cunning gesture certain to internationalize a petty, parochial murder, Baab sent emissaries not only to the viceroy in Goa but to the king in Lisbon as well. Baab's envoys traveled to Malacca by *kora-kora*, then boarded a Portuguese ship bound for Europe, and returned to Ternate in similar fashion, after making an extraordinary personal appeal that the Crown could not ignore. Under pressure from Lisbon to placate the sultanate, the viceroy acted. He ordered Mesquita imprisoned in the hold of a cargo vessel bound for Ternate, where he would face charges for murder.

Had Mesquita actually been delivered to Sultan Baab to face Ternatean justice, the Portuguese might have been spared their ignominious departure that was to follow. But fate played a strange hand. On a provisioning stop in Java, the ship in which Mesquita was imprisoned was boarded by pirates masquerading as merchants, and a fierce hand-to-hand battle raged before the ship was looted and burned.

The prisoner Captain Mesquita, though he was chained below to a

cannon, fought with Herculean strength, killing ten Javanese before he
was slain. Except for a handful of survivors, the rest of the ship's party
were slaughtered. Two of those spared have a place in Javanese legend, for
they were taken to the palace of the emperor of Java, where they spent the
rest of their lives chained as "white monkeys" at its entrance.

After five years, many of the Portuguese in the besieged fortress had
died of dysentery or starvation. Keenly aware of their desperation, Baab
sent his brother with an ultimatum. If the Portuguese would surrender
the castle, he would spare their lives. The command negotiated a conces-
sion from the intermediary, namely that Sultan Baab would deliver those
who surrendered to the island of Ambon to the south, where a small Portuguese contingent was constructing a fort.

With no choice but to comply, the Portuguese agreed to give up the
castle. Led by a priest, they stacked their arms and walked out in columns,
a motley assortment of half-castes known as Black Portuguese, native
wives, children, soldiers, and merchants, all carrying whatever personal
possessions they could to a world they had not seen in half a decade.
Some of the refugees accepted Baab's offer to enter his service. Others
joined the few Spanish on Tidore, while still others took ship south for
Ambon. But the majority boarded cargo ships to return to Malacca.

Thus, on July 15, 1575, the Portuguese surrendered the island they had
dominated since the arrival of Francisco Serrão sixty-three years before,
while Ternate began to prosper anew under the Baab sultanate.

Baab rigorously developed the alliances among islands near and distant
that he had used to defeat the Portuguese. In his fleet of *kora-kora*, he
made state visits to every island of the alliance, garnering support and
pledges of loyalty, even venturing as far as Macassar on southwestern
Celebes, where he signed a peace treaty with the most powerful regional
king outside of Java. Most important, he scrupulously avoided overrun-
ning Tidore, the ancient enemy but recent ally, allowing the handful of
Europeans to remain there for purposes of trade.

The annual fleet from Malacca continued to call, but at Tidore, while
Sultan Baab oversaw the commerce from across the channel. Envisioning
a golden age of Moluccan monarchy, realized in himself, he introduced a
new protocol informed by his own royal self-importance.

Any Western visitor to Ternate was required to remove shoes and hat.

Baab granted audiences in what had been the great hall of the Portuguese castle, which he renamed Gammalamma, and dictated the terms of trade. Once in a royal display of temper, he angrily and memorably drove the bearers of a personal letter from Philip II from his sight. The messengers had stalled in bestowing on the sultan certain rich gifts mentioned by the Spanish king in his letter until Baab agreed to their trade proposals, and his monarchic dismissal of them was worthy of Philip himself.

SO RAN THE affairs of Ternate under Sultan Baab's stewardship, while other European nations waited, poised like a parliament of eager suitors with new, affectionate proposals for this island of cloves. Four years passed. Then, on November 3, 1579, the first expedition after Magellan's to circumnavigate the globe dropped anchor at Ternate. It was, however, an English undertaking dispatched by Queen Elizabeth, and its commander was the notorious Francis Drake. The event signaled the imminent arrival of yet another player in the high-stakes spice game: England.

Though England's maritime awakening in the sixteenth century was behind that of Portugal and Spain, it came to glorious fruition during the reign of Elizabeth. Richard Hakluyt's great collection *Voyages* gives graphic life to the notable seamen who moved to the fore in this time. One such sea captain stands alone above the others. Like his contemporaries Shakespeare and Raleigh, Francis Drake served an age that gave full rein to his special genius as well as his legend as the popular nautical hero who provoked and humiliated Europe's greatest monarch by "singeing the King of Spain's [Philip II] beard."

John Stow's *Annals* provides a contemporary sketch of Drake. "He was more skilful in all points of navigation than any ever was. . . . He was also of a perfect memory, great observation, eloquent by nature, skilful in artillery, expert and apt to let blood flow and give physic unto his people according to the climates." Drake, thirty-six years old, was short and strongly built, with a large head covered with brown hair and a full beard on his face, highlighted by large clear eyes that gave him "a cheerful countenance."

This description, however, belied the terror synonymous with his name to the French, and especially to the Portuguese and Spaniards. Stow goes on to say, "In brief he was as famous in Europe and America as Tamburlane in Asia and Africa. . . . In his imperfections he was ambitious for honour, unconstant in amity, greatly affected to popularity."

It must also be added that Drake knew how to handle sailors, who were largely ignorant, superstitious, and mercurial. "I know sailors to be the most envious [suspicious] people of the world," he commented. As his predecessor Magellan, Drake had firsthand experience with attempted mutiny and how to deal with such treachery. Earlier in Brazil, he had ordered a conspirator decapitated and the severed head to be seized out of the dust and held aloft, himself saying, "Lo, this is the end of traitors."

Little of the hazards of ocean voyaging, and the seamanship required to match them, had changed in the sixty years since the ragtag remains of Magellan's Spanish expedition finally managed to find Ternate. In that earlier adventure, four ships were lost. Drake likewise had lost four, with the sole survivor the one-hundred-ton flagship *Golden Hind*. But considering their circumstances, its crew was a fat and happy one. Aware of the Portuguese expulsion, Drake elected to put in at Ternate, where he counted on a friendlier welcome than would be accorded at neighboring Tidore, for the Spanish knew at first hand the piratical exploits of the widely known Drake.

Sultan Baab was at once delighted and mystified by Drake's visit. Here were Europeans seemingly uninterested in colonizing his islands or joining in an expedition against the handful of Spaniards on Tidore or even in filling their ship's holds with spices. For his part, Drake kept his own counsel. Baab did not have to know that the *Hind* was already rich from privateering on the Spanish Main to the tune of one million pounds sterling. Having plundered Valparaiso after traversing the Straits of Magellan, the English captain was eager to return home with the booty via the African cape to the welcoming court of Queen Elizabeth.

In fact, Drake's visit may be seen as an early reconnoitering by the English Crown of colonial possibilities in the Spice Islands, though England's East India Company, or the Honourable Company, to be chartered on December 31, 1600, would not foray into these waters for twenty more years.

It was not an easy reconnaissance. The English captain would likely have missed the Moluccas but for two fishermen in canoes off the small island of Siau, north of Celebes, who agreed to guide the *Golden Hind*.

According to English accounts, Drake's decent, gentlemanly pose seemingly impressed Baab, who saw these new Europeans as superior in manner to the loathed Portuguese and dispatched three large *kora-kora* to the flagship riding at anchor. A shipboard chronicler recorded the scene: "In each whereof, were certaine of the greatest personages that were about him (the sultan), attired all of them in white Lawne, or cloth of Calecut, having over their heads, from one end of the Canow to the other, a covering of thinne and fine mats, borne up by a frame made of reedes, under which every man sate in order according to his dignity; the hoary heads of many of them, set forth the greater reverence due their persons, and manifestly shewed, that the king used the advice of a grave and prudent Counsell, in his affaires."

Then arrived Sultan Baab himself in the company of six "grave and ancient fathers." The sultan was "of a tall stature, very corpulent and well set together, of a very princely and gratious countenance: his respect amongst his own was such, that neither his Viceroy . . . , nor any other of his counsellers, durst speak unto him but upon their knees, not rising again till they were licenced."

Drake provided Sultan Baab with a noisy reception, firing cannon and small arms as well as sounding trumpets and drums and other musical instruments. The latter so pleased the sultan that he asked that his *kora-kora* be attached to the stern of the *Golden Hind* and towed around the harbor, "being thus in musicall paradise." Before the sultan's departure, Drake lavished gifts on the royal party, and Baab reciprocated by sending out stores of food for the ships, promising a return visit the next day to enjoy a scheduled shipboard entertainment.

The next day the sultan did not appear but instead sent his brother as emissary bearing an invitation to visit Gammalamma Castle, the very fortress Baab had wrested from the Portuguese. Drake pondered his options. Fearing treachery, he personally declined the sultan's invitation, sending instead his own emissaries while holding the sultan's brother hostage aboard the flagship.

The sultan received the envoys in the *baileu*, the reception hall of the former Portuguese fortress, and Drake's men were bowled over by the lush elegance of the scene. The large, square room was open on all sides and draped in colorful cloths, with the grand throne, covered with a richly textured tapestry, prominent to one side, surrounded by layers of the same rich fabric. Attending the court in anticipation of the sultan's arrival were red-turbaned elders, whose sole purpose was "to keepe continuall traffique." The emissaries were amazed to discover among the courtiers two Turks, one Italian, two Muslims from the Middle East, and a Spaniard. The presence of outsiders with specific tasks at court was a measure of Ternate's superior international trade under its present sultan.

A thousand spectators crowded to see Sultan Baab make his impressive entrance in a golden sarong, red-dyed leather shoes, a headdress "wreathed in diverse rings of plated gold," and a large gold chain necklace. Diamond, emerald, ruby, and turquoise rings adorned his fingers as he mounted his throne, attended by a page with a fan "richly embroidered and beset with saphires."

Drake's men were mightily impressed by such a show of wealth that symbolized Baab's power as "Lord of an hundred Ilands thereabout," far greater than any enjoyed by a predecessor; and though the presence of elders remained a constant in Ternatean court ritual, the Englishmen were struck by how palace ceremonies seemed designed to underline the vast social gap between the sultan and his subjects. This was the Ternate monarchy's golden age, for it oversaw a vast trading empire that made the sultanate a name to be reckoned with far beyond its shores. Ternate was unquestionably the most prosperous trading center in the eastern part of the Malay Archipelago, and the Englishmen immediately grasped that fact.

Drake's expedition lingered in these waters for only a few days, and with his holds already filled with earlier plunder, the six tons of cloves he did take on was essentially to please Sultan Baab, in exchange for fabrics and weaponry. Spanish historians, however, paint a different picture of Drake's dealings with the sultan during his short visit, recounting that Drake behaved arrogantly with Baab and refused to pay the sultan's export tax of 10 percent until the English captain was threatened with death. Though there was no recorded treachery on the part of Baab, Drake's sense of his vulnerability might account for the brevity of the *Golden Hind*'s anchorage off Ternate, for he waited days later until landfall at Crab Island off the northeastern peninsula of Celebes to careen his flagship.

Drake's most lasting contribution to clove-perfumed Ternate was a curious one and laden with an odd symbolism. When he prepared to sail from Ternate in late autumn 1579, a squall erupted. With an already overloaded flagship, Drake, ever on the alert, feared that the reef outlying the island would rip the bottom from the *Golden Hind,* and so he ordered his men to jettison a major weight, a mighty and handsome cannon.

Sultan Baab watched the huge weapon plunge into the sea and sink to the bottom. After escorting Drake's ship beyond the hazardous reef and when the flagship stood out on the horizon, he ordered an ingenious salvage operation, sending divers off the reef with buoyant segments of thick bamboo. The cannon was floated to the surface and towed to shore on a raft. It was then taken and mounted on a rampart of the sultan's fortress, where it remained for centuries as a ceremonial and decorative reminder of the famous Englishman's only visit.

Drake's benign Ternatean idyll, though quiet and unnoticed amid the contentious bloodletting in the Spice Islands, had a subtle play two decades later when the English and Dutch supplanted the Portuguese and Spanish for control of Moluccan waters, and the English would insist, with no formal documentation, that Sultan Baab had accepted Ternate as an English protectorate.

THREE YEARS LATER Ternate's fortunes were altered with the bizarre death of Sultan Baab. Believing himself immune to Portuguese treachery, the sultan had allowed himself to be lured aboard a Portuguese ship, where he was taken hostage while the vessel sailed for India. Baab was beheaded, quartered, then his parts were preserved in brine and his head presented to the Viceroy in Goa.

Baab's successor, his son Said, shared his father's ambitions but lacked his diplomatic cunning. In the strange aftermath of his father's murder, Said somehow arranged for the return of the preserved remains of his father from Goa, organized a lavish state funeral attended by the Sultan of Tidore, and after oaths of peace and friendship, ordered each of his guards to draw his *kris* (short, curved sword) and cut down his royal neighbor and a dozen of his courtiers. Once again the two sultanates, equally lurid in their court intrigues and murders, were at war, and as a result each was

eminently exploitable by Western powers for Western interests. But those
Western powers were soon to change.

DRAKE RETURNED TO England in late September 1580 not only with
loot to please his queen, accounts of "the world encompas'd," and a tale to
tell of humiliating the Spanish, but with important geographical discoveries as well. He had learned that the *terra australis incognita,* if it existed,
was not where the familiar atlas of Ortelius showed it to be; and that the
Atlantic and Pacific Oceans came together not far to the south of the
Straits of Magellan. His most significant gift at homecoming, however,
was a notion for his queen, who later knighted him, that would lead to
the founding of the Honourable Company and England's first colony on
the tiny Bandanese island of Run in the Southern Moluccas.

In the meantime, the Spaniards, who had begun in 1571 to build the
fortress and walled city of Manila, learned in the Philippines of Francis
Drake's visit to Ternate and dreaded the terrible consequences of his presence in the Far East. And so one practical result of Drake's world-ranging
expedition was that the Portuguese and Spanish realms in 1580 became
united in Asia as well as Europe. This unification occurred under the
stronger, more aggressive Spanish crown for the most practical of reasons:
to check England's expanding role and its potential as a world power.

England was in fact becoming what Spain feared, and largely because of
the incorrigible Drake. Under a commission from his queen, he voyaged to
the New World and sacked Santiago and burned Vigo in 1585 before taking Santo Domingo and Cartagena. In 1587 he destroyed a Spanish armament in Cadiz Harbor and the next year as vice admiral commanded a
division of the English fleet against the armada, which he destroyed.

MEANWHILE, TERNATE'S commercial and military renown was to have
an effect the Europeans could not have anticipated: the increase of Islam's
prestige in the Spice Islands at the expense of Christianity. The Spanish
Jesuit Antonio Marta, a distinguished soldier turned priest, noted with
despair that despite the warring sultanates, the Muslims were now showing greater unity than before. But Marta and other followers of Francis

Xavier perhaps misperceived what was truly happening when a community was "lost" or "saved."

As both religions maintained a certain flexibility regarding native practices, so did the natives manage to weave Christian or Islamic practices into their ancient tribal practices: spirit worship and the possession of many wives, the latter the most effective way the Moluccans had of assuring allegiances. Generally speaking, the Spice Islanders managed quite easily to accommodate aspects of both systems of belief. A given community on a given island, in the absence of a continuing religious authority to force a strict adherence to teachings, would move with some fluidity back and forth between Christianity and Islam because its fundamental beliefs had not been altered, especially in the event of a mass conversion.

To these extremely tenuous bondings it must be added that commitment to a faith in one Moluccan community almost inevitably assured for its rival neighbor the embrace of another as a matter of expediency. Faith determined political loyalty and vice versa.

But Father Marta's perception of religion in the Moluccas was a despairing one, and he returned to Manila with grim counsel. It was his belief, he told the secular authorities, that the total of forty thousand Christians in the Spice Islands were doomed in one last great jihad. To convert more natives to Christianity, he believed, would simply mark them as victims. Marta's was an eerie prophecy, for it presaged that Francis Xavier's "islands of divine hope" would be a spiritual loss, while the Jesuit's military counterparts were vigorously prosecuting that they not become an earthly loss as well.

Ternate, then, was not yet done with Iberia, for the Spanish in the Philippines still coveted the extraordinary commercial realm. In the wake of the dreaded Drake's visit, they sensed that Far Eastern waters had not seen the last of the marauding English. Time and again, however, the Spanish were beaten back from Ternate by the native alliances that had been forged by Sultan Baab and upheld by Sultan Said.

The years 1599 to 1606 were to be the most momentous in Moluccan history, with the advent of the English and Dutch, then with the Spaniards playing a final hand. Aided by the Tidorean sultanate, in 1606 the Spaniards, with a superior force, managed to overrun Ternate, seize Sultan Said from Gammalamma Castle, and send him and his court into lifelong exile in Manila, allowing the Spaniards for a time to be the dominant European force in the Northern Moluccas.

It was a desperate but anticlimactic move. Their success was short-lived, and the Spaniards were soon forced to return to the Philippines from the Spice Islands, eclipsed by two northern European Protestant nations, who, while discovering their own sea routes to the East around Africa's southern tip, saw the papal authority that had divided the world between the two Iberian nations as "insolencyes."

NORTHERN DESIRE

. . . by equinoctial winds
Close sailing from Bengala, or the isles
Of Ternate and Tidore, whence merchants bring
Their spicy drugs . . .
—JOHN MILTON, *Paradise Lost,*
Book Two (ii, 683), 1667

In matters of commerce, the fault of the Dutch
is giving too little, and asking too much.
—ENGLISH SAYING

Chapter 9

THE GLOBE
AND THE WORLD

THE LONDON that greeted Francis Drake in the autumn of 1580 after his circumnavigation of the globe was a rip-roaring beehive of a city, whose ground had already shifted from the churchly to the worldly. The theater was in flower, and the hundreds of old inns and taverns, advertising themselves on elaborate, colorful signs with such names as the Bear and Ragged Staff and King Harry Head, were themselves a theater of sorts through which the world passed. "The immoderate drinking of fools," a time-honored pastime since the twelfth century, had emerged as popular public sport at these "great and sumptuous places" scattered throughout England's capital, bulging against the banks of the Thames.

But this conventional picture of Elizabethan London is at odds with the city's background: inauspicious beginnings on an unpromising river site with an early history shrouded in mystery. By Chaucer's day, the last half of the fourteenth century, London, with a population of forty thousand, already had endured a thousand years of history. Now there was an invasion of exotica flavoring a former savage wilderness with contrary sweetness and pungency. There was talk, and much of it, of new flavors and tastes. The poet recounts in "The Merchant's Tale" the antics of exuberant revelers, who "danced and drank and, left to their devises, . . . went from room to room to room to scatter Spices about the house."

During the two centuries from Chaucer to Shakespeare and Queen Elizabeth's "gentlemen adventurers," whose mariners were poised to sail for spices, London's old town bore the stamp of the ages, while new settlements began to scatter headlong beyond it like straws caught in a gust, with Fleet Street and the Strand reaching to Charing Cross in pastureland.

Surrounded by a wall, London snaked for about a mile along the river's north bank, the city's southern boundary, with communities rooting themselves a half mile inland. At its eastern end stood the royal, imposing Tower of London, from which the wall circled about to the northwest, before arcing south past St. Paul's Cathedral and Blackfriars, the great Dominican monastery, and returning to the river. Where the Thames dipped sharply south stood the royal residence known as Whitehall. Nearby was the separate community of Westminster Abbey and Parliament buildings.

A traveler coming up from Canterbury entered the city by crossing London Bridge, a mile to the east, marked in midstream by a chapel dedicated to St. Thomas of Canterbury and lined with thriving shops and dwellings. High towers stood at either end, where the heads of traitors were roosted on pikes after execution. On the Southwark side of the bridge stood the Tabard Inn. This comfortable hostelry was typical of the best that London had to offer and served as a gathering place for Canterbury-bound pilgrims.

Cheapside was the great parade ground stretching from the Tower of London to Westminster, wide enough for the "boast of heraldry, the pomp of power." It was also the center of trade, where small shops and open-air markets flourished in the confusion of such byways as Stinking Lane and Seething Lane converging on it. Garbage and offal were swept into the streets, and on the vigils of festival days in June and July, bonfires were lit to purify the air.

A city of merchants and traders, pilgrims and penitents, London had grown used to travelers and strangers, who stowed away food in prodigious quantities at taverns and inns. There was no touch of irony in Chaucer's description of the charming table etiquette of the Prioress, for such delicacy was quaintly at odds with the manners and style that cut through society's every level in a crude, roisterous age. It was a spirited day, heralded by the common field laborer and the menial shopkeeper caught up in a rising tide of assurance, as a common language, English, was in the ascendancy. This notion of opportunity for the ordinary man, nurtured within the chrysalis of a rich language, kindled the era with new energy, a passion for life and its possibilities.

London town had evolved into the mecca of the main chance; and for a Londoner, to possess the moment was to display it. The profane festivals on the heels of pious holy days, especially May days, were the gaudy processions of no despondent people. This Chaucerian spirit sowed a legacy of muscular expansiveness and broad-shouldered risk that would mark the day of Shakespeare and court of Elizabeth and continue, despite the greatest domestic upheavals England has ever known, through the reigns of James I, his doomed successor and son Charles, the Commonwealth of Cromwell, and the Restoration court of Charles II.

By the early seventeenth century London's population had grown to about a hundred thousand; and though the old walled city remained intact, with Cheapside still the center for trade, the city by now had reached beyond itself. Southwark, across the Thames, was now a thriving community. Just below London Bridge was the terminal for oceangoing ships bound to and from the Americas and soon to the Indies. A great fleet of sailing ships was usually to be seen in this part of the river, known as the Pool, with Billingsgate the busiest of shipping points and the timbers of its docks and warehouses in time to be infused with the aroma of cinnamon and other spices.

The city's swelling population was matched by a burgeoning spirit of not only confidence but independence as well. With Drake's destruction of Spain's armada in 1588, the island nation was for the first time unintimidated by any continental power, and none of this assurance was lost on her cocky citizens.

More important than native swagger, the England and London of Elizabeth had thrown off the yoke of the Roman Catholic Church, so prevalent in Chaucer's time, to embrace secularization. With the dissolution of the monasteries under Henry VIII, vast piles of architecture owned by the Church throughout the land reverted either to the Crown or to powerful individuals for worldly ends, while others, such as Tintern Abbey, its window lead melted for other purposes, decayed into magnificent ruins. More effect than cause, England's nod to the profane signaled a profound change in the national character, and man's relation to God became less absorbing than his relations to his own fellows and circumstances.

The Thames, London's artery to the world's seas and soon the Spice Islands, was seen anew as a splendid stream and duly celebrated in drawings and poems for its fair water, abundance of fish, and myriad swans plying the river's currents. Nature was tamed into formal gardens, to be immortalized in verse later in the century by Andrew Marvell and others. The language, words with disparate spellings on a single page, sang in the streets, the taverns, the theater. They flowed from the pen of pamphleteers and poets, among them England's monarch Elizabeth, whose courtiers praised highly her poetry and ready wit.

Thus awakened, the Elizabethans saw themselves as a new race, keen to savor the wonders of the material world, with the spirit of the day summed up in Hamlet's lines: "What a piece of work is man! how noble in reason! how infinite in faculties!" Such sentiments found flesh and blood in the rough-cut Drake or the more refined Raleigh, Renaissance men by any measure, whether in or out of favor in the eyes of a fickle, mercurial court.

The Tudor English were known for their love of abundant food and drink, and by then the bounty of the Spice Islands was essential to their enjoyment of both. Robert May's *The Accomplisht Cook, or the Art and Mystery of Cookery,* the most complete and enterprising cooking manual of the age, scarcely details a recipe without the inclusion of spices. To bake a turkey, he advises: "Bone it, and lard it with pretty big lard, a pound and a half will serve, then season it with an ounce of pepper, an ounce of nutmegs, and two ounces of salt, lay some butter in the bottom of the pye, then lay on the fowl, and put in six or eight whole cloves, then put on all the seasoning with good store of butter, close it up, and baste with eggs, bake it, and being baked fill it up with clarified butter."

And to make ipocras, a wine fortified with spices and a popular drink of Elizabethan England among nobility and commoners alike, May explains, "Take a gallon of wine, three ounces of cinnamon, two ounces of slic't ginger, a quarter of an ounce of cloves, an ounce of mace, twenty corns of pepper, an ounce of nutmegs, three pound of sugar, and two quarts of cream." John Partridge's *The Good Huswifes Handmaide for the Kitchin* offers a variation: "Take a gallon of wine, an ounce of synamon, two ounces of Ginger, one pound of Sugar, twentie Cloves bruised, and twentie cornes of pepper big beaten, let all these soake together one night, and then let it run through a bag, and it will be good Ipocras."

Feasting was raised to the level of a high art among the wealthy during Elizabeth's reign. A wedding scene detail from a painting hanging in London's National Portrait Gallery—*Life of Sir Henry Unton* (1557–1596), by an unknown artist—depicts a brightly colored feast, with guests, musicians, and entertainers before a spice-laden table. Shakespeare's plays and poems likewise abound with references to spicy food and drink, and spices lend an engaging description even to a spirited horse in *Henry V* (act III, scene 7): "He's of the colour of the nutmeg," declares Orleans. "And of the heat of the ginger," responds the dauphin.

It is important to remember that, with the exception of Drake's cargo and whatever piracy Tudor sailors could manage to acquire them, spices before the year 1600 were a priceless bounty that had changed hands countless times before reaching England's shores, thus multiplying their value astonishingly. At once ubiquitous and rare, they inspired chef and poet alike. It followed that if spices had infused the zeitgeist and the whole world was a stage, with the aptly named Globe Theater emblematic of a larger play, the distant seas leading to the land of spices awaited England's sailors.

When Drake returned from his circumnavigation in 1580 with the hold of the *Golden Hind* filled with Spanish booty and spices from the Moluccas, two things had been proven to Queen Elizabeth and her advisors. First, the Spanish confidence in their monopoly of Pacific navigation had been severely shaken, Magellan's expedition on behalf of Spain sixty years before notwithstanding. The second piece of evidence crystallized more gradually, taking the form of a revelation. The Portuguese, earlier thought to be masters of the East by virtue of their seizure and occupation of Malacca and their subsequent colonization of the Spice Islands, held the unenviable position of defending their long sea-lanes to Asia, which were dotted with strongholds against a host of envious enemies.

Drake's historic voyage, returning him to England and a hero's welcome, had been the most noteworthy, though not the only expedition to expand England's horizons for trade. John Cabot had reached the heavily wooded shore of the Newfoundland Banks' Cape Breton Island only five years after Columbus discovered America, and this Venetian, learned in Renaissance geography and commanding an English ship, returned to England believing he had touched the eastern edge of Cathay.

In the last half of the sixteenth century, English ships had also doggedly pushed into Canada's frozen wastes, with Frobisher and Davis plumbing the Arctic Circle in an attempt to find the fabled northwest passage; Henry Hudson's fatal voyage followed in 1610 and was soon succeeded by Bylot and Baffin. Earlier Willoughby and Chancellor had sailed beyond Norway's North Cape to discover a northeast counterpart, only to be beaten back by the ice floes of Nova Zembla's frozen hell. But the search continued. When the attempts to find northern passages to the East failed, Whitehall by the 1590s was seized by a new energy, and the goal to establish contact with the East and maintain it without an intermediary became urgent.

This urgency was further inflamed by the union of the Spanish and Portuguese crowns enduring from 1580. Protestant England's hatred of Spain now included Portugal, as England herself was a potential victim of the combined Iberian forces. Diplomacy gave way to intrusion and plunder. As a result of a 1579 treaty with the Ottoman sultan, English ships were moving trade goods, especially spices, from Syrian ports, but they were now challenged at the Straits of Gibraltar by Iberian warships. The twin horns of politics and economics spelled a message to Whitehall, and there was no mistaking it. The time was ripe for England to forget about a northern passage. Her Crown must risk an attempt on the East Indies trade by sailing the Portuguese routes, thus challenging the combined Iberian nations in earnest.

The queen's first consent for her mariners to intrude directly in the Indies trade via the cape route was issued in 1591, but the expedition commanded by James Lancaster came to grief as two of three ships were lost, while the third reached Ceylon and the Malay Peninsula to take on a cargo of pepper. When she returned to England, there were only twenty-five scurvy-ridden survivors, including Lancaster himself.

But Tudor merchants and sailors still dreamed of playing at commerce on the world stage. That dream was kindled in part by a galvanizing incident involving Sir Walter Raleigh. This enterprising courtier was destined to be a great explorer and colonizer, but his lofty bearing and bold spirit had already marked him as a favorite of the queen. Elizabeth had soon bestowed wealth and power upon him. At thirty-five already a master of great estates in England and Ireland, this knight was named lord-lieutenant of Cornwall as well as a vice admiral, among other honors. But Raleigh was also haunted by impetuosity and ill luck that gave his life a strange and tragic intensity. When he seduced and later married Elizabeth Throckmorton, one of the queen's ladies-in-waiting, he so angered his mercurial monarch that she had him imprisoned in the summer of 1592.

On September 8 of that year an East Indian carrack was escorted into the West Country port of Dartmouth by a fleet Raleigh had organized and intended to sail with, before he ran afoul of Queen Elizabeth. The Portuguese-Spanish *Madre de Dios* was a floating fortress-palace afloat with seven decks, a six-hundred-man crew, and the richest cargo taken by English sailors during Queen Elizabeth's reign. Dazzled by such unprecedented wealth, the townspeople began looting the ship, until Raleigh, "the especial man," was summoned from the Tower to restore order among his fellow West Countrymen.

The huge carrack, which had crossed the Indian Ocean and navigated Africa's southern cape, was sighted by the fleet lying in wait off the Azores, and Raleigh's own *Roebuck* was the first ship to give chase and open fire on the vessel. When the *Madre de Dios* was boarded, the English privateers discovered in her hold a fantastic booty the like of which they'd never seen: 537 tons of spices, including 8,500 hundredweight (one hundredweight equals 112 pounds) of pepper, 900 hundredweight of cloves, 700 hundredweight of cinnamon, 500 hundredweight of cochineal (red dye), 59 hundredweight of mace, 59 hundredweight of nutmeg, and 50 hundredweight of benzoin; 15 tons of ebony; and two great crosses and another large piece of jewelry, all studded with diamonds. This was alongside chests overflowing with musk, pearl, amber, calicoes, drugs, silks, ivory, tapestries, silver, and gold.

It was half a million pounds of treasure, according to Sir John Hawkins, treasurer and controller of the navy—more than a king's (or queen's) ransom. Dartmouth was transformed into a St. Bartholomew's fair, with London merchants holding cash aloft and distribution of the profits from the spoils making the Crown and fleets' shareholders numb with exhilaration. "My Lord, there was never such a spoil!" wrote an amazed Robert Cecil back to the Privy Council in London. There was more where this came from, it was said aloud in the corridors and chambers of Whitehall.

ON DECEMBER 31, 1600, "The Company of Merchants of London trading into the East Indies" was given a royal charter by Queen Elizabeth in the name of free trade. Spelling out her convictions in a letter for the eyes of any potentate her seamen might encounter, east or west, Her Majesty stated England's case in the dawning light of a new era: that no nation under God was self-sufficient, and that nations however far and remote from each other should through the interchange of commodities become friends.

By the same token, England's monarch warned, insistence by a European nation on exclusive trading rights anywhere on the globe was a prelude to trouble. Proof had been given in the previous century by the Borgia pope, who had carved the world in half exclusively for Spain and Portugal, giving those two nations singular trading rights within their spheres, to the exclusion of all others. It followed that with the formal establishment of the Church of England under Henry VIII, God was now an Englishman and Rome no longer the universal authority for ecclesiastical truth, least of all trade restrictions. Thus the Holy See's pronouncements were "insolencyes" in the eyes of England's court and her intrepid Tudor merchant-sailors.

When in June 1602 Captain James Lancaster, commander of the English East India Company's first fleet, put in at Aceh on Sumatra's northwest tip with a copy of the queen's letter for Ala-uddin Shah, Aceh's sultan, the die was cast. Aceh's century-old hatred of Portugal, which had monopolized trade in the region since the conquest of Malacca in 1511, was no secret in London. Only a half century earlier the warrior-priest Francis Xavier had rallied Malacca against the Acehnese fleet, and the defeat remained a bitter memory. As expected, the Acehnese sultanate welcomed a new ally against the detested Portuguese.

If there was a nagging question at Elizabeth's court—namely, had England moved too late?—the gusto of the age insisted it had already been answered by Drake two decades previously, when he struck terror in the hearts of Spanish and Portuguese alike by sailing to the Spice Islands after sacking Valparaiso, and by the resounding success of Raleigh's privateering fleet in 1592 at the Azores.

But this was a contradictory age of not only pertinacity and vigor, but of sinuosity and vacillation. Though the issue hardly mattered to sailors toiling against storms on the remotest seas of the earth, there had been protracted peace talks between Elizabeth and Philip II of Spain, and they remained a sensitive issue with both monarchs. In the crucial year 1599, before the charter for the company was issued, Elizabeth hesitated to compete in the spice trade. If England were perceived by Spain as that nation's competitor in the East Indies, she reasoned, any chances at peace would be abolished. So it was that the queen procrastinated, with her delays bringing much dismay to her impatient petitioners on behalf of missions to the East Indies.

Elizabeth's concerns, however, were misplaced in this perplexing day of sudden jolts of fortune, as they would be with her successor James I. With the waning of the Iberian powers in an astonishingly fluctuating world, another northern European nation, Holland, was in no mood for such diplomatic niceties. Complicating the picture was England's ambivalent attitude toward Holland, already the distributor of spices throughout northern Europe. Siding with a fellow Protestant nation against a common foe, England had supported Holland's revolt against Spain. So while the English crown's eagerness for trade was crossed with caution, it had not passed unnoticed at London's court that the Netherlands, finally freed from Spanish domination, had designs similar to England's on the spice trade, with an aim to realize the broadest possible commercial yield, whatever the costs. By observing Holland's example, Elizabeth finally saw reflected the dying organism that was Spain. Though late in the day, England joined the hunt.

IN MARCH 1603 a forty-ton pinnace, a lone reconnaissance craft from Lancaster's expedition seeking spices at their source, fetched up on Pulau Run of the Banda group and disgorged a skeleton force of scurvy-ridden, bedraggled Englishmen to hoist a flag on the newly claimed island—all of two miles long and a half mile wide—and attempt an outpost among the scented groves of nutmeg trees. This tiny speck of an island was England's first colony anywhere. But the new settlers discovered that they were not alone in Banda waters. Three years before, the Dutch had arrived with similar expectations on the islands of Neira and Lonthor, a mere ten miles east of Run.

Chapter 10

"BY TREATY

OR BY FORCE"

THAT TWO SMALL, ostensibly friendly European nations whose East India companies, created nearly simultaneously by profit-motivated directors, came to loggerheads on the other side of the world is a revealing story of a savage, exuberant age, whose only certainty was its incongruity. In its telling, the similarities and differences between the English and Dutch, the extraordinary successes and bloody bungles of their iron-nerved adventurers crazed with ambition and greed, write a vivid chapter in the darker embroilments of the spice trade.

Holland had ignited the Elizabethans' competitive spirit in 1599 by making inquiries to purchase ships from a supposed ally—England—to swell the numbers of its Eastern fleets. This challenge of one-upmanship rankled in the Tudor breast. Suddenly the race was on, with the English, citing national interests, entering the game late but with no shortage of gusto. Only weeks after the return to Amsterdam of the second Dutch fleet with its holds loaded to capacity with spices, the petition to found what was to become the English East India Company was presented to Queen Elizabeth. But stymied by the peace talks with Spain, she hesitated for a crucial year before the royal charter was finally granted, with the parent firm of the Honourable Company modeled after its Dutch counterpart, Holland's East India Company.

In vivid contrast to their later deeds, the first incursions by the Dutch in the Spice Islands were benign ones. The main sea route for Holland's "Indiamen" was the months-long trek down Africa's west coast, then around the Cape of Good Hope (where the Dutch would later establish a provisioning colony at Table Bay [Saldania] in 1652), before sailing across the Indian Ocean. Dutch strategy dictated that the Hollanders give wide berth to such Portuguese strongholds as Goa and Malacca, instead entering East Indies waters far south of the Malay Peninsula through the Sunda Strait separating Sumatra and Java.

Nonetheless, word of the northern European interlopers quickly spread, raising alarm among Portuguese contingents scattered through the islands as the Dutch followed the successful example of this nation that had preceded them. They commandeered Malay prahus, Chinese junks, pinnaces, and galleys wherever they could be found, for these island vessels were essential in negotiating island reefs and shallows to reach such remote corners of the archipelago as the Spice Islands.

The Java Sea and contiguous waters to the east were to the Dutch largely a mystery, much as they had been to the Portuguese in the day of Francisco Serrão nearly a century before. But with ships and weaponry superior to those of the Portuguese, the Dutch consolidated their forces at Bantam, a settlement they established on the swampy northwestern Java coast, a tactic enabling them to isolate Portuguese-held Malacca for the time being.

Bantam as a staging area had a dual advantage: it was closer to the Spice Islands than Malacca, and it guarded the Sunda Strait, the western approach to the Malay Archipelago. But the settlement was also a cursed place and would prove for many to be a fatal posting, for it lay in a fetid, malarial marsh that bred disease and death.

While Queen Elizabeth two years before her death sought to bring about peace between her nation and Spain, four small Dutch ships sought the Spice Islands. Sailing east from Bantam, they tracked the Portuguese route beyond the islands east of Java, with two of the ships reaching Banda in early 1599, while two others reached Sultan Said's kingdom of Ternate later that spring. While business proceeded slowly as the natives appraised the eccentric strangers, both missions in the end were success-ful, with the Banda expedition finally settling for a fifty-percent inflation in purchase price before returning to Holland, satisfied that the number was still 1/350 of their projected profit on the Amsterdam market, and with the Ternate squadron sailing for Holland, their holds loaded to capacity with cloves.

This squadron also sailed with a strange farewell present from Sultan Said, who had every reason to distrust Europeans after the disastrous occupation of his kingdom by the Portuguese. But Said was sufficiently shrewd to realize that he was in a global chess match and that the stakes were indeed high. The gift was a box of earth to be offered to either the queen of England or to Prince Maurits of the Netherlands, the offering a symbol of the sultan's desire to have either as Ternate's "lord." It was in fact a subtle gesture designed to see one European power played off against its rival. The implications of the gesture were not lost on the Hollanders, for they left with the realization that Francis Drake had called here twenty years before and with the mounting suspicion that the English, not the Portuguese, would become Holland's adversary in the unfolding great spice game.

The Portuguese on Tidore, however, were determined to be more than merely idle onlookers. Incensed over Sultan Said's kowtowing to the Hollanders, the command quickly dispatched a letter to Ternate's Gammalamma Castle. "They [the Dutch] seek only to drive the sultans from their realms," wrote the Portuguese commandant from his beleaguered contingent on the neighboring island. "They have neither law nor religion; the son sleeps with the mother; the brother with the sister; and the men themselves commit the most abominable acts with one another."

The letter gave Said grim satisfaction. Solicitous of the Dutch, Said continued his role as a grateful host to the Hollanders' successive fleets, a seemingly naive but actually crafty stance. In light of Portugal's menacing presence in the islands for nearly a century and the havoc they had raised in Said's own sultanate, together with the islanders' own proclivity for intrigue and betrayal, Said saw no harm in currying favor with the Dutch, as presumably his own father had with Sir Francis Drake and his English sailors two decades before.

Said knew that the European presence—whether Portuguese, Spanish, Dutch, or English—was a continuing reality in the Moluccas. If Ternate was now the islands' major entrepôt for spices, it was to his kingdom's advantage to encourage rivalry among the Western powers while remaining aloof from the contending nations. With luck and Allah's will, the Christian unbelievers were certain to checkmate each other.

So it was that the Dutch soon returned to Moluccan waters from Bantam with a fleet of seven ships and fifteen hundred men. Bypassing Ternate, the fleet's admiral settled on Ambon, just south of the large island of Ceram at the nucleus of the Spice Islands, for an invasion. Ambon's strategic importance was clear. With one of the finest natural deepwater harbors in the East, a long, fjordlike inlet that nearly bisected the island and was capable of sheltering entire fleets, Ambon (today the capital of the Moluccas) was easily within striking distance of Ternate and Tidore in the north and the Banda group to the south.

Most important, there was the Portuguese fortress guarding the harbor to consider. Given Ambon's ideal location and natural configuration, if the fortress was taken and either shored up or replaced by another fortification capable of repulsing a siege with modern, more lethal weapons, Ambon would be unassailable.

Upon discovering the castle undermanned with a hundred soldiers, the Dutch easily took it, confiscating brass cannon and storerooms filled with trade goods, spices, and munitions. And so, with the Dutch having seized Ambon and with "factors," or company merchants, already established in Banda, Holland now effectively controlled the Southern Moluccas. There remained only the business of consolidation at the twin volcanoes in the north.

The Dutch factors who had remained in Banda to continue the trade with the islanders gradually saw the complexion of their business begin to change, as trade and territory were becoming synonymous. The factors, mindful of security on an island inhabited by a people they considered head-hunting savages, ordered their factories strengthened to the point where they became as defensible as forts, while the islanders, used to coming and going as they pleased in their own land, were appalled at what they perceived to be the Hollanders' brazen overreaching.

All would have been well for the Dutch but for the discovery of serpents in their Eden. Two English ships commanded by Captain Henry Middleton had shadowed the invading Dutch fleet out of Bantam to the Spice Islands and actually reached Ambon first, in time to buy spices from the Portuguese.

Withdrawing just before the Dutch attack on the Portuguese fortress, the English witnessed from the horizon its fall. For his part, the Dutch admiral grimly realized that the Spice Islands had another suitor (and Holland a new competitor) in the wretched English.

The earlier benign attitude on the part of the Hollanders toward the islanders began to change as well. The Dutch on Banda had from the beginning been irritated by the fluidity of prices set by the natives, with the seemingly whimsical altering of what had been agreed upon running counter to the way Europeans did business. Now the disagreements spread to other matters. To the alarm of the resident factors, the islanders coveted Dutch weapons and resented the Christian contempt for Islam and their lust for island women. But business continued, however uneasily.

As for Sultan Said's precious box of earth, it is not known whether the gift was ever delivered to either Holland's or England's crown, as its donor had intended.

MEANWHILE, on the other side of the world at the headquarters of the Compagnie van Verre in Amsterdam, there was spirited discussion of an approaching dilemma. The company directors cautioned in their assembly that Portuguese-style territorial conquest would only dissipate energies and funds that would best be spent on trade.

The Dutch then should replace Portuguese arrogance with circumspection and courtesy, a stance that was reflected in the manner of the first visits to the Spice Islands. It was inherently difficult to establish confidence and trust in the wake of the deceitful Portuguese; on this point the directors enthusiastically agreed.

But in 1602, the year before the bedraggled contingent from James Lancaster's expedition fetched up on Banda's Pulau Run to hoist a flag over England's first colony, the Compagnie van Verre was supplanted by the notorious Vereenigde Oostindische Compagnie, or United East India Company. The ruling body of this new firm of merchants were called the Heeren XVII, or Lords Seventeen, and disagreements arose as the ablest directors of this elite group began to reason more aggressively.

The most assertive members of the Lords Seventeen were quick to point out that embracing a soft policy in dealings with the natives of the

Spice Islands would prompt a more serious problem. It was a given, they held, that spices were cheap and plentiful throughout the islands. With as many alternative sources of supply as there were local sultanates, there were also different ways and routes of shipping the produce to Europe. History had proven that.

It followed that if the Dutch were to enter the spice game as simply another player, prices would rise in the islands. If left unchecked, the European market would become glutted. Successful trade demanded maintaining a high price in Europe while ensuring a cheap, regulated supply in the Moluccas. Given these circumstances and one important additional one—the threat of the English as potential spoilers—establishing a monopoly was essential.

This end could be achieved only by succeeding where the Portuguese had failed. Strict control over the sources of the supply of spices was vital to the company's, and Holland's, success. As the company evolved to embrace this hard-line approach, the Dutch presence in the Moluccas would alter radically from the benign to the tyrannical over the next few years. The apotheosis was reached by the end of the new century's second decade under the ruthless governor-generalship of Jan Pieterszoon Coen.

AT FIRST the English threat to Holland, which had preceded England's arrival in the Spice Islands by three years, seemed negligible, but it intensified as the early years of the new century wore on. By the time Henry Middleton witnessed the fall of the Portuguese fort on Ambon in early 1606 the contest was clearly joined, while the first half decade of the new century provided a study in mounting tensions.

Five years earlier to the month, in February 1601, James Lancaster's fleet—led by the *Red Dragon,* his six-hundred-ton flagship designed for war as well as cargo—together with three smaller vessels went to sea from Woolwich, England. Saldania, at Table Bay, near the Cape of Good Hope, was their first destination, a six-month voyage. With a daily dose of lemon juice, the flagship's crew fared as well as could be expected, while the other ships, whose crew were not similarly replenished with vitamin C, lost more than a hundred sailors from scurvy.

Saldania was a welcome provisioning and recuperative stop before the fleet pushed around the cape for Madagascar, where still more men weakened and died. In March 1602 the ships hauled out across the Indian Ocean, arriving at Aceh on Sumatra's northwestern tip in early June, sixteen months after sailing down the Thames.

Then as now, Aceh was the Malay Archipelago's "Gateway to Mecca," and the Acehnese were among the most militant Islamic people in the world. Separated from the rest of Sumatra by geography and pride, they had ascribed to themselves a fierce individualism crossed with a thirst for mercantile supremacy and piracy that made them feared as *orang laut* (sea people) throughout the seas of Southeast Asia. "I am the mighty ruler of the Regions below the wind," had written the sultan of Aceh to Queen Elizabeth as early as 1585, "who holds sway over the land of Aceh and over the land of Sumatra and over all the lands tributary to Aceh, which stretch from the sunrise to the sunset."

It was the Acehnese who, in their zeal to control the Straits of Malacca, had for a century been bitter enemies of the Portuguese. And it was an Acehnese fleet whose destruction the Jesuit Francis Xavier had seen in a vision from his pulpit in Malacca, an event that came to pass.

In the spice trade the Acehnese role was not as farmers but merchants. They controlled distribution of Sumatra's monumental pepper crop (which was actually grown by Minangkabau tribesmen far down in Sumatra's interior) and would continue to control it for two centuries. The Acehnese were a force to be reckoned with, and the English knew it.

Ala-uddin Shah did not economize in his role as host, sending "sixe greate ellifants with many trumpets, drums and streamers" to greet the English and bear them to his palace. The queen's letter was wrapped in silk and placed in a golden bowl borne within a resplendent howdah on a separate elephant.

Having duly presented Elizabeth's letter as a prelude to opening trade, Lancaster and his men were feted with sumptuous banquets, drink, and elaborate gamelan presentations, with bejeweled female dancers swaying to the percussive instruments. The trade agreement having been reached, the English were crestfallen to discover that the season's pepper crop had not yet reached Aceh from the south. So Lancaster filled his holds with cargo in the time-honored manner of Eastern waters: piracy. Promising the ruler Ala-uddin Shah a supply of maidens for his harem, Lancaster ordered one craft down the Sumatran coast to the Minangkabau port of Priaman to trade for pepper, while two other ships homed in on stray vessels in Acehnese water, waylaying a Portuguese carrack with an especially rich cargo.

The two fully loaded ships returned to England, arriving in June 1603, while the *Red Dragon* and its smaller escort set out for the Dutch settlement at Bantam on the northwest coast of Java, confident that they had won a lasting patron in the sultan of Aceh.

Except for the occasional thievery of the Javanese, the initial signs at Bantam were positive. A regent acting for the ten-year-old sultan gave the English trading rights and permitted them to establish a factory, England's first in Asia, and post factors on a permanent basis, allowing spices to be gathered for the next English fleet.

Lancaster then dispatched a forty-ton pinnace for the Moluccas, a ship that eventually found its way to nutmeg-growing Pulau Run in the Bandas, the outermost of the tiny group and ten miles west of the Dutch factors on Neira and the adjacent island of Lonthor, a mile to the south across a curve of water.

The storm-whipped pinnace returned to Bantam after two months, but not before the English gained a claim in the Spice Islands and their first colony anywhere on the island of Run, a point noted with consternation by the resident Dutch commander on Neira. This resentment, at first a minor irritation, would fester in time.

After a difficult return voyage in which the *Red Dragon*'s rudder was lost off southern Africa and a makeshift one was made to replace it by its companion's crew, the two ships arrived in England by mid-September 1603. Lancaster with his stores of pepper quickly discovered that the London market was swollen with the condiment, with the Crown selling its overages, perhaps the spoils of a captured galleon, while a resentful company was made to sit on its own. This development caused a near panic among the young company's directors, who were counting on a quick return on their investment in Lancaster's voyage.

Had the directors envisioned a longer-term commitment to their new company the glut on the market would have been less threatening. But a fair share of these gentlemen adventurers were short-term investors in a single expedition who wanted to see an immediate return, while wealthier merchants were eager to reinvest and finance another profit-seeking adventure. The result of these disagreements was that funds for future voyages were slow to materialize. For his part, Lancaster was knighted by his grateful new sovereign James I, who had succeeded the seventy-year-old Elizabeth after her death earlier in the year.

Finally, Henry Middleton, whose brother John had been the second in command of Lancaster's expedition and died of dysentery and malaria in the backwash of Bantam's mud flats and marshes, was given command of the second voyage with the same four ships. This time his orders were more specific, with a priority of reaching the Spice Islands to trade for its produce.

He sailed from England in March 1604, and again the outward-bound expedition nearly came to grief. The crew, including Middleton himself, was scurvy-ridden when it reached Saldania, and more so when the fleet finally made harbor, driven by "diseased cripples," at its destination on Java's northwestern coast just before Christmas 1604. "They had hardlie fiftie soound men in theire foure ships," observed a factor who came aboard.

Bantam had already begun to prove itself untenable as a staging area for the shorter runs east to the Moluccas as well as a repository for spices awaiting the next fleet's return to Europe. Chroniclers noted the thick swarms of mosquitoes hovering in the sullen, windless air and the endemic typhoid, malaria, and cholera. It was no place to linger, for here a well man sickened and died. Later, the Dutch would leave Bantam to the horrendous elements and move their factories fifty miles east to the ancient port of Jacatra, to be renamed Batavia by Governor-General Coen, and still much later to revert to an approximation of its original name, Jakarta, which it remains today as Indonesia's capital.

But for the time being the English remained at Bantam, the only staging area for reaching the Spice Islands. There the atmosphere, already pervaded with disease and death, was poisoned as well by other unfriendly realities. The Dutch, first to establish their factories in the city, had made themselves unpopular with their Javanese hosts through high-handed dealings in trade. Of greater offense was the manner of their randy sailors, who habitually ravished the native women upon arrival in port.

The Javanese responded by staging nighttime raids against the stockades with arcs of flaming arrows and burning torches, and the newly arrived English suddenly discovered to their horror that they, whom the natives had understandably thought to be simply another contingent of Dutch, were subjected to the same sieges. "Oh this worde fire!" wrote an agent with dread. "Had it been spoken in English, Malay, Javan or Chinese, although I had been sound asleep, yet I should have leapt out of my bedde."

A simple parade in England's national colors of red and white to a drumbeat through Bantam's streets, with the banner of St. George waved aloft by a handful of English, had the desired effect of differentiating for the Javanese between the two North European rivals. "Their redde and white scarves and hatbands made such a shew that the inhabitants of these parts had never seen the likes," wrote the head factor. "Ever after that day we were known from the Hollanders."

Bantam presented an uneasy situation at best. Strictly speaking, England had lost the first leg of the contest to Holland, but the Stuart sailors reminded themselves that the race had hardly begun. The two nations glaring at each other across the English Channel were in an uneasy alliance, as England had supported Holland's bid for independence from Spain. But it was a different tune in the Moluccas and would be played so for decades.

The relationship at that time between England and Holland was a complex one, rife with ambiguities. One might begin sorting them out by noting that these nervous allies were an ancient nation competing in trade with an emerging one recently unyoked from foreign rule. The former had a long memory, duly celebrated by a distinguished lineage of poets, including Chaucer and Shakespeare, while the latter, unencumbered by tradition, was creating its destiny anew. Keen to gain favor in the eyes of the world, Holland contracted with East Indies kingdoms to be their protectors in exchange for exclusive trading rights. But such treaties were more often than not got by force, and dissension was severely dealt with. Holland's Far Eastern forts were not to protect the natives but to subdue them.

By the same token, the English company of "gentlemen adventurers" sought "a quiet trafficke" in the East Indies and built only one fortification: on Run, not as protection against the natives but to repulse the Dutch when the stakes grew dangerously high. The occupation of India would be another story; but in the East Indies of Middleton's day, such men, though patriots willing to fight if pushed, were interested only in commerce to profit their company. The Dutch, on the other hand, were intent on building their nation's future and would use force in the Indies to achieve that end. Armed conflict in the Spice Islands would be inevitable.

But for now at Bantam the sailors and merchants of both countries were joined as brothers, however unwillingly, in a fraternity of outcasts and interlopers in a swampy wasteland. Whatever support could be afforded to a sworn enemy of national trade was given by each side—English and Dutch—by tacit, mutual agreement. "Though we were mortal enemies in our trade," noted an English factor, "yet in other matters we were friends and would have lived and died for one another."

Captain Henry Middleton, however, painfully aware that his brother John had met his end from disease in Bantam, turned his gaze eastward, where the company's business lay. Two of his ships, the *Red Dragon* and the *Ascension* (of Lancaster's original voyage), sailed past Java, Bali, and the islands of Nusa Tengarra to enter Moluccan waters, where, after trading for spices in Ambon, the English witnessed from afar the Dutch siege of the Portuguese fortress in February 1606. Aware of the small contingent of his countrymen on Pulau Run, Middleton quickly dispatched the *Ascension,* commanded by Captain Colthurst, south to the Bandas to investigate the Run colony's well-being.

What Colthurst discovered was hardly a colony at all but tiny, lonely factory outposts—huts of bamboo and thatch—on Run and its island neighbor Ai. These two islands were scattered to the west of Neira, Lonthor, and the volcano Gunung Api and so were separated from Banda's nucleus by a deep, ten-mile-wide trench of open sea. Banda's history told of first Asian traders, then Portuguese, and finally Dutch concentrating their trade at the close configuration of islands and settlements hugging the foot of smoldering Gunung Api. They had remained aloof from Run and Ai for good reason.

Though only a few miles divided these outer islands from Neira's harbor, which was protected by the close proximity of Lonthor and the volcano island, the distance might have been a hundred, so fierce was the chop. These conditions worked heavily in the favor of the English. The open seas, strong in any season, made the comfortably removed English virtually immune to attack, especially during the west monsoon, when the two islands were all but inaccessible to vessels from Neira to the east.

For the Dutch, the English were out of sight but hardly out of mind. The locals of Run had received them courteously; and because their new competitors were undermanned and poorly armed, the Hollanders considered them too ill-equipped to wage war or large-scale trade. So in splendid isolation the English gathered stores of nutmeg from islanders eager to barter with no strings attached.

Colthurst's arrival in Banda, however, angered the Dutch command. Though the Dutch East India Company's holdings in the tiny group were scarcely more substantial than those of the English, the Dutch flag had flown there first, and its bearers were proprietary about their claims. By way of enforcing them, the Dutch in 1602 had insisted that island *orang kaya* (chiefs) sign a contract ceding all trading rights to Holland in return for "protection" against the Portuguese and English, an agreement that the Dutch deemed irrevocable.

But the islanders' way in business was circuitous at best, and while the chieftains agreed to the Hollander-proposed contract in principle, it was another matter when tested. Feeling that any reservations expressed would be an offense inviting reprisals, they signed the agreement oblivious to its ramifications.

With the Dutch already in Banda, the presence of the English as a counterforce was altogether welcome to the islanders, as was continued trade with regional merchants a necessity. Asian traders brought rice and sage, as well as Chinese porcelains, metal wares, and medicines. Many of these items were eschewed by the Dutch but were essential for traditional island life, such as Javanese batiks and Indian calicoes, which made clothing more agreeable in the torrid climate than velvets, damasks, and woolens from Holland. Then there were Banda's long-standing domestic and political considerations, which were markedly different from those of the clove-producing sultanates north beyond the equator.

Unlike the more worldly kingdoms of Ternate and Tidore, Banda, while strongly Muslim, was comparatively primitive. The tiny group of islands had neither an acknowledged chief who ruled over the group nor a federation of councils. Each village was a republic of sorts, governed by its *orang kaya,* who mediated long-ingrained customs that predated the arrival of Islam to these remote shores; the occasional island war was of sufficient threat to foster mistrust among the mercurial local chiefs.

How, then, could one local *orang kaya* who was a signatory to the agreement speak for another who was not? For the chiefs, such a contract with Holland was at best an expedient piece of paper. How it bound the islanders within the fluidity of their daily affairs was another question. But the Dutch regarded the agreement as inviolate, and that different interpretation would lead to more misunderstandings and eventually hatch tragic consequences for Banda in the next decade under the rule of Jan Pieterszoon Coen.

After ensuring the well-being of the English skeleton force on Run and Ai, Captain Colthurst with the bravura of his day sailed the *Ascension* into Neira's harbor with the intention of trading with local merchants. There, in a strange turn of events, he accepted an invitation to dine with the Dutch admiral aboard his flagship. In the early evening Colthurst arrived with a chicken pie, which the two men shared over polite, guarded conversation. The Englishman stated his intention, which was to load the hold of his ship and then depart.

Seemingly satisfied, the Dutch admiral voiced another concern, a domestic matter. There was the threat of mutiny at the Dutch fortress at Ambon, requiring his immediate presence there. Colthurst offered support, but the admiral declined such brash English opportunism. He had been sent to the Moluccas with orders to establish trade supremacy, a goal realizable only by the expulsion of the competing Portuguese and English. Now here he was exchanging pleasantries with a potential enemy. When Captain Colthurst departed Banda, he left the Dutch admiral at a loss as to English intentions, beyond those of the handful of merchants eking out a living on Run and Ai.

But the insolent English colonists on those two islands were in fact thriving in trade with wayward native suppliers. They were no longer an annoyance but a constant affront to the Dutch, and their differences couldn't be resolved over a shared chicken pie. Quite simply, something had to be done.

• • •

IN THE MEANTIME, Captain Henry Middleton sailed for Ternate in the *Red Dragon*, hoping to arrive at the twin-island volcano sultanates before the Dutch, who were now consolidating their victory in Ambon after seizing the Portuguese fortress. Middleton realized that he had only one card to play, as it would have been folly to attempt to match the superior forces of the Dutch. His only hope was to seek friendly relations with traders of whichever island, gather whatever cargo he could, and make his departure trailing a modicum of goodwill in his wake.

Fate played a hand in Middleton's designs. Unbeknownst to the English captain, the waters surrounding Ternate and Tidore were a war zone, with the Dutch and Ternate forces allied against those of Portugal and Tidore. As the *Red Dragon* approached the clove-bearing islands, Middleton's crew spotted what he first thought was a state procession of two *kora-kora,* before realizing that one of the paddle-driven canoes was being pursued by another whose armed warriors were smelling blood.

Intervening, the English saved the fleeing craft, taking the survivors aboard his ship only to discover that they included none other than Sultan Said and four Dutch "advisors." All hands professed gratitude for Middleton's intervention, and Said made welcome the English sailors at his court with lavish feasts and a house ashore where they could live and trade.

For his trouble, Middleton was awarded a holdful of cloves, while from a discreet distance he witnessed the drawing of battle lines without taking either side. A waiting game ensued until a Dutch fleet out of the south appeared on the horizon. The fleet's commander, eager to complete the unfinished business with the Portuguese begun on Ambon, began lobbying at Said's court for an invasion of Tidore. Middleton's English already on the scene were not only competitors: The Dutch believed them intent on siding with the Portuguese.

Confronted with the dilemma of two European nations vying for power in his own house, Said exercised his characteristic cordial evasiveness, while the Dutch launched a brutal attack on Tidore, ending when a ship's cannon shot happened to ignite the fortress magazine, razing much of the structure and blowing seventy Portuguese defenders to pieces. The island was quickly overrun, with Middleton given the unenviable role of negotiating the Portuguese surrender, while Said's Ternate natives swarmed through the island in the invasion's aftermath to pick it clean of whatever spoils they could find.

Middleton with his negligible force aboard the *Red Dragon* could only invoke to Said the visit of Sir Francis Drake as an early precedent for conducting trade. The sultan countered that more than twenty years had elapsed since the *Golden Hind* had threaded the channel between Ternate and Tidore. He reminded Middleton that his own father, Sultan Baab, had given Francis Drake a ring for Queen Elizabeth "in commemoration of their alliance," but the queen had not responded.

Baab had therefore written to Holland's Prince Maurits pledging that he would sell Ternate's fruit exclusively to the Dutch, his "friends and liberators" whose guns Said now eagerly awaited. Another item for barter had entered the picture, and the sultan was now less interested in luxury goods than he was in the latest weaponry.

Confident that any number of European nations wanted his cloves, Said had learned the dangers of such maneuvering from trade with the Portuguese. Simply put, the English had come too late. Were he to trade openly with the English, the sultan insisted, his kingdom risked terrible retribution from the Dutch, who except for one merchant and four soldiers as a token force had withdrawn to Ambon to quell the mutinous doings there. Then, giving Middleton bland reassurances, Said noted that the *Red Dragon*'s hold was now filled with cloves and that he was sending a letter to England's monarch James I stating that the English would always be welcome on Ternate.

Middleton, for his part, was anything but mollified by such double talk, especially as he had been ordered away by the Dutch commander before his leave-taking for Ambon. Told that it was Dutch policy to forbid any other nation trade with Holland's island subjects, Middleton sailed the *Red Dragon* for Bantam, there to rejoin the *Ascension* for the return to England by May 1606.

Though on the homeward voyage Middleton had many practical concerns to occupy him, among them the *Hector*, crippled by a depleted crew, he could hardly contain his rage. He wrote: "If this frothy nation [Holland] may have the trade of the Indies to themselves (which is the thing they hope for) their pride and insolence will be intollerable." It became increasingly clear to English sailors, if not yet to company directors, that "a quiet trafficke" was as impossible as it was repugnant. Cast as underdogs, the English were keen to become gleeful spoilers, insofar as they were able.

The Dutch commander's ultimatum to Middleton, however, was only the latest card in a long-standing game. Since Francis Drake's world-ranging privateering mission two decades earlier, the English were perceived by competing nations as a dangerous underdog. Twenty years before, it was the combined Iberian nations who quaked with alarm over the freebooting Drake's piratical activities, which signaled the death of the Portuguese century in the Spice Islands. Now that Holland was acutely aware that the English had entered the spice trade formally as a direct competitor, Dutch intentions grew more hardened and inflexible. When a new force of fourteen heavily armed Indiamen arrived in the East Indies from the Netherlands in 1608, its admiral bore a commission from the Lords Seventeen that put a finer point on Holland's interests.

"We draw your special attention," the order read in part, "to the islands in which grow cloves and nutmeg, and we instruct you to strive after winning them for the company either by treaty or by force." The Dutch were determined to use both, especially the latter, and Banda became the stage on which the drama was acted out.

Chapter 11

"VILE TREACHERY"

THE ARRIVAL IN early April 1609 of the Dutch fleet in Banda signaled the hardening of an attitude on the part of Holland that had been evolving from the beginning: a demanding realization that the rules of the spice trade must change as the game progressed. Expediency rather than principle became key, even as the Dutch in the Moluccas were receiving mixed signals from Amsterdam. The Lords Seventeen of the Dutch East India Company were insisting on a monopoly, whether by treaty or force, by hook or by crook, which the sailors and merchants in the Spice Islands were expected to achieve, but the mandate was an ambivalent one.

While the fleet's admiral had every intention of implementing his marching orders, European intellectuals of the day were seeking to encode a new-world system of ethics. Holland's Hugo Grotius, the jurist, statesman, and theologian, held forth in the defense of freedom on the seas against the Portuguese and Spaniards, and later against the English.

In the widening century, Grotius insisted, the world would be thrown into chaos if commerce were delivered into the hands of belligerent states exercising arbitrary power. It was a revolutionary notion, whose logic demanded that the piracy of a Serrão or Drake or Raleigh, carried out in the name of national interests, was anathema. Put simply, Grotius held that the flag covered the goods. Or so it was in theory.

In practice, however, there were questions. How would such a legalism support itself when tested in a world thrown into disarray by Western expansion into Asia? *Whose* goods and *what* flag? Within a few years the Netherlands had already assumed a mighty position on the vast curve of earth beyond the Indian Ocean and China Sea. How sound was this position in an unstable, tumultuous world with its conflicting interests and shifting forces?

It is important to note that from the beginning, any attempts at trade needed the backing of force, and therein lay the germination of empire building. Just as the commercial enterprises of the Portuguese had led to the founding of a colonial empire, so did the expeditions of the European nations—the Dutch, English, and French—lead to similar though undesired and undesirable ends. Why was such imperialism inevitable?

No small part of the answer to the European's lust for dominion lay in the nature of the native people with whom they were dealing. It was one thing for Holland to sign the Twelve Years' Truce with Spain, for the European mind and sensibility, despite diverse nationalistic and religious differences, could seek and find a common ground. But it was quite another matter for a European nation to seek an alliance with a culture that by Western standards was socially and politically backward.

The innumerable kings, rajahs, and sultans of India, Southeast Asia, and the Malay Archipelago held their authority only too insecurely, threatened from without by rival neighbors and from within by the intrigues of pretenders to the throne. Power existed in no vacuum. It had to be seen to achieve its desired effect; and while it lasted, it was often exercised most arbitrarily and admittedly so. Typical was Java's sultan of Mataram's response to a Dutch envoy's query about his methods of governing: "My people, unlike yours, have nothing which they can call their own, but everything of theirs belongs to me; and if I did not rule them harshly, I would not be king for a day longer."

Difficult to consolidate under the best of domestic circumstances, a sustained native rule was all but impossible in the face of European traders competing with one another in the deadliest rivalry. The clove-producing sultanates of Ternate and Tidore are a textbook case in point.

How could Grotius's thoughts incorporating a harmonious fusion of economic interest and political idealism, noble principles that rang in the ears of all Europe, be applicable half a world away, where the buying of ministers and harbor-masters and princes occurred routinely? What treaty —even that conceived by the great Hugo Grotius, the founder of the science of international law—could withstand the pecuniary temptations over which Portuguese, Dutch, and English traders fired their cannons and crossed their swords?

The meeting of West and East in commerce, each with selfish ends, unleashed a new global force. European capitalism, in fleeing its safe harbor of relatively stable political conditions and societal values that allowed it to flourish in the first place, fanned across Asia's seas to find itself adrift in a topsy-turvy no-man's-land, where the pink dawn of the future was clothed in vestments of the dusky, feudal past.

Under such conditions, trade inevitably had to protect itself, a necessity that was becoming a self-fulfilling prophecy. Jan Pieterszoon Coen, a man who would become a malevolent force in the Spice Islands and ever the choleric pragmatist, put the matter succinctly and in cold light to the Lords Seventeen in 1614: "Your Honors should know by experience that trade in Asia must be driven and maintained under the protection and favor of Your Honors' own weapons, and that the weapons must be paid for by the profits from the trade; so that we cannot carry on trade without war nor war without trade."

Security led to consolidation, which in turn encouraged expansion and finally monopoly, where sea power became the readiest weapon against undesired competition. For the Hollanders—Lords Seventeen and common sailors alike—intent on achieving their unparalleled position in the Indies, Grotius's defense of the freedom of the seas was a bracing, intellectual spectacle for the salons of Amsterdam, London, and the other European capitals. In the lonely, contentious world of the Malay Archipelago (quickly evolving into the Dutch East Indies) its argument, having no place, was conveniently forgotten.

THE FLEET of fourteen heavily armed Indiamen in the spring of 1509 carried a force of a thousand fighting men, mostly Dutch with a handful of Japanese mercenary samurai. Upon his arrival in Banda, the Dutch admiral, whose name was Verhoeven, was ready for anything except for what he saw: the English ship *Hector*, captained by William Keeling. Verhoeven knew the ship well, for it had trailed the Dutch fleet from Java to the Moluccas.

Keeling had preceded Verhoeven in Banda by two months and had hardly been idle. Upon his arrival, he presented a letter from his sovereign, James I, to Neira's *orang kaya* requesting trading rights. He also presented them with gifts of tribute: a gilded beaker, an ornamented helmet, and a fine musket. Welcomed by the Bandanese headmen, Keeling was also befriended by resident Dutch merchants on Neira and Lonthor, lonely and bored in the remote island backwater and eager for civilized company over a glass of good Dutch gin. Verhoeven was not amused by the Englishman's audacity at winning Banda over with fine manners and a single English ship, while his own fleet, fitted for war, seemed absurdly out of place.

Verhoeven quickly countered Keeling's early successes at trade by undermining the Englishman: he paid Neira's aristocracy a gratuity of twelve thousand pieces of eight on behalf of Holland's government by way of persuading the locals to sell exclusively to the Dutch at lower prices than those offered by the English. Keeling withdrew the *Hector* to the outer islands of Ai and Run, where with the ship's thirty musketeers he offered protection to any merchant seeking it.

At this point the early hospitality extended by Dutch traders to the English cooled, and the interlopers were denied the essential rice and fresh water that were unavailable on Ai and Run, which have no natural springs and wells, a condition requiring that the islanders subsist on rainwater. Suspected of fomenting Bandanese hostilities against them, Keeling was ordered by the Dutch to leave at once. As he prepared for departure, a chronicler noted the "most unkindlye" dealings on the part of the Dutch with Keeling, "searching his boate disgracefullye both going for fresh water and retourning, and not suffering him to haue any furthr trade, nor to gather in his debts but wth a pemptory comaund, to be gone, wherunto (through necessitye) he submytting himself, was enforced to dept, wth out his lading, or any furth trade."

Receiving this ultimatum, however, Keeling was not so easily intimidated. The English captain agreed to leave, but not before the *Hector*'s hold was brimming with fifty-six tons of spices. As a parting gesture,

Keeling stationed more men ashore to collect spice stores for the next English ship.

Verhoeven hoped to make much of the *Hector*'s imminent leave-taking. If the English on Ai and Run could not yet be expelled, at least they could be made ineffective in the spice trade: a humiliation, he reasoned, greater than expulsion.

The admiral had another notion as well. With official documents in hand from the Prince of Orange and the Dutch East India Company, he crossed the mile-wide ribbon of extended harbor from Neira to Lonthor with a force of 250 men prepared for war and with great ceremony lavished gifts upon the chieftains. Stressing that he wanted to build a factory on Neira to process more spices, he added that construction of a fortress to ensure the factory's security would also provide the Bandanese protection from their enemies.

The *orang kaya* were suspicious, and their responses were characteristically evasive as they sorted out their options in a world where dreams and spirits had their say. They had not forgotten the prophecy holding that an army of blond knights would attempt to conquer the islands, a prediction that Captain Keeling had striven to associate with the Dutch. Nor could they ignore the voice of Gunung Api, suddenly and ominously erupting, scattering hot ashes upon Neira's thatched dwellings, setting several afire. There were other considerations to be hashed over by the chiefs. Lonthor's elders did not speak for Neira's, and vice versa, so consensus among the island rulers was difficult if not impossible.

On one point, however, the elders did agree. Despite their differences among themselves, the Bandanese far preferred as trading partners the Arabs, Chinese, Bugis from southwest Celebes, and the Javanese, all with whom they had dealt for hundreds of years. Asian merchants understood one another. Junks and other native craft were always to be seen in Banda's ports, and they carried cargo that always met with local favor.

Better, Asian merchants tacitly knew the rules of the game. Bargaining was best done at leisure, for relaxed conditions fostered a marriage of business and pleasure in the best possible sense. It was the way things were done. Recriminations over breaches of faith after the Dutch manner simply had no place in the pursuit of trade nor in the scheme of life.

The English were now a reality, admitted the chieftains in their councils, but what if the Portuguese and Spanish returned? What would it profit Banda, its diversity of leadership notwithstanding, to form an unnatural and exclusive alliance with the Dutch? Unsurprisingly, negotiations stalled, and the headmen for the second time asked for an extension of deadline.

Admiral Verhoeven's patience was becoming sorely tested. There was work to be done to stabilize the clove production in Ternate, but the tedium of negotiations in Banda must first be resolved before his fleet could carry north. With high-handed aloofness, the admiral removed himself as a negotiator and on April 25 ordered a force of 750 soldiers to begin construction of a fort on Neira. It was an inauspicious move, and the *orang kaya* were appalled at this callous breach of diplomacy. The building of a fort in their own islands was a provocation that needed to be answered. In the meantime, they waited, while arguing amongst themselves in council, and ultimately vowed to pay Verhoeven out in coin the admiral knew.

After false starts, the admiral finally settled on a spot facing Lonthor where massive stones from a similar Portuguese effort a century before, Fort Nassau, would be a reliable foundation. A second, far stronger fort would be erected by the Dutch East India Company on the hilltop behind, Neira's highest vantage point. As construction got under way, Dutch soldiers ousted Bandanese from their homes, taking the shelters for themselves, while the natives fled to watch from the wooded hills.

As Verhoeven suspected they would, the headmen made overtures to conduct new negotiations, and a meeting place under a large tree on the eastern side of the island was selected. On May 22 the admiral proceeded with his counselors and an armed guard escort to the site only to find it deserted. The admiral dispatched an interpreter to find the chiefs, who were discovered in a nearby grove. Explaining that they had been frightened off by the approach of the armed contingent, the headmen suggested that the admiral and his advisors join them without the unseemly show of force.

Verhoeven agreed, and in so doing the Dutch invited a betrayal, ignited by what the headmen saw to be a breach of courtesy and faith. The admiral and his party were ambushed; Verhoeven and a senior merchant were killed outright, decapitated, and their heads mounted on battle lances, while twenty-six other Dutch officials were cut down on the spot. Two hostages, whom Verhoeven had turned over to the islanders pending negotiations, were similarly beheaded and their bodies deposited at the water's edge. The action was so fast-paced that the guards, upon hearing shouts of "We are betrayed!" and "To arms!" rushed in too late for intervention. Discovering the carnage of their own, they searched but could not find any sign of the attackers, who had fled.

The lethal surprise attack sent shock waves through the Dutch community in the town and aboard the ships of the fleet. "The vile Bandanese treachery of 1609," as the incident came to be known, was witnessed by a young junior merchant under Verhoeven's command, who narrowly escaped death in the ambush. Jan Pieterszoon Coen, to become governor-general of the Dutch East Indies nine years later, would seek retribution for the slaughter many times over.

In the meantime, the Dutch took stock of their situation, elected a new leader, and, anticipating a major Bandanese offensive, rushed efforts to complete the fortress. Soon emissaries from Lonthor crossed over to Neira, professing innocence in the slaughter and offering to protect the Hollanders against similar uprisings.

Their conditions, however, demanded that the Dutch dismantle their fort and recall soldiers to the ships, leaving only merchants ashore. The Dutch naturally refused, but signals became mixed as two *orang kaya,* believing that terms had been reached, arrived from Lonthor, accompanied by a slave. The chiefs were immediately clapped in irons and imprisoned aboard ship, with the slave dispatched back to Lonthor carrying an ultimatum that all Dutch hostages were to be immediately released.

The chiefs managed to escape their shipboard chains and swim to shore, and the next news to reach the Dutch was that two of their Lonthor merchants had been savagely murdered. A stalemate ensued, during which the Dutch kept to the safety of their ships and Fort Nassau, which was rapidly nearing completion. Then, in early July, Verhoeven's successor sent a series of punitive expeditions sweeping through Lonthor's coastal villages to loot or burn property and boats.

Emboldened by these successes, he tried a more ambitious campaign. Closing on a fortified position on July 26, the Hollanders suffered nine dead and seventy wounded, a humiliating defeat that they blamed on the English on Pulaus Ai and Run for alerting the defenders.

The Dutch admiral, whose men were in a mutinous frame of mind and whose merchants were quarreling, quickly changed his tactics. He ordered a blockade of the coasts to prevent both provisioning and escape, thus prompting certain of the chiefs to sue for peace by early August. By the middle of the month a legal document was completed outlining a plan for peace and trade. Though the document was signed by only a scattering of headmen, to the Dutch mind it applied not only to Neira but the entire Banda archipelago, the first of such dominions in the Indies to be so claimed by Holland.

While the issues of religion, monopoly, and fugitives-at-large were addressed, the Dutch insisted on other checks designed to increase their control. Inspection was required of all incoming craft to Banda. Dutch passes became necessary for traffic among the islands, and no one could settle in Neira without an official permit.

Assuming he had fulfilled Verhoeven's original mandate, the admiral and the majority of his fleet set out for Ternate and Tidore to bring the clove-producing twin sultanates in the north officially into the Dutch sphere, while a strong garrison manned Fort Nassau and merchants filled its storerooms with spices.

With Neira and Lonthor now under Dutch control, the natives of Ai and Run grew more hostile toward the Dutch's claim to monopoly, while the English merchants there thrived, acquiring nutmeg and mace grown on nearby islands within the Dutch claims.

As THIS WAS transpiring, Captain David Middleton, the youngest of the three brothers who would leave their bones in the East, was making a mockery of Dutch pretensions to monopoly by sailing in cavalier style among the islands of Ceram, Ambon, and Banda, several times calling upon the bewildered Dutch command at Fort Nassau, as though he were daring his rivals to stop him.

Middleton's bravura was based on his own precedent. He was an intrepid sea captain who in 1608 had taken just eight months to reach Bantam from England. Avoiding any confrontations with the Dutch, he had traded for spices at Macassar, the port near the tip of the southwestern peninsula of Celebes. This stronghold was controlled by fierce Bugis tribesmen, strongly

Islamic seafarers who developed a fierce hatred for the Dutch. The English East India Company would find use for Macassar, a menacing city with a mingling of races and castes, as an opening in the spice trade, and the company quickly dispatched a factor there.

With his ship, the *Consent*, laden with spices, Middleton had returned to England with sufficient riches to underwrite his voyage ten times over, and by early 1610, under full sail in the *Expedition*, he was closing on the Banda Islands.

In mid-February, Middleton sailed his *Expedition* into Neira's anchorage easily within range of Dutch cannon opposite fiery Gunung Api. Peremptorily, he rejected a Dutch summons to Fort Nassau to present his commission. Meanwhile, Bandanese elders were allowed on board his ship, where Middleton promised them protection should they repudiate the Dutch boycott on trade. Finally, the English captain did go ashore to call on the governor, reading him a paragraph of his commission stating that he was no corsair but a legitimate agent of his crown. Invited in turn for dinner aboard the *Expedition*, the governor held firm, refusing authorization for trade and threatening force if the Englishman insisted on it.

Middleton then sailed the open-sea trench to Pulau Ai, shadowed by three Dutch pinnaces that came about only when the *Expedition*'s cannon were trained on them. Approaching Ai, the English captain ran afoul of adverse winds and changed course to bear down on Ceram to the north, after sending his second in command in a smaller ship, a pinnace, to mobilize trade on the island. When Middleton returned, his mate had acquired sufficient spices to require chartering an additional junk to export the cargo.

By now Middleton, ever the entrepreneur, had hatched a scheme. Shrewdly, he established a safe harbor for the *Expedition* on Ceram and managed to fill her holds by shuttling smaller craft—pinnaces, local junks, even a skiff—loaded with spices on the one-hundred-mile, south-to-north crossing from Ai and Run under the noses of the Dutch. The islanders allied themselves with the Englishman against the implacable Dutch, acquiring spices from the other islands for Middleton, whose unprepossessing native boats in turn slipped through the thin line of Dutch blockade ships and headed for the mother ship north on Ceram, at most a two-day sail.

Middleton's ingenuity was matched by his toughness and courage. Once a typhoon caught his skiff off Ceram, and he was lucky to be washed ashore. Eluding head-hunting cannibals as he tried to make his way to the *Expedition's* safe haven, he swam a crocodile-haunted river only to be swept out to sea. Believing himself lost, he managed to survive by clinging to a coral head, and battering waves nearly claimed him before help arrived. After a rest he declared himself well, "to the amazement of all my company."

Once Middleton's ruse of smuggling contraband spices to Ceram was discovered, the Hollanders in a fury sent a fleet to attack Ai, but the same adverse winds that had prevented Middleton from landing also aborted this mission by scattering the ships. Thus the game continued.

The outer islanders of Ai and Run, as well as other pockets of Bandanese hoping for an alliance against the Dutch, were mystified about one characteristic of the English that had distinguished them from the beginning. Unlike the Dutch, the English never arrived in force but in ones and twos, with the occasional trader and chartered junk. So far, the understated maneuvers of Middleton and others—the stance of the underdog—had worked to their advantage. They insisted on no monopoly or forts, only on the opportunity to compete in trade, and it was an attitude the Bandanese found to their liking.

A lone, fearless ship plying Moluccan waters with the banner flying the Cross of St. George streaming from its masthead, while hardly a threat, was effectively tweaking the nose of the Dutch command in the face of incredible odds. Nor was the defiant posture lost on the Bandanese, who, while admiring the likes of Middleton, found themselves coveting foreign intrigue.

The Dutch, with their large fleets and talk of protectorships and monopolies, were maladroit in their dealings, bringing both themselves and the Bandanese to grief. The dash of the English appealed to the islanders' own sense of finesse in the presence of risk. In this spirit one *orang kaya* sailed as far as Bantam in northwestern Java, a distance of nearly two thousand miles, to ask formally for English provisioning and arms. The request came in the form of an extraordinary letter written in late 1615: "Wee all desire to come to an agrement wth the kinge of England, because (as yett) we have never heard any hurt, that he hath donn to any Nacon," read part of the document.

Therefore wee all desire to come to an agrement wth the kinge of England, because that nowe the Hollanders doe practize by all meanes possible to conquer our Country and destroy our Religion by reason whereof all of vs of the Islande of Banda do vtterly hate the sight of theis Hollanders, sonnes of Whores, because they exceede in lying and villany and desire to overcome all mens Country by Trechery. . . .

That if soe be the kinge of England out of his loue towarde vs will haue a care of our Cuntry and Religion and will help us wth Artillary powder and shott and help us to recover the Castle of Nera, whereby wee may be able to make warr wth the Hollanders, by Gods helpe all the spice, that all our Ilande shall yeald, wee will only sell to the king of England, and to noe other nacon in the world, wherefore if you shall please to accept of what you haue here written, Wee doe all intreat to make agreement wth the king of England, that there be noe discontent betwixt vs even from this tyme forth *for evermore* to the end of the world.

The final condition elicited smiles from the letter's recipients.

We all desire that you doe not seek to overthrowe our religion, and that you doe not comitt offence wth our Weomen, because theis Twoe onely wee are not able to endure, Yf therefore the king of England out of his Loue shall please to assiste vs, wee doe all then earnestly request that you would come vnto vs, wth what convenient speede may be.

The letter, which spread joy through every English heart in Southeast Asia, was carefully considered, prompting a measured directive not to Bandanese elders but to the English merchants dispatched from Bantam to Banda in early 1616, the year of Shakespeare's death:

At your arrival at Pooloroon [Pulau Run] show yourselves courteous and affable, for they are a peevish, perverse, diffident, and perfidious people and apt to take a disgust upon small occasions, and are, being moved, more cumbersome than wasps; their councils are public, their resolutions tedious, and their dispositions quick to change. . . .

As concerning commerce . . . put not your goods in the forts, castles, or houses of the Bandanese, as formerly has been, lest you never see them again, for believe me and you shall find it that they will be more secure in your hands than theirs.

Whatever their true sentiments, the islanders of Run and Ai voluntarily sought England as an overlord in 1616, taking oaths of allegiance and presenting as tribute a potential grove of nutmeg saplings rooted in balls of earth, a gift rich in symbolism. It was an extraordinary gift, for another 150 years would pass before it would become common knowledge in Europe that trees could be transplanted to places other than where they were naturally found. One can only assume that the Bandanese had already mastered the horticultural art of transplanting, so the gift was practical as well as symbolic. Thus did Bandanese machinations ensure that one Western power was pitted against another and the ends played against the middle.

The effect of this diplomatic conundrum upon the Lords Seventeen in Amsterdam can easily be imagined. Quick to heap damnation on the scheming headmen and the upstart gentlemen adventurers of London, the Amsterdam directors ordered nothing short of a conquest of the recalcitrant Bandas, with massive fleets embarking for the Southern Moluccas in a convincing parade of power.

After a series of false starts, the Dutch mounted an offensive and managed to overrun Pulau Ai, slaughtering the islanders who opposed them, while escapees fled their English-planned strongholds and made for the sea on the western side of the island, where dugout canoes lined the beach and small sailboats rode at anchor in the surf. They pushed off in the dark toward an invisible Run, where the English were building a stone fort on a coral head just east of the island overlooking the sea lane from Neira. In the distance Gunung Api glowed like a great smoking god surveying a dark, stormy scene. But strong seas had boiled up with the seasonal squalls, and that night alone four hundred people drowned, followed by as many who had survived.

Hundreds of hostages were taken by the Dutch, among them prominent island aristocrats, as leverage to ensure that the elders sign a contract stipulating new prices in favor of the Hollanders. The islanders had little choice but to comply. Though Bandanese promises to honor the Dutch protectorate by selling exclusively to its factors were readily spoken, the Dutch command soon came to the familiar realization that a true monopoly would never be realized as long as the English were in Moluccan waters. Not only were they in Dutch-claimed seas, but they were ten miles away from the seat of Neira's governor, thriving on Pulau Run, and enjoying the whole affair as a huge joke.

• • •

MIDDLETON'S RETURN to England and his report on the imbroglio in the Spice Islands steeled the English East India Company's directors. Men like Middleton were proving that the high-value trade in cloves, nutmeg, and mace, bringing profits of several hundred percent, was making England abundantly richer. Consequently, the crown began to see the Honourable Company as less of a gamble and responded by giving it an indefinite monopoly on Eastern trade, replacing the original finite charter of fifteen years. Shareholders who were stingy at first began to beam with confidence now that Whitehall's commitment to their enterprise had been won.

There was, however, another vital step to be taken. Recognition of His Majesty's citizens' right to trade on the seas and in the ports of the world was one thing. Having the Dutch acknowledge and respect that right was something else. In London and Amsterdam, as the English government pursued extended negotiations with the Dutch States General on behalf of the Honourable Company's well-being, discussions were civil. The affair became a reasonable matter between reasonable men. But the fruits of these ongoing negotiations were slow to ripen and even slower to reach the other side of the world. The governments of England and Holland were smugly at peace. Not so their East India Companies in the Spice Islands.

With some trepidation modifying his characteristic pride, Middleton had noted that his reliable little fleet plying between Run and Ceram provoked the Dutch to go "starke madde." As a Bantam factor put it, "The Dutch envy is so great towards us that to take out one of our eyes they will lose both theire own." To the Hollanders the English upstarts were "a pernicious, haughty and incompatible nation." The two companies shared an unleashed competitiveness, and it was forging a white-hot mutual hatred leading to war.

Chapter 12

THE TATTERED
CROSS OF
ST. GEORGE

NORTH OF AMSTERDAM on the Zuider Zee lies the small seaport of Hoorn. Today the shallow "South Sea" is enclosed, the harbor serene, and Hoorn has settled into a mellowed antiquity whose quietude and quaintness give it the burnished air of a former age to be savored by summer tourists. But during Amsterdam's golden age this was one of the city's busiest satellite ports, giving its name to the great cape at South America's tip.

Hoorn was equally important for its shipyards. Here one of the most efficient ships ever built—the *fluytschip*—was first laid and launched in 1595. The vessel contrasted sharply with the lumbering Portuguese carrack and Spanish galleon of the sixteenth century, which functioned as both a merchantman and warship. With two or three tiers of cannon and gunners to man them, however, there was relatively little room on these old ships for cargo.

But the fluyt had been designed by traders to fill Holland's merchant fleets. It was a unique ship with unusually great length, six times the width and twice as long as the standard, a clear deck for cargo save for a small deckhouse aft, a nearly flat bottom allowing a large square hold to be more efficiently filled, and shorter masts of pine with smaller sails and sufficient blocks and pulleys for easy handling. There were eighty fluyts at sea by 1603, a number rapidly multiplying, for the fluyt—as Holland's

Indiaman—was to be the final word in bulk transport for the next two centuries.

With a low center of gravity and a weight rarely exceeding 500 tons, the craft was amazingly stable in bad weather and capable of sailing Holland's shallow inland waters as well as navigating around the southern capes of Africa and South America. The Dutch mercantile empire was built by the fluyt, and in its day the ship could be seen in the world's great harbors from Constantinople to Canton.

Near the center of Hoorn, within sight of the defunct wharves, lies the old headquarters of the United East India Company, now a museum. Adjacent to the building is a traffic circle dominated by a taciturn statue of a favorite son of Hoorn, the infamous Jan Pieterszoon Coen, who would become the agent of Banda's terrible destiny, as well as that of the English in the Moluccas.

If any figure can stand for the brutal implementation of Dutch colonial excesses in the East Indies, that person is Coen. The statue of him erected in Hoorn, his birthplace in 1587, casts this colonial figure in a heroic pose. He stands defiantly over the cobblestones, resolute in a posture of swagger with one hand on his hip and a cape draped cavalierly over his sword arm.

Another likeness, a portrait taken from François Valentijn's contemporary encyclopedic, five-volume history *The Old and New East Indies,* provides more clues to the man. This three-quarter rendering of Coen is more formal: a fashionably dressed figure of the day in an embroidered doublet and a full-lace collar, holding in his left hand a scepter of power. But it is the long, oblong face that draws the viewer's attention. Framed by closely cropped hair, a thin goatee, and centered by a prominent nose above a firm but sensual mouth, the subject suggests a contemporary courtier—a Dutch Essex or Raleigh—but for the eyes, which are penetrating, disdainful, judgmental, uncompromising.

The posturing elegance is deceiving, bordering on parody, but there was nothing comic about the rough-cut Coen. The final impression of this portrait is of strength and intelligence without compassion or subtlety, an embodiment from history's melancholy tale of the Spice Islands.

Coen's apprenticeship had prepared him well. As a young man he spent at least a year in Rome in the house of the famous Piscatori merchants.

Here he acquired skills in trade, but it was a calculated education untempered by a warmer, more agreeable and leisurely Mediterranean pace. In 1607 Coen sailed from Amsterdam to the Indies as a second commercial agent, where he remained four years and endured the "vile Banda treachery of 1609," after which his superiors deemed him so capable that he was sent out for a second time in 1612.

His career suddenly spiraled upward, as the Dutch East India Company became his life. (He did not marry until the age of thirty-seven.) The following year, 1613, he was made the director-general of East Indies trade at Bantam; his appointment as governor-general reached him five years later, just four months before Raleigh's execution in London on October 29, 1618.

The players in the spice adventure were developing out of rude Dutch stock into a new breed of vividly drawn personalities. Opportunities were ripe in the East Indies for young men, even those of mean birth. While the directors of the Dutch East India Company were drawn from the ranks of the merchant aristocracy, there was no precedent in colonial Holland for posting the well-born to the higher posts in the Indies, as had been the case with the Spanish and Portuguese. With ability and ambition, a middle-class seaman or trader or administrator could raise himself to the highest ranks.

Coen was such a striking personality, a quality that was not lost on the Honourable Company's Englishmen who crossed his wake. On April 1, 1613, he was confronted in the Moluccas by John Jourdain, the new English factor at Bantam. David Middleton had effectively opened Macassar, on Celebes, for English trade, and Jourdain had served there, amassing spices smuggled out of the Moluccas by local traders as well as his own countrymen. Now assigned to Bantam and emboldened by the exploits of Middleton, Jourdain regarded the Spice Islands with zealous ambition.

"The Hollanders say we go aboute to reape the fruits of their labours," Jourdain wrote. "It is rather the contrarye for that they seem to barre us of our libertie to trade in a free countrye, having manie times traded in these places, and nowe they seeke to defraud us of that we have so long sought for."

Once face-to-face with Coen, he recorded the memorable scene of one-upmanship in his journal:

I was received by their comander and the rest with a fained welcome, which
by their gesture bee easilie discernd; where the camamder in a collericke
manner beganne to accuse me of misbehavinge myselfe in offringe to buye
cloves in the countries that were under their proteccion, as itt were in
dispight of them; which he said was contrarie to comission given by Sir
Henrie Middleton; whereunto I replyed that I wondred much that hee
should bee soe well aacquainted with my comission; but seeinge he knew it
soe well, his long beard (for he had none att all) could not teach me to fol-
lowe my comission; advisinge him to looke well to his owne buysines and
comissions, for if I had done otherwise then my comission I was not to
yeild accompt thereof to him, but to his betters.

The issue about which the Dutch and English were at such cross-
purposes was, of course, trade of spices. Coen was only twenty-six when
this exchange occurred, a point obliquely noted by the forty-year-old
Jourdain when he made a jape of Coen's youth by referring to his nonex-
istent whiskers. The lines were clearly drawn and enemies made at this
standoff of verbal jousting and parrying. In a letter to the Lords Seventeen
dated January 1, 1614, Coen supplied his own version of the encounter
and its implications: "Here the said Jardyn [Jourdain] gave us much trouble, and I had many disputes with him; for he is a clever fellow and left no
means untried which would in any way serve his designs, which were to
establish a factory and start trade. We on our side did everything in our
power to frustrate his endeavours, for it would have been all up with us
had he succeeded."

Coen later in the same letter described the results of a meeting with several island *orang kaya,* who pledged to have no further dealings with the
English: "that any individual trading with that nation should be punished
with death, and that, should the community offend again in like manner,
we should be at liberty to destroy their town and build a fort there."

Coen continues, "Having carefully considered the proceedings of the
aforesaid Jardyn, we came to the conclusion that we were justified in
regarding his attitude as hostile and in taking forcible measures to prevent
any further action on his part. We therefore sent him a summons in writing to desist from his unreasonable proceedings or he would be compelled
to do so by force."

But Jourdain, who had sought adventure and riches for the company in the Indies partly to escape a failed business and an unhappy marriage in his native Dorset port of Lyme Regis, was not easily cowed. If anything, his efforts to undermine the Dutch in trade intensified. Time and again he reports hostile, often lethal encounters with the Hollanders, while confiding to his journal his intentions of beating the enemy at their own game, "in seekinge by subtiltye to hold us underhand with faire words to beate the bush, while they would cinninglie carrye awaie the birde, if they were not prevented . . . from . . . defameing us secreetly and abusinge us openlye in viewe of the world."

Jourdain was only too happy to turn the tables on the Dutch, and for a while he was successful. His tenure at Bantam, however, was checkered with difficulties. Malaria and dysentery hovered over the port, and there were now three separate and competitive factories to accommodate the numerous ships plying the harbor's foul waters. "Pickers, thievers and fire raisers" were creating havoc among the legitimate businesses, while their merchants were laid low by fever.

Tempers flared easily, provoking the drawing of steels, and Jourdain made the sober observation of "our people dangerously disordering themselves with drinke and whores ashoare." The upshot was that Jourdain was so distracted by the travails of his own people, with the Dutch presence a threatening reminder of an alien menace, that voyages to Ai and Run were haphazardly scheduled, if at all.

Meanwhile, English resident merchants, factors, had remained on these tiny Banda islands for at least six years, and except for the occasional trader they might have been all but forgotten were it not for John Jourdain, who saw the English presence in the nutmeg gardens as legitimate in the eyes of international law, as defined by the great Dutch legal scholar Hugo Grotius. The English, not the Dutch, had settled these two islands—Ai and Run—first, and it was arrogant of Holland to claim them by virtue of their proximity to Neira and Lonthor. It was a question not only of trade, but of crown and its prerogatives.

In early 1615 Jourdain dispatched two captains in a merchant ship and pinnace to reconnoiter the Moluccas with a notion of fomenting insurrection against the Dutch. Before, the underdog English had managed to survive by their wits. Now their missions were purposely more provocative, with more ships to come.

Then in late 1616 Jourdain sent Captain Nathaniel Courthope, an old Borneo hand for the company, from Bantam. Courthope entered Banda's waters with the four-hundred-ton *Swan* and the three-hundred-ton *Defense*. His mandate was simple: the Dutch were to be outwitted or outfought or both, and the Cross of St. George was to be flown anywhere in the archipelago it could be raised, most especially where it had already been flown—on the island of Run.

Courthope, acting quickly, ordered the original trading posts on both Ai and Run to be shored up, and on the narrow spit of exposed coral rock pointing toward the Dutch island holdings his men completed construction of the low-lying stone fort begun earlier. Taken with the natural defenses afforded by wind, surf, reef, and strong seas, and commanding the sea-lane from the Dutch-held Neira and Lonthor, the fortress, with twenty-five brass cannon manned by fifty gunners, made Run easily defensible.

Predictably, the Hollanders were incensed over these new affronts. The Dutch governor of Banda formally protested in writing to the English, who rejoined with a catechism about freedom of the seas and trade, as advocated by Holland's own Hugo Grotius. Ambon responded to a plea of help with a single ship, the unseaworthy *Morgenster* with an inexperienced crew, which moved on Ai and Run only to be defeated by strong winds and the sight of British cannon guarding the treacherous reefs.

Meanwhile, the English holding out were getting perilously low on supplies. Whether Courthope authorized a foraging party remains unclear, but the *Swan*'s master took his vessel off in search of water, setting his sails north for Ceram, thus hoping to avoid the Dutch defenses around Neira and Lonthor. The ship was immediately waylaid by the decrepit *Morgenster*, hovering in Banda waters. Hostilities might have been avoided, but for poor judgment on the part of the English skipper, who fired his cannons at the large Dutch ship bearing down on them.

It was no match. The Dutch retaliated, killing five men while taking the ship and chaining the others in the hold to use as bargaining chips in their negotiations to oust the English from Run. Then the English suffered a second loss. The *Defense*'s anchor cable was mysteriously severed, and the ship drifted to Pulau Lonthor, where it was apprehended and its crew seized. But the wretched treatment of the sailors failed to move Captain

Courthope, who stood on principle. In desperation, he sent a prahu to Bantam urgently begging for reinforcements. But there was no answer.

Months passed while the Dutch harassed Run with cannon barrages almost daily. Finally, in mid-March 1618, the islands suffered a major earthquake, provoking a devastating eruption of Gunung Api, which rained its fiery fury upon Neira across the harbor. The natural catastrophe seemed a signal to the hapless English. Two weeks later three tall sails were spied making for Run before a west wind. The men lined the beaches and rocks, and a cheer went up. The ships were English.

But the celebration was short-lived. It was near the end of the west monsoon, and the wind suddenly shifted, giving the advantage to four Dutch vessels out of Neira that closed on the heavily loaded English ships riding low in the water. With superior cannon, the Hollanders easily over-came the small fleet and, their sterns decorated with English colors, sailed the captured vessels to Neira.

By this point in the struggle between England and Holland for the "spiceries," the stakes had been raised in the Bandas to a level where chivalry had no place. Incarcerated in Neira's fort, the prisoners were held in a dungeon with iron crossbars at the top, which allowed the Dutch at their pleasure to urinate and defecate on the unfortunate inmates to the point where their bodies were covered with sores. The English sailors managed to subsist, barely, on "durtie rice and stinking raine water," while they willed themselves to live on the thin hope that deliverance might be imminent.

Meanwhile Courthope waited on Run, placing the blame for the failed rescue on the chaotic situation in Bantam. He was convinced that had the fleet with reinforcements sailed sooner—perhaps even a single day ear-lier—the west winds would have prevailed in their favor, and Run would have been saved. John Jourdain, however, had sailed for England, leaving Bantam in a state of quarrelsome indecision. Eighteen months passed—time for Jourdain to have visited England and return for a second term as head factor—and still no word from Bantam reached Run. Nathaniel Courthope continued to wait, while he told himself and his men that sur-render to the Dutch was out of the question. It was hope against hope.

• • •

As the year 1618 wore on, it became a momentous time for the spice trade, marking the ascendancy of Coen to the governor-generalship of the East Indies and the implementation of his iron rule in the Spice Islands. But it was also a year that portended a grim fate for some heroic Englishmen, high and low, who had raised England's stakes in the spice game. In the East Indies the fates were weaving for Jourdain and Courthope a skein of darkness and misfortune, while in England they witnessed the tragic, heroic end of one of the great Elizabethan players who had the misfortune of outliving his queen: the dashing and splendid (to Elizabeth) but wily and dangerous (to her successor) Sir Walter Raleigh.

The early years of the seventeenth century were heady but a turbulent time politically as the crown passed on Elizabeth's death in 1603 to James of Scotland, known as "King of England, Scotland, Ireland, France, Puloway [Pulau Ai], and Puloroon [Pulau Run]." Despite the inevitable upheavals in a maniacal time, these years were remarkable for their richness, multiplicity, and peculiarity of accomplishment. James I, the first Stuart monarch, witnessed both the famous translation of the Bible by a parliament of bishops in 1611 and John Donne's ascendancy to the deanship of St. Paul's in 1621.

But the court of James I had its ignoble moments as well. James lobbied furiously and blunderingly for Raleigh's execution in 1618 after the latter's years of imprisonment in the Tower of London on largely trumped-up charges of high treason. Here the seaman-soldier-courtier, whose strategy in 1592 had reaped for England the spoils of the spice-laden *Madre de Dios,* was writing his *History of the World.* His musings were scholarly but immediate, speaking to life's ephemera. "For there is no man so assured of his honor, of his riches, health or life, but that he may be deprived of either or all at the very next hour or day to come," he wrote in the preface. His words define more than the vicissitudes of his own personal fortune and fame: They circumscribe the winner-take-all bent of a drunken age flooded with avarice and determination.

Nowhere is the political turmoil of the day better illustrated than in the fate of Raleigh. A onetime favorite of Elizabeth, knighted by the queen in 1584, this soldier, sailor, and poet-scholar was a veteran of the Continental wars of religion, campaigns in a rebellious Ireland, and privateering expeditions against the Spanish of the sort that won his countrymen the spicy loot of the *Madre de Dios*. With his boundless energy continuing to assert itself in politics and exploration, Raleigh was instrumental in sending voyages of exploration and colonization to Virginia and in 1595 led a mission to South America in search of gold, while remaining active in the intellectual and literary life of London.

But Raleigh's intransigent hostility toward Spain earned him the enmity of James I, who, eager for a Spanish match to ensure peace between the two antagonistic nations, had Raleigh committed to the Tower of London shortly after his accession to the throne in 1603. Paradoxically, the long uncertain years of Raleigh's Tower confinement witnessed an intimacy that existed under James's very nose. A mutual admiration existed between the Tower's "guest" and James's son Prince Henry, in whom Raleigh saw the promise of a great king. For his part, Henry had begged his father "not to keep such a bird in a cage." But Henry, Raleigh's patron, died in 1612 at the age of eighteen, leaving the knight, who once rivaled Essex in the eyes of Elizabeth, vulnerable on James's watch.

In the Tower of London Raleigh remained under sentence of death for thirteen years, until he was released by his fiscally strapped monarch to undertake one more voyage of exploration in search of El Dorado, a gold mine he claimed to have discovered in Guiana twenty years before. "It is in the present time that all the wits of the world are exercised," he noted in his *History*. Raleigh sailed again to Guiana (now Venezuela), ventured up the Orinoco River, and in a battle with the Spanish, witnessed the death of his eldest son, Wat. His chief lieutenant, Keymis, committed suicide on this dangerous mission.

The skirmish also sealed the fate of the father. On Raleigh's return to England (he had remained a dead man under the law, subject to his king's pardon), James, still eager for a Spanish queen to cement relations between the two contentious countries, yielded to the demands of Spain's ambassador, Gondomar. A commission of inquiry set up under Spanish pressure determined that the gold mine was a fabrication, and the old charge of high treason was reestablished.

When on the bracing morning of October 29, 1618, Raleigh emerged from the gatehouse adjacent to the scaffold, he was immaculately turned out in a fine satin doublet, black taffeta breeches, a black embroidered waistcoat, ash-colored silk stockings, a ruff band, and a finely worked black velvet cloak covering his person—courtier's raiments. Offered a bowl of strong wine, most likely ipocras flavored heavily with spices, he drank deeply of it. Asked if he liked the mixture, he responded, "I will answer you as did the fellow who drank of St. Giles's bowl as he went to Tyburn: 'It is a good drink, if a man might but tarry by it.'" It was a day given to such epigrams.

"For I have been a soldier, a courtier, and a seafaring man," he summed himself up from the scaffold for the gathered crowd. "And the temptations of the least of these are able to overthrow a good mind and a good man."

Then to the point. "I say here that never in my life did I harbor any evil or disloyal thought against the King. Not in my most secret heart. . . . If I speak falsely, let the Lord blot out my name from the book of life. . . . So I take my leave of you all, making my peace with God. I have a long journey to take and must bid the company farewell."

Offering his forgiveness and purse to the headsman, he asked to see the axe and felt the well-honed blade. "This is sharp medicine," he said with a smile before resting his head on the curved block, "but it is a sure cure for all diseases." Thus Raleigh embraced a memorably dramaturgical death in the spirit of an expansive, theatrical age—a gesture that would have brought a nod of approval from his late queen.

THE YEAR 1618 also witnessed Coen's ascendancy at age thirty to the enviable position of governor-general of the Dutch East Indies. Austerity and acumen for business came naturally to his nature, and one cannot read his dispatches to the Lords Seventeen without realizing his extraordinary tenacity. Coen knew what he wanted. His interests were those of the Dutch East India Company and Holland, and he was not above chiding his superiors for the laxity of mind and faintness of heart that frustrated his own efforts to achieve them.

Of the initial task that had been set before his countrymen in the Indies—preventing the English from trading in the Moluccas, while using no force against them—Coen wrote of the impossibility of such folly: "If some daring thieves should night and day break into Your Lordships' houses, what measures would Your Lordships take to meet such fellows and defend your property, if not by using force against them? This is

what the English do commit against Your Lordships' estate in the Moluccas, Amboina and Banda. Wherefore we are surprised that it is ordered
not to use force against them. If the English have this privilege above
nature and all creation, then it is right good to be an Englishman, and
true indeed the slander and the calumny which they spread among all
princes against the Dutch." The directors, while chagrined at being
rapped over the knuckles by one so junior, knew that they had their man
in Coen. By the time of his appointment in 1618, the situation in the
Indies had become most critical.

One of Coen's first moves in the shadowy game between the English
and Dutch was to shift the center of the Dutch East India Company
activities fifty miles east from sickly, troublesome Bantam to the small
port of Jacatra. Here the governor ordered a fortified castle built under the
nose of the ruling Javanese prince, who, like the Bantamese sultanate, was
already resentful of the growing power of the Hollanders. Coen ignored
the *pangerang's* protests and pushed ahead with the fort and other fortifications to protect Jacatra from siege.

Meanwhile, John Jourdain's trailing English, hoping to profit by a
schism between the Dutch and Javanese, matched Coen with bravura if
not in manpower by building and manning a fort on the opposite side of
the river.

Jourdain's reassignment to the Indies at least brought him the hope
that he finally had the means to sail against the Dutch. Realizing that the
English had more ships in the Java Sea than the enemy, he decided to act.
Just before Christmas, the English captured the *Zwaart Leeuw,* its holds
filled with spices.

This provocation, together with the hostile attitude of the natives,
infuriated Coen. He wrote to the Lords Seventeen, hinting of Holland's
impending successes in the spice race while stating his own resolve:
"Despair not, fear not your enemies, there is nothing in the world can
hinder or cast us down, for God is with us. And hold the former defeats
in no consequence, for there are great things to be wrought in the Indies
and every year there can be dispatched rich returns."

Scarcely had the ink of the letter dried when Sir Thomas Dale's fleet of
fifteen ships, an unusual massing of forces for the English, threatened
Bantam and then Jacatra. Coen had only seven ships. Not wanting "to

hazard the whole state of the company," he shrewdly withdrew east to Ambon, base of the main Dutch fleet, to garner support to retake if necessary his beleaguered castle from the newly allied English and Javanese, who were bound now by fortune.

Nathaniel Courthope on Pulau Run had counted on John Jourdain, convinced that Jourdain would never desert him. Courthope, however, had not reckoned on Sir Thomas Dale. Jourdain and Dale fell to arguing over priorities and strategies, and the entire English operation was at cross-purposes. Instead of sailing to Banda to resupply Courthope's harassed forces on Run or to force another confrontation with Coen by surprising him at Ambon before he could refit his ships, Dale patrolled the waters off Jacatra to little end.

With a shaky, ill-conceived, and poorly coordinated alliance at best, the combined siege by the English and Javanese was lackluster and feeble, dragging on for week after week, then month after month. The attackers bickered and were divided among themselves against an undermanned objective that should have been easily taken. It was a crucial tactical blunder, as valuable time wore on in the Hollanders' favor.

Dale sailed for India before Coen's strengthened fleet returned. It was Courthope's fate after three years on Pulau Run to learn of the fleet's withdrawal, and he learned of it from a regional trader. Courthope could hardly believe his ears. Pulau Run was left high and dry.

A year and a half passed, and the castle at Jacatra still flew a Dutch flag when Coen returned with his force of sixteen vessels. Most of the English fleet had fled, and the Javanese were easily routed. Revenge became the order of the day. Coen torched both the English fort and the Javanese palace by way of punishing the conspiring natives into submission.

Then, at sea on July 17, 1619, he surprised two English ships, and a furious battle ensued, with the English getting the worst of it. Under a flag of truce the English commander, on Coen's orders, was dropped by a Dutch sniper's bullet. The murdered man was John Jourdain, and Coen personally rewarded the marksman with fourteen hundred guilders in a chain of gold and with the words "You have now, Hendricke Janson, given me good satisfaction, in that Captain Jordayne is dead." Though it was one of the savage acts that the governor-general's name carried until the end, Coen was jubilant in writing to the Lords Seventeen: "In this wise have we driven those of Bantam out of Jacatra and become lords of the land of Java. It is certain that this victory and the flight of the proud English will spread great terror throughout all the Indies. Hereby will the honour and repute of the Dutch nation be much increased. . . . The foundation of the long-wished-for *rendezvous* is now laid."

After this victory the town and castle of Jacatra took the name Batavia, as specified by the directors, honoring the Netherlands nation as a whole. Coen next moved his fleet to blockade Bantam's harbor, about which the scattered English ships could do nothing. He had effectively laid the foundations not only for the "*rendezvous,*" but for strategic and economic dominance of the entire Malay Archipelago.

The English forces were too meager and scattered to stand up to the Dutch navy for long, and in the western part of the Malay Archipelago—the Sunda Straits and the pepper ports of Sumatra—losses were especially heavy. When finally the English fleet returned from India in March 1620, news from Europe greeted it that the Anglo-Dutch truce had at last been realized, in fact signed days before Jourdain was killed, and that both nations and companies were now allies. It was a sobering announcement in the Spice Islands, and by this point the losses on both side were so irrevocable that neither wanted to hear the inconsequential when the word did finally arrive. The news, however, did not reach Coen and the Dutch until later.

NEGOTIATIONS IN EUROPE to reach this truce had been ongoing for years, while rivalry and strife raged in the Indies. Hugo Grotius, the exponent of freedom of the seas, had been dispatched to London to argue the Dutch claim that although the Hollanders had come to the Spice Islands initially as peaceful traders, they had been required to forfeit blood and money to dispute Portugal's claim that excluded all other nations, and as a result, Holland was forced to keep warships and fortifications in the Moluccas. The logic followed that the Netherlands could not allow third parties—to wit, the English—to profit at no cost to themselves from a situation that Holland alone had engendered.

Having been dealt a weak hand, James I was amazingly resolute in his defiance of Grotius's argument. The English king protested vehemently to the Dutch envoys in London over Coen's acts of war and addressed a letter to the Hague. "Your men have robbed my people of their possessions, you have made war on them, you have killed and tortured several of them," he wrote. "You never considered the benefits you have received from the Crown of England who made and maintained you as an independent nation. You have a man in the Indies [Coen] who deserves to be hanged. Your people present your Prince of Orange as a great king in the Indies while they picture me as a small ruler and the Prince's vassal. You are masters of the sea wide and large and can do what you want."

The upshot was that with Holland's having already won victory in the Indies, the Dutch States General, eager to continue cordial ties with England, allowed themselves to be badgered into acceptance of a union of rival companies.

As THE SECOND decade of the seventeenth century came to a close, the Englishmen of Pulau Run were far too distant from the civilized corridors of power in Amsterdam and London to appreciate a truce that had little if any meaning in the Moluccas. Ironically, concord in Europe had fueled enmity in the Spice Islands.

The contestants now were not national navies but antagonistic traders of nations committed to mercantile success, and the clubby alliance between Amsterdam and London had ensured an uneven field for unequal players. The Lords Seventeen had prevailed over their Honourable Company counterparts—with government support for the Dutch East India Company, but none for the Honourable Company on Pulau Run—and no one would be more aware of this vacuum of power than Coen.

For Courthope, three and a half years had passed since he had first taken his heroic stance, and still he sent messages to Bantam pleading for relief so that he could discharge his obligations to the natives of Run. No news of the peace now eighteen months old had reached him, and Courthope would wait for such news in vain.

For motives unclear, Courthope in mid-October 1620 made a clandestine voyage by prahu along the ten-mile sea-lane to Pulau Lonthor, and on his return two Dutch vessels overtook his small boat with twenty-one men aboard. The English fought back. For their steel-spined captain surrender was no option. Courthope took a bullet in the chest, rolled overboard, and somehow marshaled the strength to begin swimming. "What became of him, I know not," recorded his second in command. But the Dutch managed to recover his body and give their enemy a decent state burial "only fitting for such a man."

Though hardly a Lawrence of his day, Courthope's defiant but failed defense of Pulau Run was classically heroic but remained obscure. When two months later news of the "new" treaty finally did reach Banda, it came as a tremendous blow to English and Run islanders alike, with the latter seeing it as a betrayal by the English king to whom they had so eloquently pleaded by letter.

The treaty, ironically, appeared to give England what it had worked for. Having been included in a share of the spice trade, they quickly posted factories throughout the Moluccas and removed their Eastern headquarters from Bantam to Batavia. But there was a rub, and it was a big one. The "Treaty of Defense" required both parties to contribute to the defense of the Indies, a clause the London directors thought suspicious, though it was lauded by the Dutch. As a practical matter, with their numerically superior ships, men, and money, the Hollanders had the grim pleasure of seeing their former enemies bound to policies over which they had no control. For the English the treaty was a ticket to misery.

Meanwhile, a young governor-general's dream was crystallizing: to realize a Dutch colonial empire spreading across the long fold of seas and earth from India to Japan, and to achieve it through any measures necessary, however harsh. From the beginning Coen embodied the aggressive, darker policies of the Dutch East India Company, policies that had been feverishly debated among the Lords Seventeen of Amsterdam. Coen's faction had won, and now he could proceed with a murderous mandate brought from the other side of the world. Foremost in the new governor's grandiose scheme of things was his intention to subdue Banda by whatever means it took.

Essentially, Coen's strategy was to seize the tiny Banda group with a superior military force and make the islands over in his own vision. If the natives were capricious and untrustworthy, a truth Coen himself had borne witness to in 1609 when his fellows were cut down before his eyes, then they must be either destroyed or transported in favor of new replacements. His scheme allowed the import of slaves with Dutch overseers to ensure the production of nutmeg and mace.

The plan was neither new nor original. Other company officials had tried to implement a similar policy, but they were neither as determined nor as ruthless as Coen, who sought to bring the matter with the English as well as with the Bandanese to a head. Coen became a law unto himself, as when he ordered the killing of John Jourdain under a flag of truce.

But before these plans could be implemented, Coen was in for the same shock that had stunned Nathaniel Courthope on Pulau Run. When a Dutch merchant traveling on an English ship arrived in Batavia on March 20, 1620, with news of the pact signed by both nations the previous July, Coen's determination to oust the English from Pulau Run became an obsession crossed with fury. The treaty, in which the English company was to supply one third of the force and expense to maintain a shared spice monopoly and the Dutch two thirds, with a similar sharing of profits, was to Coen sheer madness. It was a cockeyed arrangement, and Coen felt betrayed by his superiors.

The question haunted and taunted him: why should Holland share with England what the Dutch had already won? The treaty bore the noisome odor of hypocrisy and soft-mindedness, and in his mind it had been spawned by an assembly of fops and coxcombs—by featherbedding, posturing politicians with little experience of how hard the game was fought in the Indies and how matters were settled there. Better an English enemy, it became Coen's burning conviction, than an English ally. He resolved to drive a stake through the heart of the English. In a tone of biting sarcasm he wrote to the Lords Seventeen, chiding the company directors for having acquiesced to a destructive political expediency: "If the English laugh for gratitude your labour has not been in vain. Their great thanks are due to Your Lordships, for they had properly let themselves be thrown out of the Indies, and Your Lordships have set them back in the midst thereof. . . . Wherefore the English have been granted a third of the cloves, nutmeg and mace, we cannot well understand. They had no claim to a single grain of sand on the coast of the Moluccas, Amboyna or Banda."

Coen would not allow his hands to be bound by such a treaty. An ally in name only, the English in the Indies were now little more than supplicants in a land where the Dutch were masters, and Coen wasted no time in exploiting their predicament. Acutely aware of the English paucity of resources and ships, he proposed on New Year's Day 1621 a joint Anglo-Dutch expedition to subdue the Bandas.

Unable to contribute to this ambitious campaign in any meaningful capacity, the English were reduced to the role of humiliated bystanders, with a few resident agents in Batavia, a toehold and factory on Ai and Run, and a handful of malcontent native sympathizers on Lonthor who wanted to escape the Dutch monopoly and proclaimed the king of England their sovereign.

Coen pressed ahead with his invasion. The English managed to man and equip three vessels, little more than a face-saving presence in the eyes of the truce, but practically to shadow the large Dutch fleet as it prepared to descend upon Banda and their own meager colonies on Ai and Run. By the terms of the treaty, Run still belonged to them, with or without the benediction of the company and the English navy. At this point, the English may well have asked themselves what they stood to lose.

Their ships proceeded via Macassar and Ambon, maintaining a distance from the Dutch fleet, a necessary aloofness at this stage of the adventurous game in which the English might yet play a card or two. Through their network of factors and traders throughout the Moluccas, they could advise the Banda natives of Coen's plans, thus preparing the islanders to resist. As important, the English could disassociate themselves from Coen's Banda campaign and the horrors they imagined that would follow.

Whatever else Coen was, he was no fool. He knew what the meddlesome English were up to. As his fleet shoved southward from Ambon, he seethed with rage that a piddling force flying the banner of St. George was sailing in the wake of what he believed was about to be the greatest conquest ever in this part of the world. But he would deal with the English later. There were other matters at hand now that Gunung Api's perfect green, smoking cone materialized on the southern horizon with a scented landfall carried on the breeze.

Chapter 13

"THUS WAS POOLORUN LOST . . ."

ON FEBRUARY 21, 1621, Coen arrived at Fort Nassau on Neira and immediately began to augment the fighting force he had sailed with from Batavia. Within ten days he had gathered a squadron of thirteen large ships, several smaller reconnaissance craft, and nearly forty junks and barges. His army consisted of over 1,600 Europeans, plus the 250 men of the Banda garrison.

Rounding out Coen's invasion force were nearly three hundred Javanese convicts taken when Batavia fell, a hundred Japanese mercenaries and swordsmen-executioners, and several freed slaves and *burghers* who were the townspeople of Neira. It was the most formidable expedition of any kind to ever converge on the tiny Banda group.

In an unlikely nod at protocol, Coen sent his messenger craft with an invitation for the score of Englishmen on Run and Ai to serve with him, but both sides knew the gesture to be empty. It gave Coen grim satisfaction to learn from his intelligence sources that the ever-watchful English gunners were training island natives in defense tactics. He bided his time until March 4, when he sent his yacht with an escort of junks to reconnoiter the coastline of adjacent Lonthor.

This tiny fleet began to circumnavigate the island cautiously at first, then crept closer to the surrounding reef for a better look at the large island's defenses. Now within cannon range, the patrolling boats were suddenly hit with a storm of native gunfire from redoubts hidden on the forested slopes. The boats quickly beat back to open sea, but two crew members were dead and ten wounded. After completing his two-day mission, the yacht's commander reported to Coen that not only had he discovered at least a dozen fortified positions concentrated along the southern coast and in the wooded hills, but he had also sighted an English gunner directing cannon fire.

The following day, March 7, Coen sailed his entire fleet around Lonthor to search out a potential beachhead, but none was readily apparent. The next day he ordered a small probing party to land, but it was immediately repulsed, resulting in one dead and four wounded.

The governor-general pondered. The morale of his officers was poor. It was not going to be easy, but once finished, the job had to remain done. Coen summoned his staff and exhorted them to rise to the task at hand. A glorious destiny was within Holland's grasp, but to realize it they must proceed with faith and courage. "There is nothing in the world," he wrote to the Lords Seventeen, "that gives a better right than power and force added to right." He set March 11 as the date for his decisive invasion.

Coen's strategy was to divide his forces into several assault groups. Early on that morning his troops reached Lonthor's beaches at a half dozen widely scattered points, immediately creating havoc and confusion among the defenders as the invaders converged upon the key strongholds. Within the day the Dutch had secured the lowlands on the north side of the island as well as the rocky promontories to the south.

A spine of precipitous highlands rises abruptly from sea level to bisect the island. When the islanders were driven back from their posts near the shore, they fled to high fortified positions with the Dutch in hot pursuit along the narrow, treacherous trails that traversed the face of sheer cliffs several hundred feet high.

The Banda natives were furious defenders. Many, choosing death rather than surrender, leaped to where the surf pounded the rocky shoreline below. Others, sensing imminent defeat, offered their services to the invaders for money. By the end of the day the Dutch were in control of most of the island, and by March 12 they had all of Lonthor at a cost of six dead and twenty-seven wounded.

As Coen fully expected, Lonthor's *orang kaya* began immediately to seek peace talks, offering as tribute a golden chain and a copper kettle. Coen accepted the gifts, while acknowledging to himself that the real treasure he was after was Banda's golden fruit. The bargain he drove was by now the traditional one. He demanded that the natives destroy all their fortifications and surrender all weapons, as well as hand over the chieftains' sons to be held aboard ship as hostages against further provocations.

It was no surprise that the headmen agreed to these terms, which, as Coen knew, they would violate. But the agreement was now codified into a document in which the Banda leaders were promised protection for their people, freedom from molestation, autonomy in their local affairs, and respect for their Islamic faith. For their part, the elders promised to tithe an agreed-upon portion of their annual harvest to the Dutch and to sell the remainder of their crop to the Dutch East India Company at a set price.

For most of the islanders, however, the agreement was only between the chiefs and the hated Dutch. The weapons handed over were only the rusted, malfunctioning ones, while the rest were hidden in shallow graves where they could be easily recovered. Urged to harvest and process the nutmeg crop, which was beginning to rot on the trees, the natives remained in the forested hills, choosing the privations of cold, rain, and potential starvation over acquiescence to the invaders.

No sooner had the meticulously refined agreement been signed than Coen ordered construction of Fort Hollandia, a massive castle atop Lonthor's central ridge and a rigorous climb from the beach by heavy stone steps. The Bandanese response was to band themselves into groups of guerrilla fighters and attack a work party constructing the fort, resulting in nine Dutch dead and twenty-five maimed, more casualties than were suffered by the invading force.

For once, Coen was at a loss as to what to do. His original scheme—to level villages, deport the inhabitants, and replace them with a more efficient imported slave labor force—was challenged by his staff. Meanwhile, he resorted to uncharacteristic half measures by razing vulnerable villages and herding their inhabitants into work parties. Still the natives resisted, with arms or morose passivity in their labors, while a fretful Coen began to see his grand scheme go awry.

In an extraordinary meeting Coen received one *orang kaya* with whom he might have gotten satisfaction. Joncker Dirck Callenbacker, a half-breed who spoke Dutch fluently and affected European airs, took it upon himself to lecture Coen about his nation's cruelty and avarice. His people, he emphasized, were only responding the way any people would who had been enslaved by invaders, while Coen countered with a catalogue of native perfidies and agreement violations.

This remarkably frank exchange lasted several hours. At its end Coen, recalling the villainy of 1609, was more convinced than ever of the workability of his original plan. Only blood would tell. Still, he waited for provocation to strike.

In the meantime, he began to consolidate Lonthor by establishing a headquarters in a village and appointing an island chief as its head, while stationing a troop of soldiers there under a captain's command. Coen's bloody obsessions, now far from Holland in this remote Eden-like corner of the globe, became infectious among his staff.

The commander ordered the chief to bring the recalcitrant refugees out of the hills and into the nutmeg forests for work, promising an amnesty if they complied and dreadful punishment if they did not. But the natives remained in hiding, while the fruit continued to decay on the trees.

The impasse became desperate as the Dutch set about to consolidate their grand design, triggering a pattern of behavior that overrode their own Protestant nature. The Dutchmen's "melancholy of the East" began a strange transmutation that was about to unleash a terrorizing sequence of events.

The commander took over the village meeting pavilion where elders sorted out and adjudicated *adat,* or custom, as his own personal command post, as well as the adjacent mosque as a billet. Thus immediately were the town's oldest, most venerable structures defiled by unclean strangers. The best native dwellings were requisitioned for billeting Dutch troops. Armed guards with little sense of local custom patrolled the narrow streets and ways, looting as they pleased.

It was a martial scene enveloped by nutmeg groves with branches laden with rotting fruit to which no native was keen to return. The chief protested vehemently on behalf of his townspeople, but to no avail. The Dutch commander would deal with the villagers in his own way.

As he sought to bring them to heel, the commander ordered the boats and thatched house of recalcitrant workers to be torched. Gathering village treasures looted by his soldiers, he had them burned in bonfires. At times he made examples of his own men. When three of his own soldiers resisted this wanton, wholesale destruction, they were seized and sentenced to death.

When their comrades pleaded for their companions' lives, the commander, whose name was 't Sionck, relented in part: He allowed the three condemned to draw lots to determine who would hang. Likewise, a Japanese mercenary was beheaded by a fellow samurai on 't Sionck's command for an infraction of discipline. It was essential to Coen's scheme that Dutch justice be *seen* to be carried out, and 't Sionck pursued it with a vengeance.

The fateful night of April 21, 1621, arrived with savageries that still are burned in Bandanese memory today. 'T Sionck was sleeping in the old mosque when a hanging lamp crashed to the floor, suddenly rousing the household. The commander summoned sentries, who had little sense of what had happened or who was responsible. The only certainty was no certainty at all, but the Dutch were panicked with suspicions that mischief was afoot.

Armed, the soldiers swept through the village, rousing all from sleep. Confusion ran in the streets. Fearing reprisals for some imagined crime, many of the villagers took to the hills, a flight that only enraged the Dutch, who anticipated ambush and massacre. Answers were wanting, and 't Sionck would have them.

They came from a frightened child, who under torture confessed that the crashing lamp had been a signal for nocturnal attack with the villagers intent on slaughtering the Dutch as they slept. 'T Sionck quickly had the town's *orang kaya* seized and tortured to exact confessions.

The headmen were systematically bound spread-eagled on a door frame, while lighted candles were held to the soles of their feet. Then a sleeve of cloth was bound tightly about the head and filled with water to the point where a futile attempt to draw breath filled nose, mouth, and lungs with water. Freed momentarily to regurgitate the water, the prisoner was subjected again to the alternating trials by fire and water until confessions of a conspiracy were gained.

The chiefs, reluctant spokesmen at best, were ordered to coax the fugitives from the hills. When they failed, Coen ordered war parties to sweep Lonthor as well as the other islands to burn villages and force surrender.

Subjugation now was not enough for Coen, who still had vivid memories of the ambush he had survived in 1609. Convinced that the islanders "would quickly rebel again, so soon as the fleet had departed," he decided to transport them "willingly or unwillingly" to Batavia, where they would be sold as slaves. Those who surrendered were quickly herded aboard ships together with the captured, with the first consignment totaling 883 men, women, and children. Others fled to join those who had escaped the sweep in the hills, while still others managed to slip through the blockade and sail south to other islands—Ceram, Kai, and Aru—in their prahus and junks.

Many of the escapees were later discovered dead from starvation. The most desperate fugitives, despondent over loss of their people and way of life, hurled themselves from Lonthor's cliffs, while "a good party of women and children" were taken alive. Coen himself kept the count: "About 2,500 are dead either of hunger and misery or by the sword. So far we have not heard of more than 300 Bandanese who have escaped from the whole of Banda. It appears that the obstinacy of these people was so great that they had rather die all together in misery than give themselves up to our men."

There was another estimate by a contemporary chronicler. Of the total islands' population of fifteen thousand, only a thousand survived within the tiny archipelago, mainly having made their way to Pulau Ai and Pulau Run, where they found English protection from Dutch atrocities.

As for those deported to Batavia, some of their leaders suffered a grim fate. Forty-five chieftains were sentenced to die for conspiring with Javanese malcontents to burn the city and flee to Banda. One eyewitness at the execution of thirteen of these leaders recounted that four victims were beheaded, then quartered, while the nine remaining were quartered before decapitation. Coen coolly noted, "All the other male persons, to wit 210, have been thrown into chains here and the women and children, namely 307 souls, we have sent to Banda to be shared and sold among our people there."

The Banda Islands, now essentially depopulated—"altogether as fair an orchard as may be seen in the world," in Coen's own words—had to be peopled afresh if the Dutch East India Company was to exploit the nutmeg and mace for the sake of which the Bandanese had been brought to ruin. Coen envisioned a Dutch settlement with new emigrants from Europe served by imported slaves.

But Coen's vision was crossed with what he saw as a need for a terrible retribution. Convinced that certain *orang kaya* must be eliminated as an example, Coen ordered over two score native men and aristocrats seized. Among them was the half-breed fancier of European ways, Callenbacker. Taken aboard his flagship, the *Dragon,* the prisoners were placed upon the rack to extract confessions. Some managed to escape by leaping overboard, while as many died in agony. Others were coerced to confess that the fateful lamp crashing to the mosque floor on the night of April 21 had been a signal for attack. Thus broken under torture, the "plotters" were convicted for conspiring to overthrow the Dutch regime on Banda and condemned for their seditious scheme.

On the morning of May 8, 1621, preparations were made for a grisly mass execution. Forty-four young men of Banda, their arms tightly bound, were herded by guards within the walled compound of Fort Nassau, built by the Portuguese a century before. Eight of the group were *orang kaya,* the islands' aristocracy, and they were dressed in finer garments—pantaloons, doublets, and turbans—than the others who wore sarongs. Fathers and mothers and wives were already assembled in the fortified enclosure. They were gathered not to give final comfort to the condemned but to witness at close hand a brutal colonial butchery meted out. Six Japanese samurai, hired assassins who had accompanied Coen from Batavia, cavalierly stood nearby, leaning on their long, finely honed swords.

When the sentence was read out, charging the accused with conspiracy and breaking the terms of the peace, the sullen air was filled with rising wails and cries as the butcher's work began. Wives, mothers, and fathers were forced to watch as their husbands and sons were sliced to pieces. The dusty grass of Fort Nassau was awash in a swill of blood and tears.

A naval lieutenant, Nicolas van Waert, witnessed the events he would forever remember: "All that happened was so dreadful as to leave us stunned," he recorded of the sickening scene. "The heads and quarters of those who had been executed were impaled upon bamboos and so displayed. Thus did it happen."

Van Waert's vivid report of this grisly mass execution eventually found its way, unsigned, to Amsterdam and the Lords Seventeen, and then it circulated through all Holland, outraging its citizenry. This alone among the bloody, terrible spectacles that transpired in the East Indies attracted any attention in the West, but it led to such revulsion on the part of the Lords Seventeen in Amsterdam that Coen drew an official rebuke from that assembly before it awarded him three thousand guilders for his conquest of the islands.

Not lost on Coen was the sobering effect news of the methodically rendered carnage would have on the English of Ai and Run. Having always suspected collusion between the deceitful natives and malicious English, he could now gloat, "Pride, presumption, falsity, and, in short, all vices are too great in them [the English]. . . . If Your Lordships desire something great and notable to be done for the honour of God and the welfare of the country, then deliver us from the English."

Coen himself very nearly delivered his countrymen from the English. Courthope had seen it as his duty to preserve at any cost Pulau Run, England's first colony and perhaps her last. Obscurity and shame attended his death after forty-two hopeful months defending an island holding that the company he had served now wanted to forget. Forgotten with no honors in England, Courthope, with his steely determination in the face of death, galvanized his less gritty followers. Cut adrift by the Honourable Company, a score of Englishmen on Run were still alive.

Having declined to participate in Coen's conquest of Banda, those same Englishmen now petitioned Coen to learn his intentions regarding them. Coen's response was peremptory. The English, he said, exposed themselves at their own peril and in doing so would receive no more favored treatment than the Banda natives.

Exposing themselves was hardly necessary to make Coen as good as his word. A Mr. Randall was the English factor stationed on Pulau Lonthor, and by his own account he did not leave his house during the invasion. After Randall's two weeks of voluntary confinement, a force of Dutch soldiers and Japanese mercenary-executioners seized the factory, Randall himself, his two English and eight Chinese assistants, and the godown filled with spices and fabrics worth a fortune.

After the looting, the Japanese amused themselves by binding and beating their prisoners. Then on impulse they beheaded three of the Chinese and kicked their severed heads about at the feet of the other terrified prisoners. Randall later said that he was spared only because the Japanese failed to understand the Dutch order that he likewise be killed. He and the other survivors were clapped in irons aboard ship for eighteen days, uncertain of their fate.

In the meantime, from Run a force of five hundred Dutch soldiers was sighted approaching the island. Run's *orang kaya* appealed to their English compatriots, vowing that with support the islanders would fight to the last man, but that without it they were doomed. The head factor, a Mr. Haies, flatly refused, citing Courthope's pitiful death as embodying the hopelessness of their cause. A later investigator summed it up: "Thus was Poolorun lost, which in Mr. Courthope's time by his good resolution and with a few [men] maintained itself to their [Dutch] disgrace, and now by the fearfulness of Mr. Haies and his irresolution is fearfully lost in the time of peace."

The island was thus taken by the Dutch, who forced the English and the tiny island's natives to dismantle their fort and factory and jettison their cannon at sea. Afterward, the natives were corralled for deportation.

As for the English, the stately burial of Nathaniel Courthope had been an aberration, for the Dutch still regarded their undermanned and under-supplied "allies" as despicable enemies and treated them as such. In a calculated gesture of mock generosity, Coen allowed the English to eke out a subsistence in their fort perched on the coral spit. Here a few loyalists survived for several years cut off from the other islanders and virtually unable to trade.

One figure remained to play a last hand with Coen. Captain Sir Humphrey Fitzherbert, commander of English naval forces in the Moluccas, had stationed himself in Ambon just before Coen's invasion of Banda. He sailed for Banda on March 10, arriving too late to give any support to either the hapless Randall or the spineless Haies. Employing his diplomatic skills, he managed with difficulty the chained Randall's release from his shipboard confinement as well as the freedom of other English hostages.

Coen had not encountered an Englishman of Fitzherbert's mettle since his old adversary John Jourdain; though it was late in the game, the naval commander exercised some leverage in his dealings with the governor-general. More than a handful of Dutch deserters had found refuge with the beleaguered English on isolated Run. Coen demanded their return to face Dutch justice, but Fitzherbert refused to budge on the issue until the English aboard ship were freed.

One final hostility would hover as a lasting, brutal memory in England's role in the spice game. In February 1624 a bizarre sequence of events followed a conversation between a Japanese mercenary and a Dutch soldier standing the night watch at Holland's fort in Ambon. When questioned about the fort's defenses, the guard became suspicious. The Japanese was arrested and under torture confessed to being a party to a planned mutiny in which he implicated the English.

The handful of Englishmen, fifteen in all, stationed at their factory in Ambon were invited unwittingly to the Dutch fort, where they were seized and for days systematically tortured with rack, lighted candles, and water as they were forced to betray their leaders on trumped-up charges. Sentenced to die on February 25, some scribbled their last words in the pages of their prayer books, while others embraced martyrs' death as they were led off to be beheaded by sword. "If I be guilty, let me never partake of thye heavenly joyes, O Lord. Amen, for me," the condemned men cried in turn.

The Ambon Massacre, as it became known, caused a furor in England as well as a mighty embarrassment in Holland where protests were lodged. Most Englishmen wanted payment in blood, but it was not to come. When in 1625 a Dutch fleet returning from the East was permitted to sail past Dover while the Royal Navy watched and did nothing, the gentlemen adventurers of the Honourable Company, already suspicious of the government, were convinced they were backed by a paper crown. Not long after, as their subscribers withheld payments, the directors announced that the government's lack of participation had forced them "to give over the trade of the Indies."

AND WHAT OF England's first colony on Run, seized by the Dutch without so much as a shot being fired? Having forfeited their claims to Run, as they had earlier with Ai, and irrespective of written agreements in Amsterdam and London, the English were losers. Ever mindful that they might revive their claim, Coen, with little use for Pulau Run, introduced there the practice of "extirpation," as he would throughout the Moluccas to control the source of spices. The Dutch leveled every nutmeg tree on the island, and the British in 1623 were compelled to seek Dutch assistance with ships to remove officials and property.

Run's spirited defense had ended ignominiously, and its heroes lie largely forgotten in unknown graves. Thus any discussion of the heroism of Courthope and Jourdain and their vain deaths seems moot, for Jan Pieterszoon Coen was commended by the Lords Seventeen for achieving what he had set out to do: oust the English and wage genocidal destruction upon the Banda islanders.

Revisionist Dutch historians, however, would take a different view as the facts of Coen's conquest came to light in succeeding generations, and the reputation as an empire builder Coen enjoyed during his lifetime would be supplanted by charges of inhumanity, barbarity, bloodthirstiness, and monstrosity. "His name reeks of blood," wrote Luc Kiers as late as 1943.

Even so, Coen is a considerable figure by any measure, for the governor-general secured for his nation the Malay Archipelago, which came to be known as the Dutch East Indies. Had he done so specifically for trade? As a man of his merciless age, the success for Coen of the Dutch East India Company became synonymous with the conviction behind the phrases that slipped so easily from his righteous pen: "the honor and repute of the Dutch nation," "the welfare of the country," and not least "the honor of God."

To give the devil his due, Coen's methods were commonplace in the seventeenth century, as Cromwell inflicted no less bloody penalties on the Irish. While the effects of what Coen wrought will be seen, one outgrowth in particular would belatedly reward the fatal heroism of two gritty Englishmen.

Courthope and Jourdain's claim for a share of the spice game with the colony of Run became suddenly an empty claim. But an empty claim is a claim nonetheless, and it spawned another issue of rightful due more promising a half century later and half a world away in North America. It was preceded by other visits by the English to Pulau Run—in 1636,

1638, 1648, and 1662—amid claims and disputes. All were ill-fated attempts to revive the cultivation of nutmeg. But inspired by the Ambon Massacre of 1623 and the earlier heroism of Courthope and Jourdain, the English persevered.

Then unrest in Europe played a hand as old cross-Channel resentments came to a head. In 1664 England passed the Navigation Act, favoring the English navy and provoking the first declaration of war against the Netherlands. As an interim settlement in 1665, Run formally reverted to the English, who were intent on sending in a new generation of settlers.

Then later that year followed a second conflict in which Holland's Admiral de Ruyter torched the English fleet based in the Thames. When word of the renewed hostilities reached Banda, the Dutch again seized— but peacefully this time—Run and amiably transported the new settlers back to Bantam, frankly to the relief of the newly arrived English. It is one of history's paradoxes that peace in Europe in Coen's day signaled war in the Spice Islands, and forty years later the reverse was true.

When hostilities in Europe ended, the treaty known as the Peace of Breda in 1667 required that the English relinquish their vestigial interest in Run in exchange for another small island halfway around the globe, where a settlement had been founded in 1625 by Peter Stuyvesant at the mouth of the Hudson River. Ironically, Pulau Run had been so thoroughly ravaged by the Dutch, they would have little use for it over the next two centuries.

Even so, the Dutch considered it a fair swap. They would give up their stake in North America to keep the bothersome English out of the Bandas and the spice trade. In so doing, they guaranteed that future Americans would speak English rather than Dutch, and that the new island would be known no longer as New Amsterdam but Manhattan.

Chapter 14

"WAREHOUSE OF EAST AND WEST"

IF HOLLAND'S North American colony of New Amsterdam was eventually ceded by that nation to England, what of the city for which it was named? Unlike London, the Dutch metropolis by the early seventeenth century was not an ancient place, and its citizens seized on this point with pride. In Coen's day the comparatively new Amsterdam became the richest city in Europe: an achievement due in no small part to Coen himself and the United Dutch East India Company he served.

The city had developed from a fishing settlement of reed hovels founded in the thirteenth century at the confluence of the Ij and Amstel Rivers. Such a lowland geography prompted its earliest inhabitants to build a dike across the Amstel as protection against the floods that constantly invaded the vast marshland crisscrossed by a maze of channels and canals. By the early 1600s Amsterdam was transformed into a nexus of islands and waterways united by bridges and Calvinistic fervor for trade as a single, mighty port. This is the Amsterdam that greets one today.

The first thing the visitor to Holland notices is the sky: masses of dark-fringed clouds streaked with blue in perpetual change, gathering and releasing, promising rain but withholding it for the moment. This moving canopy is suspended over a benign, green stillness of flat fields divided by canals that gathers the city of Amsterdam in from its ancient nemesis, the Zuider Zee. The Dutch masters painted this sky over their pastoral settings more than three centuries ago, as they rendered townhouses and their interiors, as well as the city's inhabitants dressed for work and leisure, the tiny country's waterways frozen in winter and verdant in summer, and just about everything in their fervent recording on canvas of scenes from a growing culture.

A vast tidal wave of riches had swept through a Holland finally free of the Spanish yoke, as Amsterdam very nearly overnight became the most important city on the continent. A map dating from 1597 reveals that the urban concentration of open water and inland quays was already taking its present crescent shape. Amsterdam's population doubled in increments of ten years, and when the city began building in earnest in the year 1600, stone and brick began replacing oak structures as different racial and ethnic groups began blending into the Netherlands' culture. "I am lodg'd in a Frenchman's house who is one of the Deacons of our *English Brownists* Church," wrote James Howell to his father in 1619. "It is not far from the synagogue of the *Jews,* who have a free and open exercise of their Religion here."

As the city expanded to the south and west, construction of its three most famous canals—the Harengracht, Keizersgracht, and Prinsengracht —attended this development, with the new districts protected by a combined defensive barrier of canal and ramparts known as the Singelgracht.

Though some travelers did not always find a visit appealing (the Englishman Owen Feltham saw the country as the "great Bog of Europe . . . as universal quagmire and the city itself a place where a skittish horse might cause two deaths at once, breaking your neck or drowning"), the merchant port became a favorite destination with most foreign travelers mainly because they saw Amsterdam as a city without precedent. The French poet and economist Antoine de Montchrétien observed in 1615 that "the art of industry had made a masterpiece out of nature's miscarriage." A familiar saying then was coined: "God made the world, but the Dutch made Holland."

Amsterdam's warehouses, as well as those of the outlying ports, bulged with every type of commodity imaginable—grain, timber, hemp, pitch, tar, iron, fish, and furs from the Baltic, salt and wine from Spain, Portugal, and southern France, woolens from England, cottons from India, silks from China, and of course spices from the East Indies.

The key to such wealth was obviously trade with the rest of Europe and the far corners of the world. Holland was a tiny nation that colonized large, but within the strictly defined limits of mercantilism. By the end of the sixteenth century, it had essentially ousted from Far Eastern waters Asia's first European colonizers, the Portuguese, and gained a trade monopoly in spices a world away at the eastern end of the Malay Archipelago.

A clue to the magnitude of wealth pouring into seventeenth-century Amsterdam is provided by the English Restoration diarist Samuel Pepys. In the fall of 1665 (the year of London's Plague before the Great Fire of 1666) during the naval war with Holland, Lord Sandwich led an attack on and captured two heavily laden Dutch East Indiamen returning to Holland. The ships were instead escorted to Erith, Kent. There Pepys, as surveyor-victualer to the Royal Navy, appeared on the scene to supervise the distribution of the royal cargo.

It was, as he confided to his diary of November 16 after visiting the ships' holds, "as noble a sight as ever I saw in my life, the greatest wealth in confusion that a man can see in the world. Pepper scattered through every chink. You trod upon it and in cloves and nutmegs I walked above the knees, whole rooms full. And silk in bales and boxes of copper plate, one of which I opened." Pepys admits that he was not above trading for spices with the coarse, disreputable seamen he encountered in the taverns of the port.

Amsterdam, the city of islands, enjoyed a varying rhythm in its weather, with Atlantic storms bringing series of intermittent rains to northern Europe. A fastidious city with a mania for cleanliness, it contrasted sharply with the smelly, vaster London of the gentlemen adventurers. Amsterdam and its citizens were of another mold.

William Carr put a fine point on the difference between the two peoples when he noted that the Dutch "were not addicted to such prodigality and wantonness as the English are." The English were crude by comparison, especially in their unrefined manners. Charles II once laughed aloud at the poor singing at divine services, and the sermons were so paralyzing that the courtiers openly amused themselves in church with flirtation.

The Vermeers of the day provided a living record of their countrymen's house interiors, and that they were spotlessly clean was not always appreciated by foreign, especially English, visitors. Feltham noted that "their houses they keep cleaner than their bodies; their bodies than their souls." On this point his countryman Sir William Temple's willingness to assume the butt's role in a story is revealing. At a state dinner party Temple was made to feel uneasy because every time he spat on the floor, which would not have been unseemly in London, it was wiped up. When he complained, his host rejoined that it was well that his wife was not there, for she would have kicked him out of the house.

The English were as galled by Dutch fishing fleets off their coast as they were by the Netherlands' monopoly in the spice trade, and there were many attempts by Parliament and Privy Council alike to exclude the Hollanders from English waters, prompting Grotius to publish his *Mare Librum*, which in turn was countered by John Selden's *Mare Clausum*. Complaints about Dutch competition from the likes of Sir Walter Raleigh and Josiah Child, however, fell on deaf ears in Holland.

The Dutch, quite simply, were more enterprising than any other people when it came to the sea, and they worked harder. This case was made by a social chronicler of the age, William Aglionby: "They never complain of the pains they take, and go as merrily to the *Indies,* as if they were going to their Countrey Houses." The English poet Andrew Marvell put a fine point on it with his characteristic wit: "How could the Dutch but be converted, when / The Apostles were so many fishermen?"

The area of the city known as the Western Islands was an important shipbuilding quarter in the early seventeenth century, with its warehouses on boat-lined canals plied by swans, ducks, and other waterfowl. Amsterdam's warehouse is a unique expression of Low Country engineering, with large stone-arched windows rising one atop another six floors in a narrow brick building with a remarkably simple but efficient pulley and windlass at the top for hoisting merchandise, and with each of the windows framed with large, brightly painted wooden shutters. The visual effect is of hundreds of giant butterflies poised to take flight, doubly so with their reflections in the canal bordering the street, lending a static scene vibrancy and color.

These warehouses, strewn throughout the city—many of them still reeking of nutmeg and cloves—remain Amsterdam's most vivid architectural face, and they gaze on canals of a city reclaimed from the sea, a reminder of a popular dictum of three centuries ago: "He who cannot master the sea is unworthy of the land."

Today the treasures of the Rijksmuseum—the paintings of Van Dyck, Vermeer, Frans Hals, and the towering figure of Rembrandt—are pictorial records of this extraordinary time, when trade fueled the culture that produced these master painters, enabling a rare confluence of wealth and taste to produce great works of art.

Amsterdam's famed red-light district dates from this period, more than a century before the English writer and philanderer James Boswell in 1764 prowled its streets in search of lowlifes and lechery, recording his adventures in a diary. It was an era when sailors were rewarded with illicit female companionship after months or years at sea, and its existence is a fair reminder of how liberated a city Amsterdam became in the early decades of the seventeenth century. Here sailors, resting and recuperating between voyages, squandered their hard-earned back pay on sex and gin, earning for themselves the nickname "lords of six weeks."

In 1630, the year before Rembrandt settled in the city that was to be transformed into a vast art market, freedom of worship was instituted. Only a few years after the scourge of the Spanish Inquisition, the waning of anti-Semitism seemed to have inspired other freedoms. Women had unprecedented liberties, professionally as well as privately. Art academies by and for women were not uncommon. The merchant city fathers sponsored orphanages, homes for the elderly as well as lepers, and societies where fallen women could learn a trade, thus elevating their status in society.

The Dutch East India Company was a unique marriage between government and merchants. Governed by its board of directors, the Lords Seventeen, the company essentially controlled trade, and its coat of arms adorned the headquarters in the city as well as in the smaller ports, Enkhuisen and Hoorn to the north of Amsterdam on the Zuider Zee, as well as the larger ones of Delft and Rotterdam to the south with more direct access to the North Sea. The Dutch East India Company accounted in large part for Amsterdam's supremacy in trade, which infused the city with such fantastic wealth. As early as 1561 the Italian visitor Lodovico Guicciardini counted five hundred ships in the harbor.

The Dutch company surpassed the English East India Company as the world's most important trade organization of its time, giving rise to the

Bank of Exchange as early as 1609 and by extension the notion of "futures" and investment in expeditions to bolster international mercantilism. The poet Jeremias de Decker describes the Exchange:

> A strolling place where Moor and Northman bargained
> A church where Jew and Turk and Christian gathered
> A school of every tongue, a market field of every ware
> An exchange which swells all exchanges in the world.

One acute observer was the aforementioned English diplomat and writer Sir William Temple (1628–1699), whose works include *Observations upon the United Provinces of the Netherlands,* published in 1672. Temple ultimately helped negotiate the treaty known as the Peace of Breda in 1667 (ceding New Amsterdam to England and Pulau Run to Holland); effected the triple alliance between England, Holland, and Sweden, aiming at the protection of Spain from French ambition; and in 1674 brought about the marriage between William of Orange and Mary. A graduate of Emmanuel College, Cambridge, and a close friend of Jonathan Swift, Temple's perceptive detachment makes him a reliable reporter of the Dutch scene.

When the Exchange Bank of Amsterdam opened its doors for business and concerned itself largely during the Golden Age with deposit banking and exchange, it also advanced sums to the Dutch East India Company for its expeditions to the East Indies. Temple marveled at this unrivaled institution as "the greatest Treasure either real or imaginary, that is known anywhere in the World. The place of it is a great Vault under the Staathouse, made strong with all the circumstances of Doors and Locks, and other appearing cautions of safety that can be."

A thriving Amsterdam demanded admiralty buildings, naval docks, and new fortifications, and with the Reformation came new churches as well. Much of the destiny of the world beyond Amsterdam was directed by the Dutch East India Company headquarters in conjunction with the New Town Hall, dating from 1655 and adorned with a cupola crowned with a ship atop a pineapple, a symbol of expansion borne by one of domestic welcome. That union between the familiar and the exotic was the city's essence.

If the Rijksmuseum is distinctive because it houses many of the finest works of the Dutch masters, the Historical Museum, just off the Spuis-traat, provides the best record of the impact spices and other exotica had on Amsterdam's economic growth. Its holdings are a mosaic of Amster-dam's past. Portraits of wealthy grain and spice merchants and their fam-ilies clad in black robes and lace collars engage the viewer with unsmiling demeanor, revealing traits that enabled the new republic of Holland to prosper: modesty, sobriety, diligence, and personal piety.

A typical still-life canvas of the day might include a rendering of a wine-glass, an earthenware jug, clay pipes, and as the central subject a ceramic bowl filled with nutmegs, whole and split to reveal the priceless mace enclosing the kernel. More arcane is the silver work of the period: a cham-bered nautilus from the Spice Islands, prized for its rarity, held aloft by a silver child astride a silver dolphin base, topped by a miniature putto rid-ing a triton; this elaborate eighteen-inch-high configuration functioned as a beaker. The extravagant of Amsterdam's golden age was also functional.

Such domestic objects in the museum are frequently juxtaposed with distant seascapes, often shipwrecks and other disasters that were daily realities of the long voyages through the South Atlantic and Indian Oceans to the Indies as well as a series of urgent, fateful northern voyages to find a shorter way to the same eastern islands.

Perhaps the most unusually arresting exhibit of the Rijksmuseum and the one most illustrative of the Dutch mania for mercantile expansionism is the series of cases devoted to Nova Zembla, the notorious glacial island north of Siberia that became for some explorers the final resting place as they searched for a northeast passage to the Spice Islands.

Willem Barentsz (1555–1597) made three unsuccessful voyages to find this northern passage to the Spice Islands. In 1596 Barentsz discovered Bear Island and Spitsbergen, from where he ventured east to Nova Zem-bla. Trapped by the ice, Barentsz and his men were forced to spend the winter of 1596–97 in a house they built from scraps of driftwood. They managed to survive this first winter in total Arctic darkness by trapping bear and fox, while discovering the medicinal benefits of "lepel leaves," known as scurvy grass, by which they managed to ward off the worst symptoms of that dreaded seaman's disease. In the June thaw the men rowed their way to the civilized world, arriving in Amsterdam in Novem-ber of 1597, though Barentsz himself died of scurvy along the way. The objects they left behind on Nova Zembla are now housed in the museum, and they are a fantastic story in themselves.

After the Barentsz party left Nova Zembla, the remnants of their winter's stay remained untouched for nearly three hundred years, until 1871, when a Norwegian expedition discovered the collapsed remains of the driftwood shelter. These items—a pair of leather shoes, a wooden plate, two books on navigation, sextants, pieces of rigging—speak to the spirit of that ferocious, expanding age when expeditions, however unwillingly undertaken, were part of life's vast risk that might yield a fortune in spices. The most striking inclusion of all is a map drawn by survivors of the expedition showing Polus Arcticus dominating the vast northern wastes like a frozen sun at the center of an icy wilderness inhabited by sea monsters and anything else a cruel nature could inflict.

For many years Arctic knowledge to the east was confined to Nova Zembla, Vaigich Island, and the mouth of the Ob River at the Kara Sea. Even though the ice precluded further exploration, the Dutch persevered in their efforts to search out a northeast passage until 1624, though their bold expeditions brought home only information about the north coast of Russia. Such lore, finally, was determined to be useless to spice merchants but invaluable to whaling captains. The northern routes, both east and west, were failures in the immediate sense, for ships so routed could not reach the Spice Islands. However, these frozen adventures were undertaken by the best seamen of the sixteenth and seventeenth centuries, and whatever success they realized added greatly to navigational confidence and experience and ultimately, however slowly, opened new trades in fur and whale oil.

BY THE mid-seventeenth century the spice trade and its ramifications had embossed a new iconography on the European sensibility, and the farthest horizons invoked by new discovery were now names to conjure with in the highest caliber of artistic expression. Barentsz's final, ill-fated voyage to Nova Zembla was an aberrant expedition that ended in disaster, and it became the talk of Europe. When Shakespeare's Fabian tells Sir Andrew in *Twelfth Night,* "You are now sailed into the North of my lady's opinion, where you will hang like an icicle on a Dutchman's beard," his audience could not fail to make the connection. Likewise, England's metaphysical poets drew upon the current cosmology as a reservoir of imagery in their sacred and profane verse, as well as in their prose. Paradox, incongruity, muscular rhythms, and the use of novel comparisons in writing were now legitimized by an expanding world, with the new worldview infusing the intellectual and theological conceits of such writers as John Donne. "As west and east in all flat maps (and I am one) are one, / So death doth touch the resurrection. . . ."

Canvases depicting vivid pictorial representations of voyages on the proven southern route around the Cape of Good Hope were enormously popular, while the day's literary taste demanded thrillers of voyage reading. These were the golden age's best-sellers, aimed at an audience that expected the unexpected, usually a striking calamity from which only the virtuous and stalwart escaped. In such stories, the victims are bound by community and submission to God's will, both severely tested, whether among the icebergs of Nova Zembla or the monsoons of the Indian Ocean. The Dutch publishers who turned out books describing adventures and misadventures in the eastern seas, usually published in Latin, French, German, and occasionally English as well as Dutch, were the first mass-marketers of escapist reading, and they published with a keen eye to the foreign market.

If not so vast in scope, the navigating manuals and atlases drew an equally broad readership. As early as 1584 such books were published, introducing standardized symbols for navigational concerns, from buoys to safe anchorages to hidden shoals. Then there were the numerous ships' journals, often lavishly illustrated, with accounts of ports and peoples seen for the first time. These provided hard information for the merchant and seaman as well as diversion for the armchair traveler at home.

Amsterdam was more than a market for the world. It filled its warehouses with material goods, but it had intellectual storehouses as well and drew the learned, creative outsider like a magnet. A formidable mind of the day was the famous German scientist Georg Rumphius, "the Blind Seer of Amboina," who served the Dutch in the Moluccas for fifty years and wrote of the flora and fauna of the Spice Islands. His works were published in Amsterdam to great success and remain highly valued in scientific circles for their exacting expertise.

There are few instances in modern history when the historical, the esthetic, the social, the economic, and the metaphysical blended so completely as they did in Amsterdam in this age of Rembrandt, Descartes, Locke, and Spinoza. The poet Constantijn Huygens, their contemporary, provides a poignant coda to the city's golden age, for Amsterdam would not remain Europe's richest city forever, or even for very long: "How com'st thou, golden swamp, by the abundance of heaven: / Warehouse of East and West, all water and all state, / Two Venices in one, where do thy ramparts end?"

Enveloping an Amsterdam bracing itself against the ever-threatening sea is orchard country, with roadside canals mirroring the brooding windmills and castles dating from the fifteenth century that hover nearby. They mark a time when Europe was still largely barbarized, and the fortresses stood like sentinels of another age, guarding their dominions against invasion by rival petty nobility. The inexorable invaders, however, would come two centuries later: an invasion not of militiamen carrying pick and musket, but of flower buds, dried pieces of bark, and small aromatic seeds infused with the scents of Eden.

Chapter 15

"NO TEN
COMMANDMENTS SOUTH
OF THE EQUATOR"

AFTER HIS CONQUEST of Banda, Coen returned to Batavia not as self-styled conqueror but as architect of a new society, to attend Holland's flourishing business concern in Banda. Now that "by God's grace" the Dutch East India Company possessed a cluster of virtually unpopulated and unproductive islands, Coen pinned his hopes to a dream he'd had all along: that Dutch settlements would rise from the ashes of the obliterated native ones. In this spirit, he and the company began encouraging applications for land grants in Banda, as in the rest of the Moluccas, if the applicants were willing to emigrate from Holland and settle permanently in the islands to grow and process spices for the company.

The first applicants were largely men who had already served in the military or mercantile branches of the Dutch East India Company and remained in Batavia or Ambon after completing their service contracts. Now as "free burghers" they brought the skills and trades that would allow such small, potentially thriving towns as Neira and Ambon to expand and prosper within a northern European plan.

The grantees would be given the status of tenant-vassals of the company and would be held responsible for maintaining their groves and delivering their crops at fixed prices. In return, the company would purchase all the spices and provide such staple necessities as rice at cost plus a small duty. Most important, the company would provide slaves to work the plantations.

From the beginning, relations between these *perkeniers,* or planters, and the Dutch East India company were sticky. There was, to cite one example, the question of profits. If the company was able to buy a planter's crop at a negligible cost and resell it in Amsterdam at a markup of, say, 1,220 percent, the planter could complain that he was being treated less generously than had been the native growers who preceded him. This basic conflict between the company and its producers, colored by an interdependency as well as a myriad of other issues, continued for the better part of two and a half centuries.

Coen, his Italian training as a bookkeeper notwithstanding, eschewed precise accounting to avoid delaying the harvest of spices, and the company was eager to recruit planters at the expense of character or professional assessment, while the planters grew and processed the "golden fruit" on terms that were at best shaky. Bitterness and contention were inevitable.

Central to the animosity was the nature of the planters themselves. Coen was a rough fellow from rude Dutch stock, but he had a keen aptitude, intelligence, and a driving will to see things through to his company's and nation's profit. On the other hand, the planters, with some exceptions, were life's drifters and misfits, rakes and scoundrels, who had washed up in the Indies like flotsam.

Repeatedly and insistently Coen petitioned the Lords Seventeen for "honorable men," good peasant craftsmen with their wives and children "to plant colonies." What he got was "a godless crowd instead." "Let the soldiers and seamen be used against the enemy, to which task they were created of God," he lectured his directors. "Few or none can be expected to make good citizens." But Coen had to take what he could get and was forced to work with unsound material to provide "free men, for the sake of keeping people in the country."

If maintaining sound relations between the drunken, demanding, disrespectful *perkeniers* and the arrogant, often incompetent, and corrupt company hierarchy was difficult at best, with fraudulent claims insisted upon by both sides, the presence and status of women in the Moluccas produced unprecedented tensions.

The planters had hardly stepped from the highest stratum of Dutch society into their new life of tropical adventure, and they brought with them a randy appetite for the yeoman's country pleasures. These arak- and gin-swilling, lusty young men unsurprisingly discovered carnal pleasure in the islands.

A mutual accommodation between the planters and their slave girls was soon fostered on the basis of cohabitation, which was strictly forbidden by the government, or intermarriage, which was barely tolerated. Both planter and military man alike were forbidden to marry local women without the governor's consent, on pain of being whipped in public for such transgressions. But an eager young "free burgher" soon learned the trick of sowing his oats without risking a visit to the flogging post.

It became commonplace for a planter to buy or adopt a fetching slave girl and, after seeing her baptized, apply to the governor for a marriage license, which was usually forthcoming. Often slaves were brought from as far away as New Guinea, thus introducing a darker-skinned people. The concubines of choice, however, were Bugis women of southwest Celebes, whose sex appeal one Dutch voyager inimitably explains:

> The Bouginese women are, in general, much handsomer than those of any other Indian [Asian] nation. There are some among them, who, for the contour of their faces, would be esteemed beauties even in Europe; and did they but possess the lilies and roses of our northern fair, they would be equal to the handsomest of the sex. They are all most ardently addicted to the sensual pleasures of love; and, goaded on by the hottest fires of lust, are ingenious in every refinement of amorous enjoyment; on this account the Bouginese girls are preferred throughout the east, for concubines, both by Europeans and by Indians. Mr. Van Pleuren, who had resided here for eight years, and several other credible people, informed me, that among these women, and those of Macassar, were many who, in common with some of the Portuguese women at Batavia, possessed the secret of being able, by certain herbs and other means, to disqualify their inconstant lovers from repeating the affront to them, insomuch that the offending part shrunk entirely away; with other circumstances, which decency requires that I should suppress.

Thus in a generation or so the planter's household took on a new racial composition, as Dutch fathers sired their offspring from native women, recalling the English East India Company proverb of a later day: "Necessity is the mother of invention and the father of the Eurasian." A new social system was spawned as the so-called mixties in time began to find acceptability in the planter hierarchy.

The situation was naturally exacerbated by the paucity of "worthy" women dispatched from home. Coen was horrified at the inexorable progression toward the mingling of races, and his pleas to the Lord Seventeen to supervise the quality of European women sent out became more urgent. "If the Indies, if we and other Your Lordships' servants are worthy of no better women than the scum of the Netherlands," he curtly put it, "then do not count upon keeping good people in the Indies or founding a prosperous state there."

Most of these so-called company daughters emigrating to the Indies did not make it as far east as the Spice Islands, and this alone accounted for the plethora of mixed marriages in the Moluccas. The choicest of these "daughters"—orphans, paupers, servant girls, prostitutes—arriving in the strange East with their modest dowries (courtesy of the company) were claimed at Batavia, the first of their destinations.

Ternate, Ambon, and especially remote Banda were another fifteen hundred miles farther east, the end of the line, and the women who finally arrived there were inevitably a homely, charmless, uncouth lot; according to reports, they were soon regarded as more lowbred than the commonest slave girl. As one contemporary put it, "the scum of our land are marrying with the scum of the Indies." Peter Both, the first governorgeneral of the East Indies, as early as 1612 advised the Lords Seventeen not to allow any more "light women" to emigrate from Holland "since there are far too many of them here already leading scandalous and unedifying lives to the great shame of our nation."

Adventurous women sometimes disguised themselves as sailors to get to the East from a Holland where there were few prospects for them. Governor-General Specx wrote to the Lords Seventeen in 1629: "The crew are all fit and well, and we lack nothing save so many filthy strumpets and street-walkers who have been found (may God amend it) in all the ships. They are so numerous and awful that I am ashamed to say anything more about it."

There was a school of thought in Holland which held that there was "a hidden force of the East which permeates and disintegrates the European, who cannot, or will not, stand apart and above races which, be their natural merits what they may, can never combine with his, but only poison and corrupt." As a definition and defense of apartheid, this belief took root early on in the pioneering days in the tropics. Interestingly, it was counter to the Portuguese view. But gradually this Dutch attitude altered as experience taught the Lords Seventeen that respectable women from Holland simply would not emigrate in sufficient numbers to provide the basis for a colony.

As Holland's colonial society evolved in Banda, a unique hybrid community came into being, as recounted by unblinking contemporary chroniclers. One such observer was Johan Sigmund Wurffbain, a German from Nurnberg who lived in the islands from 1633 to 1638 and kept a journal for those five years, recording methodically and exactingly his observations of a rare, evolving community.

Wurffbain had served the Dutch East India Company as both a soldier and a junior merchant, and from him we learn of the curious racial mixture of an island society whose total population in 1638 was 3,842, a third of what it was when the Dutch had arrived nearly forty years before. He noted that in five years the total export of nutmeg came to 3,097,209 pounds and mace to 890,754, whose markup value in Europe was dazzling to contemporary economists.

The most striking and sobering aspect of Wurffbain's journal are the entries in which he describes the frontier justice of a wealth-mad society crumbling in the face of domestic upheaval, where punishments rarely fit the crimes they were visited upon. Wurffbain noted twenty-five executions during his tenure, counting two persons burned alive, one broken on the rack, nine hanged, nine beheaded, three garrotted, and one "arquebussed." In addition there were routine whippings, mutilations, expulsions, and banishments to uninhabited islands.

The chastisements he lists are as bizarre as they are repellent, and more often than not the crimes to which they speak are unspecified. One might expect that the most heinous executions were the lot of Banda's lowest societal stratum, but that was not exclusively the case in this volatile powder keg of a colony.

On July 14, 1633, for example, we learn of the fate of a group of prominent residents at the hands of the executioner. A local company factor was beheaded, and he was followed in death by the popular dandy Rocques Risemenor, who was burned alive. His sister was then strangled, followed by a brother-in-law and an Englishman who were hanged. Others were branded and exposed in the pillory.

This cabal on that fateful day were implicated in so bizarre and unlikely a plot involving the cream of Banda's society that it would seem fanciful, were it not true. Rocques Risemenor, the son of a Portuguese father and Malay mother and a young man of good looks and keen intelligence, had been anointed by Dutch authorities as one who could go far in the service of the company. A favorite of both Banda's governor and chief merchant, Risemenor had risen to become a leading figure in the islands' Eurasian community.

On June 15, 1633, a rumor was abroad that Risemenor and his family had gathered their belongings and provisions and set out under cover of night in a boat manned by rowers. Dispatched by the governor, a lieutenant with an armed guard gave pursuit to overtake the fugitives, who were apprehended just beyond Banda waters. A mystified Risemenor explained that the governor had given him leave to voyage on a trading mission to the islands east of Banda. Unimpressed, the officer returned the group to Neira to await charges and judgment.

Placed on the rack, Risemenor implicated a company factor who allegedly had conspired to defect and join the Portuguese in Macassar on the southwestern peninsula of Celebes. Promising to finance Risemenor's trading expedition, which would become his own means of escape, the factor planned poorly. He failed to join the outgoing boat at the eleventh hour, thus prompting Risemenor to panic and flee with his family.

Himself now strung to the torture wheel and hoping to gain sympathy from the Dutch authorities, the factor came clean. He was born of an aristocratic but poor Flanders family, and to increase his circumstance deserted his wife and children to seek employment first overseas with the Spanish, then with the Dutch East India Company, while never ceasing to yearn for his family. With disarming frankness he admitted his plan to desert to the Portuguese in Macassar, hoping to make his way by merchant ship to Malacca with the plans of Banda's defenses in hand. Thus having ingratiated himself with the Spanish-Portuguese allies, he foresaw a safe passage home to join his people.

The level of justice meted out nine days later was not atypical in its severity. Indeed, the death penalty was awarded soldiers sleeping on duty, slaves attempting to escape, as well as thieves, murderers, and adulterers caught red-handed. The brand punished island women who suffered baptism only to revert to Islam, while a female slave who attempted suicide, thus defrauding her master, was given a permanent frozen smile as her cheeks were laid open mouth to ear.

Infractions against the monopoly, such as engaging in private trade, brought retribution of a different sort with heavy fines, even enslavement for officials, while the offending contraband spices were consumed in a public bonfire. Still, in this lonely outpost of European civilization, scarcely civil at all, the Dutch authorities continued to strive for the half-remembered, longed-for order of home half a world away. Capricious and repressive cruelty was the order of the day to achieve it, when a governor could decree a man to be burned at the stake, with or without the consensus of his judicial council.

Wurffbain was not the only chronicler of seventeenth-century Moluccan life. François Valentijn, a *predikant* or pastor employed by the company, spent only a year in Neira (1687–88), but he saw and collected much and became known as the historian of the old East Indies.

His aforementioned five-volume *The Old and New East Indies* contains voluminous descriptions of daily intercourse, especially regarding financial transactions and the recompense for officials within a rigorously drawn hierarchy: their shares and profits; their foodstuffs, including Rhine, French, Spanish, and Persian wine; and seemingly mundane perquisites such as highly lucrative privileges regarding trade. Quite simply, if an official was careful and keen-witted and played his cards accordingly, the man could amass a fortune by diverting official funds into his private account or in numerous other ways. It did not hurt his prospects that the relatively stable Dutch currency of the day, the *rijksdaalder,* was as strong as any coinage on the globe.

AND WHAT OF Jan Pieterszoon Coen, whose brutal legacy was Banda's? In one sense the conqueror's dream had been fulfilled, for the nutmeg gardens of the tiny islands indeed realized undreamed-of wealth for the Netherlands. On the other hand, not even the Dutch could sustain the sort of civilization Coen wanted to impose on the Indies, such a vast country of islands and their seas, so densely populated with alien tribes-men divided by language and custom. Trade, by definition, had to con-form to an economic system that was trusted on all sides, and when he was recalled to Holland in 1623, Coen assiduously lobbied the Lords Sev-enteen for certain reforms.

He argued vehemently that the well-being of the Dutch in the Indies depended upon certain basic premises: the necessity of European immi-gration; development of direct trade with China (before the English got there first); more efficient colonial government; and above all the promo-tion of free trade and cultivation of gardens to produce spices. On this last point, upon which the others were dependent, the Lords Seventeen balked. Encouraging such freedoms without the confines of the Dutch East India Company would amount, the governing body insisted, to an infraction of the monopoly upon which the company, and Holland, had always depended.

Even so, the directors knew that they had their man of the Indies in Coen, and so in 1624 he was reassigned to Batavia for another term as governor-general while his proposals were being debated in the domestic halls of power in Amsterdam. Sensing defeat of his initiatives, Coen asked for delay in his appointment so that he could be married in Holland.

Sickness delayed his appointment further, and in the interim the champions of monopoly seized the opportunity to thwart Coen's plans. When he was finally sent out again in 1627, the energetic governor was deprived of the opportunity to put in place the management reforms he believed essential to realize the colonial society of his vision.

Another and darker cloud came to envelop Coen, and it haunted him for the rest of his short life: the fiercely critical reaction at home of his merciless subjugation of the Banda islanders during his conquest. The Lords Seventeen, alarmed when the facts gradually came to light, wrote that such actions must be "once and enough."

A critic in Holland put a finer point on the argument against coloniza-tion: "What honorable men will break up their homes here to take employment as executioners and jailers of a herd of slaves, and to range themselves amongst those free men who by their maltreatment and mas-sacre of the Indians have made the Dutch notorious throughout the Indies as the cruelest nation of the whole world?"

Coen, having returned to Batavia, never again visited the Spice Islands. Now ensconced in the West Java fortress, he had spun a web about himself and was trapped in it. Once he had written that a sovereign Dutch "*rendezvous*" would attract people from all sides because "the merciful free manner of our nation" contrasted so vividly with the "tyranny" exercised by these Eastern kings who "held all their dominions by force." Coen, however, had been the architect of a system in which neither mercy nor freedom had any place, and least of all for the islanders of the Indies. Bitterness and hatred became his legacy.

Coen died in 1630 at the age of forty-two, though the circumstances surrounding his death are disputed. Valentijn attributes the cause of death to dysentery or cholera. Another less plausible source suggests that Coen died of sheer terror over the impending confrontation with his successor, Governor-General Specx. Specx was the natural father of Sara Specx, Coen's thirteen-year-old Eurasian foster daughter, whom he had publicly whipped and executed for fornication. Death by poison, however, always remained a possibility in the East Indies, because tropical illness was such a convenient cover for the intriguer poised with a nasty vial in hand.

Other Dutch accounts provide the governor-general with a more heroic end, recording that he died in 1629 defending his castle during a siege ordered by the sultan of Mataram, the self-styled emperor of Java. The fastidious attackers were eventually driven off when defenders emptied their chamber pots upon the heads of the Javanese.

A fatal illness, however, seems the most plausible explanation.

MEANWHILE, THE DUTCH had to control the monster they had created: their spice monopoly. On Banda it would seem to have been nicely in hand. The English had officially departed, and the islanders had been all but eradicated through Coen's genocidal policies. But this new society was evolving out of Holland's colonization, and it was a radical, dichotomous one at cross-purposes.

The Dutch were unhappy, homesick colonizers and complained from distant climes of the malaise they knew as "the melancholy of the east," a malady often leading to madness or suicide. There is irony here. While spices were the lifeblood of Europe, assignment to the clove- and nutmeg-producing Moluccas was not a happy one, except for an adventurer of Francisco Serrão's stripe or a savage conqueror such as Coen.

Instead, the East Indies were seen as a peripheral posting, even a place of exile for the European administrator or military man. What made the assignment bearable was the opportunity it afforded. One could prove oneself and be duly rewarded, both with riches and no small measure of national pride.

An essential part of an assignee's personal baggage, however, was this dichotomous attitude of abroad and home. An English East India Company official writing from Bantam in the early seventeenth century might have been writing for his Dutch counterpart:

> Many [Englishmen] are invited out by golden rewards but none stay, indeed it were madness to do so. At home men are famous for doing nothing; here they are infamous for their honest endeavors. At home is respect and reward; abroad disrespect and heartbreak. . . . At home is content; abroad nothing so much as griefs, cares, and displeasure. At home is safety; abroad no security. And, in a word, at home all things are as a man may wish and here nothing answerable to merit.

Nonetheless, Holland's large, fortified Indiamen, far more formidable than the Portuguese caravels they supplanted, controlled the spice trade for more than 150 years. If their crews and merchants were unwilling sailors, they were successful ones in the name of trade, in which they participated with a religious passion. The planters, of course, had their slaves, and together they became a unified force against the Dutch East India Company. The latter demanded profit, but it was a profit that could be generated only by the indolent, insolvent lot who were the planters.

By this time, the threat of a slave uprising was real enough to require the manning of every fort and outpost in the Bandas, while with their planter masters the slaves began to seek opportunities in private enterprises that excluded the company. A slave could become a sailor, then a trader, and, if he was shrewd enough, buy or will his freedom. An enterprising slave could feather a crafty planter's nest and so be rewarded for his trouble.

Thus the game took on a new turn as planters and their slaves smuggled out nutmeg and mace as they secretly brought in, with the help of regional traders, the essential staples of rice and fabrics as well as such regional exotica as pearls, sandalwood from Timor, tortoiseshell, or sea cucumbers, sharks' fins, birds' nests, ebony, and feathers from the bird of paradise. Such luxury items were status symbols of a new class that enjoyed putting on airs. They also traded in "long nutmegs" from other islands, deemed inferior to Banda's round variety by connoisseurs but eminently exportable to Asia and to an unwary clientele in Europe.

What could the company do but accuse the planters, on whose well-being the company depended, of failing to cultivate their nutmeg gardens assiduously while electing instead to engage in individual trade? Though since Magellan's day the cunning sailor risked his life in Asia with a sea chest full of goods that would be traded for a trunk of spices as his essential return baggage, the Dutch East India Company officials (those who were not bribed) could only look on helplessly at the shenanigans of the planters. The latter exported privately and at great profit the necessities required for the running of their plantations, which they acquired at subsidized prices from the company. At the same time they forced their field hands to eat sago rather than rice.

Speculation became rife with the planters. Arab and Chinese traders were only too happy to lend them money at usurious rates of interest so that they could invest in mad schemes and outdo each other in matters of social extravagance. As collateral, the planter pledged the plantation, despite the fact that under the auspices of the Dutch East India Company the property could not be so encumbered. But even this worked to the planters' advantage, for if a plantation was a highly conditional leasehold and not a readily disposable property, it was guaranteed by the company against dispossession by an Arab or Chinese creditor.

Ironically, though the company was created by the Dutch state, in many ways it evolved into its very antithesis. The Netherlands had chosen a republican form of government, which upheld the virtues that Hollanders believed placed them among God's elite.

The Dutch East India Company, by contrast, was perceived by many as the Antichrist, and its servants as casting shadows over the upright society at home. "Jesus Christ is good, but trade is better" was a popular saying of the day, but to many, if not most, of the God-fearing Dutch, it was as impious as it was vulgar. Even so, the Amsterdam merchant and his East Indies counterpart alike were unabashed profiteers who, if they could make a commercial profit "by passing through hell, would risk the burning of his ships' sails" to do so. "For love of gain, the wide world's harbors we explore," sang the poet Vondel.

In the Far East the top Dutch East India Company officials soon learned to live as opulently as Asian potentates. If frugality was admired at home, it was perceived in the distant outposts as a sign of poverty or stinginess, a judgment the company was quick to dispel. The use of golden parasols (a sign of Malay royalty), carriages, and large retinues of slaves became commonplace among leading company officials, and their wives were suitably bedecked in silks, satins, and jewels.

The Amsterdam in the age of Rembrandt, sobered by its Calvinist spirit, hardly knew what to make of such posturing. Batavia, the "Queen of the Eastern Seas," was known in Holland as "an honorable prison," while a less charitable assessment of the company had it as "a good refuge for all libertines, bankrupts, failed students, cashiers, brokers, bailiffs, secret agents, and such like rakes."

Greed, debauchery, and corruption came to be a natural extension of the expatriate's life. A Leiden professor in 1678 referred to the East Indies as "a real sewer of a country into which flows all the garbage of Holland." Even the Lords Seventeen expressed concerns in their letters over the ignoble character of those serving their company in Asia.

One company official cynically observed: "The directors in the fatherland decide matters as it seems best to them there; but we do here what seems most advisable to us." There was a general conviction that "there were no Ten Commandments south of the equator." Or as another official put it, he "had not come out to Asia to eat hay."

Meanwhile, the majority of planters left plantation life to paid overseers, while they lived in idle pretense in Neira, where the order of the day for the *arrivistes* was social one-upmanship. One skeptical observer noted that "they began their day with gin and tobacco and ended it with tobacco and gin." Coen himself had written in 1620 that "our nation must drink or die," and he was hardly referring to water.

Brightly colored tiles and slabs of marble, brought in as ballast, were laid in as floors for the ever-expanding town mansions and polished to a fine sheen to reflect the crystal chandeliers, gilt-framed mirrors, and other European furnishings reminiscent of a distant homeland.

Life, however, was not all paradise in Eden. When the planters were deeply in debt because of ill management or because of such natural disasters as earthquakes, tidal waves, or typhoons, the company had no choice but to reduce their debts and advance more money, for the company's livelihood depended upon the planters, the plantations, and their spices.

The most visible and menacing threat was Gunung Api, rising two thousand feet in a nearly perfect symmetrical cone a half mile off Neira. When the mountain was at slumber its beauty was serenity itself, but when awakened the volcano was terrible in its wrath. As if to bring in the new century, Gunung Api had responded to the first Dutch visit to Banda in 1599 with a major eruption.

Throughout the seventeenth century—in 1615, 1629, 1638, 1691, and 1693, Gunung Api's most vengeful years—the volcano erupted, wreaking memorable devastation. As if the mountain were capable of harnessing other natural forces, eruptions showering hot ash down upon houses of thatch and bamboo and the grander, less vulnerable dwellings of stone were often accompanied by attending disasters. Earthquakes took their toll of living quarters, factories, and godowns, while typhoons wreaked the most havoc in the nutmeg gardens, where trees were uprooted and stripped of their fruit by violent winds and drenching rains. In quieter times the mountain emitted "noxious vapors" and "poisonous miasmas" that crept over Neira's cowering community like a plague, bringing sickness and death.

Most vicious was the 1615 eruption, in which great boulders were hurled down upon Fort Nassau. Then, in 1629, while the mountain belched its fury, a tidal wave descended upon Neira, sweeping boats over the embankment, destroying heavy pavement and dislodging brass cannon from the fort and carrying them to sea, along with several houses. During one especially pestilential period, vapors and ash permeated Neira for a full five years, and epidemics were rife. Yet, however strange life was for the transplanted Hollander in these tiny islands so far from home, it continued for two and a half centuries.

Chapter 16

HOLLAND AND ENGLAND: TWILIGHT AND DAWN

BY 1636, WHILE Banda prospered with its nutmeg gardens, the northern sultanates of Ternate and Tidore began to decline as a result of a process that had been gathering momentum since Portuguese times: the dissemination of the culture of cloves to the islands to the south, most notably Ambon and Ceram. The Dutch East India Company by now had gained the power to restrict production to meet Europe's demand for cloves, thereby maintaining high prices and forestalling a glutted market. To achieve this end, the company engaged in a ploy it had perfected in Banda, but with uncertain results: balancing off the islands' supply of spices against what it perceived to be the world's demand for them. Such a scheme introduced the practice of obligatory cultivation of spice trees in groves officially authorized and the careful extirpation of those the company did not approve.

This aim did not sit well with the planters, who were made to fear that a surplus was less desirable than a shortage. Nor did it please the spice-growing sultanates, who had little appreciation for the fickle European market and resented the disturbances it imposed on their own way of life. For the natives whose livelihood had depended upon spice production, the company's policy of controlling the source of spices willy-nilly by leveling forests of clove trees was as baffling as it was cruel. Facing starvation at the hands of blond oppressors, the islanders rebelled, leading to a pro-longed series of conflicts fought sporadically between 1618 and 1657 and known as the Ambon Wars.

Despite their problems with the natives on Ambon, the Dutch in the meantime were broadening their horizons as they began establishing bases in Formosa (Taiwan) to exploit the China trade, as Coen had intended. It was their intention to break the Portuguese monopoly, which was con-ducted out of Macao. Europe had just got wind of another priceless com-modity that had been described by a Persian traveler and recorded by the secretary to Venice's governing Council of Ten in 1559. Of a Chinese drink we learn: "One or two cups of this decoction removes fever, headache, stomach-ache, pain in the side or in the joints, and it should be taken as hot as you can bear it. He said besides that it was good for no end of other ailments which he could not remember, but gout was one of them." Another Venetian writer, assessing the character and health of an urban population, noted in 1589: "The Chinese have an herb from which they press a delicate juice which serves them instead of wine. It also pre-serves the health and frees them from all the evils that the immoderate use of wine doth breed in us."

By 1615 an English trader named Richard Wickham wrote to his col-league in Macao: "Mr. Eaton I pray you buy for me a pot of the best sort of chaw in Meaco, two Fairbowes and Arrows, some half a dozen guilt boxes square for me to put into bark and whatever they cost I will alsoe be will-inge accoumpatable unto for them." Thus we have the first reference in English to *chaw* (also *chai*), or tea. Whampoa Reach, the anchorage for for-eign ships just south of the river city of Canton in southern China, began magnetizing European sails intent on acquiring this strange new obsession.

With their vastly superior sea power, the Hollanders knew little fear of enemy or rival. In 1640 Dutch forces moved upon Ceylon (Sri Lanka) to capture yet another valuable spice monopoly: that of cinnamon (*Cin-namomum cassia*), which, along with the produce of the Spice Islands, was a staple of the sixteenth-century Portuguese trade.

Though not counted among the holy trinity of spices that grew only in the Spice Islands, cinnamon (indigenous to Ceylon and China and later transplanted throughout Southeast Asia and the Malay Archipelago), nonetheless possessed as impressive a lineage as cloves, nutmeg, and mace.

The ancient Chinese believed this tropical evergreen tree to be the Tree of Life, which flourished from the beginning of time in Paradise, a garden at the headwaters of the Yellow River believed to rival Eden in its exquisiteness. It was held that a pilgrim entering Paradise would gain immortality and eternal bliss by eating the tree's fruit, though it was the bark, peeled during the rainy season (as it was more pliable when wet), rolled into "sticks," and dried that was the famous trade commodity. The spice's pungent flavoring had given it special status as a cargo among the trans-Asiatic caravans from biblical times.

Cinnamon is mentioned on several occasions in the Bible. Moses was told by the Lord on Mount Sinai to make an anointing oil of cassia and sweet cinnamon. The spice is likewise honored in Psalms and Ezekiel, and in the seventh chapter of Proverbs, we learn that a woman lured a young man into a seduction by assuring him that her bed was scented with "myrrh, aloes, and cinnamon."

As with the bounty of the Spice Islands, the source of this priceless bark was kept secret by the Arabs who traded in it, and as early as the time of Solomon, around 1000 B.C., potential rivals in trade were warned of dangers in the distant lands where cinnamon grew. The Greek historian Herodotus, writing in the fourth century B.C., notes attacking bats, fierce birds, and steep, dangerous precipices guarding the lofty, inaccessible gardens of this spice, lost somewhere in the mysterious East.

By allying themselves with Ceylon's inland kingdom of Kandy and procuring steady payments of elephants and cinnamon in exchange for their protection of the Sinhalese monarch, the Dutch in 1640 were able to overcome the Portuguese factories on Ceylon's coast in a decisive fashion. By 1658 the weakened Portuguese were expelled from the island, giving Holland control of this crucial halfway house of East Indian trade and its most precious export, cinnamon, which, ground or whole, had universal appeal as a flavoring and was used in countless ways.

Once the Dutch had ousted the Portuguese, the "high government" at Batavia began to see successful possibilities beyond this island off India's southeast coast, namely the subcontinent itself. The governor-general wrote to the Lords Seventeen: "The time is come to throw the Portuguese out of India. . . . The opportunity presents and offers to Your Excellencies the mastery of the Orient."

But the Portuguese in the face of such odds were surprisingly resilient, a quality recorded by the Dutch leader: "The greater number regard India as their fatherland, thinking no longer of Portugal; they trade thither little or not at all, living and enriching themselves out of the treasures of India, as though they were natives and knew no other fatherland."

This is an insightful observation. Despite having been ousted from the Spice Islands and losing their monopoly to the Dutch, the Portuguese were scattered in pockets throughout Asia. No longer the great colonial force they had been in Serrão's day, the Portuguese—despite the reprehensible acts committed by some—were unique among European colonizers of the Far East in their ability to involve themselves deeply in the social and cultural lives of the Asian peoples among whom they did retain a foothold. Serrão's career on Ternate is illustrative of this attitude. By the same token, such expatriation was repellent to the Dutch, who distrusted the Malays less on religious grounds than for their alleged dishonesty in trading. Catholicism, while hardly supplanting Islam, had taken root here and there from India to the Malay Archipelago thanks to the Portuguese, and the Portuguese language rolled more easily off Malay tongues than did Dutch or English. Ironically, if any European tongue was the language of merchant intercourse, even in Batavia, it was Portuguese, much to the displeasure of the Dutch, who had overridden the Portuguese in matters of trade but made little effort to regard Eastern cultures sympathetically.

Then there was the question of Malacca and the continuing but weakening Portuguese presence there since they conquered the port in the summer of 1511. With Lisbon's monarchy in decline and the government in serious debt, even with the Spanish alliance, it was only a matter of time before the Acehnese of Sumatra, the perennial rulers of the Straits, reclaimed their control. As the Dutch presence in the archipelago strengthened, Malacca dwindled in importance and Batavia grew, attracting foreign traders and gradually supplanting the Malayan port as the chief emporium of the region.

Batavia's government, however, knew that it was essential for the Dutch to control the passage from the Indian Ocean to the China Sea. Entering into an alliance with Malacca's ancient enemy, the sultan of Johore, the Dutch seized the port in June 1641 after a six-month blockade that "cost much human flesh," forcing the surrender of the last Portuguese governor. Over the next 150 years, Malacca took on a Dutch character and facade, but its glory days were in the past.

As the seventeenth century drifted into the eighteenth, there was little marked change in the succession of Dutch governor-generals in Batavia or in the manner by which they attempted to exercise their monopoly in the Spice Islands. The conflicts continued with a new and varied cast of characters.

Then a development at home signaled a new direction for Holland. On the morning of April 12, 1713, there was an unusual commotion in the marketplace of Utrecht, when at ten o'clock two cannon were fired and a great cheer went up. Delegates from England, France, Holland, Spain, and Sweden had concluded a peace that ended the War of Spanish Succession, and a curious and unprecedented transformation began to occur in the Dutch Republic. Having been for more than a century one of the most aggressive powers in Europe, the Netherlands volunteered to retire from so active and contentious a life among the great nations. Long-wigged diplomats began to supersede admirals and generals in the country's scheme of business. Peace and prosperity became the order of the day, as Holland, having accumulated vast amounts of wealth in the seventeenth century, became Europe's banker. Having loaned money to the great powers of Europe, the Netherlands realized that peace and friendship with other nations were essential to her well-being. It was said that Holland was now a counting house defended by a fleet.

The old prosperity that had built Holland did remain, and for decades to come trade remained quite profitable. But the national will had shifted. Energy was replaced by caution as financial speculation became key. If the seventeenth century had seen the accumulation of wealth, the eighteenth witnessed its enjoyment. Men of courage and initiative—leaders of Coen's mettle—were figures of the past. Even so, the Dutch East India Company reached its zenith in the mid-eighteenth century, when in 1756 the Banda enterprises were realizing an annual profit of over one million guilders. As the company was urged by the Lords Seventeen toward more efficient and humane measures, the plantations in the Spice Islands became more productive. As we shall see, however, Holland was destined to lose her 150-

year monopoly of the spice trade by the audacious actions of a Frenchman under tensely dramatic circumstances.

The decline of Holland may be seen in the erosion of the Dutch East India Company. There were more than 4,700 voyages from the Netherlands to Asia between 1602 and 1795, and during this time nearly one million people took ship from Europe, while only a third of that number boarded in Asia to return to the Dutch Republic. These are extraordinary numbers, especially when one considers the demographic effects such mass migrations had on Holland. The figures are all the more amazing when it is considered that the Dutch Republic had only 1,500,000 to 2,000,000 inhabitants during this period, with the implication that the company relied heavily on foreigners for its rank-and-file personnel.

In any event, the Dutch company surpassed any other company in dispatching sheer numbers to Asia—in fact, twice as many as all other European companies together. Likewise, its ships carried more men, with adequate supplies of food and drink to sustain them through the long voyage, than any other European East Indiamen.

The likes of Courthope and Jourdain had English pluck and heart; but the Dutch always had superior manpower, and the Dutch East India Company's activities in Asia explain why so many people were needed. The Dutch company required sailors for their Asian fleets, merchants, clerks, and craftsmen for its overseas settlements, and above all soldiers for its campaigns and to protect its factories.

The Dutch East Indiamen on the outward voyage from Europe carried not only their crews to sail the ship but personnel to be employed in Asia, from Ceylon to Ambon. The numbers for such human flux are not evenly divided between the two centuries, for the migration was far greater in the eighteenth century as voyages increased.

These figures are revealing because of their enormousness, for they make understandable the monstrous charges against the Dutch East India Company: that the organization devoured its own personnel. Only one out of three of those persons departing Holland ever saw home again. The voyage itself demanded a toll, but most of those not returning died during service in Asia, sometimes as casualties of war but more prominently of such diseases as scurvy and typhus. The gaps had to be filled.

As for the voyages themselves, the concentration of so many men of diverse backgrounds and nationalities during a long sail on a single ship created a hellish environment for the crew. Such tensions often led to mutiny, though in nearly all cases the offenders were caught and severely punished. Penalties included the death sentence for murder, mutiny, and homosexuality (usually by being thrown into the sea bound to the body of the victim or other culprit); keelhauling; ducking from the yardarm; nailing the culprit's hand to the mainmast; flogging, up to five hundred lashes; and imprisonment in irons on bread and water in very confined quarters. Far more soldiers and seafarers found a way out of misery aboard ship and the frightening prospect of rotting away in some sickly Asian outpost in company service by deserting, especially in a port such as Bengal where a deserter could enlist in the service of a rival company.

The happiest ships, however, were those whose crew and passengers shared the social or family ties of a single background, be it Delft, Hoorn, or Enkhuizen. These were men who had a home to which to return, while poverty-stricken vagabonds from the German hinterland, say, had no future in Europe at all and were more likely to succumb to shipboard disease or end in up an obscure Eastern grave.

There were other developments at home that led to the decline of the Dutch East India Company. Since the company's inception, the Lords Seventeen had run it free from government interference. Also, the small investor effectively had no say in the company's affairs, as stockholders' meetings were unknown. It was inevitable that such a classically oligarchical arrangement would eventually invite inefficiency and corruption. If during the seventeenth century the riches of the Indies had kept company dividends high, at the end of the eighteenth the company was desperate for money, while its representatives had lost their taste for battle.

Ships began to rot in Holland's ports, and her shipyards, which had guaranteed employment and a lot of it, went to seed. For such smaller ports on the Zuider Zee as Enkhuizen and Hoorn, the craft and machine shops, godowns, and building yard activities that were essential to a seagoing trade declined, severely punishing the local economy.

Late in the eighteenth century, when the American Revolution was raging, the Dutch East India Company tried to maintain its commerce with Asia by hiring ships under neutral flags, while the old yards were dismantled and the smaller ones of Delft, Enkhuizen, and Hoorn closed down. In February 1778, after France made a secret treaty with America, hostilities broke out between France and England. That same year Commodore John Paul Jones, thirty years old, sailed into Dutch waters, a personification of the revolutionary spirit of the day sweeping through continents on both sides of the Atlantic.

The impact of this American gentleman pirate on the Dutch consciousness, along with the noteworthy presence of avuncular Benjamin Franklin, was infectious but destructive for the country. A fervent Holland was swept into a disastrous war with England, suffering greatly in the conflict, which lasted from 1780 to 1784, for the English destroyed most of the Netherlands' fleet. Having complete control of the English Channel, the British forced the Dutch to transport their goods to French ports by sailing the dangerous, long route around the north of Scotland. Dutch ships became easy prey.

By 1785 the Dutch Republic was in a sorry state. Though the war with England had ended, the public debt had increased to the point where it was nearly impossible to pay the interest that had accrued. Holland's ships captured during the last four years were still in English hands. The practical result was that the Dutch East India Company was eclipsed by its rival across the channel. Holland's citizens faced destitution, and many of them fled to France and Belgium to greet the French Revolution as the last great hope.

Thus there were other cataclysmic changes at work in Holland's decline. The French Revolution, which had begun in 1789, and the subsequent rise of Napoleon placed Holland in a shadow from which she never emerged. The Napoleonic Wars reignited hostilities between English and Dutch, and Banda after nearly two centuries was again fair game for the contentious English, who had nearly but not quite forgotten the heroic stands of Courthope and Jourdain. In 1802 the decision was made to stop all ship construction in Holland and sell the remaining ships together with the dockyards.

Thus did the Netherlands' glorious and infamous years of supremacy in the Far Eastern trade drift into a quiet, brackish backwater, "and the startling beauty of its waterborne cities, so modern and functional in the 17th century, acquired the patina of age," as the Cambridge historian J. H. Plumb memorably phrased it. "A country without a history began to live in the past."

• • •

WHAT OF THE mercantile fortunes of England? The island nation followed Holland's decline as a spirited contestant in the spice trade, but with one important difference: England prospered through other lucrative avenues of trade, while Holland, as we've seen, foundered and never recovered.

The signs of England's future in world trade were made clear to the English East India Company back in Coen's day. Even as early as 1625 in the wake of the failed heroics of Courthope and Jourdain, the Honourable Company subscribers and directors, angered by the crown's inaction against the Dutch, essentially gave up the trade of the East Indies for the next 170 years. While an English factory acquiring cloves would last in Macassar until 1667 and Bantam would survive as England's source of pepper until 1680, the fate of Pulau Run, depopulated and shorn of its nutmeg gardens, best illustrates the island nation's disillusionment with the spice trade as an exclusive mercantile endeavor. The company looked elsewhere in Asia for Eastern riches, for England had discovered "a politer way of living, which passed to luxury and intolerable expense," as the churchman diarist John Evelyn, Pepys's friend, phrased it in 1685. Not long after Evelyn, Daniel Defoe, the author of *Robinson Crusoe* and *Moll Flanders,* observed more pointedly, "The general fansie of the people runs upon East India goods."

Ships occasionally brought back to Europe's shores unwanted cargo as well, and in this regard Defoe's name evokes a darker side of the spice trade. In 1721 a great plague swept like an evil tide across Europe from the East, reaching Marseilles and spreading through Provence. Both England and Holland feared that another widespread epidemic—a new Black Death—would devastate the continent and England. The Dutch acted first, imposing a strict quarantine on all shipping from Asia, even torching cargoes and compelling sailors to swim ashore naked. The equally fearful English government placed an embargo upon Eastern shipping, angering the merchant classes. If the memory of the Great Plague of London in 1665 had dimmed for the traders, it had not for the shrewd journalist Defoe, for that earlier scourge had been the most acute memory of his childhood.

Seizing the opportunity to write a cautionary tale in anticipation of the impending disaster by dramatizing the events of the earlier epidemic, Defoe created his *Journal of the Plague Year,* a mingling of fact and invention by a quick and observant eye of the marauding pestilence Defoe indeed remembered. The memorable images—London's afflicted houses marked with a large red cross, the gruesome carts bearing the dead to yawning grave sites, the constantly tolling bells—place a human face on a vast, incomprehensible tragedy. But the plague of 1721 never reached London, and Defoe's journalistic warning for Georgian England became a page-turning, bleak remembrance of things past.

England's supreme day in the East would come later in the century and in the next, with Captain James Cook's Pacific voyages, Sir Joshua Child and Lord Clive in India, and Sir Thomas Stamford Raffles in Malaysia and Singapore, as well as in other far-flung tropical outposts, from Bencoolen on Sumatra to the West Indies. Opium grown and processed in India became a huge cash crop for the Honourable Company, which oversaw the entire production but had no direct hand in its shipment and resale to China. Such flouting of official Chinese restrictions against the contraband drug would have jeopardized trading relations between the two nations, the last thing an expanding England wanted. Rather, the opium crop was sold at a premium to independent agency houses in India, which passed the drug to Chinese smugglers at Whampoa Reach. They, in turn, bribed conniving Chinese officials in Canton, who turned a blind eye as the narcotic entered the mainland. Nonetheless, the company in British India profited mightily from opium sales, enabling it to purchase tea for an insatiable domestic consumption.

Of paramount importance to the company was this burgeoning, legitimate China trade, which had become England's obsession. The English were even trading silver for tea and porcelain, a practice that at once baffled and delighted the mandarins of Canton. In a happy turn at doggerel, John Cawthorne captured the spirit of the age in 1756: "Of late, 'tis true, quite sick of Rome and Greece, / We fetch out models from the wise Chinese."

England had developed other geographical diversions as well that modified her frustrations in the spice trade. In the mid-eighteenth century Captain Cook's exploration of the Pacific coincided with a number of other cultural developments that effectively elevated that great ocean to a fashionable as well as a scientific vogue. On his first Pacific voyage, Cook sailed for Tahiti to measure from that island the transit of Venus across the sun's face on June 3, 1769. Cook had no chronometer, but he did have an array of other instruments aboard the *Endeavour* with which to observe this heavenly alignment. If properly measured, the configuration would help establish earth's distance from the sun.

Sailing with Cook were a number of important civilians, including the astronomer Henry Green and the brilliant young botanist Joseph Banks. (After celestial measurement, the voyage's purpose would be exploration, leading to landfall at New Zealand and afterward the discovery of Australia, and Banks would have the study of the South Pacific's flora all to himself.) The transit of Venus was observed; however imperfectly it was achieved, the observation contributed to navigational techniques that were being constantly refined.

It was not until two years after she had left Tahiti—July 1771—that Cook's *Endeavour* returned to England after a voyage that witnessed a third of her crew die from malaria and dysentery. But the cost of the expedition was scarcely counted, for all England wanted to hear about the strange, new world of the Pacific. That ocean was as great a mystery in Cook's day as the Far East had been in an earlier one. Not unlike Africa, the Pacific had been only vaguely known. Was it haunted by demons and monsters? Were its islands inhabited by a people blessed by an abundance of natural resources in paradisaical surroundings? Cook brought back the answer that there did exist an unspoiled tropical haven whose people knew nothing of the restraints of civilization. At least, that was the evidence of a better life most English and Europeans wanted to hear.

Banks, an attractive young aristocrat, was particularly feted, with a royal interview with George III, an honorary degree from Oxford, kudos from the Royal Society for his botanical discoveries, a portrait painted by Joshua Reynolds, a lunch hosted by Dr. Johnson, and a number of dinner parties at which the young scientist exuberantly displayed the tattoo on his arm acquired in Tahiti. (Years later, in 1778, when Banks was made president of the Royal Society, it was his suggestion that Lieutenant William Bligh command the *Bounty* on an expedition to Tahiti to acquire breadfruit seedlings for transport to the West Indies, where they were to provide a staple diet for the African slaves.)

Cook likewise had an audience with the king and won praise from the Admiralty, for his years on the Pacific had enabled him to fill in a great blank map with newly discovered islands. But it was the philosophical implications of Cook's voyage that proved to be the most intriguing. Rousseau had written his *Discourse on the Arts and Sciences* in 1749, and by Cook's return the theory of the noble savage was the talk of Europe. Tahiti was soon regarded as the happy, unspoiled Arcadia, where simple, sophisticated man prospered far from the shores of the corrupt, fallen West. Sailor and philosopher alike were seduced by the delights, real and imagined, of this Pacific Eden, thus fulfilling a need of the time: the realization of an earthly paradise where civilized men might escape their bonds. Even Boswell was not above yearning, half in jest, for a life of nostalgic escapism. He wrote to a friend in 1757: "You are tempted to join Rousseau in preferring the savage state. I am so at times. When jaded with business, or when tormented with the passions of civilized life, I could fly to the woods."

But London was a city not only of Boswell and Johnson, but also of Horace Walpole and Fanny Burney, not to mention other such skeptical wits as Gibbon, Burke, Garrick, and Sheridan. Such keen minds were hardly capable of letting such romanticism pass without recourse to satire. It was the pious moralizing about the virtues of enchanted islands in the South Seas that induced them to take up their pens. The point is that a false, idealized picture of Tahiti had formed in the minds of people, and Cook's scientific data about these and other matters could do little to correct it. People idealized Tahiti because they wanted it to be as true as what they dreamed, while their opposites boasted of the wonders of their technological age.

It was in this day of Newton that a great discovery was made in navigation: the invention of the chronometer as a means for determining longitude.

Long before Captain Cook, back in the time of Magellan and later in the day of Coen, long voyages in eastern waters were possible because of the dependability of the monsoons, enabling vessels to maintain a course by running before the wind. The act of fixing positions by astronomical methods, however, was slow in coming. A latitude was fairly easy to determine by "shooting the sun" at noon with an octant, then using tables converting that figure for the day, month, and year into distance north or south of the equator.

Appraising a ship's longitude, on the other hand, was exceedingly difficult, beyond the very rough method known as "dead reckoning," or estimating the run of the ship by determining nautical miles traveled over a compass-set course. Distance equaled elapsed time multiplied by speed, measured by a chip log and reel. A crew member tossed the log overboard and counted the evenly spaced knots in the rope as they were pulled over the stern during one turn of a twenty-eight-second log glass. This measurement was converted to nautical miles per hour (knots), while pegs inserted each thirty minutes in the traverse board recorded the time run on each dead reckoning course.

Later it became essential for sailors bound east and west to know the time, because the star tables with which they sailed informed the navigator what position the moon or sun or a star should be in the sky at a certain position on Earth at a certain time of day or night; for as the heavens moved, the angles of their components changed by a known amount. These tables were computed on a meridian: the north-south line that ran through the location where they had been computed. Thus, a vessel making its way south or north on the Greenwich meridian could use the tables to find out how far south or north of Greenwich the ship was. If a ship moved east or west, however, it was a different matter entirely, because the position of the stars as specified by the tables would differ by the longitudinal (east or west) distance of the vessel from its home meridian. Because the earth revolves once every twenty-four hours, it follows that for every fifteen degrees east or west, sunrise will be one hour earlier or later. The position of the stars will be similarly altered.

This realization was gained through a most dramatic and startling discovery at the end of the greatest voyage in history. What was left of Magellan's expedition, the *Victoria* and her ragtag crew, anchored in the Cape Verde Islands off Santiago to learn that the date was not Wednesday, July 9, 1522, but Thursday, July 10. The mariners were puzzled, for an exacting log had been kept for nearly three years, and they finally decided that the Cape Verde time was erroneous. However, when they arrived at Sanlucar on what they believed to be Saturday, September 6, before sailing up the Guadalquivir to Seville in triumph, they were told that it was Sunday,

September 7. Somehow the *Victoria* had lost a full day from its calendar, though this was inconceivable to her crew.

None of the great geographers from ancient times onward had foreseen this conundrum, and sixteenth-century scientists were as baffled as the men of Magellan's expedition until their studies allowed them to conclude that Copernicus had been right. The earth was spinning eastward, finishing a cycle each day. Because Magellan's voyagers had been sailing to the west against that motion and had completed a circumnavigation, they had gained exactly twenty-four hours.

Without a clock to tell him what time it was at his home meridian, the navigator could not make the required adjustment to compute his position. Each minute that the navigator's clock was fast or slow would give him a position that was, at the equator, inaccurate by about fifteen miles. As civilization became increasingly dependent on transoceanic trade, such errors became unacceptable. It was imperative to find a clock that would tell the time accurately over long periods at sea. A pendulum clock was not the answer because it was useless in strong seas. There were also the inherent problems of salt and corrosion.

The rise of modern methods of navigation may be dated from 1735 and the invention of the chronometer, whose springs were made of crucible steel, enabling ships to carry Greenwich Mean Time on board. The difference between ship's time and Greenwich Mean Time could be converted into the distance from Greenwich. But chronometers for nearly another century were too expensive and fragile for common use, though an exact instrument that could stand up to conditions at sea was nearly perfected by John Harrison in 1764.

ON JULY 13, 1772, a year to the day after the *Endeavour's* return to England, Cook sailed again. This time his mission was to sail as far southward as possible toward the undiscovered South Pole, then to withdraw to the tropics (Tahiti) during the long Antarctic winter. The expedition was successful. England's expectations on the eve of the American Revolution were high, and Cook's voyages—especially their legacy after his murder at the hands of Hawaiian natives in 1777—proved to be an exotic dream of a distraction, and an obsessive one, from the ongoing mania for spices.

But England was still not yet done with the spice trade. The Crown's star briefly rose in the Spice Islands at the end of the eighteenth century during the Napoleonic Wars, when her forces seized French possessions in India and moved on France's ally Holland in the Far East. By then, Holland as a mercantile power had declined drastically since Coen's aggressive stewardship in the early decades of the seventeenth century, and the Dutch East India Company by the 1790s survived in name only.

Ambon fell to an English fleet in 1796, which then proceeded to seize Banda, and by 1801 Ternate was also in English hands. But these conquests, successful and with little resistance, were anticlimactic. As we shall learn, a series of smuggling operations—an impudent scheme hatched by a reckless Frenchman—spirited clove and nutmeg seedlings out of the Moluccas under the very noses of the Dutch, thus breaking Holland's long-standing monopoly. The transformation was immediate and catastrophic, changing the way the world had done business from the beginning. Simply put, spices were no longer the potent force driving the global economy they had been since ancient times. The English managed to export seedlings to their own colonies, such as Penang off Malaysia. As well, they transported the Moluccan bounty to Canton, thus contributing to the Anglo-Chinese balance of payments.

England's possession of the Spice Islands so late in the day, however, was short-lived. The Peace of Amiens in 1802 stipulated that all the former Dutch possessions in the East Indies be returned to Holland, though Ceylon (Sri Lanka) and the Cape became colonies of the English crown. Further hostilities were to come as a direct result of Napoleon's campaigns in Europe and Egypt, and the aforementioned Raffles of the Honourable Company, a wiry, energetic man with his own ambitions of company expansion, began to cast a longer shadow in Far Eastern waters. Realizing that Penang would never assume the strategic importance of Malacca, successively held since 1511 by the Portuguese, Dutch, and British, Raffles eventually, on January 28, 1819, put ashore at the tiny cluster of islands at the tip of the Malay Peninsula. Negotiating with the local sultan, Raffles quickly established a settlement, the Union Jack was raised, and within weeks thousands of Malay and Chinese merchants had established their shops and godowns in Singapore (the name is from the Sanskrit, meaning "lion city"). It was an ideal location on the Straits of Malacca for safeguarding British commerce from India to China. In effect, Singapore became the new Malacca.

"Our object is not territory but trade," Raffles wrote in a now familiar litany, "a great commercial emporium and fulcrum whence we may extend our influence politically as circumstances may hereafter require. . . . One free port in these seas must eventually destroy the spell of Dutch monopoly; and what Malta is in the West, that may Singapore become in the East." In any event, Singapore, Raffles's brilliant invention of an offshore Eastern entrepôt, enabled England to consolidate and sustain its success in the China and India trade.

This mercantile focus intensified after the dark days of the Opium Wars, provoked by a Chinese blockade of British merchants in their Canton factories until they had surrendered their stores of opium. The British responded with the deployment of forces with weapons and gunboats superior to the antiquated ones of the Chinese. The practical result of the hostilities and the peace that followed was that opium and tea as goods for trade became more valuable than ever, inviting wild speculation at home and abroad. Following the Honourable Company's fall from grace in Canton in the early 1840s as a result of these skirmishes, a major entrepôt on Hong Kong Island at China's very door was founded. Notwithstanding the loss of the American colonies nearly three quarters of a century earlier, the bright sun of Queen Victoria's empire shone the world over.

Chapter 17

THE BROKEN GOURD

UNTIL THE MID-EIGHTEENTH century it was generally believed that trees and plants could grow only in places where they were discovered growing naturally. The German botanist Georg Eberhard Rumpf (1627–1702), writing a century earlier, had put a fine point on the notion that spices had been given by God to the Spice Islands, "beyond which, by no human industry, can they be propagated or perfectly cultivated." However, Rumpf's theory had in fact been disproved, though it was not universally known. In 1585 a West Indies ship arrived in Europe with a first cargo of Jamaica ginger *(singabera),* a flavorful root originating in India and southern China and the first Asian spice to be grown successfully in the New World. Whether other such early transplanting experiments were successful remains a mystery.

Rumpf without question was the most prestigious botanist of his day. Moreover, he had spent years of research in the Spice Islands and published volumes on his findings, literary accomplishments that gave weight to his authority. While it is true that cloves native to Ternate and Tidore had been successfully propagated to the south on Ambon, these were local transfers closely and jealously monitored by the Dutch.

As a practical matter, few thought to challenge Rumpf's pronouncements by attempting to remove seedlings from the Spice Islands, largely because of the nature of the plants themselves. Cloves presented a particular problem, for as commercial stock, it is a dried flower, not a fruit or seed, and thus is useless for planting. Cloves normally grow from seedlings scattered by a parent tree, and they obstinately refused to survive during transport, so the young plants habitually were in a sorry state on arrival at their destinations. The problem of transplanting was complicated by the uncompromising Dutch, who made the export of seedlings a crime punishable by death.

Nutmeg seedlings were almost as difficult to cultivate elsewhere, especially the round variety, which grew only on Banda. The Dutch headed off the potential threat of illegal export by shelling and roasting the nut and then coating it with lime, thus preventing its germination elsewhere.

But the challenge of transplanting spices to gain unrestricted access to them as trade commodities, thus enhancing the wealth and prestige of a rival nation, was too enticing not to go unanswered. Enterprising Englishmen sought to test Rumpf's accepted theory by carefully packing a ship hold's worth of the best clove and nutmeg seedlings and sailing them to the southwest Sumatran port of Bencoolen, which they called Port Arthur. Pepper plantations were already laid out there, and the new nutmeg seedlings likewise thrived, with the first commercial shipment of Sumatran nutmegs reaching Europe in 1815. Similar experiments were tried in England's new island colony of Penang off the Malay Peninsula, established in 1786 as a pepper port, as well as Grenada in the West Indies. The tests were successful to the point where by the mid-nineteenth century these upstart colonies collectively rivaled Banda's exports.

The English, however, were not the first to transplant clove and nutmeg seedlings. They had been anticipated by a Frenchman in the mid-eighteenth century, and if anyone can claim to have broken the long-standing spice monopoly held by the Dutch, that man is Pierre Poivre, a French adventurer who began his career as a missionary in China but eventually rose to become administrator of Île de France (Mauritius). One of the most curious and colorful figures in the saga of spices— and seemingly destined for greatness in the spice trade (*poivre* means "pepper")—Poivre's exploits are the stuff of romantic fiction.

•　•　•

BORN IN LYON in 1719, Poivre was educated in the place of his birth and then in Paris, where he distinguished himself as a student of theology and philosophy as well as of drawing and painting. At twenty-one Poivre was sent by the Paris Society of Foreign Missions to Canton, where misfortune struck. Unwittingly carrying a letter of introduction intended for someone else, he was jailed for a year in a case of mistaken identity.

Under these circumstances, as he would later under vastly different conditions, Poivre displayed a talent for exploiting a bad situation to his own good. Assiduously studying Chinese, he mastered the language and so impressed a mandarin that he was awarded both freedom and patronage. After traveling for a year in China's interior, he spent two years at the imperial court of Cochin-China (Vietnam), where he dazzled the royal house with his sophistication and knowledge.

From Cochin-China he made his way back to Canton, where he took passage back to France in a convoy of three ships passing through unfriendly waters patrolled by the hostile English and Dutch. In the Straits of Banka the convoy was set upon by an English fleet, and in the course of battle before he was captured, Poivre's lower right arm was taken off by a cannonball.

Imprisoned in an English hold, he quickly developed gangrene. This was a day when instruments were not sterilized and anesthetics were unavailable for an operation, and to go under the knife in any circumstance was to gamble with death. Poivre was saved only by an emergency amputation performed by the ship's surgeon during a fire that had all other hands occupied. Putting in to Batavia, the English sold the vessels to Dutch authorities and gave them custody of the prisoners, including the maimed Poivre.

Poivre had a natural aptitude for languages, and as his wounds healed he managed to learn the Malay language in Batavia. Exposed to the extraordinary commerce of spices that had made Batavia into a port to be reckoned with Poivre was struck by an idea similar to the one that had engaged Courthope and Jourdain nearly a century and a half earlier. If Holland had prospered because of the spice trade, why should France be denied a share of such lucrative activity?

From Batavia Poivre and a few of his fellow countrymen took ship for Pondicherry, in southeastern India, via the Malay Peninsula. A skilled navigator, though largely a self-taught one, Poivre contributed to the success of the voyage by guiding the ship through storms and shoals, while by lamplight he composed his journals, noting with exacting detail his observations on the ways of life and livelihood in the ports of call.

Europe was still curious about Eastern exotica—silks, lacquers, spices—and Poivre's compendium of diary entries became the genesis of a literary work, *Voyages of a Philosopher,* that came to be celebrated not only in Europe but in America as well. He arrived in Europe via Île de France and Martinique, but not before encountering on two different occasions French and English pirates.

With such adventures behind him and the panache to exploit them for personal gain, Poivre used his linguistic brilliance to secure a royal appointment in 1749 and return to the East on behalf of the French crown and the French East India Company. Barely thirty years of age, he was given a range of assignments. Most important, he was to ingratiate himself with the Cochin-China royal court in Haiphong, while plotting to realize his primary goal: that of thwarting the Dutch by smuggling nutmeg and clove seedlings out of the Spice Islands, thereby breaking Holland's 150-year monopoly in the spice trade.

It was a dangerous task. If caught, he would be found guilty of a capital offense and executed. Seeking official sanction for this secret mission, Poivre sailed back across the Indian Ocean to Pondicherry on the Bay of Bengal. Though he had been promised financial backing from the French East India Company he served, he met personal opposition from the company's governor, the famous Joseph François Dupleix, France's greatest figure in India and adversary of the legendary Englishman Robert Clive. Dupleix was an arrogant and complex man, and he was determined to sabotage the venture.

While the reasons for Dupleix's antagonism toward Poivre's daring enterprise remain obscure, one might conjecture about them. England and France were competing on the battlefield for the spoils of India, and for Dupleix, who did nothing by halves, France's Asian destiny was tied to his own vanity. Saddled with inferior recruits sent out from France, he faced in the unruly, quarrelsome Clive a brilliant guerrilla leader, who with a small force captured and held Arcot, the capital of Dupleix's Indian factions.

The French East India Company was determined to remain a trading organization and not to be led astray by a man of Poivre's stripe, an ambitious, wild-eyed visionary who promised nothing but trouble. As for the French company's English rivals, Dupleix, with an Indian wife and the style and dress of a potentate, mistakenly thought he could eradicate them. When Poivre appeared on the scene to garner support for his mission from Dupleix, the lines were already drawn between the forces of the French governor and the English troops of Clive. (In 1753 Clive would return to England with a fortune, while Dupleix, a ruined man, lost his post.) Dupleix, witnessing the erosion of his influence and power, was not about to see France's glory carried forward by an upstart adventurer such as Poivre.

But Poivre finally succeeded in collecting from the company the tidy sum held for him to finance the expedition. Moving on to Mauritius, he encountered more bureaucratic obstacles set in his way by a resentful Dupleix, angry at having been circumvented. Skirting them, Poivre journeyed on to Manila via Canton and Macao, gathering goods and garnering money as he traveled to support his masquerade as a merchant.

Arriving in Manila on May 17, 1751, aboard the *Santa Rita,* a small ship he had chartered out of Macao, he found a sympathetic ear in the Spanish governor, Ovando Solis, who wanted nothing so much as to see the Dutch get their comeuppance. Another friendly listener was the sultan of Jolo, who offered his hospitality on behalf of the islanders of the southern Philippines.

Solis, wise to the ways of official backbiting, even managed to derail a scheme by Governor Dupleix, who bitterly resented Poivre's royal support. Dupleix had bribed a Spanish merchant to secure a score or so of spice trees at a hefty price, thus giving him the credit while embarrassing Poivre. But Solis managed to discover and suppress the plot.

Poivre then decided that he must proceed somewhat cautiously. He spent eighteen months in Manila foraging among the waterfront wharves and godowns for the spice seedlings, which failed to materialize—an indication of Holland's relentless grip on the monopoly. He waited and waited. Finally, to expedite matters he bought and fitted out two small craft and sent them south to the Moluccas.

As time passed, the boats failed to return, and Poivre's resources were rapidly dwindling. Additional financial resources were due him, and he appealed repeatedly to Pondicherry only to be frustrated by Dupleix. If only he were given an armed frigate, he wrote, he himself would sail to the Moluccas for seedlings. His entire life had been a risk, proof given by the loss of an arm. Why should it be any different now?

But he was spared any further risk when, through a middleman in Manila, he was able to acquire nine rooted nutmeg trees. Though he was unable to determine their condition for sea travel, he resolved to return to Mauritius with the seedlings, then to strike out for more.

Setting out in February 1753, Poivre voyaged back to Pondicherry, where he was ignored by Dupleix, whose problems with the English and with his own company were mounting. When Poivre arrived in Mauritius, his nine trees had dwindled to five, but he carefully planted them in a garden plot, then sought the help of Acting Governor Bouvet, a sympathetic official but hardly in command of the resources Poivre needed.

Nevertheless, Bouvet helped. He provided Poivre with a decrepit sixty-ton vessel called *La Colombe,* which barely pushed into Manila Harbor four months later ready to be beached and shored up. In January 1755, with a completely rebuilt though barely seaworthy *Colombe,* Poivre was determined to sail her to the Spice Islands. If smugglers, fearing the unforgiving laws of the Dutch, were afraid of providing him with the necessary seedlings, then he would procure them himself.

Sailing southward with a crew ignorant of his purpose, Poivre entered Moluccan waters with the *Colombe,* and it was only then that Poivre explained to his men what he was about. His crew to a man was solidly against the plan and enraged at having been duped. Why should they face the noose for Poivre's insane scheme?

Poivre risked mutiny and desertion with each passing day as the *Colombe* plowed southward. Meeting a Dutch patrol ship, Poivre ordered a Dutch flag raised so his ship wouldn't be boarded. The deception almost failed when a crew member attempted to jump ship and turn informer to save his own neck, but Poivre managed to have him restrained, and the *Colombe* continued on her way before a south wind.

The misadventures of the *Colombe* might have been comical to a disinterested observer, as the ship was at the mercy of any contrary wind, which spun the craft this way and that over the eastern rim of the Moluccan archipelago. Not once was the *Colombe* to find a sheltered landfall in the Spice Islands, despite sheaves of charts and intelligence reports Poivre had gathered in Manila. With a hostile crew and conniving winds, the *Colombe* might have been lost to mutiny or storm but for a chance landing at the port of Lifão on Portuguese Timor, the large island southwest of the Banda Sea, only three hundred miles from Australia.

Received by the governor, Poivre admitted what he was about, and the former was only too happy to conspire against Portugal's ancient enemy, the loathed Dutch. If Poivre would return in a year with sufficient funds, the governor advised, he would see what stock might be accumulated from Dutch-held islands. Meanwhile, the governor presented Poivre with a token gift of eleven nutmeg trees and a handful of clove seeds.

Poivre urged the *Colombe* back to Mauritius, where to his horror he discovered that the nutmeg trees he'd planted earlier had died of neglect or vandalism by the hand of envious colleagues of Dupleix's camp. After overseeing the planting of his new cache and ensuring their well-being in his absence, he sailed for France to report on his niggling successes and to plead for more funds. A new expedition, however, was not forthcoming.

It was only several years later that Poivre was officially recognized for his labors with a pension. Returning to Lyon from Paris, he bought a house and married Marie-Françoise Robin, a young woman who bore him three daughters. Meanwhile, the French East India Company, which had entered the highly competitive spice game late in the day and was riddled with intrigue and corruption from its inception, was dissolved. The result was that the government would now see to its territories. Its foreign minister, the duc de Praslin, appointed Poivre as intendant of Mauritius and the nearby island of Bourbon, and it was to here that the adventurer, now in his late forties, returned with his wife and children in late 1767.

Here, Poivre's experience and aptitude as an administrator enabled him to overcome the obstructionist tactics of disgruntled company men who had presided over its ruin. In just three years he transformed the island into a model agricultural community to the point where he was able to support some six thousand French troops billeted there with no official provision for doing so. On a piece of newly acquired property in the hills, he built a mansion, which he called Montplasir. It became the centerpiece of a magnificent botanical garden, laid out under Poivre's supervision with the aid of a gifted local gardener named Cère.

Cère and Poivre experimented with a plethora of exotic fruits and plants—breadfruit, mango, durian, avocado, mangosteen, and many others. The renowned botanist Commerson was attracted by what Poivre had created and came to take up residence. Soon Poivre discovered a clerk called Provost who shared his passion for cultivation and spices and who in fact reminded the intendant of his own passions as a young man. It was an immediate and lasting friendship. Because Poivre's second garden of spices had fared no better than his first, he charged an eager Provost to embark on another adventure to bring back the forbidden fruit—nutmegs and cloves—for cultivation.

Provost set out in May 1769 for the Spice Islands with Lieutenant Evard de Temignon in command of the *Étôile du Matin* and Lieutenant Sieur d'Etcheverry commanding the corvette *Vigilant* as escort. The small expedition put in at Aceh on Sumatra's northwest tip, then Kedah on the Malay Peninsula, before crossing the South China Sea to Manila, their staging area for reaching their destination in the Spice Islands from the north. Poivre had been a tireless collector of intelligence on the islands, and his sources informed him of the discovery of a small, uninhabited island northwest of Ternate called Miao, where spices grew in abundance and the Dutch were not especially vigilant as to its security.

When the two ships anchored off the tiny island and put in to explore it on March 8, 1770, they were crestfallen to discover that the Dutch had themselves discovered the hidden spice-forested gem. Two days of exploring the island brought them the grim realization that the Hollanders had cut down every spice tree on the island. The futility of the voyage thus far steeled Provost, as it would have Poivre.

It would be necessary to penetrate more deeply south in the Moluccas, so Provost concocted a plan. He and d'Etcheverry would push on south in the *Vigilant* for Ceram, while Temignon would skirt the Moluccas in the smaller boat and make for Timor, where the party would rendezvous.

Provost's party sailed the five hundred miles to Ceram. Their main fear, after negotiating the treacherous shoals surrounding the island, was the hostility of the natives, who had remained a wild and aggressive lot since Francis Xavier's visit two centuries before. But luck was with Provost, who had hoped that things might go well for a Frenchman.

Encountering an embittered Dutchman who resented his high-handed treatment at the hands of the Dutch East India Company, Provost was delighted and relieved to accept the man's genuine offer of help. Forthcoming with maps and instructions, the Hollander pointed the French party in the direction of the small island of Gueby. There, emphasized the Dutchman, grew quantities of prime cloves and nutmegs. What's more, the company had no clue as to this trove of botanical treasures.

On April 6 the *Viligant* hove to at Gueby. Upon putting ashore, the ship's boat was met by a band of enthusiastic natives, whose chiefs deeply resented Dutch avarice and brutality. In much the same spirit that the Run and Ai islanders of the Banda group had befriended the English as an ally against the Dutch, the *orang kaya* immediately took to the strangers and urged the establishment of a French base on the island.

Festivities with prodigious amounts of food and drink followed that loosened a generosity of spirit on both sides. Provost, with a show of gallantry, presented his ranking host with a French uniform and flag while onlookers cheered. The chief preened in his new costume, and while he unfurled the new colors, he trampled the Dutch flag into the sand. Inviting Provost to herald the existence of his new adherents to the king of France, the chief then queried him as to what gifts from new vassals would most please their new king.

One can imagine the question stirring Provost's blood and the restrained enthusiasm with which he answered it as he stood on the beach with sweat on his brow and sand in his stockings. The French king, Provost responded carefully, would be interested in many island curiosities. But nothing, he said, would please the royal house more than a bevy of well-rooted clove and nutmeg trees to adorn the royal gardens.

So it was to be. The delighted headmen proposed a voyage together southward to the island known as Petani. There, they insisted, were the best specimens to be procured, and though it might take a few days' time, a great number could be collected.

As expected, the welcome at Patani was as warmly heartfelt as had been the reception at Gueby. Lavish entertainment was the order of the day, with food, drink, and women for the strangers, while parties were dispatched overland and in *kora-kora* to explore the hidden coves for access to the perfumed woods. Days passed during which no seedlings were brought in, and Provost's apprehensions mounted. As Lieutenant d'Etcheverry advised him, the changing monsoon was nearly at hand, and it brought a double specter: They might miss the winds that would return his party to Mauritius, and their ship might be taken by the Dutch. The latter possibility especially would seal their fate.

Bitterly disappointed, Provost had d'Etcheverry prepare the sails for departure. Suddenly, the islanders of Gueby approached with hundreds of nutmeg trees with firm but pliable rootings to be carefully loaded on board the *Vigilant*. Just as the sails were set and Provost despaired of receiving any clove trees, another party arrived with enough seedlings and seeds to fill the ship's hold. Farewell speeches and embraces followed, and a great cheer rose from the beach as the *Vigilant* weighed anchor and cleared the green inlet for the indigo of the open sea.

The risks, however, were not yet over. Several days passed as they sailed northwest. Then, off the southwest Celebes port of Buton, the *Vigilant* was hailed and halted by a Dutch patrol party borne in a fleet of native *kora-kora*. Two Dutch officers boarded, eyeing the French officers and crew curiously. Provost spoke up. They were en route from Manila to Batavia, he explained, and with the shifting monsoon had been blown off course by a storm.

Seemingly satisfied with this explanation from a Frenchman (an Englishman would have invited more suspicion), the officers declined to search the ship and escorted the *Vigilant* through treacherous reefs to see her back on a westward course. Once the boats were out of sight, Provost gave the nod to d'Etcheverry to backtrack southeasterly for Timor. In days the rendezvous occurred with the *Étôile du Matin,* which was berthed safely in port. Provost divided his cargo between the two ships for security's sake, and the expedition rode the east wind across the Indian Ocean to Mauritius.

It was a triumphant homecoming on June 24, 1770, when Provost presented his patron, Pierre Poivre, with a cargo of four hundred rooted nutmeg trees, seventy rooted clove trees, and thousands of seeds and nuts. Poivre had most of the plants distributed in his own gardens at Montplaisir and dispatched the remainder to the botanical gardens at Cayenne. Recalling the failure of his own meager imports years before, he sent

Provost back to Gueby one year later for another successful expedition.

The consolidation of Poivre and Provost's dogged determination and achievement was less auspicious. Factions arose and clashed. Poivre's long-standing belief was that the seedlings should be distributed far and wide throughout France's tropical possessions, while others held that cultivation should be rigorously restricted to Mauritius. Eventually, but not without heated opposition, Poivre prevailed. By the 1790s Zanzibar had its spice gardens, as did Madagascar and Martinique, and they were yielding a quality of clove many thought superior to those of Ternate and Tidore, while nutmegs thrived on the Caribbean island of Grenada, yielding a larger and better crop, many insisted, than Banda.

In any event, the secret vessel so carefully protected by the Dutch for a century and a half was shattered, and Holland's monopoly, so firmly entrenched by the likes of Jan Pieterszoon Coen, became a memory. After Poivre's departure in 1773 spices did not fare so well on Mauritius, but this failure was the result of bureaucratic factionalism. The gardens of Montplaisir, which Poivre sold to the government at cost, were badly neglected. Some bureaucrats even lobbied for their abandonment.

Poivre returned to France and retired to his home and garden at La Fréta near Lyon, where he wrote, gardened, and entertained a parade of distinguished visitors interested in his exotic specimens, excepting clove and nutmeg, which could not withstand the harsh winter climate of central France. Pierre Poivre died at La Fréta on January 6, 1786, survived by his widow and daughters.

Nine years later the vivacious Madame Marie-Françoise Poivre was courted by Pierre Samuel Dupont de Nemours, her late husband's biographer. "I wish I could forget her," the suitor wrote in a letter. "But her husband, who was my friend, entrusted her to my care when he was about to die. . . . Sometimes I think I will end it all by writing to Citizeness Poivre, getting her to come here, and marrying her. But that is a very radical step to take."

Dupont de Nemours, a liberal politician, publisher, and advisor to the king, who had escaped the guillotine only by the death of Robespierre in 1794, took that radical step. The couple, at President Jefferson's urging, eventually emigrated to the United States.

Pierre Samuel Dupont de Nemours in France had known both the wonder of luck and the joy of a windfall. The former saved his neck by the narrowest of margins, for unbeknownst to Dupont de Nemours, he had missed his appointment with the guillotine by a single day. As for the latter, his marriage to Marie-Françoise Poivre, wealthy from her late husband's daring successes in the spice trade, enabled this enterprising former French politician/publisher to flourish as a businessman in Thomas Jefferson's America. "I have very good cards to play in this country," Dupont de Nemours wrote to Madame de Staël. Before him sparkled the promise of great riches and honors: a bustling import-export business, a teeming shipping line, and, most important, a thriving gunpowder factory on the Brandywine River near Wilmington, Delaware, to serve the raw, new nation. Dupont de Nemours died on August 6, 1817, after having founded an American dynasty of considerable wealth.

Ironically, it apparently never occurred to Dupont de Nemours that one of the cards he might have played was the one that had won for Pierre Poivre *his* fortune—spices—which, in turn through marriage to Poivre's widow, enabled the Frenchman to succeed in the United States. Others in America, however, had a less restrictive vision about spices, and about one spice in particular. At the time of Dupont de Nemours's death, the New England port of Salem, Massachusetts, was thriving in the pepper trade with Sumatra.

NEW ENGLAND PASSION

"L'arzento va dove e il piper" (silver goes where the pepper is).
—THE VENETIAN PIERO ZEN TO
THE TURKS AT CONSTANTINOPLE IN 1530

The pure Walden water is mingled with the
sacred water of the Ganges. With favoring
winds it is wafted past the site of the fabulous
islands of Atlantis and the Hesperides, makes
the periplus of Hanno, and, floating by Ternate
and Tidore and the mouth of the Persian Gulf,
melts in the tropic gales of the Indian seas, and
is landed in ports of which Alexander only
heard the names.
—HENRY DAVID THOREAU, *Walden*, 1854

Chapter 18

"TO THE
FARTHEST PORTS
OF THE RICH EAST"

EARLY ONE FINE MORNING in 1789, not long after his inauguration on April 30 at New York City's Wall Street, George Washington departed Boston for Salem, Massachusetts, in a large four-horse coach, followed by a baggage wagon with black lackeys and outriders in rich livery, his white horse haltered behind. Their pace was brisk, for this was another leg of a continuing journey through New England, and there were engagements planned for the day. Standing aloof from party divisions, the unanimously elected nation's first chief executive was keen to emphasize his role as president of the entire country by a tour through the northern states, as later he would travel through the South.

The president was especially enthusiastic about visiting Salem, for there was a strange, unprecedented force at work in this modest New England port that had all but overshadowed its larger neighbor, Boston, just a few miles to the southeast. In time, the successes of the two ports would be reversed. In the meantime, while Boston's day was yet to come, foreign trade had for more than a century brought great wealth to Salem, and the influence of the Washington administration would see it continued. When the Salem Federal Custom House was opened in 1789, the vast seas east of the Cape of Good Hope awaited exploitation by Salem's merchants. Though the British, having eclipsed the Dutch, still traded in spices, the dissemination of clove and nutmeg seedlings had already reduced the dearth of the "holy trinity." Likewise, the pepper trade was for the English a routine commerce in this bustling era, when tea and opium commanded a premium. But for the traders of Salem, Massachusetts, pepper, as we shall see, was anything but a routine commerce.

It was two o'clock in the afternoon when the fifty-seven-year-old president stepped down from the coach on Salem's Federal Street to take in his large hands the reins of his horse, already bridled and saddled. His party looked on, enjoying the ease and authority with which the old general placed his foot in the stirrup and swung his sturdy-shouldered, six-foot three-inch frame atop his old charger. Washington, an experienced rider and foxhunter since his youth, was at home on horseback and cut a commanding figure. People liked to watch him ride. Then, preceded by an honor guard, the former head of the colonial forces rode up the line in review of the troops to Boston Street.

Since the bleakest days of the Revolution, when Massachusetts troops had stood firmly in support of him, a Virginian, thus solidifying the link between the two most powerful colonies, Washington had maintained close ties to this port city. Hurrahs rang out as the president appeared on the balcony at Town House Square to receive a welcoming address and to hear a choir sing an ode composed for the occasion.

Washington made a brief reply, ending with these words: "From your own industry and enterprise, you have everything to hope that deserving men and good citizens can expect. May your navigation and commerce flourish, your industry in all its applications be rewarded, your happiness here be as perfect as belongs to the lot of humanity, and your eternal felicity be complete." When he had finished, a chorus of loud cheers went up.

The cheering din followed Washington as he retired from the Town House balcony to the home of Joshua Ward, one of the city's most distinguished merchants. Ward's house was a large, new brick structure well off the street, facing the water. Terraced up in front, the property afforded at the top a stunning view of the busy harbor. As one stood and gazed, there was nothing to impede the vista out to Naugus Head save the long reach of Derby Wharf.

The foreground of the harbor as seen from the house provided a lively tableau, as if to illustrate the sentiments expressed in Washington's remarks spoken earlier. At Derby Wharf a large East Indiaman, which had arrived earlier that day from the waters east of the Cape of Good Hope, was berthed and off-loading, her keel embedded in harbor mud. A roar of incessant noise rose from the docks—shouted orders, creaking windlasses, shrieking seagulls, the cacophony of vessels under construction from nearby shipyards—while prostitutes beckoned to sailors from nearby windows and the aromas of cinnamon, clove, coffee, tea, and pepper wafted on the strong-smelling sea air at low tide.

Crew members shouldered bags of sugar from Île de France and bolts of cotton from India to be weighed on the customs scale and the merchant's scale, while dunnage now stacked by the merchantman's bow had been packed around the cargo as a preventative against its shifting in bad weather. Berthed just forward of the off-loading ship was a coasting schooner having its hull coppered; behind Derby's counting house and warehouse on the wharf itself, a lumber schooner was putting in at a shipyard with a load of timber.

Down the harbor another merchantman was docked in front of the large, striking, and somewhat eccentric dwelling later to be known as the House of the Seven Gables, and beyond it was planned a great finger of construction reaching into the harbor just where it widened. It was to be called India Wharf or Crowninshield Wharf, depending on one's preference, and it promised to rival that of Captain George Crowninshield's arch-competitor Mr. Elias Hasket Derby, who owned by far the most prominent of Salem's swelling number of wharves. Coaches plied the narrow waterfront streets seeking fares from among the shore parties of the several visiting frigates.

In the early evening, with powdered hair and dressed in a black velvet suit with gold buckles, yellow gloves, a cocked hat with an ostrich plume in one hand, and a sword in a white leather scabbard, President Washington arrived at the Assembly Hall on Federal Street, where a party was already gathered. Like the courthouse across town, another notable building of this enlightened day, the hall with its noble Federalist lines was an anomalous structure flanked by gambrel-roofed houses; for it had been built only a few years before expressly for the social events of Salem's most prominent citizens.

On this evening the proud building beamed with neoclassical confidence and promise of intoxicating possibilities. The Reverend Dr. William

Bentley, the local chronicler who kept a finger on Salem's pulse, noted the scene glowing beneath the candlelit chandeliers with gentle irony: "The ladies were numerous and brilliant, the gentlemen were also numerous!" Washington confided to his diary that there were a hundred handsome, well-dressed people assembled to pay him homage.

The cream of Salem's society parted for the presidential party entering the hall, withdrawing left to right with curtsies and bows, as the lofty guest of honor was escorted to a fine armchair at the end of the spacious room offered for the occasion by Mr. Derby and his wife, Elizabeth Crowninshield Derby. French tapestries and portraits of persons and ships adorned the walls; fine silver, crystal, and porcelain pieces graced the tables and hunt boards; Khotan, Samarkand, and Tabriz carpets decorated the floor. In one corner hung a highly polished mahogany spice cabinet where the precious condiments were kept under lock and key.

There followed an evening of dancing until the distinguished visitor retired at nine, as it was his custom to rise at five, but not before promising well-wishers that he would be riding out into Essex County at eight the next morning to inspect a new bridge. The festivities continued late into the evening, for if the citizens of Salem knew one thing apart from diligence and hard work, it was how to live and enjoy themselves.

One of the most sedate of the revelers was Elias Hasket Derby Sr., who had lent the hall for the evening. Mr. Derby was a bold, visionary maritime merchant and the head of Salem's most prosperous family, a house that had emerged from the Revolution measurably richer, with Derby's privateers having captured nearly 150 British prizes at a profit of one million dollars.

"King" Derby has been described as "a tall man, of fine figure and elegant carriage. His deportment was grave and dignified, his habits regular and exact." His contemporaries were especially struck by his eyes, for one was blue, the other brown, and the arresting contrast is vividly revealed in a contemporary portrait. The son of Richard Derby, he had entered his father's business at age fifteen not by way of the quarterdeck, which was the normal way to begin a merchant's career, but with the account books in the counting house. His sons John and Elias Hasket Jr. and other prominent captains and merchants, known as "Derby's Boys," would serve a similar apprenticeship.

By the age of thirty-three in 1772, he was running the business, and after his father's death at war's end, when Derby was forty-four, he had complete authority over the port's greatest merchant house, with wharf, warehouses, stores, a distillery, brigs, and ships: all without ever having been to sea or abroad. Refitting his privateers as merchantmen, he began to broaden his vision, being the first Salem merchant to dispatch ships to such distant ports as Calcutta, Bombay, Madras, and Manila.

An innovator, Derby established for Salem ships the role of supercargo, or traveling business agent. He was most likely the first American merchant to send ships to sea with coppered bottoms. Having envisioned a centralized global trade network and developed a system that allowed the consignment of cargoes to a foreign house, he relieved his supercargoes of the task of dealing with a succession of buyers. His life was lived in luxury, a style mostly promoted by his wife. The most envied man in Salem, he was also the luckiest, having lost but one ship at sea during his entire career. In the approaching decade, the 1790s, one third of the vessels out of Salem to round the Cape of Good Hope were to be Derby's vessels. Dr. Bentley wrote with some awe of America's first millionaire, "Wealth with full tide flows on in that man." Other merchants looked to Derby as an example to follow in Far Eastern trade.

Derby, unsurprisingly, had his enemies present that evening, most notably Captain George Crowninshield, the patriarch of a rival clan of seafarers and from whose family had come Derby's own wife. Crowninshield's rise in the merchant arena had been quick, aggressive, and occasionally litigious. Moreover, the Crowninshields were Republicans, an affront to the aristocratic, Federalist Derbys. Crowninshield had been a captain for Richard Derby before the Revolution and was described as a "bluff, warm-hearted chivalrous seaman" and "a son of nature [with powers] such as are employed only in seafaring."

George Crowninshield had a toughness that matched his ambition, and both these qualities helped to elevate his firm to a competitive level with that of Elias Hasket Derby. His five sons who followed him in the family business were diverse and complemented their father's character. Each had mastered navigation at age twelve, sailed to the East Indies at fifteen, and captained a ship by age twenty.

After independence their father began acquiring ships of his own, much to Derby's displeasure, who branded the Crowninshields as "base plebeians" and "sons of pride." Derby brought a suit against his brother-in-law for a wharf that extended too far into the channel, causing the bottom adjacent to his own wharf to silt in. After an acrimonious contest, Derby prevailed. A court decision forced Crowninshield to remove twelve feet of his wharf, fueling the animosity. Bitterness between the patriarchs was so rife that when Elizabeth Crowninshield Derby died in 1799, not one Crowninshield attended the funeral.

Henry David Thoreau undoubtedly had these two dynamic families in mind when he described the ideal merchant in *Walden*, published over a half century later, in 1854:

> If your trade is with the Celestial Empire, then some small counting-house on the coast, in some Salem harbor, will be fixture enough. You will . . . keep up a steady dispatch of commodities, for the supply of such a distant and exorbitant market . . . keep yourselves informed of the state of the markets, prospects of war and peace everywhere, and anticipate the tendencies of trade and civilization—taking advantage of the results of all exploring expeditions, using new passages and all improvements in navigation. . . . It is a labor to task the faculties of a man—such problems of profit and loss, of interest, of tare and tret, and gauging of all kinds in it, as demands a universal knowledge.

Many of Salem's maritime achievements and domestic conflicts were to be embodied in these rival dynasties of Derbys and Crowninshields, whose fates were intertwined through collaboration and competition in trade, politics, and marriage. Their story is the story of a growing Salem, for the two families gave great and lasting shape to an American city whose development is indelibly linked to the East Indies pepper trade.

As determined by the first census taken in the United States in 1790, the year after President Washington's visit, Salem, with a population of eight thousand, was the sixth-largest town in the new independent confederation. Boston was larger, as were New York, Philadelphia, Baltimore, and Charleston, and these ports to the south had far greater natural advantages than Salem. Before the day of the railroad, water transportation was essential for transporting heavy goods to and from the interior, and these ports, unlike Salem, were situated on fine harbors with access to mighty rivers.

This geographical fact would finally defeat Salem, as she was off the main trade routes of the developing country and had an inadequate harbor with no access to the interior. Of the New England ports only Boston, with its large deepwater harbor and principal lines of inland communication, would survive and eventually attract many of Salem's merchants. Boston's prosperity would come in the 1830s, when foreign ships had slipped away from the smaller ports to convene at her splendid docks, prompting Oliver Wendell Holmes's observation in *The Autocrat of the Breakfast Table* that "Boston State-House is the hub of the solar system."

Salem, however, for three generations over half a century, would come to surpass all the other American ports in world commerce, and in fact engender more foreign trade with ports in Africa, Asia, and South America than the others combined. It was a free period in American life, as laws of trade, business, and labor, apart from foreign restrictions, were as yet unheard of. Opportunities for able, courageous, and willing men nurtured in Puritan ideals of faith in God and industry were abundant. The distinguished local historian James Duncan Phillips has offered a reason for the port's rise: "It is possible to account for Salem's success in just one way. She had a greater number of intelligent, courageous, industrious people at that period than any other town in America: they were Puritans of the Puritans." There was as well a profane side of Salem's character, for the port had grown to love wealth, and its most influential people were those who had attained it.

This Salem temperament was never preening and self-infatuated, nor even self-proclaimed. The British consul in Philadelphia, assigned to monitor the new country's affairs for London, wrote the duke of Leeds in 1789, "The inhabitants of New England may be said to be a peculiar people; they have more public spirit, more enterprise, energy and activity of mind and body than their neighbors." It was an age when Americans deemed the individual capable of controlling his own destiny this side of heaven; and if he did not rise in the world, he had only himself to blame.

On the other side of the world there were strange cities with temples and pagodas, people of different races and castes dressed in silks, sarongs, and turbans, and exotic-looking women. There were also the "flower boats," the floating brothels of the Pearl River near Canton. A sailor fresh out of Salem, who might never visit the city of New York down the coast, would observe that some islanders of the South Seas were a "stout robust treacherous voracious gluttonous naked set of wretches," while reassuring himself in light of his mercantile mission that they were "regular Yankees for trade." As Salem opened its arms to the world, the embrace was reciprocated; on Sumatra's pepper coast Salem came to be regarded as a sovereign nation such as England or Holland.

Salem's seamen were confident that they could sail their vessels faster and closer to the wind than any others of their day, and the Far Eastern waters, neither too distant nor too dangerous, beckoned with their promise of excitement and wealth. The Latin motto of the city's seal was an appropriate one, and reads in translation, "To the Farthest Port of the Rich East."

SALEM HAD BEEN settled by English Puritans in 1626 on a secluded bay guarded by a severe, rocky coast known to the Indians as "the fishing place." By the mid-seventeenth century, in the wake of a series of conflicts with the French and Indians, and afterward with the British, Salem's so-called codfish aristocrats had established for the port a remarkable trade with Europe, the West Indies, and the Atlantic coast. But the biggest gain was the transoceanic routes as Americans, and Salem traders in particular, began to overtake the English.

This was the day of the dark "triangular trade," in which sea captains collected sugar and molasses in the West Indies and brought them to New England. Here the cargo was distilled into rum, which in turn was sailed to West Africa, where the spirits were exchanged for a holdful of slaves to work the plantations of the Caribbean.

Confident with their success in the "Sugar Islands," Salem merchant captains continued to look eastward across the North Atlantic. Soon they were making port in the Netherlands and the British Isles, trading timber, hides, wool, and rum for salt, linen, and iron. From southern France and the Iberian peninsula as well as the so-called Wine Islands (Madeira, the Azores, the Canaries) they secured wine, fruit, and pieces of eight for cod and tobacco.

Then the British Navigation Acts of 1660 and 1663, which had such a profound impact on Dutch-English relations, gave American shipping a virtual monopoly on commerce between the colonies and the West Indies. Such a development was a boon to New England shipping, for the competitive Dutch, from their port of New Amsterdam at the mouth of the Hudson River, had been keen rivals. This impetus to trade became Salem's lifeblood until the American Revolution over a hundred years later. The success of such trade was realized through two contrary factors: the risky cargo of sugar, for its price was notoriously unstable, and the boldness of Salem merchants in acquiring and transporting it. The risk paid off, making Salemites very wealthy; the English adventurer John Josselyn even commented on the "very rich merchants" he met in Salem. Such boldness in the face of great risk would become a hallmark of Salem's pepper trade with Sumatra in the port's expansive years following the Revolution.

Like the contemporary Dutch sailors, these Salem seafarers were tempered in much the same hearty way. Having been nurtured in Puritan soil and savage winters, they built and sailed their ships under the banner of a God who rewarded industry, sobriety, and thrift with success. If wealth resulted from a marriage of profits and piety, it was a sign of God's favor. Three prominent men figure in Salem's rise during this period. Philip English, who immigrated from the Isle of Jersey in the 1660s, soon controlled twenty ships that sailed to the Channel Islands, Suriname, Newfoundland, and Barbados. Though Captain John Turner was dead at thirty-six, he made a fortune with his ships in the Barbados trade and built the house with seven gables destined to be immortalized by Nathaniel Hawthorne. Then Roger Derby emerged as progenitor of Salem's most illustrious merchant family. Such men became prominent and influential as they brought trade goods and wealth into the fishing port, ensuring that Salem's rising merchant class was firmly in place by the end of the century.

In the eighteenth century, as the port grew from a provincial fishing village into a prospering market town of five thousand inhabitants, the Puritan underpinnings of this scene of the infamous witch trials of 1692 became unfastened. Georgian-style houses replaced the steep-angled, casement-windowed dwellings. More wharves were built, and Wharf Street at the bend of the South River became congested with schooners and three-masted merchantmen. The richest merchants had slaves as servants in their houses. When the still-unpaved streets were thawing in spring, carriages could not negotiate them, and it was not unusual to see the wives of these affluent aristocrats being borne about in sedan chairs by slaves.

As the century progressed, Salem became America's neoclassical gem of a port city. Enlightenment was in the air, and anti-British sentiments festered over a remote government across the Atlantic that imposed unfair trade acts and encouraged the arbitrary seizure of ships. As John Adams put it, "American independence was then and there born." Despite the sentiments of loyalists who thought of England as home, and they were not few in number, revolt against England was inevitable.

When mercantile resistance escalated to armed conflict, seafarers carried the war to the Atlantic Ocean. Salem's new merchant captains rejoiced at the Continental Congress's move to swell its navy by licensing hundreds of commercial vessels as privateers to attack British shipping. John Adams referred to such privateering as "a short, easy, and infallible method of humbling the British."

Individual fortunes were made by privateering, but it was not the ultimate answer to the disruption of trade and a weakened economy the war had caused. The Treaty of Paris in 1783 marked the end of an era, and patriot merchants turned to rebuild what their loyalist forebears had marshaled through faith and perseverance from a storm-lashed bay on the New England coast.

The success of the port's privateering expeditions against British ships during the war had induced an attitude of vision and risk crossed with native ingenuity and enterprise that was to alter Salem's destiny. With the lapse of trade during the years of the conflict, privateering had held together the delicate web of Salem's economy. Now with independence came economic depression, as though a market had crashed, and Salem's merchants began to realize that more intrepid steps to seek out a higher level of trade would have to be taken to ensure the port's future prosperity. The codfish aristocrats had seen Salem evolve from a fishing settlement to a humming market, but a new generation was bent on seeing Salem as a center for world trade.

IN 1796, as the English in the Spice Islands were intent on avenging the deaths of their countrymen at the hands of the Dutch over a century and a half earlier, Captain Jonathan Carnes of Salem was crowding on the sail of his schooner as he rode the high seas of the Indian Ocean to close on Sumatra and its pepper crop. Carnes was the first of a succession of determined captains and traders from the New England port who were unintimidated by the nation from which they had won independence. Now they sought to corner the market on pepper by sailing the twenty-six-thousand-mile round voyage to Sumatra under the very noses of the British, who were obsessed with tea and opium. Carnes's historic voyage signaled the rise of American supremacy at home and on the high seas, while marking the success of her first millionaires, Elias Hasket Derby and Captain George Crowninshield. Fortune favored the bold.

Chapter 19

FORTUNE FAVORS
THE BOLD

THE ORIGINS OF Captain Carnes's voyage of 1796 may be found in an earlier expedition. In December 1785 Elias Hasket Derby, shipowner, had sent the *Grand Turk,* commanded by the twenty-seven-year-old former privateersman Ebenezer West, around the Cape of Good Hope to Île de France (Mauritius).

Though she was the first American ship to stop there, her captain found little enthusiasm from the natives for his cargo of butter, fish, flour, rice, and rum, and trading proceeded slowly. Approached by a Frenchman to carry a cargo to Canton, West agreed, after establishing a base on Mauritius for future Salem expeditions. Sailing to Canton was an audacious move, for the ship was not insured beyond Île de France, and West had only crude charts for the unknown waters and the pirate-infested Straits of Malacca, through which no American ship had ever sailed. But although the shipowner, Derby, was no seaman himself, he was known for trusting the judgment of an enterprising shipmaster and giving him his head. Captain West steered northeast through unknown waters for China, dreaming of an unprecedented fortune from the East.

Arriving at the mouth of South China's Pearl River in September 1786, Captain West learned that the *Grand Turk* was New England's first vessel to reach China. With a difficult voyage behind him, West faced another arduous task in meeting the complex trade regulations and customs of the Chinese, an elaborate ceremony of bribes and fees. The English East India Company had established a factory here a hundred years earlier, followed later by the French and Dutch; by an imperial decree of 1757, Canton had been made China's sole port for foreign trade.

But there were tensions. Already the Honourable Company's exportation of opium from India to China was beginning to alarm Chinese authorities by its reversal of a trade balance hitherto favorable to them. This sinister commerce would lead eventually to the rise of Hong Kong as a deepwater port, the Opium Wars, and Lord Ashley's parliamentary denunciation in 1843 that such trade "was utterly inconsistent with the honour and duty of a Christian kingdom."

Despite the frictions, however, Canton in 1786, with its coveted Chinese products of porcelains, teas, silks, and rhubarb, was the choice port of call for Western traders. A "celestial representative," or customs inspector, boarded to sail the ship upstream to Whampoa Reach, a widening in the river twelve miles south of the port proper.

Here the cargo was unloaded and carried upriver in sampans threading their way through junks and tea-deckers to Canton Harbor, where the shallow-drafted vessels were unloaded at factories. "New people," as visitors were known, were restricted to these walled compounds of warehouses called *hongs,* where goods were stored and negotiations conducted through one of a dozen imperially appointed Chinese merchants, in this case a man known as Pinqua.

William Vans was West's supercargo, or traveling business agent, and it was his responsibility to purchase goods. Soon the ship's hold was filled with diverse teas transported in boxes from eight hundred miles inland on the backs of porters, crates of porcelain, and sacks of cassia (Chinese cinnamon). With a loaded ship and the issue of the grand chop certifying that all duties and taxes were paid, the *Grand Turk* was cleared for Captain West to sail downriver.

The ship returned to Salem Harbor in May 1787 to a thunderous welcome, with gun salutes and crowds cheering over the exotic cargo. Derby had tripled his investment on a pioneering voyage, and the gaze of Salem seafarers was suddenly to the Far East.

Three years passed. Then, on a spring morning in 1788, the one-hundred-ton *Cadet,* built at Pembroke on the North River, glided down Salem's harbor "bound for Madeira and from thence to India and the China Seas: Prosperous be her voyage," according to the Salem *Mercury* of April 15. The daily newspaper celebrated the small brig's leave-taking as it did that of most ships, because in Salem her being fitted out for parts unknown was the sort of pulsating news upon which the port thrived during the heady days after the Revolution.

The *Cadet,* once owned by Derby, now belonged to the same William Vans who had sailed with Ebenezer West to Canton in 1785. Vans was aboard again as supercargo, while the brig was commanded by Vans's brother-in-law Jonathan Carnes, who was thirty years old.

A month later the *Cadet* made Madeira, and then she suddenly disappeared, presumably somewhere in Eastern seas—the Indian Ocean or perhaps beyond. Not one of the other half dozen Salem ships in that part of the world could account for her whereabouts. Then, on May 18, 1790, more than two years later, the Salem *Gazette* finally reported, "Captain Carnes, absent on an India voyage upwards of two years, was at the Cape of Good Hope, February 14, 1790, and was to sail in a few days for the W. Indies." But where Carnes's voyage had taken him remained a mystery. That he had sailed thirteen thousand miles to unknown Sumatra was this young captain's secret.

SUMATRA IS THE California-size, westernmost island of the East Indies, and it straddles the equator, reaching northward through the Indian Ocean and past the Malay Peninsula, creating the Straits of Malacca, toward the mainland of Burma. A nexus of smaller islands acting as a barrier off the west coast rises from the edge of the submarine platform of the Indian Ocean. Sumatra is as richly diversified, with its lowland swamps and jungles and rain forests and mountains, as other large islands of the sprawling archipelago. However, its proximity to the Southeast Asian mainland has given it a place on European maps since Ptolemy's time and an accessibility denied other large islands of the Malay Archipelago such as Borneo and New Guinea.

Sumatra's east and west coasts are markedly dissimilar. Because of the fortress of mountains that extends nearly the island's length along its western side, the rivers descending to the Indian Ocean flash with rapids and are rarely navigable for any great distance upstream. Sumatra's eastern rivers, however, are sullen, torpid streams passing through wide delta plains and coastal swamps, providing access to the interior for large, oceangoing ships and a haven for crocodiles. It was in one such eastern river in northern Sumatra across the straits from Kedah where the Portuguese, exhorted by the warrior-priest Francis Xavier, closed with and destroyed the Acehnese fleet in the mid-sixteenth century.

Europeans were provided with the name Sumatra by the Italian adventurer Ludovico de Varthema in 1505, the same mysterious figure to venture to the Spice Islands a few years before d'Abreu's expedition in 1512, which resulted in Francisco Serrão's self-exile on Ternate. Varthema hired himself to the Portuguese, and these first Western colonizers of Asia established a trading post on Sumatra as early as 1509, only to be driven out at the end of the century by the Dutch, who in turn withstood rival claims by the English over the next three hundred years. This rivalry was firmly in place upon the arrival of the Salem traders at the end of the eighteenth century.

Beyond its allure as an equatorial pepper garden and its reputation as a risky destination with treacherous natives and uncharted coasts for determined merchants, the Salem traders knew little of this large, westernmost island of the East Indies. Ignorant of its precolonial history, they could scarcely have imagined that the Taprobane of Pliny, as some scholars have speculated, might be not Ceylon but Sumatra.

The Americans knew not or cared little that Sumatra was the first island of the Indies to receive the Hindu migrations and that by the seventh century it was the seat of a powerful Hindu kingdom. This was a full six hundred years before Arab traders arrived in the thirteenth century with Islam to convert the northern kingdom of Aceh. The men of Salem were indifferent to the fact that the religion of Mohammed had spread the length of this vast volcano-pocked island to reach diverse tribes divided by mountainous rain forests and lowland jungles.

While in the Sumatran port of Bencoolen on the island's southwest coast (where the English had recently transplanted clove and nutmeg seedlings smuggled out from the Spice Islands, thus contributing to the end of the Dutch monopoly), Captain Carnes got wind of a major pepper source at Padang, a more prominent port about midway up Sumatra's west coast. Following directions given him by a local pilot, Carnes set a northwesterly course. Upon arrival in Padang he learned of still other, smaller ports farther north that traded in pepper. In fact, Padang's pepper supply consisted of goods sailed down the coast by prahu from these satellite ports as well as fruit raised in the island's interior and transported overland to the port's godowns.

Padang and the smaller port of Pariaman, up the coast, were the major trading centers for the Minangkabau tribe, industrious farmers who raised coffee and pepper in the rolling country of the Padang Highlands on the coastal side of a forbidding mountain range. For centuries these green hills and valleys, marked by a great triangle of smoking volcanoes, had been dotted with ornate houses, raised off the ground, with horned ridgepoles and finely carved painted wooden fronts.

Though on this voyage Carnes did not venture north of Padang even as far as Pariaman, he carefully recorded whatever information he could obtain as bags of pepper were shouldered into the *Cadet*'s hold. After lading, he sailed for the United States, and news of the brig's sighting at Africa's southern cape eventually reached Salem.

There are conflicting stories as to what happened next, for there is no surviving log. Nor are there letters home from crew members, and the Salem papers do not mention the *Cadet*'s return, an unusual omission. With the paucity of records, one can only speculate on the fate of the *Cadet*, which remains largely a mystery.

Carnes most certainly left the Cape with a fully laden ship to ride an easterly wind back across the Atlantic toward the Caribbean. A likely explanation, though it is by no means conclusive, is that the brig and her cargo were lost on a reef in the West Indies. We know only that somehow Carnes found his way back to Salem with tales of the strangest race of people he had ever seen. But more important, he returned with a profoundly rich secret: the opening of a new channel of trade in pepper, which, to say the least, was arcane cargo in this brash new nation.

THOUGH PEPPER IS not included among the "holy trinity" of spices that had earlier so galvanized the European powers of the Renaissance and the vehemently commercial age that followed it, the history of the pepper trade, its color and story, rivals that of nutmeg and cloves, cinnamon and ginger. And pepper certainly had a most prominent role in the early growth of the American republic, for trade in the "holy trinity" was already spoken for by the English and Dutch.

During the period of the Venetians' supremacy on land and sea, from the twelfth century until the Portuguese supplanted them in the late fifteenth century, pepper, a preservative and reputed aphrodisiac, was the most basic of spices; and because pepper was worth its weight in gold, demand for it kept prices high. If a nation's coinage was dubious in value, pepper became not only the medium of foreign exchange, but the currency of tribute, bribes, and gifts worthy of sovereigns as well.

When Venice had the monopoly on its transport, Alexandria was the chief port for distribution of pepper, as it had been since the first century B.C., when one of the city's entrances was actually known as Pepper Gate. Its name is believed to be derived from the Sanskrit *pippali* (Latinized to *Piper nigrum*), suggesting that pepper was perhaps the earliest known spice, a stock-in-trade as far back as two thousand to three thousand years. This perennial climbing shrub or vine was indigenous to India, specifically the forests of Malabar and Tranvacore, before merchants in ancient times introduced it to other parts of Southeast Asia, from Sumatra to the Philippines, where it has thrived in the sweltering jungles within twenty degrees of the equator.

Since the dawn of history, pepper—owing its pungency to a resin and flavor to a volatile oil—had widespread use in the Near East and was highly esteemed by the ancient Greeks and Romans. One of the articles demanded by Alaric the Visigoth in A.D. 408 as part of the ransom of Rome was three thousand pounds of pepper, and two years later he began his annual extraction of three hundred pounds of the condiment/preservative as tribute.

For five centuries during the Dark Ages, however, the spice ceased to reach western Europe, until the Venetians reintroduced it as early as the year 900. Europeans consumed it both as black pepper, whose corns were picked before they ripened and dried in their husks; and white pepper, the same berry permitted to ripen before the dark outer layer was removed, thus allowing a less piquant but subtler taste. Pepper in the house in medieval times became a symbol of solvency; if a family was poor, it was said to lack pepper.

During the Middle Ages the continent consumed thirty-three hundred tons of pepper a year. In distant and barbaric England around the year 1000, King Ethelred forced merchants to pay a tax in pepper for the privilege of trading in London, and by 1179 the Guild of Pepperers had been founded in the English capital.

At the end of the fifteenth century after Portuguese soldiers waded ashore at Calcutta with the cry "For Christ and spices!" to seize their share of the pepper trade (an invasion that prompted pepper prices to fall in Europe), Venice would still control mercantile outlets in the eastern Mediterranean ports for more than a century, so great was Europe's demand. The tart fruit remained a monopoly of the Portuguese crown until as late as the eighteenth century, thanks to Goa and its other colonies on the Indian subcontinent.

By Carnes's day at the end of the eighteenth century, if pepper was not the gastronomic obsession in America that it was in Europe (indeed, it was virtually unknown in the former colonies either as a condiment or as goods for trade), the transatlantic gaze of shrewd Salem traders told them where their most profitable market lay. Much of the Salemites' success in the pepper trade was found in the exportation of this exotic import to Europe. While Salem merchants hardly eschewed other spices such as cloves and nutmeg, European domination of the "holy trinity" trade had long since been in place. Pepper, if it could be got at its source, was cheaply acquired and represented a tidy upside in profits. As traders, Salemites certainly knew its value.

CAPTAIN JONATHAN CARNES, the erect blue-jacketed, brass-buttoned officer with blond good looks who had been master of the ill-fated *Cadet*, possessed a figure of reserved confidence and determination. The son of John Carnes, a shipmaster and distinguished privateersman of the Revolution, the younger Carnes was married to Rebecca Vans, William Vans's sister. His uncle on his mother's side was Jonathan Peele, patriarch of a prominent mercantile family of Salem.

With these connections, the captain's secret of a lucrative pepper source became a family trust, and it remained closely guarded while Carnes took the Derby-owned *Grand Sachem* out to India, an expedition that also came to grief on a Bermuda shoal. Carnes, however, was back in Salem by early 1794, in time for a return voyage to Hamburg as he bided his time with thoughts of Sumatra and its pepper.

Peele, meanwhile, had commissioned a Salisbury shipyard on the Merrimack River to build a large schooner of 120 tons. Christened the *Rajah,* she was fitted out by 1795 for a long voyage and registered on November 3 of that year with Willard and Jonathan Peele and Ebenezer Beckner as owners and Jonathan Carnes as master. Her captain undoubtedly had overseen the *Rajah's* construction on the Merrimack and was responsible for its somewhat unorthodox rigging as a schooner, but Carnes had his reasons.

For one thing, there were the contrary winds at the Cape to consider. Though with less sail than a fluyt or square-rigger, the ship compensated for its lack of speed with its versatility, for no ship could sail to windward better than an American schooner. And having had a taste of uncharted Sumatran waters with their lethal hidden reefs and shoals, Carnes knew that for coasting on that virtually unknown island, a schooner would be more responsive and easier to handle than a brig.

While the dangers of navigating were abundantly clear to Carnes, he quite rightly suspected that they had been exaggerated by English and especially Dutch factors on Sumatra as a deterrent to the new Salem adventurers. Once those eastern waters were more familiar to him, the *Rajah* could be refitted as a brig.

The "India" for which the *Rajah* was to clear on her maiden and path-finding voyage in the late autumn of 1795 was not the country known today. It was, rather, a geographical expression (and a vague one at that) with mythical overtones, conjuring up the mysteries and riches of the East awaiting discovery somewhere south of China and Japan.

In Carnes's day India might have been Sumatra or Burma, the Malay Peninsula or the Spice Islands. In time, the term would be replaced by the more precise and restrictive term *East Indies,* which are the islands of the Malay Archipelago, today the nation of Indonesia, while the name *India* took on a narrower focus, coming to specify the vast and densely populated lands of the subcontinent.

Armed with four guns and carrying a crew of ten men, the *Rajah* cleared for India on the crisp day of November 3, 1795, with her crew chanting, "We're outward bound this very day, goodbye, fare you well," as they sheeted home topsails. She was registered with an outward-bound cargo of two pipes of brandy, fifty-eight cases of gin, twelve tons of iron, two hogsheads of tobacco, and two boxes of salmon. Four months later she was sighted at the Cape of Good Hope before disappearing for more than a year. Thus commenced the first of 967 voyages over the next seventy-six years in direct pepper trade between America, principally Salem, and Sumatra.

Because of the obsession with secrecy on the part of the *Rajah*'s owners and master, not much information survives. The fact that the schooner was reported passing the cape but afterward vanished for so long a time suggests that Carnes avoided such landfalls as Madagascar and Zanzibar, on Africa's east coast. More likely, the *Rajah* sailed instead with the northeast monsoon for Île de France, where an American vessel, a French ally against the hostile English, would have been welcome to replenish victuals and refill casks with fresh water.

Even so, it is improbable that on such a secretive mission Carnes would have made port, for the *Rajah*'s crew was to remain ignorant as to the schooner's destination and were oblivious as to its position. As unlikely as that may seem, maintaining a crew's ignorance regarding navigation was a maritime tradition. Aboard English ships a sailor's unauthorized knowledge of position was a hanging offense, rigorously enforced; for after long, hard months at sea, it was believed to be an invitation to mutiny. Ignorance, then, was a deterrent to shipboard insurrection.

As for Carnes's crew, like most sailors they were more interested in seeing the sun over the foreyard, when they would receive their "nooner" of grog, which took the edge off. Carnes probably bypassed the French island and rode under full sail the dizzying swells of the Indian Ocean directly northeast for Bencoolen on Sumatra's southwest coast.

When the *Rajah* finally stood in at Bencoolen, the crew welcomed the humidity and distractions of the strange port after the numbing crossing from the cape. Carnes immediately made inquiries as to the availability of pepper at the Minangkabau ports of Padang and Pariaman, to the north. While he was made welcome in a land long accustomed to traders, what he learned was disappointing and frustrating, and may account for the long duration of the *Rajah's* first voyage.

There were precious few stores of pepper remaining from the previous crop, a scarcity necessitating that Carnes wait for the arrival of the next harvest to ensure that he return to Salem with a full hold. In the meantime, his experience and instincts as a sailor were to be tested anew, for there remained the tricky and time-consuming task of navigating the coastal waters to reach those ports.

Carnes also gathered other intelligence that gave him pause. The Minangkabau, while noted for shrewdness in their business dealings, were not known to be difficult partners in trade. But the ports north of the Padang Highlands on the other side of the equator were controlled by the fierce Acehnese tribe.

It must be stressed at the outset that the confidence, courage, and ingenuity of the Americans was crossed with a certain naïveté, laced with a tincture of hubris. Believing they would be regarded as equal partners in trade and welcomed at any of the Malay ports in peacetime, Salem traders were largely ignorant of East Indies history. As a consequence, Salemites could not have known that centuries of colonialism by Christians in a land of Muslims had bred hostility in their hosts, masked by a seeming willingness to do business. The eventual result would be an erosion of trust on both sides and a succession of violent episodes.

The Acehnese were essentially warrior-merchants whose independence and aggressive stance enabled them to control the Straits of Malacca for centuries, and their homeland was and remains northern Sumatra. Their capital, Banda Aceh, is situated on the island's northern tip in a seaside plain, a broad, flat valley of palm-covered farmland that gives way eastward to the large range of mountains that bisect the island. It is country isolated from the rest of the world by mountains and sea as well as by Acehnese severity.

Known for centuries as the "Doorway to Mecca," the city was a winding metropolis of Moorish covered sidewalks and shop signs in Arabic script, which betrayed Aceh's proximity to the Islamic world west of the Bay of Bengal: a mercantile city of vendors and mosques conceived in a Middle Eastern light. Its fabric remained unstained by the West, and the Acehnese had long since crossed their Muslim practices with animist ones

of a more distant time. A number of less important ports with such names
as Quallah Battoo, Soo Soo, Tallapoo, and Tapanooly spilled down the
island's northwest coast from Banda Aceh. These smaller trading centers
were ruled by individual rajahs, and they were the ports where Captain
Carnes and the Salem traders who followed him would seek to trade for
pepper.

The Acehnese were the people who had challenged Portuguese autonomy in the northwestern part of the archipelago, a challenge that led to
war and eventually to Portugal's abandonment of Malacca, Aceh's biggest
commercial rival across the straits on the Malay Peninsula. Any affront to
the Acehnese was tantamount to sparking a holy war that they joined
with a maniacal frenzy, as the Dutch were to learn at great expense of men
and money when Holland tried to subdue them in the late nineteenth
century. At the beginning of the same century, however, their mettle and
fierce pride would make the Acehnese a formidable trading partner for
the Salemites, as the journals kept by the voyagers reveal.

Both Acehnese and Minangkabau were shaped by alien customs that
would baffle the Yankees into wariness and finally fear. The New Englanders discovered themselves to be infidels among believers, even as they
traded in spices.

Having sailed the *Cadet* to Padang a few years before, Carnes worked
the *Rajah* in similar fashion on the first leg. Then, having cleared Padang,
he set a northwesterly course as he neared and crossed the equator, working his ship inside the barrier islands by tacking to and fro by day in order
not to lose touch with the large island, while studying the water's surface
constantly for signs of reefs and shoals. In uncharted waters a keen eye
meant survival. Late afternoon found him taking in sail and feeling his
way with lead line to avoid running aground as he used the remaining
light to seek a sheltered anchorage to pass the night.

The commands sung out were familiar ones to sailors, but Carnes's
ten-man crew heard them with clean ears as the schooner cut through the
strange bay, and the Salem seamen were alert to their tasks. Then, with sail
hauled in, the *Rajah* carried into the wind two hundred yards offshore.
The bower anchor was let go and the hemp cable played out as the anchor
fluke bit into sand bottom, urging the schooner to make sternway. At the
mate's word the cable was snubbed on the capstan, and the *Rajah* was rid-

ing in safety and snugged down for the evening. The shallop was lowered and reconnaissance made for fresh water and victuals before darkness, which came in a rush so few degrees from the equator. Watches were posted, for these were dangerous waters.

Such a routine was repeated for days on end, as the *Rajah* coasted in search of such Acehnese pepper ports as Muckie and Quallah Battoo while passing a coast backed by primeval wilderness and forested mountains whose volcanic tips were enveloped by sulphuric clouds. What had been a hitherto peaceful voyage, however, was not to last, and the following incident was the first of many violent ones to visit Salem sailors on the Sumatran pepper coast at the hands of unfriendly natives or contending European factions. What prompted this episode, however, was a case of mistaken identity.

One evening, late, Carnes was pacing the small quarterdeck while the sounds of jungle on a moonless night filled the bay. He made his way forward, dimly making out the anchor watch alert in the dense darkness before returning aft, passing two seamen of the port watch who murmured a greeting before Carnes resumed his solitary promenade on the quarterdeck.

A half hour passed, then an hour. Carnes considered turning in, but it was close and humid below, and a soft breeze made it pleasant on deck. Suddenly a shout went up from the bow watch. "Boat ahoy, who's there?" he challenged in the darkness. Carnes, suspecting Malay pirates, had just turned to sound the alarm below when he was rocked by the heavy impact of another boat. Men hurried up the ladderway, seizing pikes as they emerged from the hatch to repulse the attackers who were attempting to board.

A figure rose over the rail, and the mate fired, hitting his target, who fell backward, but another replaced the first. The bow watch, with no weapon, tried to push the intruder back, but a cutlass severed his left hand. Other mates came to his aid, and the attackers pushed off.

In the darkness the attackers identified themselves as French, having misidentified the American vessel for a British one.

Men of the *Rajah* stood to arms now under lantern light as Frenchmen came aboard, uttering exclamations of regret, while their lieutenant, who had led the attack, lay dead in the longboat and the maimed sailor was carried below.

The remainder of Carnes's voyage proceeded without incident. But as the American presence in the islands intensified in the years to follow, the Malays reverted to their tribal prejuduces. With some exceptions they came to regard the Yankees with the same contempt they had for the monopoly-seeking Portuguese and Dutch. Thus damned by association, Salemites were ripe for exploitation.

MEANWHILE IN SALEM, eighteen months had passed and there was no word of the *Rajah*; her owners feared she was lost. In fact, the *Rajah* was fully laden with pepper and lay off Sandy Hook, New Jersey, awaiting a carrying wind for New York Harbor. Journalists were waiting for her when she was warped to her berth. But her taciturn captain disclosed little.

Then, on July 25, 1797, the Salem *Gazette* reported the schooner's return with her hold brimming with 150,000 pounds of bulk pepper that had been shoveled in like coal, the first-ever such cargo to be brought to this country. The overjoyed owners were beside themselves with an excitement that infected Salem like a disease. Little else was talked about but the *Rajah*'s return, especially in the merchant countinghouses, for her expedition under Carnes's command had realized a yield of 700 percent.

The delirium soon turned to envious curiosity and speculation. Where had the *Rajah* been to acquire such a rich cargo? Canton, no source for pepper, was quickly discounted. Was it the subcontinent? Ceylon? What did Derby know? Or Crowninshield, for that matter? There were lots of questions, but the schooner's master and owners, keen on protecting their source of pepper from eager competitors, were tight-lipped. Questions were put to the crew, but not even they knew where they had been, only that it was somewhere east of the Cape of Good Hope. Given the small size of the vessel, the small number of sailors, and the length and hazards of the voyage that might force such a confidence, these were extraordinary and mighty revealing considerations.

While Carnes and the Peeles kept their own counsel, they ordered the schooner converted into a brig. After cleaning and refitting, the *Rajah* again lifted anchor in July 1798, to return in October 1799 with 158,544 pounds of pepper, and again in July 1801 with 149,776 pounds. The Peeles enjoyed their monopoly for these three voyages, but the Derbys and Crowninshields would remain one-upped for only so long. Soon other Salem merchants were into the pepper trade. By this time, however, the *Rajah*'s owners were more than 400,000 pounds ahead of their nearest competitor.

Carnes's second voyage yielded aesthetic prizes as well, including Acehnese exotica, which may be viewed today in the city's Peabody Essex Museum. The Reverend Dr. William Bentley, the Harvard-educated progressive theologian and an intellectual force during Salem's most prosperous period, confided to his diary on October 22, 1799: "Captain Carnes, from Sumatra, shew me various specimens of shells, a large oyster shell, like that given to the Historical Society, the tooth of an elephant, a pipe with two stems, a petrified mushroom cap and stem, and two specimens of boxes in gold, with open work, extremely nice, and open flowers. The work is of uncommonly thin plates of gold, by the Malays." Thus with a cabinet of curios was the Salem East India Marine Society born, a measure of the port's growing wealth and sophistication.

Chapter 20

PEPPER AND

MALAY KNIVES

IT CAN BE fairly said that in the wake of the Peele brothers' success with Carnes's voyages bringing a profit of 700 percent on a ship's cargo, the other merchants of Salem, especially the house of George Crowninshield and Sons, became pepper-crazed. Though as yet no one knew where Carnes had acquired his priceless cargo, ships were fitted out for "India," and then their masters were told to sail for wherever pepper could be found.

On February 20, 1799, icy hands and fingers worked the rigging as the *America,* commanded by Captain Benjamin Crowninshield, George senior's third son, cleared the harbor just before a violent winter storm struck. But the big ship was beating down the North Atlantic for southern latitudes and months later made Tranqebar on the Coromandel coast of Bengal on the Indian subcontinent. When Crowninshield entered his ship from Calcutta eighteen months later, 95,000 pounds of pepper were in the *America's* hold.

Others were quick to follow. Simon Forrester brought a modest load of pepper aboard the *Vigilant,* and John Derby, Elias's son, came home with a handsome cargo of 160,000 pounds in the *John,* with both ships arriving from Bombay. The Crowninshield ship *Belisarius,* noted for her clipperlike speed, also returned from India with 58,000 pounds of the same cargo. But none of these voyages was nearly as profitable as Carnes's, because the pepper had traversed the Bay of Bengal by native craft from where it had been grown, and its price was substantially higher than it would have been on the coasts of Sumatra. Carnes had voyaged to acquire pepper at one of its great growing places, as the Portuguese, Dutch, and English before him had sought out the source of cloves and nutmeg in the Spice Islands.

After Carnes returned from his second voyage, however, Sumatra, as the prime destination for pepper at a price that could make a man's fortune, was no longer a secret. By the first year of the new century, the *Belisarius* had slipped her moorings from Crowninshield Wharf eight times for Sumatra. The Essex *Register* of July 30, 1801, reports: "Arrived the fast-sailing and well-known 'Belisarius,' Captain Samuel Skerry, Junior, one hundred and two days from Bencoolen, having performed her voyage in the short time of eight months and three days, as she sailed from Salem, November 25, 1800. . . . It is supposed that the 'Belisarius' has made the shortest voyage to the East Indies that was ever made from this country."

Illuminated by these successes, Salem's merchant aristocracy was beginning to be perceived by the world as more than simply parochial posturers. It was becoming a fashion for Yankee shipmasters to be received into the upper bourgeois circles of the ports in which they traded, and it was not a rarity for them to marry young French or Italian women of good family. The Derby name carried sufficient weight that it inspired an invitation from Lord Nelson to Elias Hasket Jr. for a visit aboard the *Victory*.

It was a heady time, as the race for pepper was gearing up. Together the *Belisarius* and the *America* in a total of five voyages returned with 2,500,000 pounds of pepper before the end of 1803, paying into the United States treasury duties of $20,000 to $50,000 a voyage, while the *Cincinnatus* returned with 650,000 pounds for Joseph Peabody, and Nathaniel Bowditch in the *Putnam* with 425,000 pounds to Abel Lawrence, each ship paying a handsome duty on her cargo.

The voyages of the *America* in a single year reveal an astonishing network of world trade already in place by 1804. Built under the eye of George Crowninshield Jr., this large, heavily armed 473-ton ship was square-rigged and could reach a top speed of thirteen knots, enabling her easily to outdistance any pursuers.

In the spring of that year she returned to Salem with a hold filled with spices and pepper. Paid in specie, or coined money, from the sale, she sailed for Sumatra again in July under the command of Captain Benjamin Crowninshield and was back in the Massachusetts port again by the following June. She cleared immediately for Rotterdam, where the pepper brought a sale of $140,000 in gold, a portion of which was sent back to Salem on another ship, while the *America* proceeded back around the cape for Calcutta.

Here she acquired goods with the remaining gold, before proceeding to the Tuscan port of Livorno and Liguria's La Spezia (Spice) on the Levantine Riviera to exchange goods for another cargo, which in turn would bring a great profit back in Salem. Such plying among the globe's far-flung ports was typical of Salem merchantmen, with the Sumatran pepper ports remaining the one constant destination.

ONE OF THE towering figures of Salem's pepper trade with Sumatra was also one of its earliest, Nathaniel Bowditch. Bowditch's portrait was painted by one of the many unknown traveling artists of the day, who made their rounds and a decent living by carting brushes, paints, and easels through New England ports to render on canvas merchant, captain, and ship: components of a unique seafaring aristocracy. Bowditch's likeness, picturing a rare intelligence radiating from an impish half smile under a confident high forehead, is a becoming study in luminescence itself, for Bowditch's was an extraordinary mind ahead of its time.

He was born in Salem in 1773, the son of Habakkuk Bowditch, a ship master who had survived two founderings at sea and was at the time of his son's birth the head of a family quite destitute. Nathaniel's formal schooling ended when he was ten, and he took up work in his father's cooperage.

The work required greater physical stamina than the younger Bowditch possessed, so he was apprenticed to the ship's chandlery of Hodges and Ropes in Salem. Leisure time found him at study, for he had a precocious bent for mathematics and exercised it with problems of navigation, gauging, surveying, algebra, geometry, and trigonometry, all the while being constantly encouraged by Dr. William Bentley, the minister and anecdotist who touched so many prominent Salem lives.

By 1789 Bowditch had begun to copy Isaac Newton's *Principia*. Too limited in means to buy the publications needed to master this great work, he borrowed books and journals and began to study Latin, the language of *Principia,* in 1790. Mainly through the intercession of the Reverend Dr. Bentley, he was invited to use the Salem Philosophical Library, founded with the prize collection of an Irish scientist that had been captured by a local privateer during the Revolution. This windfall gave Bowditch access to the *Philosophical Transactions of the Royal Society of London* as well as the library's many other holdings, and he copied what he deemed relevant into his commonplace books, while learning French to read scientific works in that language.

In January 1795 Bowditch went to sea on the first of five voyages, with the *Henry* taking him to Île de France as captain's clerk. The next year he sailed as supercargo aboard the *Astrea* to Manila. On this second voyage the young autodidactic scientist spent every spare moment making observations and calculations, even teaching a dozen of his crew members the technique of taking lunars, the only method of determining longitude without a chronometer, which no Salem vessel could afford. Bowditch discovered that taking lunars was such an exacting business that any error in observation brought a thirtyfold error in the result. Without a chronometer, he stressed, accuracy on such sightings was key.

Having discovered some eight thousand errors in the standard English book on navigation, he was determined to publish one of his own. For the next two voyages he worked out his vast number of calculations, and in 1802 the first edition of Bowditch's *The New American Practical Navigator* appeared, with corrected tables; information on winds, currents, and tides; mathematical instructions; and simplified formulas for "taking lunars." The work has remained the sailor's bible through numerous translations and seventy editions. While this important treatise was making a significant name for itself and embarking on a remarkable publication history, its author went to sea again.

This time sailing as master of the *Putnam* with his destination the northwest coast of Sumatra, Bowditch was able to put his theories into practice. Under a heading titled "Weather, Currents, Bearings of the Land, and Remarkable Occurrences," the ship's log is laced with hydrographic and meteorological observations, lunar and solar calculations, and comments on how the pepper trade was carried out with the various rajahs, providing a hint of troubles to come: "He [the rajah] holds to [an] agreement as long as he finds it for his interest to do so and no longer." Though Bowditch's charting of the Sumatran coast proved invaluable to successive shipmasters, it would take another generation for Salem shipmasters to wean themselves from dead reckoning in favor of taking lunars.

But the acid test of Bowditch's theories occurred upon his entering Salem Harbor on Christmas Eve 1803 in a blinding nor'easter, the thick snow making it impossible to pick up any landmark, including the lights of Baker's Island. This achievement coined a phrase that became a password to success for ambitious young men who aspired to command a merchantman: "I sailed with Captain Bowditch, sir!"

IN AN ESSAY titled "Remarks on the North West Coast of Sumatra," Bowditch had warned against the native way of doing business (which sometimes included piracy), but it wasn't until the *Cincinnatus,* commanded by Captain John Endicott, returned in 1803 that merchants and masters learned that they had more to worry about on this score than storms or British privateers. Endicott reported that the Sumatran natives, while not yet at conflict with American traders, were at war with each other, and one reason was quite simple. In an effort to acquire pepper at its source, Salem traders had searched out small ports, thereby angering the rajahs of the more prominent emporia over the loss of their revenue as middlemen. Americans would soon be at risk, whether at tiny or major Sumatran ports.

Shortly after Endicott delivered his warning, disaster struck the same *Putnam* Nathaniel Bowditch had sailed to Sumatra four years earlier. In late November 1805 she lay off Bintan Island in the Straits of Malacca, not far from where Raffles would found Singapore a few years later. These waters harbored as many pirates as fishermen. Nearby two British brigs rode at anchor, while a Malay prahu lay off to the south.

It was the off-season, and pickings were lean. However, Captain John Carlton had discovered stores of an old crop of pepper off Sumatra's east coast and thought it expedient to see it loaded before sailing for the western part of the island and the new crop expected in January. He had completed his trading and was planning to sail upon completion of lading, which was sporadic due to a series of strong north winds.

With a little time on his hands, Captain Carlton went ashore in a pinnace and called on the English captain of the *Malcolm* before he was rowed back to the *Putnam*. Upon his return he learned that in his absence the Malay prahu had tacked over to close on his ship, and the crew of the native vessel had been allowed to board for an inspection. Carlton at first was unperturbed, for natives had been on the *Putnam*'s decks before to load pepper. But on this occasion the mate had sensed more than idle curiosity on the part of the Malays as they sized up the ship and crew, and he conveyed his misgivings to Carlton.

Carlton reassured his men that there was nothing to fear if they maintained a steady, alert watch. Then, to steel the confidence of his small force, he sent a longboat over to the prahu with the warning that no further visits would be allowed. The day passed without incident until late afternoon, when the watch reported to Carlton that another prahu was bearing down on the *Putnam*. The captain ordered his men to stand by for an attack, but when the prahu drew even with the Salem ship, a voice hailed the Yankees.

To Carlton's relief, it was a Chinese merchant wanting to board and trade with the crew for their own personal gain, a time-honored practice. The merchant was allowed to board, and after completing negotiations, left a deposit of thirty dollars to seal the agreement before casting off.

Thanksgiving Day arrived with the north wind picking up to gale force, making the final delivery of pepper highly unlikely. With a final item of business to close with the rajah ashore, Carlton admonished his men to be vigilant, then, accompanied by two crew members and his clerk, he put in to the beach. At noon the wind died, and almost immediately the *Putnam*'s lookout spotted the first prahu being readied to approach. When the native craft was within hailing distance, one of its crew of sixteen cried out that the final load of pepper for the *Putnam* was in their hold, and that they should take advantage of the calm to transfer the cargo.

As the Malays appeared to be unarmed, the mate agreed, and six Malays were allowed to board and receive the bags of pepper as they were muscled up from the prahu. For unarmed men, however, the Salem seamen were careless and neglectful, apparently having forgotten their captain's warning. They also believed that their identity as Salemites conferred on them a certain invincibility.

Suddenly the second mate saw a *kris* handed up, and then another of the short, curvy daggers. The mate had scarcely time to cry out before a blade cut him down, as Malays scurried up over the gunwales and attacked in a rush. The first mate in the bow took a slight wound, while a sailor in the forechains was stabbed several times and fell overboard, not to be seen again.

Another sailor seized a handspike and struck down two of the assailants before a third drove his *kris* into the sailor's back, while the mulatto steward was similarly dispatched, reducing the crew on the deck to its last hand. The ship's carpenter, William Brown, was a large man with Herculean strength, and he was looking for whatever weapon he could find. He seized a thick three-foot plank to which the cook had affixed the galley's coffee grinder. Wielded in Brown's hands, the contraption became as lethal as a medieval mace; he swung wildly, laying out Malays right and left. They were stunned by this vicious counterattack but soon regrouped to charge the carpenter.

A blade struck bone between Brown's shoulders, whereupon he turned and caught the man squarely in the head with his makeshift weapon. Then, taking a shoulder stab, he looked forward and saw the bow was clear. With his rear protected, Brown swung his weapon aloft like a broadsword, driving the attackers aft of the mizzenmast just as help arrived in the person of the foretopman, who had swung down from his perch aloft. Together the two men sent the Malays flailing into the water, while the prahu had dropped astern. Seizing the stern swivel gun, Brown and the foretopman tried to fire on the vessel, but the priming was wet.

By now the wind had gathered, and the prahu let out sail, soon putting it a mile downwind and out of the *Putnam's* cannon range. Brown, now beginning to feel the effects of his shoulder wound, was keen to send up a distress signal to alert the British brigs to come to their aid, but he was overruled by the first mate, who returned from his safe haven under the bowsprit and inexplicably gave the order to abandon ship. Placing their wounded in a longboat, the survivors rowed to the *Malcolm,* where they found Captain Carlton making a farewell call on her captain.

Meanwhile, the Malays in the retreating prahu saw this sequence. Quickly they turned about and close-hauled to retake the deserted Salem ship. They were skillful sailors, and in short order they trimmed the *Put-*

nam's sails and were under way to the island of Lingen, while two men lay dying of their wounds on the deck of the *Malcolm*. William Brown was the day's hero, while the name of the craven first mate was forgotten. It was a dark Thanksgiving evening that fell as Captain Carlton pondered what to do next.

Determined that such treachery should not go unpunished, he convinced the two British captains to give pursuit, which they did, reaching an anchorage at Lingen Straits that evening, and proceeding at daylight to finally catch sight of the *Putnam* and her prahu escort late the following afternoon. A stern chase ensued, but the Salem ship, now manned by Malays, was faster and better-armed than the British brigs that pursued her, and after two days of chase and exchange of gunfire, the skirmishes costing the life of a British officer, the *Putnam* was never seen again. Her captain and crew were delivered to Penang Island off the Malay Peninsula, from where they managed to get to Calcutta and secure passage to Salem, a disappointing return voyage with no pepper.

An unfortunate precedent had been set, and word of the Yankees' vulnerability soon spread across the waters, for if there was anything Malays of whatever tribe coveted beyond modern weaponry, it was an armed American schooner. But these risks did not deter the Salem seamen, for they were competing at the pepper trade in the spirit of riverboat gamblers playing for high stakes.

IN TIME, as the pepper trade grew even more competitive, a pattern of acquiring the produce began to emerge. The Acehnese ports of northwest Sumatra, each headed by a local rajah, were the most dependable source of supply, though the best fruit was grown by the Minangkabau tribesmen in the Padang Highlands, then traded to the mercantile-minded Acehnese. The season began in January with the harvesting of small berries at the foot of the vines, though the height of the crop flourished during March and April, with the best pepper taken from the vines' top in May, and good pepper transported to the coast as late as July.

As Captain Carnes had demonstrated, it was a question of a master first sailing his ship to such Sumatran ports as Bencoolen or Padang and making inquiries as to where that season's crop was the most plentiful, then setting a course for the likes of Soo Soo and Quallah Battoo, tiny ports often in bays at the mouths of small rivers.

The medium of exchange was coined money, and the currency was the Spanish silver dollar or pieces of eight, which seems on the face of it unlikely money for Salem traders. However, it was coin they knew very well, for its origin and availability to seamen in the vast sums required to compete in the pepper trade were historical, rooted in the many decades of trade on the Spanish Main. This specie was valuable as ballast on an outgoing voyage, and sacks of it found their way along the ports of the Atlantic seaboard in a coaster or under the driver's seat of a stagecoach in amounts ranging as high as $15,000.

Experience soon taught Salem traders the tricks of the trade. They quickly learned that the written contract with the captain or supercargo sought so earnestly by the local rajah was a one-sided affair. An eager, naive shipmaster would be guaranteed a load of pepper, but only if he paid in advance. Because of the great demand for pepper, especially with the competing English and Dutch on the scene, there were rarely sufficient quantities of the crop in a port's godowns to fill a ship on any captain's arrival, whatever flag he sailed under.

This reality put pressure on a captain to seek a guaranteed load of a future crop, or a crop in transport to the coast from such a hinterland as the Padang Highlands, and an advance payment to the rajah was the only way delivery would be ensured. But when the captain, perhaps sailing under a Crowninshield merchant flag, returned with his ship to pick up his prepaid load, he invariably discovered that he had been undercut by his Derby rival. The natural result was that the first captain saw neither pepper nor return of the large sum of money he had advanced.

It did not take shipmasters long to discover that the safest way of doing business was for the captain first to discover a port where stores were available, and then agree on a price per unit with the rajah, after which he would go ashore with his scales and transport bags. Both sides would examine the scales' weights, which were then locked in a chest until trading actually began. With a man or two at his side, the captain or supercargo would then make his purchases. The acquired pepper consequently would be bagged and weighed, paid for by the unit on the spot, and then transported by the rajah's prahus to the ship.

Before Captain Carnes opened up the pepper trade, virtually nothing was known in Salem about Sumatra. But as merchants became more competitive among themselves and the number of pepper voyages increased, intelligence about the island was shared by the likes of Nathaniel Bowditch. Such intelligence accounted for the forming of marine societies, whose memberships were made up of shipmasters and supercargoes who had sailed beyond the cape.

While these organizations came to function as professional, social, and political lodges, their most important function was the dissemination of knowledge about distant seas and ports. The Salem Marine Society's extensive holdings of logs, charts, and journals of past voyages became indispensable aids to captains sailing routes for the first time.

During these years Salem's merchant house flags could be seen flying in such diverse ports as Lima, Canton, St. Petersburg, and Cape Town to the point where Salem was regarded by some distant merchants as its own sovereign nation. By extension, Sumatra at the height of the pepper trade became known as Salem's East Indies, so vigorous was the commerce between these two vastly disparate peoples. In a short time the base established for Salem's merchants by Elias Hasket Derby at Île de France, seven thousand miles away from Salem, became key to the city's success as a staging area. From there ships struck out across the Indian Ocean for Eastern seas and beyond to the South Pacific, but most especially to Sumatra for pepper.

The first few years of the nineteenth century were the most profitable in Salem's pepper trade with Sumatra. The Crowninshield ships *Belisarius* and *America* brought home between them over a million pounds of the fruit. The peak was reached in 1805, when exports alone totaled seven million pounds of pepper just in that year. If New Englanders had little use themselves for pepper, there was spirited bidding for it on the other side of the world as goods destined for Europe. Americans had entered the spice game late in the day, when the "holy trinity" was already controlled by European nations. Even so, the Salemites had come into the pepper trade with sufficient vigor to establish what amounted to a monopoly of their own. At least on one occasion the condiment received the supreme test for its preservative qualities: It was in this period that a Salem seaman who had died in Sumatra of unknown causes was shipped home in a coffin filled with pepper, and on arrival he was pronounced as looking "very natural."

But the violence against Salem traders at the hands of Sumatran renegades escalated as trade intensified. In March 1807, half a year before President Jefferson's "Tyrannical Embargo" all but ruined Salem, the *Marquis de Someruelas,* named for a Cuban governor, arrived at Salem with a cargo of pepper from Sumatra. Her master, William Story, had a tale of violence and tragedy that had occurred some six months earlier in southeastern Sumatra on one of the salt branches of the great River Jamba.

Story was a large, powerful man of commanding presence and excellent seamanship. His father had been a surgeon in General Washington's army, and his half brother served on Chief Justice John Marshall's United States Supreme Court. It was said that Captain Story was strong enough to lift an anchor, a feat usually managed by several men.

In late September 1806 Story had traveled upriver by prahu some seventy miles from his ship's anchorage on the Jamba to collect the money he had made the mistake of advancing to a local rajah for pepper that never materialized. Confronting the rajah with threats, Story demanded his money back, but the rajah refused. Back in his camp, Story was pondering his options when an emissary appeared to say that the rajah would honor his part of the bargain with pepper to fill the hold of the Salem ship if Story would remain two months longer. As if to seal the arrangement, a prahu with the first load of pepper was ready to proceed downriver, and Story could accompany it back to his ship, with the rajah's promise of more loads to follow.

Story agreed. But as the prahu proceeded downstream, he found it slow going against an incoming estuarine tide. "Finding the proa [prahu] a heavy, dull sailer, I engaged a small proa which was passing by to carry me to the ship." Two of the men with the pepper load, however, were fearful of passing the sultan's fort some twenty miles downstream without Story, for this sultan was the supreme law of the land, and no prahu could pass his fort without a permit. Story then assured the men that he would stop at the fort and report that the pepper load was astern of him and that all was in order. He did so and again proceeded downriver until the tide beat his small prahu back, and at midnight the small party was forced to anchor.

Fearful of treachery, Story slept little, but there were no untoward incidents. At first light, when the tide had shifted, the prahu rode the ebb for the remaining fifty miles to the *Marquis,* which was anchored in a small branch of the Jamba. Soon there was not one but three prahus fully loaded with pepper for transfer to the ship's hold, and together they were manned by a force of about two hundred men, an alarming number in contrast to Story's crew of twenty.

But Story was cautious, "as we never admitted more than one large proa, or two small ones, at a time." The loading proceeded without incident. Story had dealt with these same men on previous voyages and trusted them. Early the next morning more prahus arrived, and the operation seemed to be going smoothly.

After dinner the crew resumed the loading of pepper into the hold of the *Marquis,* while Story remained on deck with Mr. Bromfield (the ship's carpenter), his assistant, the cook, and the steward as well as fourteen Malays transferring bags of pepper from the prahus. Captain Story then went below with orders about stowing the hold and had been down there about five minutes when he heard a terrible scream and the cry "I've been creased!"

Topside, Mr. Bromfield had approached a Malay perched on the larboard hencoop, his clothes wrapped tightly about him. Thinking the man might have taken sugar from an open canister, Mr. Bromfield accosted him, whereupon the Malay wielded a *kris* and stabbed the carpenter through the heart. Upon hearing his cries, Captain Story sounded the alarm while running aft to his cabin for his sword and pistol, then dodging two boarding pikes hurled at him when he mounted the ladderway. The rest of Story's men were either below or between decks, and *kris*-wielding Malays hovered over the hatchways.

Captain Story quickly divided his crew of twenty men to attack both the main hatchway and the companionway, and with just three pistols and three swords managed to emerge topside to discover the Malays had got off from alongside the ship. Story ordered his men to the arms chests, kept on deck for such emergencies, but the Malays had tossed them overboard. Meanwhile, the attacking party made it to shore.

Not long after, ten prahus approached the *Marquis,* ostensibly to help. Appraising the condition of Story's crew, with Mr. Bromfield dead and the cook and steward missing and presumed dead, the small armada went in pursuit of the renegades, but to no avail. "I find every attention paid me by the Sultan and the head men," wrote Captain Story. "I therefore have no reason to suspect the Sultan knew anything of such an act going forward. The men who rose upon the ship belong high up on the river Jamba."

Captain Story managed to guide his ship down the Jamba without benefit of a native pilot, and despite the episode the voyage was quite successful. The *Marquis de Someruelas* sailed for Europe, where she sold her cargo of pepper in Hamburg and St. Petersburg for $126,875.51. The cost of the voyage had been $27,123.81, so by her return to Salem a tidy profit of $99,751.70 on the pepper alone had been realized.

A sense of his priorities may be inferred from the following letter written by the rajah after Captain Story's visit. The communication, while making no mention of the contentious relations between the two men, does underscore that each rajah was a law unto himself. Addressed to the vessel's owners, John and Richard Gardner of Salem, written in Arabic script, and dated October 22, 1806, from a place called Triangano, the translated text of this document is as follows:

> Your ship commanded by William Story has arrived at this place in order to purchase a Cargo of Pepper. I have furnished him with all that I had remaining in my Country which is generally reputed to be the best Pepper of any hereabouts. As your ship is the first American ship to have been at this place and knowing that you deal largely in Pepper, I should be happy in having the opportunity of continuing to furnish you with this article.
>
> In the meantime, if you should send your ship this way again, I should be glad if you would send the following articles provided you can make it convenient: 600 muskets at the price of 8 dollars each (English company), 40 cannon of fathom long and thin at the price of 10 dollars each, 2 pieces of green woolen cloth, 2 pieces of red woolen cloth, 2 pieces of brown woolen cloth, and a pair of chandeliers.
>
> You may depend that no Rajah will be better disposed of continuing trade with you than I should. My port is open to every nation at no charges whatsoever. The best time for a ship to be here is in the month of August as at that time the Pepper is brought in from the country which is about fifteen thousand peculo [a native unit of weight] per year.

The letter, on display at Salem's Peabody Essex Museum, is signed "Lanaa Abedues Annah Sultan Marckso."

The enterprising shipmaster often brought back more than financial profit from his voyages, as did Jonathan Carnes after his second expedition, returning with sufficient Sumatran exotica to begin a society that eventually became a museum. Other voyages returned with such equally arcane cargo as Arabian camels and a tiger. In 1795 Captain Jacob Crowninshield, George senior's middle son, who would become a congressman at age thirty-two, brought back to Salem aboard the Derby ship *America* the first elephant ever seen in America. This resourceful shipmaster acquired the beast at Île de France for $450, and charged admission at public showings in Salem. The Reverend Dr. Bentley recorded that the elephant shook off would-be riders and "took bread out of the pockets of the spectators. . . . He also drank porter and drew the cork." The clever Crowninshield eventually sold his prize for $10,000.

Chapter 21

"Tyrannical Embargo"

The world's oceans of two centuries ago were not the vast, trackless expanse of indigo and emerald seen today, usually from an arcing vantage point some six miles above its surface. From an airplane window today one gazes on a vast mosaic, softened by distance and stilled save for the occasional lonely wake of the mammoth container cargo vessel etched on its glassy surface.

In the days of the Derbys and Crowninshields, however, the east wind blew, and men laboring before the mast heard the deep, contrary rhythms of the ocean with all their terror. Seas of the globe were dotted with the sails of small traders, merchantmen, and passenger ships churning and plowing watery hills and valleys to seek out harbors seen for the first time, like ocean-bound bees swarming to aquatic hives.

At the beginning of the nineteenth century, ships were everywhere, sailing this way and that, alone and in convoy, coasting familiar shores and crossing mighty oceans to the world's far-flung ports. Civilization and its well-being depended upon shipmasters of courage and resource plying the world's waters at great risk. It was an era that bore witness to Benjamin Franklin's seven voyages to Europe.

The tea trade belonged to Boston with its superior harbor, whose sea-lane of choice was around the Horn for the Pacific Northwest and a cargo of furs for trade in Canton. Though America's taste for tea had been inherited from the English, the demand for the leaves had become as much an American obsession as an English one. For their part, the Chinese Hong merchants liked the Boston traders, much preferring to deal with them rather than the officials of the English East India Company, whom they deemed arrogant. The American demand for silks, nankeens, crapes, and especially tea was so rapidly increasing, and Boston's sea merchants were so adroit in the handling and distribution to all parts of the world, that the trade grew mightily. Salem still preferred to haul its cod, salt beef, and woodenware as trade goods via the Cape of Good Hope to the Indian Ocean, Sumatra, and the South Pacific, with the occasional load of contraband Indian or Turkish opium smuggled into Whampoa Reach. It was a strangely noncompetitive, if tacit, arrangement between the two ports.

It was as though the two merchant ports, after the manner of Spain and Portugal in an earlier day, had tacitly carved the East into two halves to share, while whalers out of New Bedford and Nantucket stalked their prey in such forgotten corners as the Timor Sea in the East Indies, where their bone-weary seamen relaxed over gin and filled their chests with perfumed sandalwood in the port of Kupang.

Then suddenly sea trade ceased, ships were idled, and ports began their slide into decrepitude as President Thomas Jefferson's embargo fell.

Jefferson's solution to British and French privateering, which had reached epidemic proportions by 1806, was to keep American ships at home in port. Though the embargo would last only fourteen months, from December 22, 1807, to March 15, 1809 (the same month James Madison was inaugurated as president), it was as punishing a blow to farmers of the Middle Atlantic states and planters of the South, who were as fully dependent on foreign trade, as it was to the Yankee traders who transported the goods. In Salem the embargo's effect was immediate; it was a bitter winter, and firewood was scarce.

ON A LATE May evening in 1808, a reception was held for Senator Timothy Pickering, George Washington's old friend and cabinet member. Pickering had spoken out against President Jefferson's "Tyrannical Embargo," which had been in effect for five months. The Federalist Derbys, as well as other prominent merchants who were being slowly ruined by Jefferson's policy, were keen to aid Senator Pickering's efforts to end it.

The power and influence of the Derbys, however, had waned since the death of Elias Hasket Derby Sr. in 1799. Gone was the elder Derby's "uncommon spirit of enterprise." On top of the patriarch's passing, the younger generation of Derbys were perceived as something of a social embarrassment; Elias Hasket Jr.'s bad debts mounted, and disputes over the Derby estate became public. After Nathaniel West was awarded a divorce from the senior Derby's daughter as well as possession of the Derby farm, he and his former brother-in-law provoked each other into a fistfight on Derby Wharf. The Derbys were the old guard, and their flag eventually was to disappear in Salem. The season was ripe for a last hurrah.

It was still light with the promise of a pleasant evening when Senator Pickering was collected by coach from his Essex County farm and escorted through Beverly and across the bridge into antique Salem, where the reek of salt water hung in the air. The senator and his escort of 120 young men on horseback followed the famous half mile of Derby Street along the waterfront.

On the residential side they passed the row of hip-roofed brick and wooden mansions with their tidy gardens belonging to the older merchants, while on the harbor side were lined up countinghouses, warehouses, the shops of ship chandlers and pump makers, and sail makers' lofts hovered over by a confusion of spars, rigging, furled and brailed sails; behind them peered the wharves themselves. The destination of this high-spirited band was the late Elias Hasket Derby's mansion, and the partygoers proceeded to the tune of cannon salutes fired from vessels in the harbor decorated for the occasion.

After the reception the party moved in a noisy rush over to the concert hall for dinner with 150 guests. The food was washed down with much drink, followed by many toasts, and the ninth one got to the heart of the matter in its indictment of President Jefferson: "May seamen return from the spade to the capstan and the philosopher from the chair of state to the closet." Pandemonium erupted. As the evening continued, glasses were raised no fewer than thirty times. By its end the revelers were drunk but determined to give new life to their moribund Federalist party, as they were fiercely united in contempt for the embargo and the hated upstart Republicans, especially the Crowninshields, who stood for it.

The ever-alert chronicler of Salem's social scene, the ubiquitous and staunch Republican Dr. Bentley, whose one consolation over the embargo was that it stimulated pleasure boating in Salem Bay, had not been present at this political gathering. No doubt the cherubic bachelor minister and pastor of East Church spent that evening quietly at home. The Reverend Dr. Bentley resided in book-lined rooms, which he rented from the widow Hannah Crowninshield upstairs in the wooden gambrel-roofed house that had been built by Captain John Crowninshield between 1727 and 1730.

The house, which came to be known as the Crowninshield-Bentley House, was subsequently lived in by four generations of that family. Dr. Bentley, who lived there from 1791 until his death in 1819, had partisan feelings of his own, as he remarked to his diary about Derby's gathering on the evening of May 27, the event that became the talk of Salem. "Who the wretches were that conducted this insult to our government," Bentley wrote, "I never asked."

But "this insult" perceived by Bentley had a root cause. Necessity, not choice, had driven the sons of Massachusetts to sea to "trye all ports," risking all freights. When Jefferson's act closed down Salem Harbor, the shock of impact was that of a numbing winter nor'easter. Over time, however, the "Tyrannical Embargo" settled in like the natural phenomenon it most resembled: a dreaded belt of equatorial doldrums in which a ship suddenly found itself, inducing the mariner's nightmare of being helplessly becalmed, losing time, and consuming provisions and water, during which period he could do nothing except wait days or weeks while praying for a fair wind. Such doldrums were also known as the horse latitudes, so named because in the days of the conquistadors, horses that had consumed all the water allotted to them during this becalmed period were driven mad from thirst and became beasts of destruction, necessitating that crew members throw them overboard. Their floating, bloated carcasses became a grim but familiar sight to passing ships.

The Republican Crowninshields, who supported the embargo, came under considerable criticism, for they had $300,000 worth of property at sea east of the Cape of Good Hope when the embargo fell, and it was unjustly assumed that they had escaped the crippling decree. In theory, once a ship was in distant waters trading among foreign ports, it could do so indefinitely and continue to profit. But in fairness the Crowninshields, too, had many idle ships.

The loss in revenues from the enforced unemployment of over a hundred Salem ships was devastating to everyone, from the Essex County farmers who grew vast fields of yellow onions as an antidote to scurvy, to merchant-owners, sea captains, ship carpenters, and able seamen. The great voyages to Sumatra had netted from $100,000 to $300,000 each, and that capital, which New England agriculture was not about to replace, had made Salem a Federal jewel of a port.

But Thomas Jefferson had other things on his mind than foreign privateers and Salem's prosperity, namely a vision of America's manifest destiny. Where the word *frontier* in Europe denoted a boundary between two countries, something fixed and permanent, in America it suggested a transitory line of demarcation, ever receding. The Louisiana Purchase in 1803 and the Lewis and Clark expedition, which followed that acquisition, gave new meaning to the word *West.*

The problem the two explorers undertook to solve had its genesis in Columbus's landfall in America, which was for him a troubling find. When those who followed in Columbus's wake realized that the North American continent barred the way to the Indies, they took up the task of finding a way around or through the Americas, and for centuries this goal incited further American exploration. Deeply interested in scientific discovery, President Jefferson saw the new territory as a pretext for exploring the West.

On November 7, 1805, Meriwether Lewis, the President's private secretary, and Captain William Clark, the younger brother of General George Rogers Clark, gazed upon the Pacific Ocean. Their party had ascended the Missouri and its Jefferson fork in keelboats to the Rockies. Then they managed to cross to the Snake, following that river to the Columbia and then to the sea. On their return after crossing the Continental Divide, they split into groups, thus descending the Yellowstone as well as the Missouri. The expedition ended in St. Louis on September 23, 1806.

But a great epic in human achievement had been written, with profound implications for the new nation. The old dream of a northwest passage—a water route to the Indies—was laid to rest. But a continent of wilderness had been traversed, thus supplying an important impulse to further the extension of American trade and settlement. Moreover, important additions to the existing body of geographical and scientific knowledge were in hand. Lewis and Clark had left the tracks of empire across the wide Missouri. These successes, however, meant little to Salem merchants, whose Indiamen were rotting at wharfside from disuse, their sailors unemployed.

A bit of contemporary newspaper doggerel said it all:

> Our ships all in motion once whitened the ocean,
> They sailed and returned with a cargo;
> Now doomed to decay, they have fallen a prey
> To Jefferson—worms—and embargo.

This is an understandable attitude for a community whose forefathers had fastened themselves to New England's rocky coast. Theirs was a seaward gaze, and they had no conception of the vastness of the country behind them. When Cotton Mather spoke of New England as being bounded by the "Atlantic Sea eastward" and the "Connecticut River westward," he could scarcely have realized that beyond that river it was virtually as far to the western ocean as it was to Europe. Daniel Boone's push into Kentucky in 1775 was far removed from the concerns of Salem. Likewise, the appeal of his fictional counterpart, James Fenimore Cooper's Natty Bumppo of the *Leatherstocking Tales,* which dramatized the struggle between the forces of primitive nature and civilized society for the soul of man, would elude them. After the Lewis and Clark expedition and the War of 1812 (which opened up the gulf territories south of Tennessee as far west as the Mississippi), pioneers looked into the sunset at a stretch of earth too vast to be comprehended. By the same token, the sons of Salem gave the West no thought at all except as a coast, and to them a foreign one, which a merchantman had to round the Horn to reach for purposes of trade.

But if Salem was removed from the increasingly magnetic pull of the West's receding frontier, it was because she was naturally attracted to a vastly different one, where men not only pursued their livelihood but escaped from the pressures of social discipline. Salemites, too, were caught between what Emerson termed "the Establishment and the Movement," or "the party of the Past and the party of the Future." But theirs was the frontier to be duly celebrated in 1851 by Herman Melville's *Moby Dick,* in which the novelist's narrator Ishmael flees to the open sea by signing on to the whaling vessel *Pequod,* which is "not so much bound to any haven ahead as rushing from all havens astern."

The time of the embargo was a day when political passions ran high, and a man's opinion, freely expressed, might cost him his life. (Only four years before, Aaron Burr, the nation's vice president, had killed his enemy Alexander Hamilton in a duel.) The young New York dandy Washington Irving, possessed of a Federalist bent and repelled by what he perceived to be the noisome Republican mob, satirized Jefferson in his *History of New York* in the person of Governor Wilhelm Kieft. The poet William Cullen Bryant did likewise in his poem "The Embargo."

To Salem, Jefferson's "Tyrannical Embargo" was as polarizing as the Burr case, as well as outrageous and hypocritical. Like the Burr conspiracy, a dramatic struggle for power with obvious winners and losers, the lines were clearly drawn on the embargo issue, with excited passions on both sides. Though prosperity would return to Salem after its repeal, the issue unleashed Federalist bigotry in some quarters, taking the form of blind hatred for the Republican party. Federalists like the Derbys and the rising Joseph Peabody began to talk of New England's secession from the union. William Gray, who had grown to rival the Derbys and Crowninshields as one of Salem's most prosperous and influential merchants, was ostracized for his support of Jefferson to the point where he moved to Boston the same spring the embargo was lifted, taking with him nearly a fourth of Salem's overseas trade.

A spirit of self-complacency and superiority among Yankees was nurtured, and it was directed not only at men like "Billy" Gray, whose views were unacceptable, but at any state south of New England. As an issue, the embargo and its consequences bulk large in that time.

In addition to the damage done to American fortunes large and small, the embargo failed to punish Great Britain as its supporters had hoped. Instead, it gave her "a triumphant monopoly of the commerce of the world," and instituted a domestic foreign policy that led to another war with that nation.

Once the embargo was lifted, the U.S. pepper trade reached a second peak in 1810, though this rise was nearly nullified by the War of 1812, or "Mr. Madison's War," which was disastrous for American foreign commerce. America's entering the conflict in the name of "free trade and sailors' rights" kept pepper merchantmen at wharfside for another three years under "Madison's nightcaps," which were tar buckets thrown over masts to prevent rotting.

It was the port's anti-British Republicans who dispatched privateers for the sole purpose of preying on enemy commerce, with the Crowninshield fleet leading the way. In Salem's streets drummers and fife players marched to summon volunteers to man ships to sail that very night, with G. Crowninshield and Sons' *America* the most distinguished and successful of privateers in a war to which most people in New England were bitterly opposed.

When peace came at last in a freezing February, the news was passed to the scattering of idle Massachusetts ports by shouting stage-drivers and relayed through weathered fish horns to the meetinghouses, which tolled the news. Salem seamen greeted the tidings like condemned men granted a reprieve and turned once again to the open arms of the ocean.

THE WORLD, HOWEVER, had changed. The Napoleonic scourge had ended, and Europe was at peace and intent at recovering her own trade. Simultaneously, the westward movement in the United States was beginning to leave Massachusetts isolated anew, while ports like New Orleans, Baltimore, and New York with the Erie Canal began to prosper as conduits between the West and Europe.

New England had paid dearly, both in terms of prestige in Washington and love lost with her sister states to the south, and the Federalist Party's death knell was sounded. As the Industrial Revolution invaded America's shores, farsighted Massachusetts men began to see the state's future in manufacturing in the mill towns of Lawrence and Lowell. Meanwhile the old mercantile families retained their ships and once again retraced the old routes to Salem's Indies.

The redoubtable Dr. Bentley chronicled in his diary of July 8, 1816, a sight of shipbuilding that lifted his heart: "In passing to Beverly on Saturday, I observed a Vessel on the stocks on the Beverly side, near the Bridge, almost finished, & above 100 tons. The Master Builder from Ipswich. Our four Vessels one at Becket's & the other three in Southfields, two of them at Briggs & the other near S[outh] Bridge, by Barker & Magoon's' are said to be specimens of excellent shipbuilding. It is said that more of this work is going on in town than for many years & in superior execution."

In an uncharacteristic lull, however, Salem ships were destined for a time to be cursed by a string of bad luck. In June 1816 the *Union,* commanded by Captain William Osgood, cleared for Sumatra and was returning with a full load of pepper and tin when after midnight on February 24 the lookout sighted the Thatcher's Island light through a thick snowstorm, and the ship stood in for Baker's Island. Then there was momentary confusion and second-guessing. Should there be one light or two? Perhaps it was the Boston light, it was suggested; and if it was, then they should steer south of it. The indecision was costly. When Osgood gave the command to helm down, the ship could not regain her course and ran aground hard on the northwest point of Baker's. All hands were saved, but the Baker's Island beach was littered with peppercorns, along with the occasional box of tin, for months to come.

Two years later, when the *Hope* stood in off the northwest coast of Sumatra, her master, Captain Tate, noticed a change from previous voyages: the presence of ships from many nations trading for pepper, now that the world was at peace. Americans could no longer count on her neutrality to win her merchants a favored status. It was that very posture that had helped to make the foreign trade of the United States so successful. Moreover, the demand for pepper was so great that its price had risen to ten dollars per unit, but Captain Tate managed to secure a full hold of the cargo. On her return the *Hope* met stiff gales off the Cape of Good Hope and then the contrary winds of a circular storm, which soon brought them a following wind, then suddenly the turbulent waters flattened out in a dreaded calm.

Tate waited moments for the inevitable, and when the gale burst over the bow, it took the foremast by the board and ripped out the bowsprit by its fastening gammon, driving the stern under. The captain ordered cannon forward to stabilize the ship, while a man was lowered off the bow to clean away pinioned wreckage, and others worked at saving the main- and mizzenmasts by rigging additional stays. The young but game crew managed to jury-rig a foremast with a lowered topmast and a bowsprit with a topsail yard. Within a month the *Hope* limped into St. Helena, the residence of the exiled Napoleon, where they managed to secure additional rigging to see them home by September 12 with a saved ship and salvaged cargo of pepper.

In 1818 there were thirty-five pepper voyages made to Sumatra from Salem without serious incident, but when acts of piracy by Malays occurred, they were frightful. Tales had circulated in the bazaars of Batavia of the brutal practices of the pirates that chilled the blood. The method of these corsairs was to lie in wait for ships, slaughter the lascars, or East Indian sailors, and torture Europeans to death in the most fiendish ways imaginable. The stories were true, and they settled deep into the European imagination.

In 1822 Sumatra produced 18,630,000 pounds of pepper, and Salem continued to claim its share of it. But piracy and native hostilities visited upon the New Englanders intensified as the decade wore on, leading up to an unprecedented disaster in January 1831: the capture by Malays of the *Friendship* and the murder of five members of its crew, which was the worst tragedy in the history of the trade between Salem and Sumatra. The event became one of national importance, prompting retribution by the United States government.

Chapter 22

"MISTER KNIGHT
NO UNDERSTAND
MALAY MAN"

IN SEPTEMBER 1830 the *Friendship,* a large ship of 366 tons under the command of Captain Charles Endicott, reached the Sumatran coast after clearing Salem Harbor four months before. The seasoned Endicott by this stage in his career was an old Sumatra hand. He was thirty-seven, married with two children, and had conducted surveys and soundings on his many previous voyages that would greatly benefit the shipmasters who followed him. Unlike the young members of his crew, he was also versed in the propensity for Acehnese treachery.

The ship stood in at Quallah Battoo, a pepper port straddling the estuary of a narrow river, which spilled sandy sediment into a surging indigo surf. A mile-long beach before a backdrop of steep, forested mountains reached along the coast on either side, with rows of low thatched huts fringed by a string of coconut trees concentrated on both sides at the river's mouth. These were the bazaars where trading was conducted. The port was ruled by five capricious and contentious rajahs, who had each built a mud fort in a strategic part of the town to protect his holdings from his rival neighbors as well as foreign invaders.

With a good anchorage offshore, Captain Endicott was borne in a pinnace to the landing, where he commenced trading for pepper, which at this time of year was an old crop in short supply.

By early November stores were exhausted, so Endicott lifted anchor and coasted for other ports, but with little success. Anticipating January's crop, due in two months, he sought a safe anchorage for the wait and found it at Pulau Kio, or Wood Island, just two miles down the coast from Quallah Battoo. Pulau Kio was ruled by Rajah Po Adam, a man of trustworthy character and goodwill who had won the affection and respect of Salem traders in the past. The wealthiest merchant in these parts, Po Adam believed Salem to be a country in its own right and one of the richest and most important parts of the globe.

"One bright moonlight night, shortly after our arrival at this place," Captain Endicott later recounted in a lecture at Salem's Essex Institute, "I was awakened by the watch informing me that a native boat was approaching the ship in a very stealthy manner and under suspicious circumstances." Endicott, who knew enough of the native language to trade, then challenged the prahu in the Acehnese dialect, asking who they were, where they were from, and why they were approaching the ship in such a "tiger-like manner."

The prahu quickly sprang to life and from it came the answer that they were friends from Quallah Battoo with a load of smuggled pepper they were keen to sell. As the prahu drew nearer, Endicott quickly ordered it to back off: if the natives approached any closer or attempted to come alongside, his guns would fire on them. Keeping the prahu at a distance, Endicott held council with his crew, and it was decided that the second mate would board the prahu to inspect it for pepper. If it was a genuine load, his crew would then rig a whip on the mainyard to transfer the cargo on the condition that the Acehnese surrender their side arms for the exchange, while the Salemites would allow only one native on board the *Friendship* to supervise the loading.

The Acehnese agreed, and a single native stepped aboard to be carefully guarded, for by this time Endicott's crew had been mustered and armed with guards posted at the gangway. In the meantime, a seaman overheard the first mate, Mr. Knight, who was out of Captain Endicott's earshot, scoff at these precautions as cowardice and boast that "he could clear the decks of a hundred such fellows with a single handspike." Meanwhile, the transfer was effected, and some fifty to sixty bags of pepper were loaded. When the operation was completed, the prahu pushed off.

The next day in the local bazaars, Captain Endicott was able to garner enough intelligence to support his original suspicions. "The boat was sent, we ascertained, by a young man named Po Qualah, the son of the Pedir Rajah, for the express purpose which we had suspected, the pepper having been put on board merely as an excuse in case they should be discovered. It was only a sort of parachute, let off to see from what quarter the wind blew, as a guide for their evil designs upon us." But seeing that the *Friendship* was too vigilantly guarded for a surprise attack that night, the Acehnese were waiting for another chance.

It came subtly, in the form of a delegation which approached the ship still anchored at Pulau Kio to announce that the new crop of pepper was being transported into the port from the Padang Highlands to the south. At the rate of one hundred to two hundred bags a day shouldered into the ship's hold, the *Friendship* would be ladened in a month's time.

Captain Endicott's experience had taught him that one pepper port was likely to be no more or less treacherous than the next, so with the promise of pepper he agreed to trade. At the same time, he mustered his crew on the quarterdeck and admonished them with specific orders. A strict watch was to be maintained both day and night, and in the absence of the captain, no more than two Malays would be allowed to board. No prahu would be allowed alongside, and at eight every evening a gun would be fired as demonstration of the crew's alertness.

Having taken these precautions, Captain Endicott tacked the *Friendship* back to Quallah Battoo and began loading pepper, which was ferried out in prahus. The operation proceeded smoothly for several days. Then one morning Rajah Po Adam, who spoke understandable if idiosyncratic English, arrived at the ship in a small canoe from his own fort on Pulau Kio to ask if he could join the captain, the second mate, Mr. Barry, and four men in the pinnace bound for the settlement. As they pushed off and rowed toward the beach, Po Adam shared with Endicott some alarming intelligence.

"On our way Po Adam expressed much anxiety for the safety of the ship, and also an entire want of confidence in Mr. Knight, the first officer, which I then considered unfounded, remarking in his broken English, 'He no look sharp, no understand Malay man.'" The native elder then added that the villagers were poised for an attack and were waiting only for a chance. Endicott regretted aloud that they were not armed, just as the boat reached the landing to an enthusiastic and seemingly fraternal reception.

"A man, who was a stranger to me, of rather prepossessing appearance, pretended to be very much pleased of my knowledge of the language, for which he was profuse in his compliments, and to hear me speak it, followed close upon my footsteps through the bazaars, and was very assiduous in his attentions." Endicott later learned that this same man had put a price of $1,000 on his head, $500 on the first mate's, and $100 on each crew member.

The loading of pepper proceeded slowly, with a bag atop a native's head appearing only every now and then to be placed beside the ship's scales. At midafternoon the first boat left shore to ferry pepper to the ship, while Captain Endicott heard reassurances that more pepper was coming, with the promise of another boatload. "This was a mere subterfuge to keep us on shore," noted Endicott dryly.

The prahu approaching the ship, however, had stopped at a point downriver. Suspecting the natives were off-loading pepper already purchased for the *Friendship,* Endicott sent two men to investigate, but they found nothing amiss. What Endicott did not discover until later was that the prahu had picked up a contingent of armed men before proceeding to the ship.

"The ship lay about three-fourths of a mile from the shore, and between the scale houses and the beach there was a piece of rising ground, so that, standing at the scales, we could just see the ship's topgallant yards. . . . The instant I had proceeded far enough to see our ship's hull, I observed the pepper boat, which was at this time within two hundred or three hundred feet of her. As she rose on the top of the swell she appeared to have a large number of men in her. My suspicions were instantly aroused that there was something wrong."

Endicott then dispatched Mr. Barry for a better look from the top of a knoll, where he stopped short, turned around, and walked back as if nothing were the matter. Passing the captain, he spoke softly: "There is trouble on board, sir. I saw men jumping overboard."

"We must show no alarm, but muster the men and get them to the boat," said the captain. Then one of the men reminded Captain Endicott that he had not locked the chest where the weights were secured, so he

returned without haste to do just that for the benefit of both trading partners. "Such is the mutual want of confidence manifested in our dealings
with each other on this coast." The group was about to push off when Po
Adam suddenly appeared and sprang aboard. "You got trouble, Captain,"
he said. "If they kill you, must kill Po Adam, too."

The river was narrow, only one hundred feet wide at this point, and the
captain urged his men to row for their lives, "or we are all dead men,"
while Po Adam advised that they keep to the western bank. The current
picked up as they traveled downstream, and by now it was clear to the
natives that the Americans had discovered their treachery, for hundreds of
Acehnese were massed on a point at the river's mouth, screaming and
brandishing their spears.

Po Adam, speaking English and Acehnese in the same breath, exhorted
the rowers, "Di yoong, di yoong hi," and "Pull, pull 'trong. If got blunder-
buss, will kill all," he muttered in despair. The menacing Acehnese did not
have that weapon, but a ferry with natives was lying in wait at midriver
downstream. Captain Endicott quickly took stock. His own pinnace rode
high in the water, while the ferry was an oversized low-slung canoe. Their
only chance of escape was to run the intercepting craft down. The rowers
strained at the oars, gaining speed on the current as the gap closed, while
Mr. Barry manned the bow with Po Adam's sword, the only weapon
aboard, and the natives they were closing on raised their spears.

"But when we had approached within twenty feet, her crew, all at once,
as if by the direct interposition of Providence, appeared completely panic
stricken, and made an effort to get out of the way," digging their paddles
in water to avoid collision, while a desperate lunge with a spear was par-
ried by Endicott's hand just over the pinnace's gunwale. Now astern, the
men of the ferry were frantic over the pinnace's reaching the mouth of the
river. From both shores natives rushed into the stream, wading in the
armpit-deep estuary and screaming at the top of their voices in rage and
frustration as the pinnace was nearly clear of the river's mouth.

"Having now run the gauntlet, all danger for the present was passed,
and during the breathing spell which it allowed us, we quietly proceeded
the remainder of the distance out of the river without further molestation
or incident." Captain Endicott thanked God for His protection and
turned his attention to his "doomed ship laying tranquilly in the water,

with sails furled and a pepper boat alongside, with a multitude of natives in every part of her."

As they pulled closer, Endicott could see that the Acehnese had got to the arms chest and were standing by to shoot when the pinnace closed within range. Likewise, they were manning the stern chasers, which had been reloaded earlier with grape and canister. A glance over his shoulder told him that three prahus had emerged from the river to give chase.

Po Adam advised pulling the two miles for his fort on Pulau Kio, as a storm was sweeping down from the mountains and would foil the pursuers; but as they approached the small island, the old rajah changed his mind. His own fort's defenses were too meager, he counseled, to hold off an attack by an enraged band of Acehnese. It would be better, he advised, to strike out for Soo Soo, or preferably Muckie, an awesome distance of twenty-five miles for men who plunged their oars through the water with numbed determination.

It was nearly dark when they reached the Soo Soo River, and, not daring to make landfall, they pulled upstream past the estuary, where they dipped a cask for fresh water. Then quickly they nosed the pinnace back downriver and rode the current out beyond the breakers, only to be greeted by a fierce squall bringing torrents of rain and flashes of lightning that whitened them against the night like fleeing ghosts. Onward they pulled, with Mr. Barry and Po Adam double-manning two of the oars, while Captain Endicott counted cadence and steered clear of the thundering surf plunging upon the rocks, but the strong seas fought them on every stroke.

Endicott knew these waters and was picturing a lethal reef off North Tallapoo when suddenly they were lifted by a great roller. When they dropped into its trough, the pinnace shivered with the wave's aftershock as it pounded against rock, and they pulled seaward for dear life, riding the undertow through the surf with punishing breakers driving against the rising and plunging bow. Once they were beyond the surf, the storm quickly abated, and in minutes when they looked heavenward, they saw stars over the rising of a gentle breeze.

Quickly they fashioned a sail out of gunnysacks, and they were able to rest their oars and bail out the boat with a small dipper. One o'clock in the morning saw the bedraggled contingent in the roadstead at Muckie beneath the towering outline of three American ships. Just then they were hailed by the *Governor Endicott,* out of Salem.

"What boat is that?" challenged Captain Jenks, ship's master.

"The *Friendship,* from Quallah Battoo," answered Captain Endicott.

"Is that you, Captain Endicott?"

"Yes, and all that's left of us," Endicott replied, reaching upward to find his wrists gripped by strong, eager hands.

LATER CAPTAIN ENDICOTT would learn from the surviving members of his crew what had transpired aboard the *Friendship.* The approaching prahu was hailed by Mr. Knight and allowed to come alongside. Immediately a seaman named William Parnell sensed something amiss, because he had not seen these men aboard ship during the many days of loading. But despite the captain's orders to the contrary, Mr. Knight allowed the Acehnese free rein. When Parnell cautioned Knight on the natives' superior numbers, the mate told the seaman to mind his own business and see the pepper passed along. The loading began while the Acehnese had the run of the ship and put the ship's grindstone to good use by sharpening their *krises.*

Mr. Knight was the first to fall when at some prearranged signal two natives attacked him with their curved daggers, burying them to the hilt. In vain the mate reached for a boarding pike, but four others stabbed him until he lay dead on the deck. Another seaman was cut down at the forehatch and fell below. The steward at the galley was likewise stabbed, and when two of the crew on the stage hoisting bags of pepper tried to regain the ship, they met Acehnese blades. Wounded, they fled across the prahu but never made it to the water. Charles Converse leaped from the bow and hung on to the anchor cable, while his companion was slaughtered as he struggled in the water.

One survivor managed to conceal himself in the rigging, while four others plunged into the sea and began swimming. By now the Acehnese were too busy looting the ship to pay the escapees any mind. The men could see over the waves that the nearest beach was swarming with natives, so they decided to stick together and swim for a point some two miles distant. As they swam, their clothes and shoes weighed them down, so they stripped to make better headway.

It was still light when the men emerged from the surf and crawled across the beach to hide in a fringe of jungle beyond the sandy strip, praying that they had not been spotted. When darkness fell, they walked westward the entire night with the vague hope of reaching Annalaboo and at first light sought concealment in underbrush for the day, from where they watched the traffic of Acehnese treading on the beach.

When evening came, the four men set out again, only to come upon a broad, swiftly flowing river. Not only were they too weak to swim, from weariness and lack of food, but there was also the danger of estuarine crocodiles hunting its depths. Defeated in body and spirit, they began retracing their steps. Though the men could hardly know it, this was a fortunate turn, for they were now on a course that would eventually see them rejoined with their captain.

Their plan was to get somehow to Po Adam's stronghold on Pulau Kio. But to reach their old, trusted ally, the quartet had first to slip past Quallah Battoo, where they would be slain on the spot if discovered. They reached its vicinity just before dawn, so they hid out for the day and much of the next evening, plotting what to do next. Whatever was to be done, the men knew the later they did it the better, for there would be fewer eyes to see them.

Warily they advanced to the beach, finding it lined with canoes fashioned from almond trees but deserted of natives. Then they shivered to hear a voice pierce the harbor darkness with the familiar cry, "Eight bells, and all's well." Judging it to be a native ruse, each took a dugout and pushed it over the sand to the water. After mastering the delicate balance of these thin craft, they sliced through the pounding midnight surf and paddled over the swells to Pulau Kio.

Beaching their canoes, the exhausted crew members made for the underbrush and turned in the direction of Po Adam's fort. The men lay concealed until daybreak, then, barely able to walk, they staggered toward it to be received by the old man himself, who gave them a breakfast of boiled rice, their first food in seventy-two hours, and dressed them as far as their lacerated bodies would permit.

MEANWHILE, when Captain Endicott was hoisted aboard the brig named for his famous ancestor, he knew the Acehnese had seized his vessel, but he could only wonder about the fate of his crew. It stood to reason, however, that the sooner he retook the *Friendship,* the better chance he would have of seeing some of his men alive.

Also riding at anchor in the roadstead at Muckie were the *James Monroe,* out of New York, and the brig *Palmer,* of Boston. Immediately, their two captains joined Captains Jenks and Endicott aboard the *Governor Endicott* to strategize quickly about recovering the lost ship. Without waiting for daylight, they readied their ships, and in two hours the small fleet cleared the roads for Quallah Battoo, up the coast.

The voyage was slow for lack of wind, but by midafternoon the convoy reached the bay and sighted the *Friendship.* The captains made plans to attack her with the *James Monroe,* the ablest fighter of the three, but a land breeze and heavy rains compelled them to anchor for the night. Before darkness set in, Endicott took compass bearings of his ship with thoughts of dispatching a raiding party during the night, but the heavy rains continued, discouraging such a clandestine operation.

At dawn Endicott was astonished to see that the ship had been moved during the night, and as it grew brighter the Americans finally spotted her close to shore, inside some dangerous shoals, a position that now precluded laying the *James Madison* alongside her. Endicott hailed a prahu and sent a message to the rajah that if the *Friendship* was surrendered peacefully, the Americans would not bombard the port. Otherwise, he could expect the ships' guns to open fire. Predictably, when no answer came, Endicott suspected that the Acehnese were buying time to loot the ship.

The big guns spoke, drawing replies from the captured ship as well as the forts' six-pounders, whose rounds narrowly missed their targets, sending up explosions of spray. Soon it was over, with the forts hammered into silence, while Captain Endicott quickly organized raiding parties to retake the ship. Quickly three pinnaces were in the water, their men armed with muskets, pistols, and cutlasses; as the smaller craft approached the large vessel they fanned out, one to each gangway and the third to the bow.

Realizing that they were in for a fight with a superior armed force, the Acehnese panicked and fled, some plunging into the water and others retreating in small dugout canoes, which they left on the beach before fleeing into the jungle. These were the dugouts the four men who had escaped the shipboard massacre chanced upon, enabling them to paddle to Rajah Po Adam's stronghold and their deliverance.

The boarding parties ascended to find the ship utterly deserted of Acehnese, but in a devastated condition, high and low. The bloodstained deck told much of the story of the violence, while everything necessary to make a voyage had been taken: spare sails and rigging, charts, chronometer, compasses, other nautical instruments, weaponry, ammunition, clothes, and blankets.

Inventory of the ship also revealed what had happened during the night. Planning to beach the *Friendship,* the captors had begun raising the anchor, which they got to just above the waterline. Presumably the handlers, then keen to see it, abandoned the windlass. This was an incautious move that sent the cable running out at high speed, causing it to jump the drum and take a riding turn around the windlass. Not knowing how to loosen the mess, the Acehnese pirates could only watch helplessly as the ship drifted with wind and current toward the beach until the anchor at the end of five fathoms of cable bit bottom.

The Americans turned to kedge her off into deeper water, where she could be navigated, and in short order had the *Friendship* safely anchored in the outer harbor with the other ships. Having recovered her, Captain Endicott's remaining business was to see returned the survivors of the massacre. The next morning a prahu drew alongside the *James Madison,* and Endicott heard a familiar hail. Looking down, he saw the welcome sight of Rajah Po Adam, who identified his passengers as four of the men Endicott had believed to be dead.

"I proceeded immediately on board and found them to be William Parnell, John Muzzey and Algernon Warren, seamen, and William Bray, carpenter. Their haggard and squalid appearance bespoke what they had suffered. It would seem impossible that in the space of four days men could, by any casualty, so entirely lose their identity," Endicott recalled.

"They bore no semblance to their former selves, and it was only by asking their names that I knew either of them. They were without clothing, other than loose pieces of cotton thrown over their persons, their hair matted, their bodies crisped and burned in large running blisters, beside having been nearly devoured by mosquitoes, the poison of whose stings had left evident traces of its virulence, their flesh wasted away, and even the very tones of their voices changed. The pieces of cloth which covered them being all their flesh could bear, and these it was necessary to oil to do even that."

Shortly after this reunion, a prahu from the settlement approached the ships under a white flag, its occupants four Chinese merchants of Quallah Battoo. During the ensuing parley, the visitors explained that on the morning after the ship was raided, they had claimed the wounded and nursed them in a house that they barricaded against the Acehnese. Told that his men could be ransomed of the rajahs for ten dollars each, Captain Endicott readily agreed, and later in the day a sampan pulled alongside with four badly hurt men. The most seriously wounded was Converse, who had been on the staging hoisting up pepper and had taken several stab wounds, one through the lung.

As these survivors were debriefed, various pictures began to settle in Captain Endicott's mind. Of the first night after the *Friendship*'s capture, the ship "was a perfect pandemonium and a babel of the most discordant sounds. The ceaseless moaning of the surf upon the adjacent shore, the heavy peals of thunder and sharp flashes of lightning overhead, the sighing of the wind in wild discords through the rigging, like the wails of woe from their murdered shipmates, was intermingled with the squealing of pigs, the screeching of fowls, the crowing of roosters, the unintelligible jargon of the natives, jangling and vociferating, with horrible laughter, shouts and yells, in every part of the ship. . . .

"It is the general impression that Malays, being Mussulmen, have a holy horror of swine as unclean animals, the very touch of which imposes many ablutions and the abstaining from food of several days together. According to the testimony of my men, however, it was perfectly marvelous how they handled, that night, those on board our ship, going into their pens, seizing, struggling and actually embracing them, until they succeeded in throwing every pig overboard."

Of the goings-on in the port, Captain Endicott paints a vivid picture: "Quallah Battoo bazaar that day presented a ludicrous spectacle. Almost every Malay was decked out in a white, blue, red, checked or striped shirt, or some other European article of dress or manufacture, stolen from the ship, not even excepting the woolen tablecloth belonging to the cabin, which was displayed over the shoulders of a native.

"All seemed quite proud of their appearance, and strutted about with a solemn gravity and oriental self-complacency that was perfectly funny. Their novel and grotesque appearance could not fail to suggest the idea that a tribe of monkeys had made a descent upon some unfortunate clothing establishment, and each to have seized and carried off whatever article of dress was most suited to his fancy."

The *Friendship* was prepared for sailing in three days' time, with the small fleet clearing for South Tallapow, where they arrived on February 14. But news of the Acehnese humiliation of the Salemites had preceded them, and as the seamen wandered through the streets of the bazaar, they were followed by crowds of exultant natives hooting: "Who great man now, Malay or American?" "How many man American dead?" "How many man Malay dead?"

If the Salemites saw themselves in an extraordinary bind, they did not let on. While fortune favored the bold, experience had taught these rugged sailors that trade had its risks, from hurricanes to piracy. In ascribing a motive to Acehnese treachery, Captain Endicott once surmised that unscrupulous traders had soured the water for honest ones by absconding with loads of pepper without paying whatever rajah with whom they were dealing his due, thus introducing into the game a no-holds-barred attitude on the part of the locals.

But this speculation on Endicott's part is unconvincing. A more likely explanation is that three centuries of infidel European colonization in the Indies—the successive waves of Portuguese, Spanish, Dutch, and English —had bred a profound distrust of Christian Europeans on the part of Muslim Malays in a part of the world where word spread across the waters with the wind.

One thinks of an earlier day and the warrior-priest Francis Xavier in Malacca exhorting the Portuguese fleet to sail against the Acehnese, who to the Jesuit embodied the forces of darkness. The straight-talking, square-dealing sons of Salem had not earned the natives' contempt 250 years later; they merely inherited it from their predecessors. Nonetheless, accounts had to be settled.

"We now commenced in earnest to prepare our ship for sea," Captain Endicott recalled. "Our voyage had been broken up, and there was nothing left for us but to return to the United States. The feeling of presumptuous exultation and proud defiance exhibited by the natives was of brief duration. The avenger was at hand."

After the ship was refitted for sea, she sailed from Pulau Kio on March 4 and arrived in Salem on July 16, 1831. The townspeople were waiting for her, for a few days earlier another ship's arrival in Boston had brought news of the *Friendship*'s capture and murder of some of her crew members, and it was the sort of news that traveled quickly.

"The most intense excitement," noted Captain Endicott, "was caused by our arrival at Salem. It being nearly calm as we approached the harbor, we were boarded several miles outside by crowds of people, all anxious to learn the most minute particulars of our misfortune. The curiosity of some of our visitors was so great that they would not be satisfied until they knew the exact spot where every man stood who was either killed or wounded. Even the casing of the cabin, so much cut up in the search for money or other valuables, was an object of the greatest interest."

Immediately the *Friendship*'s merchant-owners, Nathaniel Silsbee, Dudley Pickman, and Robert Stone, lobbied the United States government furiously for retribution.

Washington's response was immediate, and it is noteworthy because it came early in the nation's history and was applied to a shore far distant from our own. The naval frigate *Potomac,* under the command of Commodore John Downes, originally fitted out for the west coast of South America to replace another warship there, was instead dispatched to Sumatra. Lest he be unclear as to his mission, Commodore Downes asked for some elaboration on his orders. The response from the Navy Department was succinct and sharp: "Give the rascals a good thrashing."

Chapter 23

"A Good Thrashing"

SAILING IN THE frigate from New York on August 15, 1831, was her assistant sailing master John Barry, who had accounted himself well in the *Friendship* crisis. During the six-month voyage Mr. Barry often recalled something from his previous experience on Sumatra. The Acehnese had been repeatedly warned by American captains that acts of violence such as piracy and the commandeering of ships trading with them would inevitably provoke the American government to send out a punitive force.

When this was suggested to them, it drew always the same response: laughter, scorn, and the response, "American gunship! No have got big American gunship." When Mr. Barry had tried to convince one rajah that the great American rajah possessed large gunboats exclusively for the purpose of redressing the wrongs done to his people abroad, the native leader called the former second mate of the *Friendship* a liar. When Mr. Barry insisted that what he said was true, the rajah responded that it could not be the case. If Americans had ships that could not be defeated by his own sampans and prahus, he asked rhetorically why they had never been on the coast. The prevalence of such a belief is not to be wondered at, for Americans had been trading on the Sumatran coast for nearly forty years without the shadow of protection from the arm of government, while other nations, most notably England and Holland, had sent armed vessels to look after their trade. But that was about to change.

· · ·

THE FRIGATE ARRIVED off Quallah Battoo the following February, disguised as a merchantman when she stood in, anchoring in the outer roads about five miles from shore. A chronicler noted: "In order that the Malays might not comprehend the real designs and character of the *Potomac*, the stump top-gallant masts were got up, the main deck guns run in and ranged fore and aft, the half-ports shut in, and the white streak so altered as to show only ten ports on a side. The frigate was thus made to assume the appearance of a merchant ship of great burden and capacity, like many of the East India traders."

The arrival of the ship soon attracted curious Acehnese in prahus eager for an inspection, but when they pulled alongside the ship they were quickly taken into custody, lest they betray the *Potomac's* real purpose. It was noted that the terrified visitors "prostrated themselves at full length upon her decks, trembling in the most violent manner, and appearing to think that nothing but certain death awaited them."

From a chart drawn up by Captain Endicott, the commander of the contingent of marines aboard was able to locate the forts. The initial plan was to send a reconnaissance party with a mock captain and supercargo ashore to make inquiries about the purchase of pepper, while gaining better intelligence about the location and strength "of the several fortresses where these Oriental princes were to be found." Then these rajahs would be seized and held as hostages until the actual perpetrators of the acts of piracy on the *Friendship* were given over.

There was precedent for this strategy in America. "Chiefs, like Black Hawk, have been retained in custody as hostages for the future good behavior of their tribes. Ought the bloodthirsty inhabitants of Sumatra be treated with any more lenity than the much-wronged and oppressed aborigines of our own country? Let justice and humanity answer the question."

But as the longboat approached the beach, some two hundred Acehnese, obviously suspicious as to the real motives of the Americans, rushed to the beach in force brandishing *krises* and blunderbusses. The longboat hovered in the waters beyond the breakers, its officers judging it imprudent to land, then returned to the frigate and a grateful Commodore Downes, whose instincts about the correctness of his mission were confirmed.

A surprise raid was planned for late that evening, and Downes briefed the force under arms on the spardeck. They were, he reminded them, in this distant part of the world as ordered by their government. Their punitive mission was not without American precedent, for the navy and marines had in 1805 fought a war against the Tripoli pirates. However few in number they were, and however humble the enterprise, much good or evil to the future safety of American interests and the lives of their countrymen engaged in commerce in these seas might depend on the success of the raid. They were stirring words and would be repeated by commanders of future generations in similar circumstances.

At two o'clock in the morning the boats were hoisted out under command of a Lieutenant Shubrick. With the guidance of Mr. Barry, the attacking force of three hundred men, armed with pistols, muskets, boarding pikes, six-pounders, and a high sense of mission, set off with muffled oars under a star-studded, moonless sky. As silent as the grave, they rowed the five miles to their landing spot about a mile north of the town.

On the command "Oars!" the boats immediately backed in through the high surf, scarcely wetting a single weapon. In fifteen minutes they had fallen into the familiar formations drilled into them on the deck of the *Potomac*, with the marines in front, and set out as streaks of light began appearing in the eastern sky.

When an Acehnese lookout was spotted ahead running from the beach into the jungle, Lieutenant Shubrick seized the instant to move his force quickly forward toward the town, which he knew well from briefings by Mr. Barry. Quallah Battoo's population was made up of two thousand inhabitants and five hundred warriors, and the port was situated on a small bay about two miles long, with a narrow river bisecting the town, dividing it into two unequal portions, with the main portion being on the northwest side, where the forces landed.

The settlement was laid out into streets interspersed with jungle and coconut trees and contained five mud forts defended by small cannon, owned and commanded by different rajahs, who relied on them for defense when engaged in their petty wars with each other or when expecting an attack from without. They had long believed that within these walls no enemy, however formidable, could get to them.

Shubrick divided his force into assault groups, one for each fort, and they fanned out through the town. One group, led by a Lieutenant Hoff, moved on the stronghold of Rajah Muley Mahomet, and the attackers were immediately met by small-arms fire. When Hoff called out in dialect for the defenders to surrender, the Acehnese answered with a hail of shouts and javelins, wounding two men.

In response, Hoff ordered his men to storm the fort, whereupon they dragged brush from the beach to build up a platform to allow scaling of the wall. At its top they were met by the Acehnese, and a vicious hand-to-hand struggle ensued in which Mahomet was killed. With no principal leader to rally them, the Acehnese could not stand up to the superior discipline and vigor of the marines, and the fort was easily taken.

Meanwhile, another group had closed on the fort of the Rajah Chedulah, and the resistance from it was fierce. As a prelude, the boats, having tracked the invaders down the beach, began bombarding the walls, which were soon set afire. Quickly the flames spread to the inner structures, igniting a powder barrel, which exploded, crippling the stronghold's defense. The Acehnese fled from its walls into the jungle, where they rallied with others for a counterattack. Shubrick's men easily beat them back, with Acehnese shot down or sabered on the spot. Except for a lone fort on the opposite bank of the river, the other fortifications were taken in similar fashion, and by now the fire had spread throughout the entire town, which was rapidly becoming a city of ashes.

As the surf rose, two buglers sounded "Yankee Doodle Dandy," the signal for the assault groups to reassemble on the beach for withdrawal in the boats with the few dead and wounded, under cover of a marine guard. As they rowed to the mother ship, the convoy of landing craft took small-arms fire from the remaining fort, and a ricocheting six-pounder nearly hit one of the launches. But by ten A.M. the force was back aboard the *Potomac*, and in the early afternoon troops and sailors witnessed the burial at sea of their fallen comrades, after which the frigate moved into a position to destroy the remaining fort.

As the frigate was readied, the men were exhilarated over their success. A small force of fighting men, greatly outnumbered, had destroyed four forts and torched the town. Now the frigate's guns were to pound the final fort into submission. The cannonade of awesome thirty-two-pound shot was brisk and constant, and in little more than half an hour, the fort of

Tuca de Lama was reduced to a pile of smoking rubble and uprooted trees.

A lull in the barrage brought the waving of white flags from every quarter of the town. Soon a prahu bearing a flag of truce left the shore for the *Potomac,* and its messengers, with Rajah Po Adam acting as interpreter, beseeched the commodore "in all the practiced forms of submission common to the East" to forgive the Acehnese for past offenses and to accept the promise that no further outrages would ever again be committed by them on American commerce.

Commodore Downes replied in this solemn interview that the town once again belonged to the Acehnese, as it formed no part of his government's policy to make conquests on foreign soil and establish colonies. However, his countrymen would continue to visit Sumatran ports for the purpose of trade, and as long as the Acehnese conducted themselves with justice and humanity, they need not fear further attack from American big ships. However, he warned, any future provocation would invite terrible retribution when they least expected it.

On this point, the commodore wondered aloud just why the five forts were as well manned as they were, if they were expecting no foreign invasion. Po Adam explained that the rajahs of Quallah Battoo were quarreling with the people of Soo Soo and Pulau Kio and needed only the slightest pretext to wage war. In fact, Po Adam himself had been branded a marked men by the Quallah Battoo rajahs for his earlier devotion and heroism on behalf of the officers and men of the *Friendship.* After the ship was retaken by the Americans, this loyal rajah suffered a number of indignities at the hands of his neighboring rajahs. They circulated stories of his conniving with them in the piracy, thus deceiving a number of American shipmasters before the truth became known. They also raided his fort of everything valuable, even taking the armlets and anklets from his wife.

Word of the fall of Quallah Battoo spread quickly, and thus as well the reputation of America as a force to be reckoned with. After describing the terms of the truce in a letter from Soo Soo to the Hon. Levi Woodbury, secretary of the United States Navy, dated February 17, 1832, Commodore Downes concluded: "Several rajahs from towns in the vicinity have visited my ship, and others who are distant have sent deputations to me. All of them have declared their friendly dispositions toward the Americans, and their desire to obtain our friendship. Corresponding assurances were given on my part, and they left the ship apparently well satisfied.

"Having wood and water and having refreshed my crew, I shall leave here tomorrow for Batavia."

From Batavia, the *Potomac* resumed her voyage around the world. When she returned to the United States, the captain found that news of the victory had preceded her, giving Americans something to cheer about. "The Battle of Qualah Battoo" became a popular broadside ballad and was so often reprinted in newspapers and magazines that it became the stuff of folklore.

It would seem that the retribution administered to the Acehnese might have forestalled other attacks on Salem vessels, but that was not the case. In May 1834 the *Derby*, commanded by Captain Jonathan Felt, had finished loading pepper on Sumatra's northwest coast. On the final night before sailing, Felt ordered a most vigilant watch. In the darkest hour just before dawn, Felt's crew drove off a marauding prahu with "90 musket cartridges and 5 cannon cartridges," according to the ship's log.

Then four years later Captain Wilkins, of Joseph Peabody's ship the *Eclipse,* was brutally murdered by *kris* stabs, as was a boy named Babbage, and their cargo of specie and opium was taken. By this time the pepper coast had grown so dangerous that Salem merchants were loath to send their ships to Sumatra when they were protected only by threats of punitive action. But this treachery, too, was avenged.

The frigates *Columbia* and *John Adams* called at Quallah Battoo, and its officers, accompanied by an aged Po Adam and followed by a crowd of screaming, *kris*-wielding Acehnese, marched to the rajah's fort and demanded satisfaction. The rajah received them courteously and told them the murderers would be delivered the next day along with the stolen money, but the ruler was not good on his promise. "Rajah is fool," said an exasperated Po Adam, as recorded in a first-person account in the rare-manuscript section of Salem's Peabody Essex Museum. "He give up murderer, he give money—then he save pepper trade. What can rajah do with pepper—no ships come and buy? He no eat pepper—he fool, he damned rascal, he buffalo."

The American ships replied with a barrage that leveled all but one fort, which had surrendered, then sailed down the coast for Muckie, where much of the *Eclipse*'s treasure had been dispersed and one of the ringleaders was under the rajah's personal protection. A similar ultimatum was delivered to no avail, and again an Acehnese port was subjected to bombardment, followed by a landing force with orders to burn the town and kill all armed men. Among the invaders were several descendants of old Massachusetts families: young midshipmen named John Quincy Adams and Robert S. Morris, commanded by Lieutenant Joseph W. Revere. When their work was done, Muckie was burned to the ground, and boats of every variety in the harbor had been torched.

Again the rajahs were terrified into signing an agreement guaranteeing that there would be no such betrayals and atrocities in the future, but the U.S. naval command was exceedingly skeptical that the rajahs would comply once the two frigates were withdrawn, and experience had taught them that their doubts were well founded. For Americans to trade successfully and in safety, a permanent post or factory backed by military force after the manner of the British and Dutch was needed. But this would have meant expansionism and colonization, which was philosophically counter to the American attitude and spirit of the day, and the reluctance of the American government to send out a protective force to Sumatra inevitably contributed to the decline of Salem's pepper trade.

Men of Salem, however, remained ardent sailors, and it remained for Captain Charles Endicott, formerly of the ill-fated *Friendship,* to compile and refine much of the data of Sumatra's coast begun by Nathaniel Bowditch. This descendant of the colonial Governor Endicott of Massachusetts was a learned man with a literary bent and a gift for telling a story well, as it is his vivid account of the *Friendship*'s ordeal that has been passed down.

Captain Endicott managed to compile his data in a large-scale chart that was published by the Salem firm of Whipple and Lawrence in 1833 and titled *The West Coast of Sumatra from Annalaboo to Sinkel Principally from Actual Surveys by C. E. Endicott.* The handsome four-foot-square map became highly valued in England and France as well as in the compiler's own country. Endicott wrote that "he filled up all the tedious and vexatious delays incidental to a pepper voyage by a laborious and careful survey of the coast of which no chart was previously extant which could be relied on."

Farther on he anticipates with a tincture of irony the next voyage by a naval vessel: "It is hoped she will be supplied with these charts—and that she will not as was the case of the *Potomac* run up into the mountains by chart before in fact she reaches the shore." Presumably, these charts were in the U. S. Navy's hands when the *Columbia* and *John Adams* made their punitive calls to the pepper coast.

Though Salem captains continued to trade on the pepper coast for another twenty years, their numbers were dwindling. Ports such as New York and Boston were now thriving, thus absorbing much of the trade in minor specialties—involving Manila, Fiji, Zanzibar, and Africa's west coast—that had been formerly Salem's. Goods from those destinations, however, were hardly substitutes for the wealth of the Indies, which had built Salem. Voyages became fewer, and the British and Dutch—with the armed support accorded their East Indies commercial activities—began to absorb the pepper trade along with that of other spices, which now counted for little in the global economy.

In the early 1870s, by way of a final effort to make the pepper trade viable for American interests, the American consul general in Singapore had held several meetings with Acehnese envoys to draft a commercial treaty that would give special protection and privileges to American traders. For their part, the Acehnese were seeking support for their autonomy from America. These diplomatic moves, however, were in vain, for America soon learned what the Dutch already knew but refused to admit: Aceh with its numerous, independently minded rajahs was virtually ungovernable, and Sumatra, though nominally a part of the Dutch East Indies, was a colony in name only.

Complicating the entanglement was Holland's fear that America might dispatch a fleet of warships already in Asian waters to the pepper coast "to protect American interests." Fear of this supposed intervention by the United States created a sensation in Batavia, prompting a series of telegrams to the Hague. Holland's "solution" to keep America at bay was a costly one. The Dutch signed a treaty with the British in 1871 by which the latter agreed to withdraw from Sumatra to Malaysia. With the British disavowing Aceh, there was no force to prevent a Dutch occupation, at least in theory. The fiercely independent Acehnese, however, rejected such a notion, and in 1873 the Dutch declared war against Aceh.

Holland was intent on quelling a rebellion, but to the Acehnese it was a holy war, which they waged for nearly forty years in some of the most inhospitable country in the Indies. The Dutch were ill equipped by any measure to prosecute such a war, and the Acehnese, who gave no quarter and expected none, were superb guerrilla fighters on a field they knew. The Dutch, nonetheless, were ruthless in their retributions and carried out a number of wholesale massacres of the Acehnese. But the cost of the war to the Dutch was high: 250,000 lives and 50 million pounds sterling.

By 1873, the last of America's 967 pepper voyages to Sumatra was completed against the canvas of this impending war.

THE SEEDS OF seafaring genius that settled and flowered in the Salem traders had found a different soil than that of their European predecessors. There was no Francis Xavier among the ranks of the New Englanders, intent on bringing God's word to an excluded people. One searches in vain for an adventurer of Francisco Serrão's cut, a man who jumped ship and went native; or a John Jourdain, who sought a rendezvous with destiny in the Indies to escape an unhappy marriage and failed business back in England. Least of all among their number were the sort of ne'er-do-wells and misfits who drifted east to become the besotted planters and Dutch East India Company officials about whom Coen had so vehemently complained to the Lords Seventeen in Amsterdam.

One explanation for the Salemites' singularity in these regards is a quite simple one: they were not colonizers, nor were they so tempted to be. With the single, benign exception of the Derby post on Île de France, a French colony, the Americans built neither factory nor fort. Shipmaster, supercargo, and common seaman alike had a hearth, home, and family awaiting him back in Salem. A round voyage of two years to Sumatra's pepper coasts or wherever else under the sun, with one hand for the rigging and the other for oneself, was a sufficient taste of the expatriate's life, thank you, so spare them the wild hopes and poignant dreams of the romantic outcast. Trade served and nurtured that familial life in Salem, not the other way around. Exile was anathema.

But there was more to it. Early in the century Lewis and Clark had extended the conception and content of the American West, stirring the nation as Hakluyt, Drake, and Raleigh earlier had excited the English. The empire of the United States lay not in Banda's fragrant nutmeg groves or Ternate's clove-scented slopes or in the vast, chaotic richness of the Indian subcontinent or Amazonia's El Dorado, distant corners requiring the exportation of destroyers and builders like Clive and Coen and Pizarro with sufficient military force to dominate trade and demolish nations while they established and maintained far-flung colonies.

Rather, the American destiny, inchoate but beckoning, reached across the wide Missouri, as Jefferson and the Republicans had envisioned it through the eyes of the two explorers. Such an empire lay within America's own boundaries, a continent of magnificent wilderness stretching from sea to sea that Jefferson believed would take centuries to settle. America's great wager with the world was that her citizens, whether easterner, southerner, or frontiersman, were people of adventurous independence with an innate moral sense who trusted themselves and each other.

There was the "unquestionable republicanism of the American mind" that made the nation "the hope of the world." In a letter to John Adams, Jefferson had written, "Old Europe will have to lean on our shoulders, and to hobble along by our side, under the monkish trammels of priests and kings, as she can." It was a new, prophetic vision anticipating Emerson and Whitman with their shared view of man in the morning of time on American earth. The nation at large seized on it, looking inward and inland. Meanwhile the occasional frigate, a *Potomac,* was dispatched to the other side of the world to bloody a bully's nose, thereby setting matters right on behalf of Captain Endicott and his like, while nodding toward the historic precedent set by the navy and marines against the Tripoli pirates in 1805.

SALEM BY THE 1830s was still unique and remained an exciting destination for world pilgrims, who traveled a well-rutted road to this American gateway to the Indies. The English author Harriet Martineau, visiting in 1834, was sufficiently struck by Salem's curious sophistication to note: "Salem, Massachusetts is a remarkable place. This 'city of peace' will be better known hereafter for its commerce than for its witch tragedy. It has a population of fourteen thousand and more wealth in proportion to its population than perhaps any town in the world. . . .

"These enterprising merchants . . . speak of Fayal and the Azores as if they were close at hand. The fruits of the Mediterranean are on every table. They have a large acquaintance at Cairo. They know Napoleon's grave at St. Helena, and have wild tales to tell of Mozambique and Madagascar, and stores of ivory to show from there. . . . They often slip up the western coast of their two continents, bring furs from the back region of their own wide land, glance up at the Andes on their return; double Cape Horn, touch at the ports of Brazil and Guinea, look about them in the West Indies, feeling almost at home there, and land some fair morning in Salem and walk home as if they had done nothing remarkable."

The port so acutely observed by Harriet Martineau had come a long way since its founding two centuries earlier (though ironically Salem *is* remembered today primarily for its "witch tragedy" rather than for its commerce). Harvard remained the university of choice for the sons of the plainspoken merchants who strove to improve themselves through refinement and display their wealth by stocking their fine homes with the riches of the East.

In keeping with the age, they were less formal than their fathers, with plaited "queues" of natural hair replacing wigs, and Eastern nankeen and seersucker supplanting knee breeches. Stovepipe hats had come into vogue, even among watermen dipping their oars in Salem Bay. Asian dress was the order of the evening for the opening of East India Marine Hall, and wives had grown fond of Eastern silk gowns when they entertained. Dances became fashionable, and prized old bottles of wine with labels showing the year and carrying vessel were happily imbibed on celebratory occasions.

But for those who knew Salem intimately, the port had begun its long decline as shipping began serving native industry, and not the other way around. The Reverend Dr. Bentley noted the slide during the last years before his death in 1819 and confessed his lamentations to his diary as he would trudge up the Crowninshields' stone lookout tower on Winter Island to witness the increasingly rarer departures of East Indiamen and ponder the "stagnation of Commerce."

The silting up of Salem's comparatively shallow harbor, accelerated in part by the longer wharves, began to deter the larger merchantmen and clippers that were on the scene by midcentury. Salem's merchants necessarily were accommodating themselves to other rising industries of Essex

County, such as the Naumkeag Steam Cotton Mills, established in 1848, which ushered in the factory era. They began using their merchantmen as coastal "trucks." But as the century wore on, the railroad dominated the coastal trade, and shipowners began to find Boston more attractive as a superior harbor. (There is an old saying that the first families of Boston—with the surnames Jackson, Endicott, Higginson, Cabot, Lawrence, Lowell, Hooper, Appleton, Phillips, Pickman, Saltonstall—made their homes in Salem and Essex County in the eighteenth century.) They were also drawn to that port's better rail connections. The railroad's impact on a developing America was as profound as it was controversial.

But not even Henry David Thoreau, who often spoke his mind about the "blind and unmanly love of wealth" during his sojourn at Walden Pond, could fail to be moved by this new impact of the iron horse on alert, adventurous, unwearied commerce. He noted in *Walden,* published in 1854: "I am refreshed and expanded when the freight rattles past me, and I smell the stores which go dispensing their odors all the way from Long Wharf to Lake Champlain, reminding me of foreign parts, of coral reefs, and Indian oceans, and tropical climes, and the extent of the globe." That Eastern trade, however, was not what it once was.

IN THE YEARS following the War of 1812 there had risen another son of Salem to become the port's wealthiest shipowner, whose influence would last until nearly midcentury. Joseph Peabody was born of a poor Essex County farm family in 1757 but went to sea as a privateer crewman during the Revolution and was captured by the British. After independence he worked his way up to captain and merchant, earning a fortune in the pepper trade like Derby and Crowninshield before him, eventually owning or having shares in sixty-three vessels. Perhaps Peabody's most famous ship was the *George*, noted for her fast passage to the Indies. The *George* became known as the "Salem School Ship," for from her decks many seamen graduated to captain and mate.

The upstanding Peabody, a philanthropist as well as a merchant, almost single-handedly carried Salem's East Indies trade in the port's declining years. Throughout his career the decks of his ships were trod by 7,000 sailors who knew the ports of India, China, and the East Indies.

His fleet calling at northwest Sumatra were Salem ships, but Salem meant America on the pepper coast. Peabody died in 1844, and his passing seemed to personify the fate of the port.

But there was another American family fortune in the making that bears mentioning here, and it is illustrative of Boston's ascendancy over Salem. In 1823 a young Bostonian, Warren Delano, sailed for Canton on behalf of his home port's Russell and Company and returned home a wealthy man, having realized profits from the opium trade. Delano made no pretense of justifying "black dirt" morally, but as a merchant he insisted on the trade's legitimacy, comparing it to the importation of wines and spirits to America. In 1851 he settled in Newburgh, New York, where in time he gave his daughter's hand in marriage to the prosperous James Roosevelt, the father of Franklin Delano Roosevelt.

When the novelist Nathaniel Hawthorne fell on hard times in 1846, his friends managed to procure for him the position of Salem's customs surveyor so that he could continue his writing while officially issuing ships' measurement certificates, supervising inspections, and overseeing weighers, gaugers, and boatmen. Hawthorne's father had been Captain Nathaniel Hawthorne, a ship's master who had died of "yellow jack," or yellow fever, in Suriname. The son held the executive position for three years and gave memorable description to "The Custom House," which became the title of the introductory essay of his novel *The Scarlet Letter,* published in 1850.

The building the novelist describes dates from 1819, was used until 1937, and still stands today. But by midcentury the port's trade had sufficiently declined for Hawthorne to work at his craft on idle days between ships' arrival. He sketched the harbor's vestigial presence before turning to the house itself:

> In my native town of Salem, at the head of what, half a century ago, in the days of old King Derby, was a bustling wharf,—but which is now burdened with decayed wooden warehouses, and exhibits few or no symptoms of commercial life; except, perhaps, a bark or brig, halfway down its melancholy length, discharging hides; or, nearer at hand, a Nova Scotia schooner, pitching out her cargo of firewood,—at the head, I say, of this dilapidated wharf, which the tide often overflows, and along which, at the base and in the rear of the row of buildings, the track of many languid years is seen in

a border of unthrifty grass,—here, with a view from its front windows adown this not very enlivening prospect, and thence across the harbor, stands a spacious edifice of brick.

A turbulent era had ended to be replaced by one of gentle decay, as Salem with its shallow harbor was overtaken by history. Sailing vessels increased their speed, giving way to the faster clipper. The master shipwright Donald McKay's first clipper, the *Stag-Hound*, launched on a cold December day in 1850, holds the record of thirteen days from Boston Light to the equator. McKay's masterpiece, the *Flying Cloud*, on her maiden voyage in the summer of 1851 made a day's run of 374 miles, logged 1,256 miles in four consecutive days, and arrived in San Francisco from around the Horn eighty-nine days out of New York.

But such beauty is ephemeral, and the clipper in a few short years succumbed to steam. After clewing up and bracing of yards to a parallel, all hands warped her to India Wharf singing the chantey:

> O, the times are hard and the wages low,
> *Leave her, Johnny, leave her;*
> I'll pack my bag and go below;
> *It's time for us to leave her.*

In 1897 the men finally did leave a ship called the *Mindoro*, and the last square-rigger registered in Salem was towed from Derby Wharf to be transformed into a coal barge.

EPILOGUE

THOUGH JOSEPH PEABODY, Nathaniel Bowditch, Jonathan Carnes, and the rest of Salem's sea-wandering traders could have scarcely known or cared that they had an American antecedent in the spice trade, there was such a person.

Born in Boston on April 5, 1649, Elihu Yale was taken to England by his family at the age of three. Educated privately in London, Yale began in 1671 to work for the English East India Company and the next year was sent out as a clerk to the port of Madras on India's southwest coast. Gradually he worked himself up from clerical jobs to become governor of the Honourable Company's installation at Madras, known as Fort St. George.

After Yale's service as governor of Madras, he prospered in that city for nearly twenty years as a merchant trading in pepper, cinnamon, cloves, nutmeg, mace, and other spices. When he sailed for England in 1699, he had amassed a sizable fortune in his spice business. Back in London he began devoting a great deal of time and money to various charities. It was not long before his reputation for generosity had spread on both sides of the Atlantic.

An American stationed in England, Connecticut's London agent Jeremiah Dummer approached Yale with the notion that the colony's Collegiate School at Saybrook, also known as His Majesty's College of

Connecticut, would welcome a benefactor. Elihu's response was a gift of sufficient books—boxes and boxes of them—to make an impressive library for the institution.

Several years passed, and in 1718 another American sought Yale's beneficence for the college. Boston's Cotton Mather, the learned, voluminous writer, most notably of a commentary on the Salem witchcraft trials of 1692, *Magnalia Christi Americana* (1702), wrote to Elihu. In his letter the Puritan cleric broadly suggested that the Saybrook School, recently moved to New Haven, would express its gratitude for another generous gift by naming the academy after its London donor.

Elihu responded to the occasion by sending more books, as well as a portrait of King George I and nine bales of East India exotica. The gifts fetched a tidy sum in a Boston sale, and the proceeds were used to begin construction on a building to be called Yale College. As for its namesake and benefactor, he died on July 8, 1721, and was buried at Wrexham in North Wales. Elihu Yale never returned to America after leaving it as a small boy, and never saw the college his munificence had engendered.

Connecticut, the home of Yale College, and for reasons having little to do with Elihu Yale, came after the American Revolution to be known as "the Nutmeg State." This is a curious alias for a northern land inherently hostile to that fruit's cultivation. The telling tale behind that alias is the stuff of folklore. It is said that in the state's early days, Connecticut's itinerant merchants were so shrewd they could sell wooden nutmegs, passing them off to gullible buyers as the genuine article, a measure of the fruit's worth in those days. The novelist James Fenimore Cooper, a New Yorker, had a marked distaste for such "tradesmen's tricks" of the Connecticut Yankees. For me, it's yet another reminder that spices were a small but pristine window through which one could see the passing world they so irrevocably changed.

IN THE SPRING of 1994 I returned to Sumatra and the Spice Islands. The province of Aceh in northwest Sumatra thirty years before had been awarded by the Indonesian government the title of Special Territory by virtue of its Islamic zeal and fierce spirit of independence. I found its people far friendlier to me than they had been to Captain Endicott when his ship was attacked a century and a half earlier. Evenings in Banda Aceh found the men socializing at curbside tables over strong, sweet coffee and curries spiked with marijuana buds, making raucous conversation in the shadow of the moonlit central mosque. Like most Indonesians, they were eager to engage a stranger.

Just offshore from the city, Sabang Island, connected to the mainland by ferry, marks the westernmost point in Indonesia. Here one can stand on its outer beaches and gaze across the Indian Ocean toward an invisible Africa, with India to the northwest, and beyond it Arabia, the Fertile Crescent, and then Europe. Salem, via the Cape of Good Hope, lies thirteen thousand miles distant.

It is not difficult picturing the sails of many centuries that had hove to here—among them Albuquerque's doomed flagship and Lancaster's *Red Dragon*—marking a pause in man's expansion over a seemingly infinite world. "Here we found sixteen or eighteen sail of shippes of diverse nations—Gujeratis, some of Bengal, some of Calicut called Malibaris, some of Pegu [Burma] and some of Patani [Thailand] which came to trade here," an English chronicler noted with wonder in 1601. But now the world seemed finite and this place a lonely outpost on its edge.

During my visit to the island, I attended an Acehnese wedding at one of the old pepper ports while huge rollers broke over adjacent coral beaches. Later, the Jeep negotiated hostile mountainous country that had been the scene of the forty-year guerrilla war fought against the Dutch at the end of the nineteenth century and the beginning of the twentieth. It rained for almost the entire nightlong journey, and my two drivers chanted hexes against the spirits that lay in wait for travelers. In the morning, when the weather cleared, a cobra in the Jeep's path rose like a black orchid and struck at the vehicle before disappearing under the wheels.

Deep in the Acehnese hinterland I enjoyed the evening hospitality of a *pawang*, or witch doctor, while the sounds of rain forest filled the night. He was the guide of a friend, a New Zealander who made his living photographing wildlife in places no man had seen since Adam, according to the *pawang*. This was the only time in Asia I ever heard a reference, however indirectly, to the Garden of Eden. Presented with a gift of a small globe, "a sign of the greatness of God," he was eager to find Mecca but had never heard of Salem, now a speck of history lost in Sumatra's great wilderness.

Still farther south, beyond Sumatra's volcanic lakes and the equator, I entered the small city of Bukittinggi, deep in the West Sumatran heartland. This was Minangkabau country, where pepper was grown, and the spice's aroma wafted on the cool, keen air. Indonesia and especially Sumatra still produced the bulk of the world's supply of the condiment, though the plant had been successfully introduced into tropical Africa and the Western Hemisphere long before. The Minangkabau still traded in pepper but were now equally famous for their coffee, which they grew and processed. Later I visited Pariaman, a pepper port of woven-thatch houses and low pastel-colored buildings of stone, discovered by Captain Jonathan Carnes in the late eighteenth century.

In the town an Islamic festival was in full swing, and the town vibrated with colorfully dressed, immaculately groomed women and men—many of them imbibing forbidden alcohol. I made my way through the crowds to the waterfront. Prahus unchanged in construction and design since Captain Carnes's day rode at anchor in the small harbor. Missing from the serene tableau was a pinnace gliding to the beach, rowed by the strangely dressed white men, cautious but eager for trade.

South at Padang, a flat, airless city whose sluggish streets were plied by pony-driven dokars, was another port of call for Captain Carnes. Today the Minangkabau rigidity was modified by the sounds of gambling—the shuffling of cards and the clicking of dice—behind windows shuttered against the heat of the day. Women in red and purple sarongs hovered in the doorways.

I sailed for the Moluccas the next day after a Chinese shopkeeper sold me a contraband bottle of scotch.

THE SPICE ISLANDS remain, of course, but with a palpable sense of a presence having fled. Ternate lies at the foot of the tiny island volcano known as Gunung Api Gamalama, which rises in a nearly perfect cone from the sea. It is a provincial city with no frills superimposed on the ghostly colonial presence, which is largely the ruins of the old Portuguese fort. This edifice had been wrested from the Iberians by Sultan Baab, thus ending Portuguese occupation of the island. Under Sultan Baab's rule, the fortress, known then as Gammalamma, had hosted in grand style Drake's crew four centuries earlier. Today it is crumbling and gone to seed, its visitors chickens and goats, the entrance guarded by a long-nosed monkey tethered to a post. The town's obvious charms are few, but its slow pace along the waterfront provides a splendid view across the narrow ribbon of sea to the twin volcano of Tidore.

Years before, I had enjoyed a memorable meal in Ternate of stewed bat and coconut crab, a large land variety that actually climbs trees to crack the shell and feed on the fruit. On this trip the crab was unavailable, as it had been listed as an endangered species. This prohibition was a reminder that Indonesia is rapidly becoming a tourist mecca, the globe's next hot spot, though the remote Spice Islands remain accessible only to those determined to visit them. Ternate's accommodations for the traveler are modest at best.

I was lucky to catch a special run to Banda. Today the islands are a popular if out-of-the-way destination for divers, who arrive on the twice-a-week, early-morning flight from Ambon. When the Twin Otter lifted off Ternate's strip in the early morning for Ambon with two intermediate stops before continuing from the Moluccan capital south to Banda, my satisfaction was double. The trip would last five hours on a diamond-brilliant day, allowing stunning views of the sprinkling of islands rising from an azure sea.

I had found my old familiar hotel in Bandaneira, a place of Moorish design that might have been plucked from some Mediterranean shore and placed on the lagoon. It was a spacious hostelry, with broad porticoes and arches and tiled walkways: a terra cotta setting reminiscent of Somerset Maugham. The hotel faced Gunung Api, a half mile offshore, and a stretch of open sea beyond the mouth of the harbor. Rare indigenous parrots, plumed in regal white feathers with soft yellow crowns, had the run of the place and sounded the daylight hours.

On my arrival at the hotel, I learned that its owner, Des Alwi, a regional chief of high birth, was in residence. Des Alwi was active in the nationalist movement led by Sukarno and Mohammed Hatta that eventually resulted in Indonesia's independence in 1945. After falling out with Sukarno, he went into exile and returned to Bandaneira only in 1967, after Sukarno was overthrown. Ebullient and London-educated, with an air of scholarly flamboyance, he was happy for English-speaking company.

"Banda has changed since you were last here," he said, greeting me with a bear hug. "Before there was a total of four motorized vehicles in Banda, all on Neira. Now there are six," he exclaimed with irony.

The hotel had no hot running water, and an early-morning shower was invigorating before the heat and humidity of the day rose and thickened. I took breakfast outside my room on the terrace, watching the sun glance off the water to fill the dark green folds of the sleeping volcano. The rich coffee was Banda's own, grown at sea level, to accompany sliced mango and papaya of the islands and warm home-baked bread sweetened with nutmeg jelly.

Lunch and dinner were communal affairs, served with platters of fresh local tuna and snapper, game hen seasoned with nutmeg, grilled sliced eggplant with a piquant sauce of sautéed almonds, garlic, onion, chilies, coriander, and cumin, and green beans with oysters and balsamic vinegar.

From my terrace I watched the shifting colors at Bandaneira's waterfront. Small tuna freighters called at the harbor from Ambon, while jaundiced interisland boats listed and idled at wharfside, taking on cargoes of the thirty varieties of bananas grown here, as well as passengers, the women as bright as flowers in vivid burnooses and caftans or homespun sarongs. From the waterside market local merchants plied the lagoon in dugout canoes fashioned from tropical almond wood that had been in use long before Serrão's day.

These days, the town of Bandaneira on the island of Neira, small enough for me to explore in an hour's time, is essentially what the Dutch left after centuries of occupation. It recedes from the waterfront in neat square blocks, essentially northern European in plan, but built to fend off the pounding subtropical sun. The typical Dutch planter's dwelling—some built over three hundred years ago—is a single-story house of stone and wood with fifteen-foot ceilings; a wide, wraparound portico provides maximum shade at any time of day. Near one such house and only steps from the market is a Chinese temple from the same period, its entrance guarded by ancient sculpted dragons, a reminder that Chinese traders had served their Mandarin courts by calling at Banda since before the time of Christ. The Chinese were traders, not conquerors; they introduced spices to the world and were a vital force in the history of the Spice Islands.

Minarets rise above a handful of mosques. Arab traders brought Islam to the Bandas in the Middle Ages. Today it remains the dominant religion. In the sixteenth century Christianity arrived with the Portuguese, and on Sunday mornings bells still ring out from a delft-trimmed, white-columned church built by the Dutch in 1680.

I walked away from the harbor to the town's edge, where the terrain rises abruptly to form a ridge, a prominent vantage point overlooking the harbor and the site of Bandaneira's grandest structure. Fort Belgica is an exacting pentagon-shaped fortification constructed by the Dutch in 1611 to guard the harbor with cannon against rival warships. Its lofty battlements supported by twenty-five-yard-thick walls and vaulted archways command a splendid view of the northern part of the island as well as Bandabesar (known to the Dutch and English as Lonthor), the larger island adjacent to Neira. The fort also overlooks Gunung Api across the harbor, the smoldering volcano rising 2,100 feet and blocking the outer islands of Ai and Run from view. I strolled around the interior courtyard, faced with a mellowed yellow brick imported from Holland and surrounded by a series of identical, almost monastic cells with doors and raised windows cleaved from the battlement walls.

While the fort, which is amazingly well preserved, is a marvel of strategic Low Country engineering, the best of its day, its resemblance to a cloister is consistent with the spirit in which it was built. Commerce was regarded by Hollanders of the seventeenth century with Calvinistic fervor, a zealousness that raised it to the status of a religion. I recalled the vulgar saying of that earlier day which put it well: "Jesus Christ is good, but trade is better." One practical result of this precept was the Dutch colonization of Banda, their ensuing monopoly of the spice trade, and the ruthlessness with which they exercised it in their dealings with the Portuguese and English, and especially with the Bandanese, whom they ruled by terror.

From Fort Belgica I descended to the foot of the hill where lies the ruined walls of the Portuguese-built Fort Nassau. This fort was seized by the Dutch after they expelled the Portuguese at the end of the sixteenth century and enslaved the Bandanese. Today, like many of the older European ruins in the Bandas, Fort Nassau, built in 1527, wears an air of gentle decay. The fierce sun and relentless monsoons have taken their toll on the dove-gray, decaying walls now overgrown with cassava plants and fern. Goats wander about. On the parapets where riflemen once stood their watches, acacia and jackfruit trees have taken deep root. Weathered by time, the place seems banished from it. But the peace of the present is at odds with Banda's bloody past.

I paused here, for Fort Nassau had been the scene of one of the most infamous episodes in Banda's history that occurred on a humid May morning in 1621: the slaughter of forty-four Bandanese natives by Japanese samurai under the supervision of Dutch soldiers. The incident was but one legacy of Jan Pieterszoon Coen.

During occasional daytime spells of rain, I settled into Des Alwi's library in his paternal family home, a yellowed old planter's house with a wide porch and wrought-iron railing a five-minute walk from the hotel. The interior doubles as a museum, and it was filled with island memorabilia: ancient Chinese earthenware pots, old Portuguese cannons, and furnishings imported by displaced Europeans to remind them of their homelands—the brass chandelier, the odd piece of delftware. Old maps and paintings hung on the walls, and a corner bookcase contained a small but rare collection of books and manuscripts from colonial times.

Though much of Banda's history manifested itself nostalgically, as shades, there was also a sign of a more disturbing homesickness for Europe than nostalgia. One afternoon I walked over to the former governor's mansion. The elegant structure, which faces the lagoon, is neoclassical in spirit, with a low-slung roof supported by Doric columns in front and back, creating broad, shady verandas. It was built in Napoleon's day, when the British briefly held the islands. The marble halls, now empty of any furnishings, echoed with my footsteps, while outside workmen listened to rock music as they busied themselves erecting a stage for an upcoming outdoor performance.

I paused to inspect a verse that had been etched in French into a windowpane by a Dutch governor's diamond ring. Translated, it read:

> When will my happiness return?
> When will the bells toll the hour
> Of my return to the shores of my country,
> And the heart of my family, who I love and bless?
> Charles Rumpley, 1 September 1834

After composing his inscription, Rumpley put a bullet through his head under the crystal chandeliers.

Another afternoon Des Alwi invited me to accompany him to Gunung Api, a short trip by outboard launch. Our destination was a cinnamon grove high on the volcano's eastern slope. We followed the overgrown path of the steep incline through a forest of fern, mango, and tropical almond trees. The cries of wild pigeons and white cockatoos followed our ascent, and we flushed deer and game hen and once surprised a boar as we climbed. The scent of cinnamon carried down through the trees, and once at the grove, planted as a cash crop but after decades seemingly reclaimed by the surrounding wilderness, we rewarded ourselves with a taste of pungent leaves and bark.

After we descended, we paused to bathe in the steaming, sulphuric waters where the surf met a molten shelf of lava, then crossed the lagoon to the neighboring island of Bandabesar (Lonthor) to inspect its towering, centuries-old nutmeg trees that were well over a hundred feet in height. As we stood in the evergreen forest under a canopy of dark, polished leaves painted with pink blossoms and ripening fruit, Des Alwi told me that Indonesia still produces nearly eighty percent of the world's nutmeg. Considering the broken Dutch monopoly of colonial times, I was surprised by that.

Grenada does grow most of the rest. In fact, when the United States invaded Grenada in 1983, production there ceased, causing world prices to climb. Indonesia invited Grenada into its cartel, little knowing that after the Caribbean island joined, the Dutch would resurrect themselves. A Rotterdam consortium gave them fits, undercutting them by encouraging a black market. Prices crashed and poor farmers have suffered. Today farmers are poorly paid for their produce by a government-controlled consortium. So while Indonesia may produce the lion's share of nutmeg, Banda has never recovered from the old days. And, in fact, only 1 percent of the country's export revenue comes from spices, so much has changed. Des Alwi smiled. "You see how the lines are drawn," he said. "It's a study of supply and demand over four centuries. It's odd how history repeats itself with new variations. Things change, but not really.

"God gave the nutmeg to Banda, and to Banda alone. That may explain why nutmeg trees here have not had the problems others have had in other places: Penang, Grenada, Mauritius. Because the nutmeg originated here. It's an ecosystem unlike any other. The climate, wind, rainfall, the volcanic soil, the pigeons that spread the seed from island to island."

He pointed to Gunung Api, standing like a warrior-god.

"Look at these trees, how protected they are. Consider the configuration of these islands. They are all of volcanic origin, rising from awesome depths. Only here where they smell the sea. Nowhere else on earth. Small wonder the barbaric Europeans came to us. It finally dawned on them that they ought to enjoy their food."

Des Alwi's concerns about Banda's plight are based on fact. In 1987 the Indonesian Nutmeg Association, known as Aspin, agreed to market their entire production through a 130-year-old Dutch trading company, Catz International B.V. of Rotterdam, which now controls 100 percent of the world trade in nutmeg and mace. The result has been higher world prices, which have not been beneficial to Banda, where it all began. The reason is that the Indonesian government, in an effort to realize the highest yield for its cartel, pays Banda's farmers below-market prices, thereby controlling the monopoly with no recourse by the growers. It is this latest cartel, the long-defunct Dutch East Indies Company in modern dress with a contemporary spin, that Des Alwi is lobbying against.

"Why don't they just give the nutmeg back to the Bandanese?" he said. "That's all we want. So I'm fighting for Banda and for history. Nutmeg is life here."

Nutmeg is life in other places as well, as are cloves, ginger, pepper, and a host of other spices grown in just about every place in the Tropics. As we've seen, transplantation, inspired by Pierre Poivre, has been the name of the global game, but it is played on a field with new rules. Seasoned professionals, who can distinguish between this clove and that, venture to source countries to acquire spices for their respective companies, returning their produce home to highly technological spice mills for cleaning, grinding, and processing. Such is how the spice industry has evolved over the last hundred years. No longer the driver of the world's cash and credit flow, as they were for centuries, spices today are faceless and tasteless to all but the most culinary of us. Though the connoisseur remains ever poised to pronounce, say, Grenada's nutmeg inferior to that of the Southern Moluccas, rare is the palate that can distinguish a Banda nutmeg from its Caribbean cousin.

At dusk as we retraced our path to the boat where Mato, the boatman, waited, the voice of a muezzin sounded over the lagoon, calling the Muslim faithful to prayers.

• • •

THAT EVENING Des Alwi and I were invited to a bungalow where elaborate preparations were under way to welcome a local chief who would be returning from Mecca the next day. It would be a hero's welcome celebrated with a warriors' dance, a ceremony rooted in the seventeenth century, specifically in commemoration of the aristocracy who died in the Fort Nassau massacre on that fateful May day in 1621.

Early the next morning, what seemed like the Banda Islands' entire population of about fifteen thousand converged on the small airstrip to pay homage to their returning chief, a widower of seventy-two whose village had invested a lifetime's savings in his pilgrimage. Smooth-shaven and dressed in white robes, he was engulfed by the enthusiastic crowd until a fire hose was brought out to clear his path. He was swept along through the town's narrow ways, preceded by spear-wielding warriors arrayed in red and yellow tunics and feathered Portuguese helmets, mimicking battle to the staccato of tenor drumbeats.

Pausing at one of the island's five mosques, a Victorian edifice with a three-tiered cupola in the delft-blue trim so favored in the Bandas, he entered to give thanks for his safe return. Later, under a rain tree the pilgrim held an informal audience over tea and cakes, speaking in dialect and telling traveler's tales.

"There was no rice to be had in Saudi Arabia," he said, "and I nearly choked on the hard, thin bread they gave me. And the prayer rugs for sale in Mecca were all made in Korea. Imagine it! They lost my luggage for eight days, too, and I would have been lost, too, had I not had my identification bracelet. Mecca was awash in a sea of people. Two million on the hajj. Black people, brown people, white people. Every kind of people."

The news of the occasional convicted thief punished by the severing of a hand brought forth an awed hush, as did the news that 621 Indonesians, mostly elderly, died during the hajj. That fifteen of his countrywomen gave birth on the pilgrimage brought murmurs of approval.

"Are you happy to be home?" I asked.

He smiled and shook my hand. "Now my life is complete," he said. "Centuries ago, Islam came to these shores, long before the Portuguese arrived; and it remains the blessing of Banda that God so chose to reveal Himself to us. I am very happy to be home."

My visit to the Bandas was drawing to a close, and I had not yet made the crossing to Pulau Run. Ten miles west of Bandaneira, the little island —two miles long and a half mile wide—had been abandoned by agents of the "gentlemen adventurers" of Elizabeth I in 1628 after a nearly thirty-year siege by the Hollanders. On earlier trips, bad weather had kept me from landing on the island; now I wanted to feel its sand under my feet. I made arrangements for a daylong expedition to see England's first colony.

Des Alwi nodded to a pink, mottled sky. "Like a fish's scales," he said. "It means good fishing tomorrow."

With Mato and two other Bandanese guides, I set out early the next morning, my last full day on Banda. With the sun still behind Fort Belgica, we cruised in the lavender light into the dark channel, passing Gunung Api's western face, pocked, scarred, and disfigured from a recent eruption, to reach the open surf of the Banda Sea.

Since the monsoons were nearly at hand—the rainy season lasts roughly from June to August—it was a bone-jarring crossing. The collision of wave and trough pitched the craft like a wood chip, and I wondered how the Bandanese traditionally made such a crossing in their *kora-kora*.

Once we shipped so much water that three of us busied ourselves bailing the deep, narrow deck while Mato alternately cursed and chanted prayers and grimly forced the boat to plane out against the chop. At one point the motor failed, and scores of gulls feeding in the wake of a school of tuna seemed to mock us with their cries, while Mato worked diligently at his repairs. Again we were under way, and hundreds of dolphins broke through the waves afar off our bow.

We passed the island of Ai, and Pulau Run appeared in fits and starts over the clash of currents, changing shape and texture as we neared. A narrow spit of land reached toward our approach where the English fort once guarded the island from the Dutch, the fortification working in concert with the natural, shallow barrier reefs. This was where Captain Nathaniel Courthope and his companions had made their heroic stand. We rounded the spit to find ourselves in the lee off Run's main settlement, and waters were calm, while the sun warmed our wet clothing.

Mato guided the boat through the quiet surf toward the beach, passing small native prahus riding at anchor. He cut the motor and the keel grated on the sand while curious sarong-clad townspeople, fishermen and farmers, looked on. They were shy but eager to pose for a picture under a bank of huts, built on stilts, each with its own cistern for storing rainwater, since there are no natural springs on the island. Behind the huts, tropical almond trees and sea pines rose out of the dunes to reach the low ridgeline. Fishing nets were spread to dry over beached boats. Apart from the settlement, the island appeared to be uninhabited. But if Pulau Run is almost forgotten today, it was sufficiently important in 1667 for England to trade it to Holland for Manhattan.

Gunung Api appeared as serene as a Buddha to the east as we beached at Pulau Ai to have our packed lunch in the shade of a small limestone cliff, watched by a group of children. Afterward, we strolled through a fringe of woods past the overgrown ruin of a fortification taken from the English by the Dutch in 1616; it was repaired, strengthened, and renamed, appropriately, Fort Revenge. We stopped at a small church with sparkling white columns, which bore the date 1611. First English, then Dutch, the church, although padlocked, was clearly still in use. We wandered in the weathered graveyard behind it, whose rain-worn Dutch inscriptions dated from the time of Rembrandt and Vermeer, when the bounty of these islands helped build modern Amsterdam. Then we turned back to the beach.

The waters of the Banda Sea had calmed, and Mato, now with the leisure to troll, hooked a yellowfin tuna for my last dinner on Banda. It was nearly dusk as we docked, and Mato pointed heavenward. The sky had turned a mottled pink, a good sign for the morrow.

<h1 align="center">Notes and Sources</h1>

In the main, sources identified in the text are not repeated in the notes. I trust that the below-named works will lead an interested reader to further study. For those wishing further clarification about sources for material in the text, I would be happy to answer queries forwarded by the publisher.

Prologue and Part I: Iberian Dreams

I would never have undertaken a book about the spice trade had I not visited the Moluccas in the course of doing research for another book about Indonesia, *Distant Islands*. Over the course of several visits I got to know quite well Des Alwi, Banda's most prominent citizen, who made available to me his invaluable archives of published and unpublished material. Especially key were two monographs: *Indonesia Banda: Colonization and Its Aftermath in the Nutmeg Islands,* by the late Willard Hanna, and *Turbulent Times Past in Ternate and Tidore,* cowritten by Messrs. Hanna and Alwi. Both works were printed locally, while drawing upon scattered rare manuscripts and highly specialized collections in Dutch. They opened for me a world and time I scarcely knew existed and are the genesis of this book.

Another helpful source was *The World of Moluku,* by Leonard Y. Andaya (Honolulu: University of Hawaii Press, 1993), a scholarly study of the centuries-old clash of European and Moluccan cultures and its repercussions.

I must draw special attention to Tim Joyner's *Magellan* (International Marine Publishing, Camden, ME, 1992, with an introduction by William Manchester). This superlative biography is as thorough a study of Magellan as we are likely to get and would be an invaluable tool for scholars for its appendices alone. The author of this highly readable life story graciously accepted a telephone call from me quite out of the blue and was instrumental in my research on Francisco Serrão. It was at his suggestion that I visited the Bibliothèque Nationale in Paris, where I perused Jean Denucé's *La Question des Molucques et la Première Circumnavigation du Globe* (Brussels: Hayez, 1911). Mr. Joyner also suggested that João de Barros's *Decadas da Asia,* a four-volume work by a Portuguese historian, was the most complete coverage on record of Serrão's discovery of the Moluccas, an assessment that proved invaluable to me. Likewise, he emphasized the importance of Chilean historian José Toribo Medina's *El Descubrimiento del Oceano Pacifico* and Francis Henry Hill Guillemard's *The Life of Ferdinand Magellan and the First Circumnavigation of the Globe: 1480–1521* (New York: Dodd, Mead, 1890). For each of the foreign titles, I enlisted a translator's aide.

Several trips to Malacca and the port's archives and historical museum were especially illuminating of that city's history, from precolonial days, the siege by the Portuguese in 1511, later the residence there of Francis Xavier, and through its occupation by the Dutch. In addition, I must cite the following works in my research on Malacca: Richard O. Winstedt's *A History of Malaya* (Kuala Lumpur and Singapore, 1956); John Dos Passos's *The Portugal Story, Three Centuries of Exploration and Discovery* (New York: Doubleday, 1969); Fr. Manuel Teixeira's *The Portuguese Missions in Malacca and Singapore 1511–1958* (Lisbon, 1960); John Bastin and Robin Winks's *Selected Historical Readings* (Kuala Lumpur: Oxford University Press, 1966); James B. McKenna's *A Spaniard in the Portuguese Indies: The Narrative of Martin Fernandez de Figueroa* (Cambridge: Harvard University Press, 1967); Francisco de sa de Memeses's *The Conquest of Malacca,* translated by Edgar Knowlton (Kuala Lumpur: University of Malaya Press, 1970); R. J. Wilkinson, "The Malacca Sultanate," *Journal of the Malayan Branch Royal Asiatic Society,* vol. 13, no. 2, (1935), pp. 29–33; and Dr. Luis Filipe F. Reis Thomaz's *Nina Chatu and the Portuguese Trade in Malacca,* translated by Fr. M. J. Pintado (Malacca: Luso-Malaysian Books, 1991).

A keen sense of Francis Xavier's extraordinary life was gained by visits not only to Malacca but to Goa on India's southwest coast as well. These journeys yielded insightful local publications: Fr. M. J. Pintado's *The Malacca Thaumaturge: Wonder Worker, 1545–1552* (Malacca, no date) and Fr. P. Rayanna's *St. Francis Xavier and His Shrine* (Goa: Panjim, 1982). Western works on Xavier that proved useful in drawing his portrait are: Fr. James Broderick's *St. Francis Xavier* (New York: Wicklow Press, 1952); Jean-Marc Montguerre's *St. Francis Xavier,* translated by Ruth Murdock (New York: Doubleday, 1963); and Marput Yeo's *St. Francis Xavier: Apostle of the East* (London: Sheed and Ward, 1931).

As for the mysterious figure and contemporary of Xavier, Fernão Mendes Pinto, I highly recommend *The Travels of Mendes Pinto,* edited and translated by Rebecca D. Catz (Chicago: University of Chicago Press, 1989).

Samuel Eliot Morison's *The European Discovery of America* (New York: Oxford University Press, 1974) was informative on Sir Francis Drake as well as Magellan. Other useful works dealing with Drake include John Hampden's (editor) selections in *Francis Drake, Privateer: Contemporary Narratives and Documents* (Tuscaloosa: The University of Alabama Press, 1972) and Norman. J. W. Thrower, ed., *Sir Francis Drake and the Famous Voyage, 1577–1588: Essays Commemorating the Quadricentennial of Drake's Circumnavigation of the Earth* (Berkeley: University of California Press, 1984).

As for books supplying a general background to my subject, I admire Daniel J. Boorstin's *The Discoverers: A History of Man's Search to Know the World and Himself* (New York: Random House, 1983); J. H. Parry's *The Age of Reconnaissance* (New York: World, 1963) and *The Discovery of the Sea* (New York: Dial Press, 1974); J. W. Jeadwine's *Studies in Empire and Trade* (London: Green and Company, 1923); Joachim G. Leithauser's *Worlds Beyond the Horizon: The Great Age of Discovery from Columbus to the Present* (New York: Knopf, 1955); C. R. Boxer's *The Portuguese Seaborne Empire, 1415–1825* (New York: Knopf, 1969); and Fernand Braudel's two-volume masterwork *The Mediterranean and the Mediterranean World in the Age of Philip II,* translated by Sian Reynolds (New York: Harper and Row, 1972).

PART II: NORTHERN DESIRE

Again, Willard A. Hanna's *Indonesia Banda* and *Turbulent Times Past in Ternate and Tidore,* the latter cowritten with Des Alwi, were excellent starting points for this section dealing with the Dutch and English and their struggles to gain the spice trade monopoly. John Keay's stylishly written *The Honorable Company: A History of the English East India Company* (New York: Macmillan, 1991) was informative and a pleasure to read. For statistics on the trade, I relied heavily on Jaap R. Bruijn and Femme S. Gaastra's *Ships, Sailors and Spices: East India Companies and Their Shipping in the 16th, 17th and 18th Centuries* (Amsterdam: NEHA, 1993).

With a translator's help in Amsterdam I was able to decipher the pertinent parts of François Valentijn's five-volume *Oud en Nieuw Oost-Indien* (Amsterdam, 1724–1726) as well as certain passages of Johan Sigmund Wurffbain's *Journal* (Amsterdam, no date). Amsterdam's Historical Museum was a repository of the mosaic that was the city's past, and its erudite and energetic director, Ludwig Wagenaar, made a number of helpful suggestions regarding my project.

As for period sources in English, I must cite Sir William Temple's *Observations Upon the United Provinces of the Netherlands* (London, 1672); John Jourdain's *Journal 1608–1617*, edited by W. Foster (London, 1905); William Keeling's *Voyage of William Keeling, 1607* (Glasgow, 1905); Henry Middleton's *Voyage to the Moluccas*, edited by W. Foster (London, 1943); and Richard Hakluyt's *Principal Voyages, Traffiques and Discoveries of the English Nation* (New York: Knopf, 1925). For my rediscovery of Samuel Pepys's *Diaries*, I should thank Simon Schama, whose book *The Embarrassment of Riches: An Interpretation of Dutch Culture in the Golden Age* (Berkeley: University of California Press, 1988) is an indispensable guide to the period. George Garrett's fine novel about Raleigh, *Death of the Fox* (New York: Doubleday, 1971); Robert Lacey's biography *Sir Walter Raleigh* (New York: Atheneum, 1974); and Lytton Strachey's *Elizabeth and Essex: A Tragic History* (New York: Harcourt, Brace, and World, 1928) were each helpful toward defining an age, as was Madge Lorwin's delectable *Dining with William Shakespeare* (New York: Atheneum, 1976).

For the research it contains on the tea trade, I am grateful to Jason Goodwin's *A Time for Tea: Travels Through China and India in Search of Tea* (New York: Knopf, 1991).

For general and specific historical narratives of the period, I am pleased to have read the following works: J. Ellis Barker's *The Rise and Decline of the Netherlands* (New York: Dutton, 1906); C. R. Boxer's *The Dutch Seaborne Empire 1600–1800* (New York: Knopf, 1965); Percy H. Boynton's *London in English Literature* (Chicago: University of Chicago Press, 1913); James Burke's *Connections* (Boston: Little, Brown, 1978); A. Mervyn Davies's *Clive of Plassey* (New York: Scribner's, 1939); Bertha S. Dodge's *The Quest for Spices and New Worlds* (Hamden: Archon Books, 1988); Sir William Foster's *England's Quest of Eastern Trade* (London: Black, 1933); Peter Geyl's *The Netherlands in the Seventeenth Century, 1609–1648* (New York: Barnes and Noble, 1961) and *The Revolt of the Netherlands, 1555–1609* (Amsterdam: Benn, 1958); K. D. H. Haley's *The Dutch in the Seventeenth Century* (New York: Harcourt, Brace, and Jovanovich, 1972); J. H. Huizinga's book of essays, *Dutch Civilization in the Seventeenth Century* (New York: Ungar, 1968); Albert Hyma's *The Dutch in the Far East* (Ann Arbor: Wahr, 1974); P. J. Marshall and Glyndwr Williams's *The Great Map of Mankind: British Perception of the World in the Age of Enlightenment* (London: Dent, 1982); Alan Moorehead's *The Fatal Impact: The Invasion of the South Pacific* (London: Hamish Hamilton, 1966); John J. Murray's *Amsterdam in the Age of Rembrandt* (Norman: University of Oklahoma Press, 1967); J. L. Price's *Cul-*

ture and Society in the Dutch Republic during the Seventeenth Century (New York: Scribner's, 1974); Hendrick Willem Van Loon's *The Fall of the Dutch Republic* (Boston: Houghton Mifflin, 1924); and for the Dupont family history, Joseph Frazier Wall's *Alfred I. Dupont: The Man and His Family* (New York: Oxford, 1990).

PART III: NEW ENGLAND PASSION AND EPILOGUE

Within the limits established by themselves, the merged Peabody Museum and Essex Institute of Salem, Massachusetts, are unique among the world's great custodial associations. The former houses a nautical collection of uncommonly broad range and interest, while the latter preserves a trove of rare archival material and exhibits as well as oversees several early houses open to the public. It was my good fortune to spend several rewarding days in Salem doing research at these facilities as well as in the rare-book room of Boston's public library. The time spent at Philadelphia's Maritime Museum was profitable as well, and I thank that institution's staff for their help in compiling data about ships in the colonial era.

Inevitably, anyone in pursuit of Salem's past, especially its East Indiamen, privateers, and overseas trade, will soon discover the work of that port's most eminent historian, James Duncan Phillips. Writing over a half-century ago, this chronicler produced *Salem in the Seventeenth Century* (Boston: Houghton Mifflin, 1933); *Salem in the Eighteenth Century* (Salem: Essex Institute, 1937); *Salem and the Indies* (Boston: Houghton, Mifflin, 1947); and *Pepper and Pirates: Adventures in the Sumatra Pepper Trade of Salem* (Boston: Houghton Mifflin, 1949). Though out of print and often difficult to find today, these books were indispensable to me.

For accounts of the voyages themselves, I relied heavily on George C. Putnam's *Salem Vessels and Their Voyages,* four volumes (Salem: Essex Institute, 1925). This ambitious and rare work, a compilation of ship's logs, newspaper accounts, etc., is even more difficult to find today than the Phillips volumes.

I am also indebted to three books by Samuel Eliot Morison: *The Maritime History of Massachusetts, 1783–1860* (Boston: Houghton Mifflin, 1921); *Sailor Historian: The Best of Samuel Eliot Morison,* edited by Emily Morison Beck (Boston: Houghton Mifflin, 1977); and *By Land and By Sea: Essays and Addresses by Samuel Eliot Morison* (New York: Knopf, 1953).

An excellent capsule history of the port may be found in *Salem: Maritime Salem in the Age of Sail* (Washington, D.C.: National Park Service, Division of Publications, in cooperation with the Peabody Museum and the Essex Institute, Salem/U. S. Department of the Interior, 1987). This publication is based on a text by K. David Goss and the Essex Institute.

For descriptions of ships and period dress, I consulted John Wilmerding's *A History of American Marine Painting* (Boston: Peabody Museum of Salem/Little, Brown, 1968).

Excellent articles may be found in *American Neptune,* issued quarterly by Salem's Peabody Museum, and the *Essex Institute Historical Collections,* published quarterly by the Essex Institute, each devoted to Salem's maritime commerce.

Other works consulted: *Concise Dictionary of American History,* edited by Wayne Andrews (New York: Scribner's, 1962); C. Merton Babcock's *The American Frontier: A*

Social and Literary Record (New York: Holt, Rinehart, Winston, 1965); *The Diary of William Bentley, D.D.,* four volumes (Salem: 1910–1914); Van Wyck Brooks's *The World of Washington Irving* (New York: Dutton, 1944) and *The Flowering of New England* (New York: Dutton, 1940); Howard I. Chapelle's *History of the American Sailing Navy* (New York: Norton, 1949); F. O. Matthiessen's *American Renaissance: Art and Expression in the Age of Emerson and Whitman* (New York: Oxford, 1941); and Henry Nash Smith's *Virgin Land: The American West As Symbol and Myth* (Cambridge: Harvard University Press, 1950).

As for spices, their uses and lore as they relate to all three sections of the book, I consulted Avenelle Day and Lillie Stuckey's *The Spice Cookbook* (New York: David White, 1964); Jill Norman's *The Complete Book of Spices* (New York: Viking, 1990); and Waverly Root's *The Food of Italy* (New York: Atheneum, 1971). On this score, I am also grateful for the time given to me by Jack Felton, a McCormick Company vice president and the firm's director of corporate communications at its headquarters in northern Maryland's Hunt Valley.

Acknowledgments

I am grateful to my agent and old friend, Fred Hill, for approaching another friend and former colleague, Paul De Angelis, the editor in chief of Kodansha America, when I proposed a book about the spice trade. Kodansha America's executive vice president, Minato Asakawa, shared Paul's enthusiasm, and the book exists today because of that original collaboration. Paul remained extremely supportive throughout the writing of the book, read an early draft, and offered a number of helpful suggestions. Then, when Paul left to establish his own editorial service, Kodansha's new editor in chief, Philip Turner, who shared some of his own cogent and welcome thoughts about the manuscript, placed me in the capable hands of Nancy Cooperman. Immediately, this exacting and scrupulous editor enthusiastically rose to the task, which I realize in retrospect must have seemed daunting because of the sprawling nature of the subject. The time she gave to the manuscript and the work she performed over several drafts, together with the skill and sensitivity attending her labors, are, I believe, rare qualities in an editor. It is a pleasure to salute and thank her. I am also grateful for the copyediting skills of Sue Warga.

I must also pay special homage to my former teacher of history at Washington and Lee University, Professor Emeritus William A. Jenks, who, after thirty-five years of our being out of touch, remembered me and offered to read an early draft of the book. Within days of my sending him a five-hundred-page manuscript, he forwarded a legal-size notebook of corrections, queries, and suggestions that surely prevented more than one black eye. Professor Jenks, a taskmaster who was known for bringing a class to its feet in spontaneous applause at a course's end, remains a giant on whose shoulders many of his students have stood.

My very special thanks, too, go to my faithful companion and collaborator, Rosalie Muller Wright, who from the outset shared my enthusiasm for the subject, often accompanying me over the last nine years to where research led: the Spice Islands, Amsterdam, London, Paris, Java, Sumatra, Sulawesi (Celebes), Malacca, Singapore, Penang, Goa, Sri Lanka, South Africa, Hong Kong, the Philippines, Guam, Brazil, Argentina, Chile, Barbados, the Iberian Peninsula, Italy, Salem, Boston, New York, and Philadelphia. I value highly her amateur's curiosity and zeal as well as her professional's determination and perseverance to get things right. These qualities are infectious. With her keen critical eye and ardent support bolstering years of work, *The Scents of Eden* is as much her book as mine.

Index

About the Author

Charles Corn is a native Georgian, graduated from Washington and Lee University, and took a graduate degree in English from George Washington University. A former officer in the U.S. Marine Corps, he has worked as an editor at several New York and Boston publishing houses, including Dutton, where he served as editor in chief. The author of *Distant Islands,* which Anne Lamott hailed as "beautiful, innocent, fascinating, and wonderfully written," and which Martin Cruz Smith called "a book to inspire your dreaming," Corn now devotes himself full time to writing. His work has appeared in the *San Francisco Chronicle, The New York Times,* and *Islands* magazine, to name a few. He lives in San Francisco and is a frequent and recognized visitor to the Spice Islands.